COMMODITIES IN CRISIS

WIDER

Studies in Development Economics embody the output of the research programmes of the World Institute for Development Economics Research (WIDER), which was established by the United Nations University as its first research and training centre in 1984 and started work in Helsinki in 1985. The principal purpose of the Institute is to help identify and meet the need for policy-oriented socio-economic research on pressing global and development problems, as well as common domestic problems and their interrelationships.

COMMODITIES IN CRISIS

*The Commodity Crisis of the 1980s and
the Political Economy of International
Commodity Policies*

by
ALFRED MAIZELS

*A study prepared for the World Institute for Development Economics
Research (WIDER) of the United Nations University*

CLARENDON PRESS · OXFORD
1992

Oxford University Press, Walton Street, Oxford OX2 6DP
Oxford New York Toronto
Delhi Bombay Calcutta Madras Karachi
Petaling Jaya Singapore Hong Kong Tokyo
Nairobi Dar es Salaam Cape Town
Melbourne Auckland
and associated companies in
Berlin Ibadan

Oxford is a trade mark of Oxford University Press

Published in the United States
by Oxford University Press, New York

© World Institute for Development Economics Research (WIDER)–
The United Nations University, Annankatu 42C, 00100 Helsinki, Finland, 1992

All rights reserved. No part of this publication may be reproduced,
stored in a retrieval system, or transmitted, in any form or by any means,
electronic, mechanical, photocopying, recording, or otherwise, without
the prior permission of Oxford University Press

British Library Cataloguing in Publication Data
Data available

Library of Congress Cataloging-in-Publication Data
Maizels, Alfred.
Commodities in crisis : the commodity crises of the 1980s and the political economy
of international commodity policies / by Alfred Maizels.
p. cm. – (WIDER studies in development economics)
'A study prepared for the World Institute for Development Economics Research (WIDER)
of the United Nations University.'
Includes bibliographical references and index.
1. Prices–Developing countries. 2. Produce trade–Developing countries.
3. Primary commodities–Developing countries. 4. Commodity control.
5. Developing countries–Economic conditions. 6. International economic relations.
I. World Institute for Development Economics Research. II. Title. III. Series.
HB235.D44M35 1992 338.5'09172'4–dc20 91-26887

ISBN 0-19-828387-3

Typeset by Colset Pte. Ltd., Singapore

Printed and bound in
Great Britain by Bookcraft (Bath) Ltd.,
Midsomer Norton, Avon

PREFACE

SINCE the onset of the severe economic crisis in the majority of Third World countries a decade ago, international economic policy has focused almost exclusively on possible measures to reduce the debt burden of the heavily indebted countries, mostly in Latin America, and of the poorest countries, mostly in sub-Saharan Africa. The role played by the catastrophic fall in the prices of primary commodities, on which the economic fortunes of so many developing countries largely depend, has been generally overlooked or downplayed, not only in the 'North–South dialogue', but also in academic analysis and discourse.

The present book is a major contribution towards re-establishing the commodity issue as a priority item on the international economic agenda and an essential element in a comprehensive strategy to overcome the continuing economic crisis in the Third World. As such, it fits well with the basic remit of WIDER, and of the United Nations University, to develop action-oriented research related to the pressing problems of the global economy.

Hitherto, academic analysis and international policy on commodities have concentrated very largely on short-term price instability, and on the consequent problems for the development process. But, as Dr Maizels shows, the predominant feature of the commodity markets since the early 1980s has been the depressed level of commodity prices and commodity export earnings of developing countries rather than short-term instability (though instability remains an important negative feature for a number of major commodities). It follows that international commodity policy should now also shift so as to deal effectively with the changed nature of the central problem.

Over the whole post-war period, the focus of international commodity policy has been the negotiation of price-stabilizing agreements based on buffer stocks and/or export quotas. A new approach would now seem to be needed, one designed to raise commodity export earnings from depressed levels, so as to alleviate the continuing foreign exchange 'squeeze' on commodity-dependent countries, and so help them safeguard their living standards while financing necessary structural adjustment to lay the basis for future economic growth. Proposals to raise commodity export earnings of developing countries, whether by market intervention or by some form of supplementary finance, have been one of the most contentious areas of the 'North–South dialogue'. This book clarifies the issues involved, and sets out the pros and cons of alternative policy options to raise depressed commodity export earnings.

If successful, such policies would also help to meet the longer-term problems of commodity-dependent countries faced with stagnant or declining trends in world demand for their traditional exports. In the longer term, these countries need to diversify their production and export structures towards processed commodities and industrial products. Dr Maizels' study considers in depth the problems and policy issues involved in export diversification, as well as those associated with technological change, protectionist barriers, and the activities of transnational corporations in international commodity trade. His analysis and perceptions of the future for international commodity policy – which emphasize the need for a greatly enhanced role for South–South co-operation – will be of particular interest for academic studies in this field, as well as for policymakers involved in current and future international commodity negotiations.

Lal Jayawardena
Director, WIDER

ACKNOWLEDGEMENTS

THIS book would not have been written without the constant support of Dr Lal Jayawardena. It was he who proposed a Senior Fellowship for me at WIDER to enable me to undertake research on international commodity problems and policies and who has given me his warm encouragement throughout the study.

I must also pay tribute to the late Sidney Dell, who made extensive and perceptive comments on many of the draft chapters, which greatly helped in improving the analysis on a number of major issues. Special thanks are due to Gerry Helleiner and Amit Bhaduri for critical comments and suggestions on the early drafts of a number of chapters, and to Yilmaz Akyüz, Mehmet Arda, Dragoslav Avramović, Adrian Hewitt, Lakdasa Hulugalle, Walter Labys, Mehdi Shaffaedin, John Spraos, Frances Stewart, Harry Stordel, and an anonymous referee for detailed criticisms of various chapters of the penultimate draft. Helpful comments on specific points were also made by Nevenka Cučković, Eduard Dommen, and Harmon Thomas. I am also grateful to Aziz Taj and Jean-Paul Marquet, of UNCTAD's Statistical Service, for their willing and competent help in constructing new indices of unit values for the commodity exports of both developing and developed countries.

A particular debt is owed to Dr Gamani Corea, who was Secretary-General of UNCTAD from 1974 to 1985, with whom, before I joined WIDER, I first discussed the idea of writing a book on international commodity policy. Dr Corea was also kind enough to let me see the manuscript of his book on the commodity negotiations in UNCTAD, on which I have drawn heavily in my own discussion of the UNCTAD IV resolution of 1976 and of the subsequent negotiations on the Common Fund. I have also benefited from many relevant points made at a Seminar at Queen Elizabeth House, Oxford, in January 1990, where I presented the main lines of argument deployed in the book. My thanks also to my wife, Joan Maizels, who contributed substantially to improving the clarity of the argument in several chapters. The editors of *World Development* have kindly given permission for the use of a good part of my article in the 1984 issue of that journal in the first two sections of Chapter 10, dealing with trading channels and the elements of bargaining power, and in the section of Chapter 3 dealing with supply management.

Finally, I would like to express my appreciation for the helpful support of the WIDER staff, both administrative and secretarial. Hema Perera, Jan Johansson, Max Bond, Vira Danvivathana, and Ara Kazandjian, of the administrative staff, all contributed to making my stay at WIDER pleasant and trouble-free. Successive librarians, including Riita Ruokonen, Timo Matoniemi, and Zsuzsanna Oinas all made great efforts to meet my need for documents, while the typing of successive drafts was efficiently and willingly provided mainly by Liz Paavolainen, Liisa Roponen, and Illeana Ganz.

A.M.

September 1990

CONTENTS

LIST OF FIGURES — xii
LIST OF TABLES — xiii
LIST OF ABBREVIATIONS — xvii
INTRODUCTION — 1

PART I. THE COMMODITY CRISIS AND THE DEVELOPING COUNTRIES — 5

1. THE COMMODITY PRICE COLLAPSE OF THE 1980s — 7
1. Commodities in the Development Process — 7
2. Commodity Prices in the 1980s — 9
3. The Causes of the Collapse in Non-Oil Commodity Prices — 14
4. The Outlook for Commodity Prices — 20

2. THE IMPACT ON THE DEVELOPING COUNTRIES — 23
1. The Magnitude of the Foreign Exchange Loss — 23
2. Imports, Investment, and Economic Retrogression — 35
3. The Impact on Human Resources — 38

3. RAISING DEPRESSED LEVELS OF COMMODITY EXPORT EARNINGS — 40
1. The Case for International Action — 40
2. Supplementary Financing — 43
3. Preferential Prices for Commodity Exports from Developing Countries — 47
4. Supply Management — 49

4. INSTABILITY, STABILIZATION POLICY, AND ECONOMIC DEVELOPMENT — 61
1. The Effects of Export Instability — 61
2. The Empirical Evidence — 64
3. Economic Theory and Market Stabilization — 71

5. COMMODITY MARKETS AND THE WORLD ECONOMY — 85
1. The Commodity and the Industrial Sectors — 85
2. The Commodity and the Financial Markets — 89
3. Commodity Markets and World Economic Fluctuations — 92

PART II. INTERNATIONAL COMMODITY POLICY — 99

6. THE POST-WAR BACKGROUND — 101
1. Early Post-war Developments and the Havana Charter — 101
2. The Emergence of UNCTAD — 105

7. THE INTEGRATED PROGRAMME FOR COMMODITIES AND THE COMMON FUND — 112
1. The Commodity-by-Commodity Approach — 112
2. The Integrated Programme for Commodities (IPC) — 114
3. The Struggle for a Common Fund — 116

8. NEGOTIATIONS ON INDIVIDUAL COMMODITIES — 125
1. The Dual Price Objective — 125
2. Price-Raising and 'Indexation' — 126
3. The Post-War Stabilization Experience: Technical Limitations of the ICAs — 129
4. The Political Economy of International Commodity Negotiations — 136

9. COMPENSATORY FINANCE — 140
1. The Origin of Fluctuations in Commodity Export Earnings — 140
2. Definition of an Export Earnings Shortfall — 142
3. The Effects of Export Earnings Shortfalls on Economic Development — 145
4. International Compensatory Financing Policies — 147

PART III. LONGER-TERM ISSUES — 157

10. THE STRUCTURE AND CONTROL OF INTERNATIONAL COMMODITY MARKETS — 159
1. The Main Enterprises and their Trading Channels — 159
2. The Elements of Bargaining Power — 165
3. Strategies of Host Countries and TNCs — 173
4. International Negotiations Related to Commodity Market Structures — 175
5. Policy Options for Developing Countries — 178

11. TECHNOLOGICAL CHANGE AND THE CHALLENGE OF SYNTHETICS — 181
1. Technology and Commodity Markets — 181
2. Dematerialization and Transmaterialization — 182
3. Post-War Trends in Raw Materials Consumption — 185
4. The Impact on Developing Countries — 191

5. The Search for an Effective International Policy	191
Annexe: Decomposition of the Change in Consumption of Natural Raw Materials	198
12. PROTECTIONIST BARRIERS TO COMMODITY TRADE	200
1. The Extent of Protection	200
2. Benefits and Costs of Agricultural Protection	208
3. National and International Policies Affecting Agriculture: The Prospects for Liberalization	213
13. NEW TRADE DIRECTIONS: SOUTH–SOUTH AND EAST–SOUTH	220
A. South–South Trade	220
1. Recent Trends	220
2. Policy Responses of Developing Countries	223
3. Policy Perspectives for the Future	226
B. East–South Trade	232
14. DIVERSIFICATION	234
1. Diversification and Growth	234
2. Horizontal Diversification	236
3. Vertical Diversification	237
4. National Policies to Promote Diversification	241
5. The Role of International Policy	247
Annexe: The Coffee Diversification Fund	252
PART IV. THE FUTURE OF INTERNATIONAL COMMODITY POLICY	**255**
15. THE FUTURE OF INTERNATIONAL COMMODITY POLICY	257
1. The Need for a New Policy Focus	257
2. The Elements of a Possible Minimum North–South Programme	261
3. Measures by Developing Countries to Strengthen the Commodity Sector	264
4. The Crucial Role of Finance	271
APPENDIX: TERMS OF TRADE GAINS AND LOSSES ON COMMODITY EXPORTS FROM DEVELOPING COUNTRIES	273
REFERENCES	283
INDEX	297

LIST OF FIGURES

1.1.	The commodity terms of trade, 1970–88	11
1.2.	The commodity price recessions of the 1930s and 1980s	12
2.1.	Gains and losses of developing countries attributable to changes in the commodity terms of trade, 1970–88	27
2.2.	Volume, prices, and terms of trade of commodity exports in the 1930s and 1980s	28
2.3.	Terms of trade losses on commodity exports of developing countries in the 1930s and 1980s	29
3.1.	Sugar exports from developing countries to the free market and through preferential channels, 1980–7	49
4.1.	Commodity prices and terms of trade of commodity-dependent countries, 1970–80	76
9.1.	Drawings and repayments of developing countries with the IMF Compensatory Financing Facility, 1980–7	148
10.1.	Hypothetical relationship between bargaining power and the division of the benefits of trade	167
10.2.	The elements of bargaining power between TNCs and governments and enterprises of developing countries	169

LIST OF TABLES

TEXT TABLES

1.1. Trends in the commodity terms of trade, 1958–60 to 1986–8	10
1.2. Trends and instability of prices of main commodity groups, 1962–87	13
1.3. Contributions to commodity price change, 1980–6	20
2.1. Commodity exports of developing countries, 1970, 1980, and 1988	25
2.2. Changes in volume, terms of trade, and purchasing power of commodity exports of developing countries, 1970–88	26
2.3. Terms of trade effects in the balance of payments of commodity-dependent countries, 1980–8	31
2.4. Terms of trade loss during 1980–8 as percentage of GDP in 1980 for commodity-dependent countries	33
2.5. Indices of trade volumes, terms of trade, and purchasing power of exports of commodity-dependent countries, 1980 to 1985 and 1988	36
2.6. Imports, investment, and GDP of groups of developing countries, 1965–88	37
2.7. GDP growth rates of commodity-dependent countries, 1960–88	38
3.1. Sugar exports from developing countries to the free market and to preferential markets, 1980 and 1987	48
8.1. Objectives and instruments of selected International Commodity Agreements	130
8.2. Commodity agreement price ranges in relation to amplitude of market price cycles, late 1970s to mid-1980s	135
9.1. Relationship between export instability indices of unit value (I_{uv}), volume (I_{vol}), and value (I_{val}), for individual countries and selected commodities, 1962–81	141
10.1. The principal channels of trade in commodities exported by developing to developed countries	160
10.2. Estimated shares of commodity trade controlled by largest TNCs, 1983	165
11.1. Peak years in life cycles of selected minerals and metals	185

List of Tables

11.2.	Consumption of the major industrial raw materials in developed market-economy countries, 1963–5 to 1984–6	186
11.3.	Materials consumption per unit of industrial production in developed market-economy countries, 1963–5 to 1984–6	187
11.4.	Major influences on the growth of consumption of natural raw materials in developed market-economy countries, 1963–5 to 1984–6	189
11.5.	Consumption and trade in industrial raw materials, 1971–3 to 1984–6	192
12.1.	Frequency of application of various non-tariff barriers to imports of agricultural products into industrial countries, 1984	202
12.2.	Net producer subsidy equivalents in the agricultural sector of OECD countries, 1979–85 and 1986–9	203
12.3.	Escalation of trade barriers in industrial countries by stage of processing	205
12.4.	Tariff rate averages for selected processing chains in developing countries, 1981	206
12.5.	Total transfers associated with agricultural policies in OECD countries, 1986–9	209
12.6.	Estimated change in world prices of agricultural products under alternative liberalization policies	212
12.7.	Estimated net foreign exchange and welfare impact on developing countries of alternative policies for liberalization of agricultural trade: regional summary	217
13.1.	Exports from developing countries by broad destination and product group, 1970–80 and 1980–8	221
13.2.	Intra-trade of sub-regional groupings of developing countries, 1970, 1980, and 1988	223
13.3.	Trade of developing countries in selected commodities, 1980 and 1987	227
13.4.	The effects of alternative GSTP tariff preferences on developing-country trade	229
14.1.	Export diversification, export growth, and GDP growth of selected commodity-exporting countries, 1964–81	235
14.2.	Selected developing countries heavily dependent on exports of 'problem' commodities, 1970, 1980, and 1985	238
14.3.	Imports of primary and processed forms of selected commodities by developed market-economy countries from developing countries, 1965, 1975, and 1985	240

14.4. Possible national policies to reduce export instability or to improve the trend of export prices and export earnings — 242

14.5. Commitments by major international financial institutions for export-oriented diversification in the commodity sector, 1980–9 — 251

APPENDIX TABLES

A.1. Exports and terms of trade of the present developing countries, 1929–38 — 275

A.2. Effect of changes in the commodity terms of trade of developing countries, 1970–88 — 277

A.3. Unit value and volume of commodity exports of developing countries by region, 1980–8 — 278

A.4. Value of commodity exports of developing countries, 1980–8 — 279

A.5. Commodity terms of trade effects by region, 1980–8 — 279

A.6. Sugar exports from developing countries to the free market and to preferential markets, 1980–7 — 280

A.7. Terms of trade, volume, and purchasing power of sugar exports from developing countries, 1980–7 — 281

LIST OF ABBREVIATIONS

ACP	African, Caribbean, and Pacific countries associated with the European Community
ATAS	Advanced Technology Alert System
CAP	Common Agricultural Policy of the European Community
CEPR	Centre for Economic Policy Research
CFF	Compensatory Financing Facility
CICT	Commission on International Commodity Trade
CMEA	Council for Mutual Economic Assistance
CRC	Commodity Reserve Currency
CSE	Consumer Subsidy Equivalent
ECA	Economic Commission for Africa
ECE	Economic Commission for Europe
ECLA (now ECLAC)	Economic Commission for Latin America (now Economic Commission for Latin America and the Caribbean)
ECOSOC	Economic and Social Council
FAO	Food and Agriculture Organization
GATT	General Agreement on Tariffs and Trade
GDP	Gross domestic product
GSP	Generalized System of Preferences
GSTP	Global System of Trade Preferences
IBRD	International Bank for Reconstruction and Development (now World Bank)
ICA	International commodity agreement
ICCICA	Interim Co-ordinating Committee for International Commodity Arrangements
IMF	International Monetary Fund
IPC	Integrated Programme for Commodities
ITO	International Trade Organization
NCU	New Currency Unit
NIC	Newly industrializing country
NIESR	National Institute of Economic and Social Research
NTB	Non-tariff barrier
OECD	Organization for Economic Co-operation and Development
OEEC	Organization for European Economic Co-operation
OPEC	Organization of Petroleum Exporting Countries
PSE	Producer Subsidy Equivalent
R & D	Research and development
TNC	Transnational corporation
UN	United Nations

UNCTAD	UN Conference on Trade and Development
UNCTC	UN Centre on Transnational Corporations
UNDP	UN Development Programme
UNICEF	UN International Children's Emergency Fund
WIDER	World Institute for Development Economics Research (UN University)
$	US dollar

INTRODUCTION

The decade of the 1980s has witnessed a double crisis in the development of the underdeveloped countries. A succession of external shocks – the severe economic recession in the Western industrialized countries in the early 1980s and their slow growth since then, together with two 'oil shocks' – has been a major cause of a sharp deterioration in the economic and social progress of a wide range of developing countries. Indeed, the majority of these countries have been overtaken by a crisis of such magnitude that only extraordinary efforts both by themselves and by the international community can restore their potential for further development in the years ahead.

At the same time, however, international support for the development process has been limited in scope and wholly inadequate in magnitude to match the severity and pervasiveness of the problem. International negotiations aimed at strengthening such support – in the so-called 'North–South dialogue' – have reached an impasse on virtually all the main issues in the economic relations between developed and developing countries. This crisis in international co-operation for development has compounded the objective economic crisis of the developing countries and has acted also as a constraint on world economic recovery.

This book is concerned with only one segment of the economic ties between developed and developing countries, namely, the production of and trade in primary commodities.[1] But since the majority of developing countries are heavily dependent on commodity production and trade for their national output and their foreign exchange earnings, a study of the problems of the commodity markets, and of the national and international policies which influence these markets, can throw light on a substantial area of the development process as a whole. Moreover, the commodity sector has important linkages with other sectors in most developing countries: as supplier of raw materials to domestic industries, and of foodstuffs to the distribution network; as purchaser of inputs and of consumer goods from domestic industries; and as provider of foreign exchange for the purchase from abroad of goods and services for consumption and investment.

The significance of commodity markets goes wider than their influence on the economies of developing countries. The developed countries are themselves major producers and traders of primary commodities. Developments in world commodity markets, often influenced by events in financial markets or in the political scene, necessarily have an impact on these countries also, as was shown

---

[1] The terms 'primary commodities' or, simply, 'commodities' are used throughout this book to include all crude and processed products of agriculture, forestry, fishing, non-fuel mining, and the non-ferrous metals industries.

dramatically by the consequences of the rise in the price of petroleum during the 1970s. Though the principal focus of this book is on the developing countries, the influence of changes in world commodity markets on the developed countries is also considered as an integral part of the global commodity problem.

Most of the issues discussed in the book have been the subject of intense controversy, both in academic circles and, in one form or another, in intergovernmental discussions and negotiations on commodity problems. Very often, these issues have been considered in a neoclassical framework of the working of perfectly competitive markets, in which resources are optimally allocated by the normal operation of market forces, and both buyers and sellers reap economic gains. This is not, however, the perspective adopted in the present book, which considers the commodity markets in the context of their impact on the world economy and, more particularly, on the development of Third World countries. Thus the typical question arising is not, for example, how commodity markets reach an equilibrium position following an initial shock, but rather how commodity markets operate to stimulate or retard the development process or the overall rate of growth of the world economy. Clearly this 'development approach' is likely to have different implications for policy than is the traditional neoclassical one. As we shall see later, this divergence in theoretical approach is related to the conflict of perceived interest between developed and developing countries on commodity issues (as well as on other major issues in the 'dialogue' between the two groups of countries).

However, the impasse in North–South negotiations on commodities, as on the wider issues of a New International Economic Order, cannot be attributed wholly, or even mainly, to differences in theoretical approach. Arguments based on economic theory are, it is true, often adduced in support of national policy towards proposals for international action, but this does not mean that such policy has been evolved because theory has demonstrated its utility. Rather, national policies reflect the 'national interest' as perceived by governments, very often reflecting a narrow and short-term view which excludes any incidental costs of such policies for other countries.

In a world of very unequal distribution of economic and political power, any clash of perceived national interest is almost certain to be to the disadvantage of weaker countries. Yet without due allowance for the exercise of national power, it is not possible to obtain a realistic insight into the dynamics of policy-making in the international arena, including the complex process of international commodity negotiations. It is hoped that the present book, by introducing a political economy element in the discussion, will go some way towards greater understanding of the reasons for the continuing stalemate in international commodity policy, and thereby assist in the evolution of new approaches and new attitudes on which a viable strategy for primary commodities may be built in the future. One major conclusion of the study is that such a new strategy will have to be based essentially on much closer co-operation than hitherto among the principal commodity-dependent developing countries, rather than on reliance on the emergence of a mutually-agreed and co-operative North–South strategy which, on present policies, seems unlikely to be achieved.

Plan of the book. The book is arranged in four parts. The first, from Chapters 1 to 5, is intended to cover the principal issues involved in the 'commodity problem' from a theoretical and analytical perspective, as well as providing, in Chapter 2, quantitative estimates of the losses suffered by developing countries as a result of the fall in commodity prices after 1980. Part II (Chapters 6–9) relates essentially to the international negotiations on the short-term commodity instability issue. A review of the evolution, in the early post-war period, of the institutional framework affecting international commodity trade (Chapter 6) is followed by a detailed discussion of the negotiations on the UNCTAD Integrated Programme for Commodities, and on its central feature, the Common Fund (Chapters 7 and 8). Chapter 9 deals with the complementary issue of compensatory finance. Part III (Chapters 10–14) focuses on the main longer-term issues, including market structure, technological change, protectionism, South–South and East–South trade, and diversification. Finally, Part IV (Chapter 15) considers the major findings in the context of the need to evolve a viable international commodity policy in the future.

I
THE COMMODITY CRISIS AND THE DEVELOPING COUNTRIES

1
The Commodity Price Collapse of the 1980s

1. COMMODITIES IN THE DEVELOPMENT PROCESS

The great majority of the population of developing countries depend for their welfare and livelihood on the production and exports of primary commodities. The economic return to commodity producers is thus a central element in the potential for economic and social progress of these countries. But, as already mentioned, the importance of the commodity sector for the developed countries must not be overlooked. These countries are themselves major producers of a wide range of commodities, as well as being the traditional markets for the greater part of the commodity exports of developing countries. Changes in the conditions of commodity production, consumption, and trade, and particularly the resultant changes in commodity prices, can therefore have important impacts on the economic situation of both developed and developing countries, and thus on the whole world economy.

However, these impacts tend generally to be asymmetrical, since the relative weight of the commodity sector in the national economy is much greater in most developing, than in most developed, countries. Equally, the dependence of most developing countries on commodities for their export earnings is very substantially higher than that of most developed countries. This much greater dependence of the majority of developing countries on the commodity sector is essentially a hangover from the period of colonial rule, when the task of the former Colonies was to supply cheap food and raw materials to the metropolitan powers and to provide an assured market for a reverse flow of manufactured goods. Though a number of countries have succeeded in modernizing and industrializing their economies—particularly the NICs of East Asia—this process has not proceeded very far in many others, which still retain essentially the same lopsided economic structures that they inherited from the Colonial period.

None the less, the potential exists in the post-Colonial period for the commodity sector to play a central role in economic development. This can be achieved in one, or both, of two ways, viz. by providing an increasing volume of food and raw materials to support domestic industrialization and economic growth; and by earning foreign exchange from commodity exports to finance the imports of capital goods and other essentials for domestic economic and social progress. Up to now, the majority of developing countries have relied essentially on the latter route, i.e. on the export of their commodities to earn foreign exchange to purchase essential imports, and this dependence on export markets is likely to continue for many decades to come.

For this reason, the economic development of commodity-exporting countries remains, to a very large extent, contingent upon changes in world commodity markets. This is not to decry the importance of domestic policies in developing countries in expanding export earnings from commodities. Such policies – including the provision of adequate incentives for export, adequate transport, credit and extension services, and adequate supplies of essential imports – have clearly been of vital importance for individual countries in expanding supplies for export. However, the majority of commodity-exporting countries have traditionally suffered from a number of serious, and interrelated, handicaps arising from the operation of world commodity markets, which have often more than offset the benefits arising from appropriate domestic policies.

The central handicap faced by commodity exporters, particularly of agricultural products, is that world demand for their exports is both income-inelastic and price-inelastic, so that the growth of real income in the main commodity-importing areas over the past two decades has brought relatively little growth to consumption. For most minerals and metals, supply can be adjusted, at least to some extent, to price changes over the short-term, but many of these commodities are subject to long-term substitution by synthetic or other materials, while short-term price cycles reflect mainly fluctuations in demand. At the same time, the efforts of producing countries to expand their supplies come to fruition usually after a time-lag, and tend to be self-defeating, since increased supplies result, other things being equal, in lower prices and earnings. It is this double-inelasticity effect on the demand side which underlies much of the continuing difficulty of developing countries in achieving any substantial expansion in the purchasing power of their commodity exports over a sustained period of time. Indeed, as discussed later, the expansion of production of many commodities over the post-war period has been an important contributor to the downward trend in the commodity terms of trade (or in 'real commodity prices')[1] suffered by the developing countries.

Low price-elasticities of demand, together with low short-term price-elasticities of supply for many commodities, also result in relatively large short-term fluctuations in world market prices. This is particularly the case for many commodities produced and exported wholly or mainly by developing countries (e.g. cocoa, coffee, and many minerals and metals), or produced in most developed countries behind high protective barriers (e.g. cereals and sugar). Commodity markets can generally be characterized as a 'flex price' sector as regards short-term price changes, as distinct from the markets for industrial products, which are normally 'fix price', adjustments in the latter case being made

---

[1] The terms 'commodity terms of trade' and 'real commodity prices' are used interchangeably throughout this book to denote the ratio of commodity prices to the prices of manufactured goods.

in the volume of output to meet changing market conditions.[2] Protection in developed countries, by restricting the scope of the world market, and by resulting in subsidized exports, thus adds to the instability already characteristic of unregulated commodity markets. Large short-term fluctuations inject substantial uncertainty into future profitability expectations, and thus are likely to reduce the level of investment in new productive capacity and, to this extent, make much more difficult the efforts of developing countries to achieve sustained economic growth.

The difficulties of coping with the inelasticities of world demand for commodities are enhanced by the structural characteristics of commodity supply from developing countries. The great majority of these countries are small or medium-sized producers, no one of which can influence the world price by varying its own supply. Thus there is an inbuilt incentive for any one such country to expand its exports, since, other things being equal, this will result in higher export earnings. But if many such countries expand their exports simultaneously, this will result in lower prices, and lower export earnings, for all producers. Moreover, for many important commodities, both agricultural and mineral, exports from developing countries move through distribution channels controlled very largely by transnational corporations, often acting as oligopsonists in purchasing from developing country producers, and as oligopolists in selling in developed country markets. For such commodity markets, the division of the benefits of international commodity trade tends to be heavily skewed in favour of these corporations.

These various difficulties faced by developing countries, which flow from the structural characteristics of both world supply of, and world demand for, their commodity exports, are discussed in greater detail in later chapters. Here it suffices to highlight the central importance of prices on world commodity markets to the success or failure of developing countries' own efforts to achieve sustainable economic growth while adjusting their economies to changing conditions in the world economy.

2. COMMODITY PRICES IN THE 1980s

The decade of the 1980s was dramatically different from earlier post-war decades in the movement of (non-oil) commodity prices. The outstanding difference was that while the general trend of the commodity terms of trade was gently downward over the two decades up to the end of the 1970s, in the 1980s the corresponding trend was drastically, even catastrophically, downward. The three indices most widely used in this regard—those of UNCTAD, World Bank, and IMF—all show a fall of as much as some 35 per cent in real terms between

---

[2] To the extent that commodity producers adjust the volume of their output after a time-lag to changes in market prices, the commodity markets can be said to contain an element of the fix price model. But this does not invalidate the general distinction between the mode of operation of the markets for commodities and for manufactures.

Table 1.1. Trends in the commodity terms of trade, 1958–60 to 1986–8[a]

	Indices (1958–60 = 100)			
	1958–60	1968–70	1978–80	1986–8
Non-oil commodities				
UNCTAD index[b,f]	100	93	92	62
World Bank index[c,f]	100	97	90	58
IMF index[d,g]	100	95	91	61
Petroleum[e]	100	70	390	211

[a] Annual averages.
[b] 39 commodities.
[c] 33 commodities.
[d] 34 commodities.
[e] Average OPEC price (World Bank index).
[f] Weighted by value of exports from developing countries in 1979–81.
[g] Weighted by value of world exports in 1980.

Sources: UNCTAD Monthly Commodity Price Bulletin (various issues), and Supplement, 1960–84, Geneva, UN; World Bank, 1988*b*; IMF, 1989*b*.

1978–80 and 1986–8, as against a decline of only 7 per cent (World Bank), 4 per cent (IMF), or 1 per cent (UNCTAD) over the previous decade (Table 1.1).

The strong downward trend in the 1980s was interrupted in 1983–4 when commodity prices staged a minor recovery as a result of sharp increases in prices of vegetable oils which, in turn, largely reflected the effects of acreage restrictions in the United States in the preceding year. This was followed by a further price decline, and though there was another minor recovery in 1988–9 (this time mainly in prices of cereals and metals), real prices in both 1988 and 1989 were still very substantially below the level of 1980, by some 20–25 per cent (Fig. 1.1).

The virtual collapse of commodity prices in the 1980s prompts comparison with the Great Depression of the 1930s, the last occasion when there was a deep slump in prices, accompanied by widespread financial losses and a sharp contraction in international trade flows. The movement of an index of the commodity terms of trade for these two periods, as recently published by two World Bank economists (Grilli and Yang, 1988) is shown in Fig. 1.2. This index, which is based on a smaller sample (24 commodities) than either the UNCTAD or World Bank indices, shows that the movement of the commodity terms of trade over the period from 1980 to 1983 closely paralleled the fall during the early part of the Great Depression (1929–32). Thereafter, however, commodity prices in the two periods followed diametrically opposite paths. By 1987, the low point of the 1980s series, the Grilli–Yang index would have been in the region of 60 (1977–9 = 100), using the more comprehensive World Bank index as a guide, or only some 50 per cent of the 1980 level. At a similar phase of the 1930s cycle, real commodity prices (in 1936) were some 35 per cent above the price nadir (in

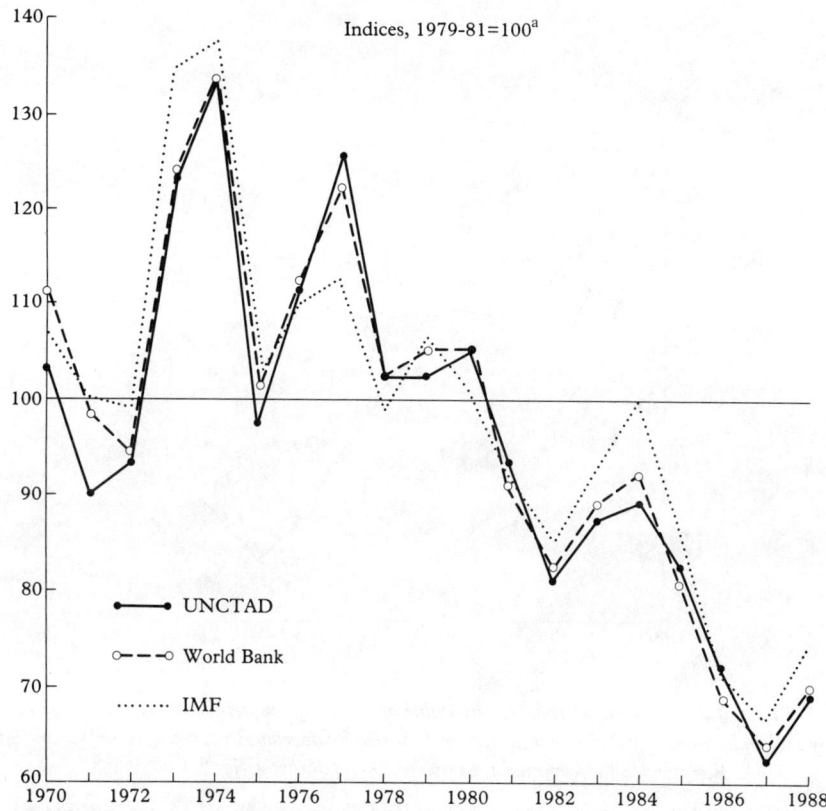

[a] Commodity price indices deflated by UN index of unit values of manufactures exported by developed market-economy countries.

Fig. 1.1 *The commodity terms of trade, 1970–88.* Source: as for Table 1.1

1932), while at the peak (in 1937) they had almost regained the pre-recession level.

As Fig. 1.2 indicates, the commodity price recession of the 1980s has been more severe, and considerably more prolonged, than that of the Great Depression of the 1930s. The 1987 low level was some 15 per cent below that of 1932, the bottom of the pre-war slump; and while there was a definite upturn in real commodity prices some three years after the beginning of the pre-war cycle, in the present recession that definite upturn is yet to come.

A second difference – considered in greater detail in Chapter 2 – is that for the greater part of the 1930s the volume of commodity exports from the present developing countries remained below the pre-recession level of 1929. In the 1980s, by contrast, commodity exports from developing countries expanded

12   Commodity Crisis and Developing Countries

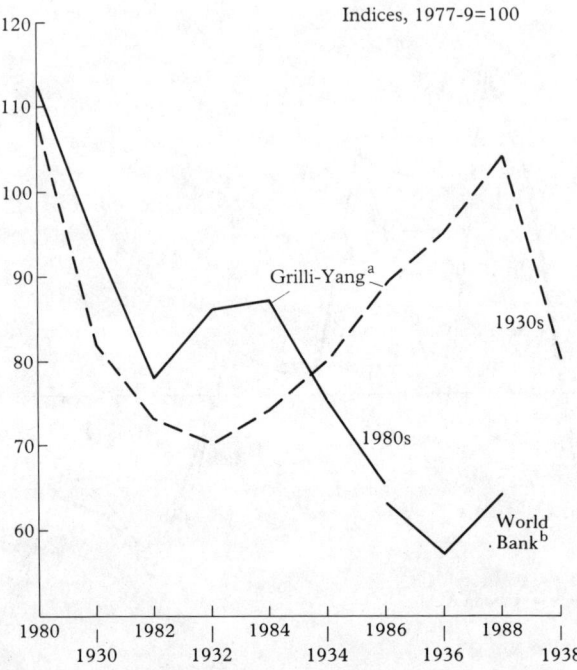

[a] Prices of 24 commodities weighted by value of exports from developing countries, deflated by UN index of unit value of manufactures exported by developed market-economy countries.
[b] World Bank index (33 commodities) using same deflator as for [a].

Fig. 1.2. *The commodity price recessions of the 1930s and 1980s.* Sources: *Grilli and Yang 1988; World Bank 1988b*

substantially and, as will be seen, this expansion was a significant element in the fall in commodity prices in that decade.

There is also an important difference between the 1980s and the 1970s in that the earlier decade was characterized chiefly by extremely large short-term price variations, as can be seen from Fig. 1.1. In this, the 1970s were similar to the 1950s, when world commodity markets had been subject to a number of major 'shocks', reflecting at first severe shortages of many key foods and raw materials, followed by a huge price cycle during the Korean War associated with rearmament programmes and the building of strategic stockpiles and, in the mid-1950s, a short, sharp price cycle for coffee which began with news of a severe frost in the Brazilian coffee-growing areas. From the late 1950s to the early 1970s, however, annual commodity price fluctuations were generally small.

The 1970s, too, was a decade of successive 'shocks' to world commodity markets, beginning with the sharp rise in petroleum prices in 1973–4, which created fears of a more general rise in commodity prices, while there was a succession of shortages in some major markets (cereals, sugar, and some vegetable oils in 1974–5, and coffee in 1977), which resulted in exceptionally high levels of commodity prices in those years. Commodity price fluctuations in the 1970s were around a modest upward trend in real terms whereas, by contrast, commodity prices in the 1980s showed relatively small annual fluctuations, the dominant feature, as already mentioned, being the sharp downward trend (Fig. 1.1), though excessive price instability remained a feature for a number of individual commodities (particularly sugar, jute, and some vegetable oils). Overall, commodity price instability in the period 1980–7 was only about one-half of the corresponding instability over the previous two decades (Table 1.2).

Another notable feature of the commodity situation in the 1980s was that the price decline affected all the main commodity groups without exception (Table 1.2), being particularly severe for foods, where the downtrend for sugar (with about half the total weighting) was as much as −21 per cent per annum.

Oil Prices

International oil prices have been subject to major shifts since the early 1970s. Periods of relative stability followed each of the two 'shocks' of 1973–74 and 1978–9 when prices rose sharply, mainly as a result of supply restrictions by OPEC member countries. Again, in the years 1983 to 1985, prices were relatively stable, but the underlying OPEC quotas were being eroded by overproduction and price discounting by a number of member countries. As a result, the largest producer, Saudi Arabia, was being forced to cut output to protect the agreed reference price. In the latter part of 1985, Saudi Arabia abandoned its role as 'swing' producer in order to regain market share and restore its former level of oil production. The consequent expansion in oil production and exports from Saudi Arabia and other Middle Eastern countries precipitated a dramatic fall in international oil prices, by some 50 per cent between 1985 and 1986.

From the end of 1986, a renewed effort was made by OPEC to agree on

Table 1.2. Trends and instability of prices of main commodity groups, 1962–87

	Trend in real prices (% p.a.)[a]		Instability index (%)[b]	
	1962–80	1980–7	1962–80	1980–7
Food (including vegetable oilseeds and oils)	1.0	−10.1	24.4	12.5
Tropical beverages	2.9	−2.4	25.5	12.4
Agricultural raw materials	0.5	−4.2	16.6	8.6
Minerals, ores, and metals	−0.5	−6.1	12.3	5.9
TOTAL	1.1	−5.6	15.2	7.0

[a] Average growth rates derived from semi-logarithmic regressions.
[b] Average percentage deviation from exponential trend.

Source: UNCTAD Commodity Yearbook, 1987, Geneva, UN.

production quotas to maintain a reference price of $18 a barrel, a policy which was supported by voluntary output or export restraint by a number of non-OPEC oil-exporting countries. Over the years 1987 to 1989, this form of supply management proved partially successful in stabilizing international oil prices at or near the reference level. Over this brief period, the oil market was thus one of very few examples of relative price stability brought about by producer actions.[3]

3. THE CAUSES OF THE COLLAPSE IN NON-OIL COMMODITY PRICES

It is important to derive a convincing explanation of the main causes of the sharp downward trend in real non-oil commodity prices in the 1980s, for two reasons. One is that without such an explanation it is not possible to develop a credible assessment of the likely future course of commodity prices, and such an assessment is crucial for a viable development strategy for commodity-exporting countries. Second, an unravelling of the various influences depressing commodity prices and a quantification, as far as is possible, of their relative importance can reveal areas in which policy changes, by both developed and developing countries, could be expected to halt, or even reverse, the price decline.

A number of studies, mostly econometric, have been published in recent years which attempt such an explanation.[4] A major difficulty in this kind of analysis has been that the dominant influences on commodity prices have differed from some years to others, and have also differed markedly from one commodity group to another. However, some general causal influences can be identified, taking the period 1980 to 1987 as a whole. The sharp downward trend in commodity prices has reflected a simultaneous decline in the growth rate of commodity demand, and a continued expansion in world commodity supply. It is convenient to consider the underlying real forces on each side of the market separately, as well as the influence of purely monetary factors.

(a) The Decline in Growth Rate of Commodity Demand

There are several distinct elements involved here: the slowdown in the economic growth rate of the world economy, and particularly that of the industrial countries; the longer-term effects of continuing technological change; and the approach to saturation levels in the demand for foods and beverages in these countries.

The slowdown in the growth rates of GDP and of industrial production

---

[3] This period was brought to an abrupt end, however, in August 1990 as a result of the imposition of UN sanctions consequent upon the Iraqi occupation of Kuwait, with renewed instability in the world oil market.

[4] For relevant econometric studies see, in particular, Englander 1985, Hartman 1985, Chu and Morrison 1986, Morrison and Wattleworth 1988 and Gilbert 1989. Useful non-econometric discussions of the various forces behind the commodity price decline can be found in IMF 1987, UNCTAD 1987a, Morgan Guaranty Trust Co. 1987, and Perlman and Gilbert 1987.

emerges from all the relevant studies as one of the main causal factors in the commodity price decline. For the OECD countries as a group, industrial production rose by 3.0 per cent per annum from the early– to the late– 1970s, but then fell to only 1.9 per cent per annum up to 1988. This sharp retardation in the growth rate of industrial output had a consequential effect in slowing down substantially the growth of demand for all industrial inputs, including primary commodities. The severity of the economic recession was undoubtedly due in part to the impact of the restrictionist monetary policies of some of the larger industrial countries – particularly those in Western Europe such as the Federal Republic of Germany and the United Kingdom – which were intended to fight inflation. A significant part of the slowdown in the growth rate of world demand for commodities can thus be attributed to economic policy decisions in the larger OECD countries, as distinct from the operation of economic forces *per se*.

A second element, relating to industrial raw materials, has been the continuance of a longer-term trend of declining consumption of natural raw materials per unit of GDP, or of industrial production. This adverse trend, in turn, reflects two separate processes. The first is a continuing displacement of natural materials by synthetics or other non-traditional substitutes in particular end-uses. This displacement has been especially great as regards agricultural raw materials (cotton, wool, jute, hard fibres, natural rubber, and timber being the most important), but metals (particularly tin, copper, lead, and many minor metals) have been increasingly displaced (optic fibres for copper wire being an important recent example), while among foods, high-fructose corn syrup and synthetic sweeteners have displaced sugar on a large scale over the past decade. In addition, for several important metals the increasing use of secondary or scrap metal has reduced demand for the primary forms exported by developing countries.

The second long-term process adversely affecting the demand for natural raw materials arises from the impact of technological innovation, and changes in economic structures, in the developed countries. Particularly since the sharp price increases for petroleum during the 1970s, technological innovation in manufacturing industry has been largely directed to saving energy and reducing costs in an increasingly competitive environment. Major changes have involved redesigning of processes and products so as to use lighter materials, the downsizing of products using new electronic devices, and significant reductions in materials wastage. At the same time, industrial structures have undergone substantial changes, with traditional heavy industries – steel, mechanical engineering, etc. – growing at a slower rate than the newer high-tech electronic and informatic sectors which use considerably less raw materials per unit of output.

A detailed examination of these two processes shows that, together, they accounted for a decline of the order of 2 per cent per annum, on average, in the volume of consumption of natural materials per unit of industrial output in the Western industrial countries between the early 1970s and the mid-1980s (see Chapter 11). Thus these adverse long-term trends added significantly to the downward pressure on commodity prices in the 1980s arising from the recession effect discussed above.

For a wide variety of foods and beverages, a major element influencing world commodity prices has been the approach to saturation levels in per capita consumption in the industrial countries. Indeed, over the past decade per capita consumption of meat and sugar, in particular, as well as tobacco, has fallen significantly, while only marginal increases have occurred in per capita consumption of many other foods and beverages.

(b) The Rise in Growth Rate of Commodity Supply

In a period of contraction, or of slow growth, in demand as in the 1980s, it appears at first sight perverse for commodity supply to grow at all, let alone to grow as fast as previously, as has been the case for many commodities. Again, it is useful to distinguish two separate elements in supply change during the 1980s, viz. supply from developed, and supply from developing, countries, since quite distinct policies are involved in each.

In the developed countries, output of cereals and other temperate-zone agricultural products is heavily influenced by the farm income support policies of these countries. These policies, reviewed in some detail in Chapter 12, have tended to generate huge domestic surpluses of major foods, and intense price competition for export markets. One result has been an abnormally high accumulation of stocks, especially in the later 1980s, to far above normal working levels and reserve requirements. World wheat stocks, for example, rose from an average of 21 per cent of consumption in the second half of the 1970s to an average of about 40 per cent a decade later. For coarse grains, the corresponding percentages rose from 13 to some 26 per cent; for sugar, from 30 to over 40 per cent; and for major vegetable oilseeds from 13 to almost 20 per cent. In total, world stocks of food commodities rose by some 50 per cent from 1980 to 1987 (IMF 1989b), the increasing stock overhang constituting a major depressive force on world food prices. As Table 1.2 shows, the decline in real prices of foods over the 1980–7 period was substantially greater than for other commodity groups.

In most developing countries, the prime force behind the expansion in commodity output and exports since the early 1980s has been the severe foreign exchange squeeze they suffered as a result of the collapse in commodity export prices, the concurrent high level of interest charges on their foreign debt, and the virtual drying-up of commercial loans after 1982. The stabilization and adjustment policies of the majority of developing countries – mostly as conditions for IMF and World Bank support – have almost always included a depreciation of the currency, among other measures, to promote exports and contract domestic demand. However, while this type of stabilization package may improve the balance of payments position of an individual country, whose expansion of commodity exports is too small to influence the world price, similar policies applied to a wide range of countries simultaneously – as was the case for many commodities in the 1980s — are likely to result in an export increase which will only add to the depressive forces in world commodity markets.[5] Gilbert (1989) takes this analysis a step further by a regression analysis which reveals a statistically significant negative relation between the magnitude of the debt service burden of producer countries and changes in agricultural food prices. Similar negative (though non-significant) coefficients were found for agricultural non-foods and for metals and minerals. His conclusion is that the efforts of individual countries to meet debt service obligations have reduced export earnings for all commodity producers, thus making it more difficult for them as a group to meet their obligations.[6]

An additional factor in the expansion in supply for a wide range of agricultural commodities has been an increase in crop yields as a result of improved techniques, increased use of fertilizers, etc. Over the period 1980 to 1988, the volume of primary commodities exported by developing countries rose by over 20 per cent, most of the increase being in food, including tropical beverages and vegetable oilseeds and oils. This expansion in export supply — most of the proceeds of which were used to meet debt service obligations — was an important factor in the sharp decline in world food and beverage prices from 1980 and 1981 levels.

For the minerals and metals industries, where the gestation period of new investment is relatively long, new capacity was coming on stream over the first half of the 1980s as a result of investment during the period of relatively favourable prices and consumption trends of the later 1970s. As a result of the economic recession, which hit the metal-using industries particularly hard, considerable excess capacity emerged, provoking much rationalization, including mine closures, particularly in North America. By 1987, metal stocks had been reduced to low levels, and increasing demand, together with speculative buying, then contributed to a substantial, though short-lived, price rise.

(c) Monetary Influences

Most internationally traded commodities are denominated in US dollars, and changes in the exchange value of the dollar have a significant, and inverse, effect on the dollar prices of commodities. As Dornbusch (1985) has shown, when the dollar appreciates *vis-à-vis* other major trading currencies, commodity prices are raised in terms of currencies not linked to the dollar, so that demand in the United States is stimulated while demand in non-dollar countries is reduced. The net effect on world prices then depends on the relative shares of dollar and non-dollar markets in world consumption, and the relative demand-elasticities in

---

[5] For an expansion of this argument, including empirical analysis, see Maizels 1988; also Wattleworth 1988.

[6] Gilbert 1989: 773–84. His results indicate that the fall in commodity prices may have reflected both increased supply and also a fall in real wages resulting from currency depreciations by commodity exporting countries.

the two markets for the commodity concerned.[7] By early 1985, the dollar had appreciated by over 40 per cent compared with its average exchange value during the second half of the 1970s. It has been estimated that this alone resulted in a fall of 25–30 per cent in dollar commodity prices over this period (Perlman and Gilbert 1987).

It was widely anticipated that a dollar depreciation would result in the opposite process, i.e. in a rise in commodity prices in dollar terms. However, the dollar depreciation of 1985 to 1987 was not accompanied by a rise in dollar commodity prices (Fig. 1.1). This reflected a further expansion in commodity supply, referred to earlier, as well as some special factors, including substantial reductions in US support prices for cereals and other foods as a result of the Farm Bill enacted early in 1986. Moreover, intense competition between the US and the European Community in world food markets resulted in significant reductions in prices of a number of important foodstuffs.

The dollar depreciation has had another important effect: it resulted in a corresponding rise in the dollar prices of manufactured goods exported by Western Europe and Japan, the principal non-dollar sources of such goods. Prices of manufactured goods exports from the industrial countries as a group rose by 20 per cent in dollar terms in 1986, and by a further 13 per cent in 1987, these increases being a major reason for the sharp deterioration in the commodity terms of trade in these two years (Fig. 1.1). From 1985 to 1988, the corresponding increase in the prices of manufactures amounted to 44 per cent.

Two other monetary factors may also have had an impact on commodity price trends in the 1980s. One such factor is the level of real interest rates, which rose sharply in the early 1980s and which substantially raised the cost of holding commodity stocks, and thereby reduced demand for commodities. An analysis by Dornbusch (1985) showed a significant negative association between a measure of the real interest rate and United States real commodity prices. Similar statistically significant associations have been found by other authors for different periods or for certain categories of products (e.g. Englander 1985 and Hartman 1985). Some analysts, however, have found little or no significant interest rate effects on commodity price changes.

A second monetary factor affecting commodity prices is the extent of speculative transactions. As expectations since 1980–1 have generally been pessimistic about the short-term trend in commodity prices, it seems likely that speculators reduced their commodity interests, and transferred their funds to more volatile markets such as those for foreign exchange or equities. However, a change in sentiment, such as in the period from mid-1987 to mid-1988, when metal prices were rising sharply, brought large amounts of speculative funds back into commodity futures, which then added to the price upturn.

---

[7] See also the analysis in Fleisig and Wijnbergen 1985 of the relationships involved.

The Relative Importance of Demand, Supply, and Monetary Factors

The various econometric studies which have been made of the movement of commodity prices in recent periods are not precisely comparable, since they cover different sample periods, use different price indices, and are based on different theoretical models. None the less, they all reveal significant contributions from the three influences of demand, supply, and monetary factors. The most recent of these studies (Morrison and Wattleworth 1988) is based on annual series for the period 1961 to 1985, and uses the IMF commodity prices index as the dependent variable. This index covers 34 commodities, and uses world export values as weights (in this respect, it differs from the UNCTAD and World Bank indices, both of which use developing-country exports as weights). The IMF price index showed a decline of 27 per cent in current US dollars from 1979 to 1986,[8] while the Morrison–Wattleworth model predicted a decline of 23 per cent over this period. The contribution of each variable in this model to the predicted price decline is shown in Table 1.3.

According to these results, the impact of the rise in industrial production on commodity demand was exactly offset by the expansion in commodity supply. However, the largest single influence by far was the trend term (the constant in the regression equation), which indicates that if there had been no changes in the variables specifically included in the analysis, commodity prices would have fallen over this period by 35 per cent (i.e. 5 per cent per annum). The monetary factor is significant, but relatively small, and relates mainly to inflationary pressures in the developed countries and to changes in the dollar exchange rate (changes in interest rates were not, however, specifically covered in this analysis).

These results generally help in understanding the reasons for the commodity price collapse, but they also raise some difficult issues of interpretation. The most important of these relates to the dominant trend term. The authors of the study suggest that this term is 'probably associated with structural shifts that tend over time to reduce demand (for example, substitution of synthetic materials for natural materials) and to increased supply (for example, technological change embodied in new high-yielding crop varieties)'.[9] However, since the supply variable in the model is defined as world commodity production plus stocks at the beginning of each year, it already includes the effect of productivity increases resulting from new high-yield crops. Thus the trend term is likely to reflect essentially the impact on commodity prices of demand factors not already subsumed under movements in industrial production. These additional demand factors can reasonably be taken as the various elements of the long-term trend to declining consumption of natural materials per unit of industrial output to which reference was made earlier, together with the influence of increases in real

---

[8] Over this period, the UNCTAD index fell by 19%, and the World Bank index fell by 16%.
[9] Morrison and Wattleworth 1988: 374.

Table 1.3. Contributions to commodity price change, 1980–1986[a]

Positive factors	%	Negative factors	%
Increase in industrial production	+19	Trend	−35
Inflation, adjusted for exchange rate changes	+16	Increase in supply[b]	−19
1983 dummy for food commodities	+7	Increase in productive capacity[c]	−11
TOTAL	+42	TOTAL	−65
		NET TOTAL	−23

[a] Based on a weighted aggregation of estimated equations for four broad commodity groups (food, beverages, agricultural raw materials, and metals) over the period 1961 to 1985.

[b] Index of current production plus stocks at beginning of year (used only for the food and beverages equations).

[c] Index of estimated productive capacity (used only for the agricultural raw materials and metals equations).

Source: Based on Morrison and Wattleworth 1988: Table 2.

interest rates. However, there is some doubt as to the derivation, and statistical significance, of this trend term.[10]

It is shown later—see Chapter 11—that the consumption of the principal natural materials per unit of industrial output in the OECD area fell by 1.8 per cent a year, on average, from the late 1970s to the mid-1980s. Applying the Morrison-Wattleworth results for the elasticity of commodity prices with respect to changes in industrial output yields a trend term of −3.0 per cent per annum, and on this basis, the effect of the adverse trend would be of roughly the same order of magnitude as that of the expansion in supply.[11]

4. THE OUTLOOK FOR COMMODITY PRICES

There is a general consensus among economists concerned with commodity market trends that, on current policies, commodity prices are likely to remain at depressed levels at least for another decade. Projections by the World Bank in October 1986 showed a fall in real commodity prices of 5 per cent from 1985 to 1990, followed by a small rise (of 5–6 per cent) from 1990 to 1995, and no change from then up to 2000 (World Bank 1986b). Later World Bank projections, in October 1988, present a considerably more pessimistic picture: a decline in real

---

[10] The trend term quoted is derived as a weighted average of the trend terms in the regressions for each of four broad commodity groups. However, for three of these groups—food, beverages, and agricultural raw materials—the trend term is not statistically significant at the usual confidence levels. For the remaining group, metals, the trend term (−7.7% p.a.) is significant at the 5% level.

[11] The importance of technological change in the market for industrial materials is discussed further in Ch. 11.

commodity prices of 23 per cent from 1985 to 1990, followed by a small rise (of 5–6 per cent) from 1990 to 1995, with no significant change from then until 2000 (World Bank 1988*b*). By the year 2000, real commodity prices were projected, in 1986, to be 25 per cent below the 1980 level, whereas the 1988 projection is for a shortfall of as much as 40 per cent below 1980.

These large changes in price level projections indicate just how great is the margin of error in such exercises, in terms of the actual outcome. Such projections depend heavily on a series of assumptions, particularly those for the future rate of GDP growth in OECD countries, future inflationary trends, future commodity supply, future rate of substitution between synthetic and natural materials, and the pace of future technological advance and the associated changes in economic structures. They also assume essentially unchanged economic policies, including no major reduction in agricultural protection in developed countries and a continuation of anti-inflationary policies.

On the basis of these, and related, assumptions it does indeed seem most unlikely that the trend of real commodity prices during the 1990s will recover to the 1980 level; rather, the continuance of recent trends and policies points to a prolongation of the 1980s experience of depressed commodity prices. World food prices rose substantially – by some 30 per cent – from 1987 to 1988, and rose further – by 6 per cent – in 1989, mainly as a result of the United States drought, and the consequent drawing down of commercial food stocks. United States production is, however, likely to increase with more normal weather, and world stocks are likely to rise again in the 1990s, even with a modest reduction in the level of agricultural protection. For many individual commodities which have in the past exhibited large short-term price fluctuations, and substantial medium-term price cycles, similar fluctuations and cycles must be expected in the future, at least on present policies based on non-intervention by governments in the international commodity markets. For raw materials, and especially for metals, low stock levels are likely to result in volatile markets, at least until there is a definite upward trend in prices.

The generally gloomy outlook for commodity prices, coming after the 'lost decade' of development in the 1980s, poses a number of urgent policy issues, both for the commodity-dependent countries and for the industrialized countries, as well as for international commodity policy in general.

A series of interrelated questions immediately arise. Can the industrialized countries, for instance, do more than they have done in the past to remedy the situation of continuing depressed levels of commodity prices? If so, should remedial action be indirect (e.g. by domestic economic expansion) or direct (by market intervention)? What can developing countries themselves do to alleviate the situation, either individually or in combination? Should they attempt to diversify their production away from commodities likely to remain in structural surplus on the world market and, if so, into what alternatives? How can diversification best be financed? What prospects, if any, are there for supply management schemes operated by developing countries only? In the broader context of

North–South co-operation, can a framework of principles be devised on which developed and developing countries could base a common strategy to strengthen the commodity sector of the world economy, and thereby promote a process of economic recovery and restructuring in commodity-dependent countries? These are the kind of questions which are considered in some detail in later chapters.

But before turning to such policy issues, it is necessary first to assess the magnitude of the commodity crisis for the developing countries concerned, and to consider its short-term and longer-term implications for their economic growth and development, as well as for the evolution of effective international remedial policies.

2
The Impact on the Developing Countries

1. THE MAGNITUDE OF THE FOREIGN EXCHANGE LOSS

The sharp deterioration in the commodity terms of trade in the 1980s has involved a massive loss in export earnings of developing countries dependent on primary commodities. There are several ways in which the magnitude of the loss can be evaluated. One is to compare the absolute loss with the total value of developing countries' commodity exports before the collapse in commodity prices, i.e. at the end of the 1970s, or in 1980. A much more stringent comparison would be to relate the export loss with what the value of commodity exports would have been during the 1980s had there been no economic recession in the developed countries, in which case a significantly higher level of commodity prices would have prevailed.

It is also of some relevance to compare the export earnings loss suffered by developing countries in the 1980s with the corresponding loss during the Great Depression of the 1930s, when the world's primary producing countries underwent a severe economic and financial crisis. Has the commodity price collapse of the 1980s created a similar situation to the great economic cataclysm of the 1930s?

A further comparison, with important implications for policy, can be made by considering the commodity exports of developing countries in the wider context of their overall balance of payments. This allows a comparison to be made between the export earnings loss from commodities and changes in the other key elements affecting the payments position, especially the rise in debt service payments and the relative stagnation in the inflow of financial resources in the form of commercial bank loans, official aid, or private foreign investment.

Finally, it is useful to relate the foreign exchange loss due to the change in the commodity terms of trade to the gross domestic product of the developing countries concerned. How large, for example, has been the commodity 'price shock' in relation to the GDP of commodity-exporting countries compared with the magnitude of the oil 'price shocks' of the 1970s in relation to the GDP of the industrialized countries, or of the oil-importing developing countries?

Before turning to consider the estimates of export earnings losses, a statistical caveat needs to be made, viz. that to apply any of the published indices of commodity market prices discussed in Chapter 1 to derive figures of export earnings losses will exaggerate these losses, probably by a substantial amount. This is so for three reasons, one specific and two more general. The specific reason is that for some commodities, of which sugar is by far the most important, only a part of developing countries' exports are sold at world market prices. In the case of sugar, a large proportion is sold at relatively stable preferential prices (Cuban sales to the Soviet Union, sales to the European Community by countries signatory to the successive Lomé Conventions, and shipments to the United States by designated Caribbean sugar-producing countries). One more general reason is that market prices for particular varieties or grades, which are used to compile price indices, tend to exhibit larger variations than do the corresponding unit values. Thus in a period of falling prices, the decline in unit values generally tends to be smaller than the fall shown by price quotations, so that the use of price indices will give an upward bias to the calculation of export volume, and thus to the terms of trade loss.

A third reason is that all the published price indices cover only a proportion of trade in primary commodities: the UNCTAD index, for example, covered 66 per cent of the value of all commodity exports from developing countries in its base period (1979–81), while the coverage is even smaller for the IMF and World Bank indices. To the extent that a general price fall encourages a shift in the composition of exports towards goods the prices of which have fallen less than average (e.g. most processed foods, as compared with unprocessed forms), there will be a downward bias in a restricted-coverage price index.

For these reasons, a new series for the unit value of commodity exports from developing countries has been computed, covering over 90 per cent of the total value of commodity exports from developing countries (see the Appendix for details). As expected, this new index shows a significantly smaller decline from the 1980 level than does the corresponding price index. Between 1980 and 1988, for example, the UNCTAD price index fell by 18 per cent, whereas the new unit value index shows a decline of only 7 per cent. Consequently, the volume increase between these two years is reduced from 40 per cent (using the price index) to 24 per cent (with the new unit value index).

Losses and Gains in the 1970s and 1980s

Estimates of the foreign exchange loss resulting from the change in the commodity terms of trade during the 1980s can now be made by deducting the value of commodity exports from developing countries at 1980 prices for any given year from the corresponding value of the purchasing power of these exports in terms of the prices of manufactured goods exported by the industrial countries.[1] Over the period from 1980 to 1988 (the latest year for which the relevant statistics were available at the time of writing), the value of developing countries' com-

---

[1] Thus for any year subsequent to 1980, the value of exports at 1980 prices can be written as $\sum_{i=1}^{n} (V_{xi1}/P_{xi})$ where V_{xi1} relates to the value of exports of commodity i in the later year, and P_{xi} is an index of the export price of i in that year with base year price as unity. Similarly, the purchasing power of exports in the later year at base year prices is $\sum_{i=1}^{n} (V_{xi1}/P_{mi})$, where P_{mi} is the index of prices of manufactured goods. The foreign exchange loss in the later year resulting from a change in the commodity terms of trade is then $\sum_{i=1}^{n} (V_{xi1}(1/P_{mi} - 1/P_{xi}))$.

Table 2.1. Commodity exports of developing countries, 1970, 1980, and 1988

Year	Unit value (US$; 1980 = 100)			Value of commodity exports ($ billion)		
	Commodities		Manufactures unit value[a]	At current unit value	At 1980 commodity unit value	At 1980 manufactures unit value
	Nominal	Real[a]				
1970	33	97	34	28	85	84
1980	100	100	100	109	109	109
1988	93	75	124	125	135	101
	Annual average change (%)					
1970–80	11.2	0.2	11.4	14.4	2.5	2.7
1980–8	−0.9	−3.5	2.7	1.7	2.7	−0.9

[a] Nominal unit value deflated by the UN index of unit value of exports of manufactures from developed market-economy countries.

Sources: See Appendix Table A.2.

modity exports at 1980 prices expanded from $109 billion to some $135 billion, an increase of 24 per cent (or 2.7 per cent a year, on average). However, over this same period the purchasing power over imports of manufactures of this expanding volume of commodity exports fell by some 9 per cent from $109 billion to $101 billion (Table 2.1). Thus the foreign exchange loss in the one year 1988, resulting from the fall in the commodity terms of trade since 1980, amounted to almost $35 billion.[2]

As Table 2.1 also shows, the experience of the 1980s was in sharp contrast to that of the 1970s, when both the volume of developing countries' commodity exports and their purchasing power over manufactured imports rose at about the same rate. Between the two individual years 1970 and 1980, then, there was no very significant foreign exchange loss due to price changes.

A more useful calculation, perhaps, is summarized in Table 2.2, which shows the mean annual changes over the two periods 1970–80 and 1980–8, as well as the cumulative totals for each period. The later period is also divided into two sub-periods, since the terms of trade loss increased very substantially after 1985. The annual changes over the whole period since 1970 are depicted in Fig. 2.1, the actual series being given in the Appendix (Table A.2).

Over the 1970s there were alternating periods of gains and losses arising from changes in the commodity terms of trade. Gains in 1973–4 and in 1976–7 totalled

---

[2] The use of 1980 as a base for calculating foreign exchange losses due to the price decline in subsequent years has sometimes been criticized on the grounds that 1980 was a peak year for commodity prices. While this is true in terms of nominal prices, it is far from true in terms of real prices (i.e. commodity prices in terms of prices of manufactures). Since the analysis here is based on movements in real commodity prices, the use of 1980 as the reference year seems justified. In fact, the general level of real commodity prices in 1980 was much the same as the average of the years 1976–9 (see Appendix Table A.2).

Table 2.2. Changes in volume, terms of trade, and purchasing power of commodity exports of developing countries, 1970–88 ($ billion at 1980 prices)

	Mean annual change			Cumulative change		
	Volume	Terms of trade[a]	Purchasing power[b]	Volume	Terms of trade[a]	Purchasing power[b]
1970–9	8.0	3.9	11.9	72	35	107
1980–8	12.3	−16.1	−3.8	98	−128	−30
1980–5[c]	7.4	−6.3	1.1	37	−32	5
1986–8[c]	20.4	−32.3	−11.9	74	−128	−19

[a] In terms of unit value of exports of manufactured goods from developed countries.
[b] Export value deflated by unit value of exports of manufactured goods from developed countries.
[c] Change from 1980.

Sources: See Appendix Table A.2.

rather more than losses in earlier years; for the decade as a whole, developing countries had a net annual gain, on average, of some $4 billion. Over the period 1980–8, by contrast, there was a mean annual loss on commodity exports of $16 billion, equivalent to a cumulative loss over this period in the region of $128 billion.[3] As Table 2.2 indicates, the rate of loss rose sharply towards the end of the period, the annual rate during 1986–8, at $32 billion, being five times that during 1980–5. Whereas in the first half of the 1980s the terms of trade loss arose from the greater decline in the unit values of commodity exports than of manufactured imports, in the later period the sharply higher terms of trade loss reflected a much more rapid rise in the dollar prices of manufactures exported by the developed countries than in the unit value of commodity exports of developing countries.

The annual loss in export earnings attributable to the deterioration in the commodity terms of trade during 1980–8 was equivalent to 15 per cent of the 1980 level; by 1986–8 the corresponding loss had doubled. On a cumulative basis, the loss over the eight years after 1980 was equivalent to almost 120 per cent of the 1980 level.

How do these rates of loss compare with the corresponding loss during the Great Depression of the 1930s? Unfortunately, no very precise comparison can be made. This is partly because of the great changes since the Second World War in political boundaries and in related Customs jurisdictions, and partly also because of the inadequacy of the pre-war trade statistics of many of the former Colonial territories, and the general difficulties of comparing differing classification systems. However, an approximate comparison can be made using the series

---

[3] For both the 1970s and the 1980s, the estimated losses are valued at 1980 prices (see Appendix).

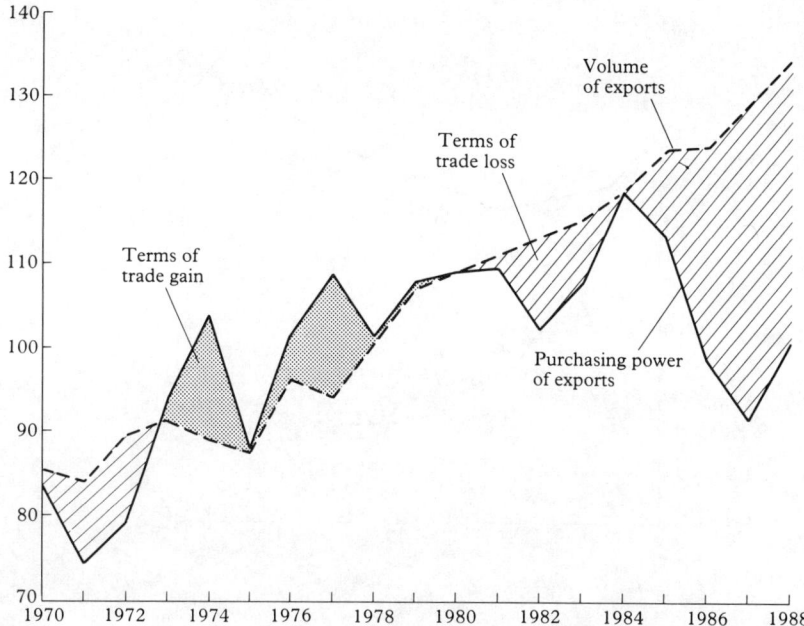

Fig. 2.1. *Gains and losses of developing countries attributable to changes in the commodity terms of trade, 1970–88 ($ billion at 1980 prices). Sources: Appendix Table A.2*

of volume, price, and value of world trade for the 1920s and 1930s published annually by the League of Nations.

The nearest approximation in the pre-war data to the present definition of 'primary commodities' exported by developing countries can be taken as the total exports of Africa (excluding South Africa), Asia (excluding China, Japan, and the Soviet Union), and Latin America, together with Turkey and Yugoslavia. In the pre-war period, these exports consisted predominantly of primary commodities, exports of manufactured goods being relatively small, nil, or negligible for the great majority of the countries of these regions, so that the volume and price series thus calculated can be taken as a reasonable proxy for primary commodities alone.[4]

Several major differences emerge between the experiences of the 1930s and those of the 1980s (see Fig. 2.2). First, nominal commodity prices fell much more sharply during the Great Depression[5] than they did in the 1980s, but the reverse was true for the commodity terms of trade. The sharp contraction in economic activity in the main industrialized countries in the 1930s, and the associated monetary deflation, resulted in declines also in the prices of

---

[4] For further discussion see Appendix.

[5] Nominal commodity values and prices for the 1930s are in terms of US old gold dollars (see Appendix).

28 *Commodity Crisis and Developing Countries*

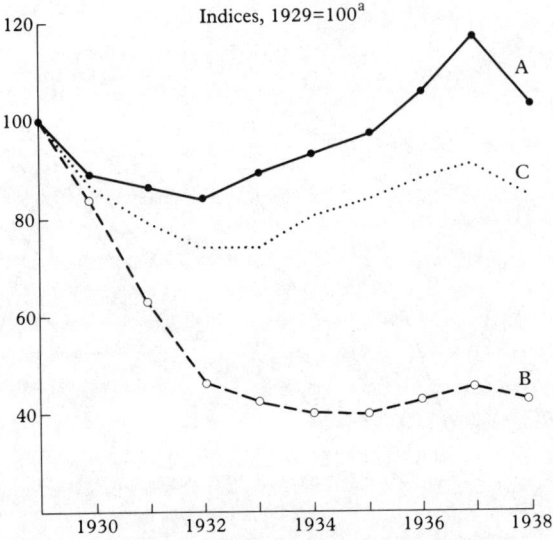

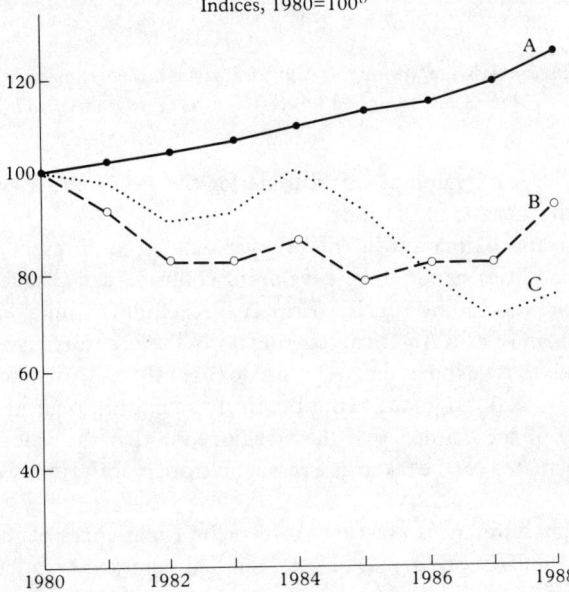

Line A = volume of commodity exports; line B = nominal prices of commodities; line C = commodity terms of trade.

[a] *Total exports from Africa (excluding South Africa), Asia (excluding China, Japan, and the Soviet Union), Latin America, Turkey, and Yugoslavia.*

[b] *Exports of (non-oil) commodities from developing countries.*

Fig. 2.2. *Volume, prices, and terms of trade of commodity exports in the 1930s and 1980s.* Sources: *see Appendix Tables A.1 and A.2*

manufactured goods during that period. Consequently, the fall in the commodity terms of trade between 1929 and 1933 — the low point of the cycle — at about 25 per cent was very substantially less than the fall in nominal commodity prices, at some 60 per cent, over the same period (Appendix Table A.1).

Second, while in the later 1930s the commodity terms of trade recovered almost to the pre-recession level, in the later 1980s the corresponding series showed a further sharp decline, a contrast which has already been discussed in Chapter 1.

Third, while the Great Depression of the 1930s was associated with contraction in the volume of world trade, including a decline in the volume of trade in primary products for the first six years of that decade, in the 1980s the volume of commodity exports from developing countries expanded throughout the decade. While this expansion in export volume has largely offset the deterioration in the commodity terms of trade, as shown in Table 2.2, this development has been a mixed blessing. This is not only because the volume expansion was itself an important factor in the commodity price decline, but also because the higher volume has inevitably resulted in a greater terms of trade loss.

If the foreign exchange loss attributable to the deterioration in the commodity terms of trade is expressed as a proportion of the value of commodity exports in the last pre-recession year, there is again a major divergence between the experience of the 1980s and that of the 1930s, as can be seen from Fig. 2.3. While the relative loss over the first five years of the recession was substantially greater in the 1930s (averaging 18 per cent a year from the 1929 level) than in the 1980s (6 per cent a year from the 1980 level), the position was sharply reversed in the

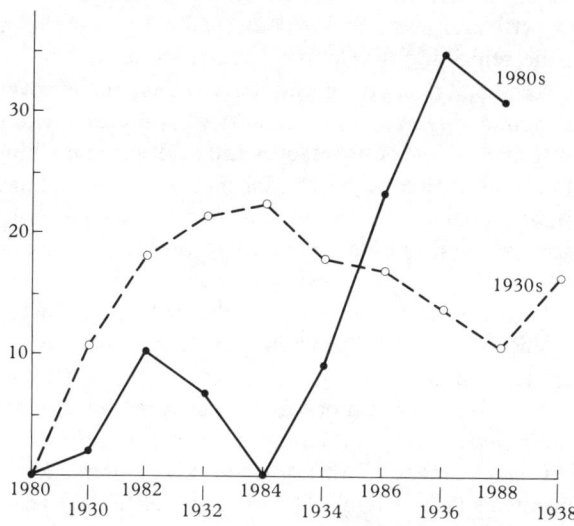

Fig. 2.3. *Terms of trade losses on commodity exports of developing countries in the 1930s and 1980s (% of export value in last pre-recession year). Sources: Appendix Tables A.1 and A.2*

subsequent three years (14 per cent for 1935–7 and 30 per cent for 1986–8).

The increased terms of trade loss in the later 1980s applied also to each of the main developing regions. Over the 1980–5 period, the loss to the African region was much greater, in relation to 1980 levels of commodity exports, than for the two other regions, while in the later years of the decade the African loss, though somewhat lower, relatively, than that of the Asian region, was virtually the same as that experienced by Latin America. Over the whole period covered, Africa's cumulative terms of trade loss, in relation to the pre-recession level, was the greatest: 134 per cent, as against 125 per cent for Asia and 105 per cent for Latin America (Appendix Tables A.4 and A.5).

Commodity Exports in the Balance of Payments

In considering the relative contributions of commodity exports and of other elements in the balance of payments to the foreign exchange difficulties of developing countries during the 1980s, it is necessary to shift from an *overall* view of commodity exports from all developing countries—which was the perspective adopted in the preceding section—to a more specifically *country* basis. This is because a number of countries which export primary commodities are, in fact, major exporters of manufactured goods or petroleum. For example, Indonesia and Mexico, both now usually classified as major petroleum exporters, are also important suppliers of tropical agricultural products and non-fuel minerals. Again, Brazil is a major exporter of a wide range of commodities, but is also a large exporter of manufactures. For such countries, developments in the world oil market or in the market for manufactures are likely to be the predominant influences on movements in foreign exchange earnings.

If the major petroleum exporters and the major exporters of manufactures are excluded, the remaining developing countries[6]—termed here 'commodity-dependent' or 'commodity-exporting' countries—accounted for over 60 per cent of the value of commodity exports from all developing countries in 1980. For these commodity-dependent countries, over 130 in all and containing over 70 per cent of the total population of developing countries (excluding China), the movements in world commodity prices and their shares of world commodity exports are likely to be prime determinants of their overall foreign exchange positions.

The changes in the main elements of the balance of payments of the commodity-dependent countries between 1980 and 1988 are summarized in Table 2.3, both for this group of countries as a whole and for the three major regions of the developing world. For the total picture, the dominant (negative) changes over this period were the foreign exchange losses resulting from the deterioration in the commodity terms of trade ($21 billion) and the increase in debt service payments ($24 billion). The principal offsetting (positive) changes were the expansion in the volume of exports, both of commodities ($10 billion)

---

[6] See Appendix for a more precise definition of the countries included.

Table 2.3. Terms of trade effects in the balance of payments of commodity-dependent countries, 1980–8 ($ billion)

	Total[a]			Regional groups: change from 1980 to 1988		
	1980	1988	Change	Africa	Asia	Latin America[b]
Foreign exchange availability						
Exports[c]						
Commodities	74.2	78.0	3.8	−0.9	4.2	0.5
Volume	...	...	9.7	1.0	6.0	2.7
Unit Value	...	...	−5.9	−1.9	−1.8	−2.2
(Terms of trade)	...	...	(−21.0)	(−5.3)	(−7.4)	(−7.9)
Fuel	19.0	12.5	−6.5	−1.5	0.6	−5.5
Manufactures	30.3	67.9	37.6	5.5	31.0	0.1
TOTAL	123.5	158.4	34.9	3.1	35.8	−4.9
Volume	...	...	58.6	10.2	48.0	1.5
Unit Value	...	...	−23.7	−7.1	−12.2	−6.4
(Terms of trade)	...	...	(−25.3)	(−8.3)	(−10.5)	(−6.8)
Export earnings[d]	122.7	158.0	35.3	−0.2	37.3	−3.8
Services, net[e] and private transfers	15.9	24.1	8.2	6.7	3.5	−1.9
Long-term capital[f] and government transfers	56.8	58.2	1.4	−0.9	6.0	−0.2
Debt service	−36.7	−60.4	−23.7	−4.7	−15.3	−1.5
TOTAL	158.7	179.9	21.2	0.9	31.5	−7.4
Imports	−167.4	−192.1	−24.7	−2.8	−28.0	3.5
BASIC BALANCE	−8.7	−12.2	−3.5	−1.9	3.5	−3.9

[a] Including commodity-dependent developing countries in Europe and Oceania.
[b] Including the Caribbean.
[c] Trade accounts basis.   [d] Balance of payments basis.
[e] Excluding interest payments.   [f] Excluding amortization of foreign debt.

Sources: Appendix Table A.5; UNCTAD 1989, 1990a and 1990c.

and, even more so, of manufactured exports (some $35 billion).[7] There was also an improvement in purely financial flows, net receipts for non-investment services, capital inflows, private transfers, etc., which in aggregate rose by almost $10 billion.

For both African and Latin American commodity-dependent countries, the foreign exchange loss due to the deterioration in the commodity terms of

---

[7] Allowing for a rise of 7% from 1980 to 1988 in the unit value of exports of manufactures from developing countries (UN *Monthly Bulletin of Statistics*, Apr. 1990).

trade was the major adverse change, exceeding the increase in debt service payments,[8] but for Asian countries the reverse was true, the rise in debt service being double the commodity terms of trade loss. Relatively to total foreign exchange availability (net of debt service payments) in 1980, the loss due to the commodity terms of trade deterioration over the period was greatest for Latin America (19 per cent), the loss for Africa being 14 per cent and for Asia 11 per cent.

The relative importance of the terms of trade deterioration is, however, understated in Table 2.3, since part of the increase in debt service payments since 1980 can be attributed to loans taken to offset, or partially offset, the foreign exchange loss associated with the terms of trade deterioration. This terms of trade element of debt service would have been particularly important for those developing countries which had not borrowed heavily on international capital markets and/or which experienced relatively large terms of trade deteriorations.

Three conclusions can be drawn from these figures. First, as was to be expected, the decline in commodity prices was a major factor in the movement in total foreign exchange availability of this group of countries over the 1980s. Second, the increase in debt service payments was not offset, to any significant extent, by an expansion in long-term capital inflows; indeed, the net inflow of financial resources (long-term capital inflow *minus* debt service payments), which had amounted to $20 billion in 1980, turned into a marginal net outflow, of some $2 billion in 1988, a net switch over this period of $22 billion. Third, in spite of the first two adverse changes, total foreign exchange credits rose, essentially as a result of a large increase in export volume, both of commodities and, even more, of manufactures.

The rise in export volume was concentrated very largely in the Asian region, from which exports of both commodities and manufactures rose substantially. By contrast, a modest rise in commodity exports from Latin American countries was more than offset by a sharp contraction in the value of their petroleum exports. For Africa, commodity exports remained virtually stagnant in volume, manufactures exports more than doubled, but petroleum shipments fell in value terms (Table 2.3).

The ability of a number of Asian commodity-exporting countries to diversify into a range of manufactured exports – assisted by a continuing and substantial inflow of private direct investment – was a notable feature of the 1980s. Total manufactured exports from Asian commodity-dependent countries almost doubled in volume between 1980 and 1988 (an annual growth rate of 7.5 per cent), as against a volume increase of under 30 per cent for commodity exports (3.2 per cent a year). Impressive rates of growth in manufactured exports were achieved by Turkey, Malaysia, and Thailand, which together accounted for about 70 per cent of total manufactures exports from the Asian commodity-

---

[8] The totals for the Latin American commodity-exporters exclude Argentina and Brazil, both of which are here classified with 'major exporters of manufactures' (see Appendix).

Table 2.4. Terms of trade loss during 1980–8 as percentage of GDP in 1980[a] for commodity-dependent countries

	Mean annual loss			Cumulative loss		
	1980–5	1986–8	1980–8	1980–5	1986–8	1980–8
Africa	1.3	3.3	2.4	6.6	9.9	16.5
Asia	–	2.1	0.8	–	6.1	6.1
Latin America[b]	0.5	2.2	1.1	2.2	6.4	8.7
TOTAL	0.4	2.3	1.1	2.0	6.9	8.9

[a] GDP in 1980 was, in $ billion: Africa, 152; Asia 384; Latin America and the Caribbean, 344.
[b] Including the Caribbean.
Source: Appendix Table A.5.

exporters in 1988. However, for both Malaysia and Thailand, the loss due to the decline in commodity prices was roughly double that resulting from increased debt service payments, though the reverse was true for Turkey.

Export Losses and GDP

Finally, it is useful to relate the foreign exchange loss due to the change in the commodity terms of trade to the GDP of the commodity-dependent countries, since this provides an indicator of the immediate, and direct, impact on the economies of these countries. Over the period 1980–8, the mean annual foreign exchange loss resulting from the fall in the commodity terms of trade amounted to some $10 billion (Appendix Table A.5), equivalent to 1.1 per cent of the total GDP in 1980 of the commodity-dependent countries as a group; over the period as a whole, the cumulative foreign exchange loss was equivalent to as much as 9.6 per cent of these countries' aggregate GDP in 1980.

In relation to GDP, the foreign exchange loss was much greater for the African region than for Asia or Latin America (see Table 2.4). This was to be expected, since the relative importance of the commodity sector is much greater in the economies of African countries than elsewhere. Over the whole period 1980–8, the terms of trade loss for the African region was equivalent to as much as one-sixth of aggregate GDP in 1980 – an enormous drain on resources by any measure. For the two other regions, the corresponding losses were smaller – 6 per cent for Asia, on a cumulative basis, and almost 9 per cent for Latin America.

A broad comparison can be made with the real income loss suffered by the OECD countries as a group as a result of the oil price increases of the 1970s, as estimated by the OECD secretariat. Both in 1973–4 and in 1978–9, the sharp increases in oil prices arising from OPEC action resulted in large real income transfers from the Western industrial countries, equivalent to about 2 per cent of their combined GDP.⁹

The real income loss suffered by the commodity-dependent developing countries in relation to their aggregate GDP in the period 1980–8 was, on an annual average basis, about one-half of that suffered by the OECD countries during the years of oil price 'shocks' of the 1970s. This result is also broadly true for the Asian and Latin American regions, but not for Africa, for which the annual terms of trade loss in relation to the region's GDP was significantly greater than the corresponding OECD loss resulting from the 1970s oil price shocks. For all three developing regions, also, the rate of terms of trade loss in relation to GDP in the later 1980s was either much the same as the corresponding OECD oil shock loss (Asia and Latin America), or substantially exceeded that loss (Africa). A further consideration in this context is that the commodity-dependent countries are also very much poorer than the OECD countries (average GDP per head in the former having been about $550 in 1980, or only 6 per cent of the corresponding figure of $8,800 for the OECD countries in that year), so that even an equal percentage loss of GDP would have been a much greater disaster for the commodity-dependent countries than for the relatively wealthy member countries of the OECD area. Moreover, the developing countries' losses due to price changes have been prolonged over a decade or more, whereas the OECD losses were largely recouped, in real terms, by subsequent increases in prices of their manufactured exports.

For the oil-importing developing countries, the increase in the cost of their oil imports in 1974, and again in 1979–80, represented on each occasion about 2.5 per cent of their total GDP.[10] The adverse effects of the first oil shock were substantially offset by the recycling of the foreign exchange surpluses of OPEC countries to oil-importing developing countries through the intermediation of the commercial banks, together with a variety of innovatory compensatory facilities established by the IMF. The second oil shock had already added some $25 billion to the import bill of the oil-importing developing countries between 1978 and 1980, and continuing high petroleum prices until 1985 added to the difficulties caused by falling non-oil commodity prices and the contraction in financial flows. Moreover, the special IMF facilities designed to support oil-importing countries in the 1970s were phased out, and the IMF Compensatory Financing Facility was largely inadequate to meet export shortfalls in the 1980s.[11]

From the various comparisons made – with exports in 1980, with the experiences of the 1970s and the 1930s, with the rise in debt service payments and with the impact-effect on GDP – the foreign exchange losses in the 1980s suffered by the commodity-dependent countries as a result of the deterioration in the commodity terms of trade have constituted a major shock to the economies of these

---

⁹ See the analysis in OECD 1980.
[10] OECD 1980: 126–7.
[11] See Ch. 9 for a review of this Facility.

countries. As the earlier analysis indicates, these losses have been largely hidden when account is taken only of the movement in actual export earnings, since they have generally been offset by an expansion in export volume.

2. IMPORTS, INVESTMENT, AND ECONOMIC RETROGRESSION

In the immediate post-war decades, developing countries appeared to fall into two broad groups, viz. those where the dominant constraint on growth was an insufficiency of domestic saving, and those where the dominant constraint was the inadequacy of foreign exchange. Countries were conceived as moving over time from one phase to another, e.g. from a phase where a 'savings gap' put a limit on growth to a phase where the 'foreign exchange gap' restrained the growth process.[12] However, during the 1970s and, more especially, since the early 1980s, the great majority of developing countries have been in a situation of foreign-exchange-constrained growth. The relatively few exceptions have been confined essentially to the East Asian 'newly industrializing countries' of South Korea, Singapore, Hong Kong, and Taiwan Province of China, whose aggregate monetary reserves increased rapidly in the 1980s (from $18 billion in 1981 to $108 billion in 1988).[13]

During the 1980s, a large number of commodity-dependent developing countries faced severe foreign exchange shortage, and many entered a phase of 'import strangulation', where domestic economic activity was perforce contracted as a result of lack of complementary imports (spare parts, intermediate products, replacement equipment, etc.). By reducing the availability of complementary imports, the foreign exchange squeeze has resulted in a reduction in the efficiency of use of resources as well as in a reduced level of domestic investment — both key elements in the economic growth process.

A close relationship can be expected, *ceteris paribus*, between movements in the purchasing power of merchandise exports and the volume of imports into developing countries. For Latin America, both the purchasing power of exports and the import volume have remained below 1980 levels since 1982. African countries' import volume has risen, in the later 1980s, at a much faster rate than the purchasing power of exports; but if the special position of Egypt is excluded, the difference between the two variables is relatively small. For the Asian commodity-exporters, by contrast, import volume has risen at a considerably lower rate than export purchasing power, reflecting in the main the sharp rise in debt service payments by these countries noted earlier. For the commodity-dependent countries in total, however, the rate of increase in import volume has closely paralleled that of export purchasing power (Table 2.5).

The empirical evidence suggests that developing countries shifted the burden

---

[12] The well-known two-gap theory of growth was first elaborated by Chenery and Strout, 1966.
[13] The monetary reserves of these countries rose further in 1989.

Table 2.5. Indices of trade volumes, terms of trade, and purchasing power of exports of commodity-dependent countries, 1980 to 1985 and 1988 (1980 = 100)

	Africa		Asia		Latin America		Total[a]	
	1985	1988	1985	1988	1985	1988	1985	1988
Export volume								
Commodities	100	105	109	124	113	109	108	113
Total	103	137	155	212	108	103	123	150
Terms of trade[b]	92	78	87	88	83	86	88	87
Purchasing power of exports[c]	93	108	135	187	91	89	107	129
Import volume	105	139	117	147	79	77	101	120

[a] Including commodity-dependent developing countries in Europe and Oceania.

[b] Unit value index of total exports divided by unit value index of total imports (including petroleum).

[c] Export volume (total) multiplied by terms of trade.

Sources: As for Table 2.3; and Appendix Table A.4.

of import compression in the 1980s largely to domestic investment. According to World Bank figures, over the period 1980–8 gross domestic investment declined, on average, by over 2 per cent a year in the low income countries (other than China and India), whereas in the preceding one and a half decades there had been an annual increase of some 9.5 per cent – a deterioration of 12 percentage points. For the middle-income countries, the corresponding deterioration was 9 percentage points; by contrast, for private consumption the deterioration was 1.5 (low income) and 4 (middle income) percentage points.[14] This result is consistent with the close relationship between changes in total import volume and changes in gross domestic investment shown in Table 2.6, also based on World Bank figures. For the low-income countries (other than the two large economies of China and India), the contraction in imports in the 1980s was associated with contraction in domestic investment, while for the middle-income countries (which include many oil-exporting and manufactures-exporting countries) both imports and investment showed only marginal changes in the 1980s, after having increased at a fast rate in the earlier period. For sub-Saharan Africa, and for the severely indebted countries (mostly in Latin America), the decline in the growth rates of both imports and investment in the 1980s has been particularly severe.

A close relationship between the investment and GDP growth rates of different groups of countries is not to be expected, since investment is only one factor – though a strategic one – influencing growth. A recent analysis of the investment and growth experience of 15 heavily indebted developing countries, for exam-

[14] World Bank 1990 (World Development Indicators, Table 8).

Table 2.6. Imports, investment, and GDP of groups of developing countries, 1965–88 (average growth rate, % p.a.)

	Import volume		Gross domestic investment		GDP	
	1965–80	1980–8	1965–80	1980–8	1965–80	1980–8
China	7.9	13.1	10.7	14.4	6.4	10.3
India	1.6	5.4	4.5	4.3	3.6	5.2
Other low-income countries[a]	4.5	−3.2	9.7	−2.3	5.5	2.0
Middle-income countries[a]	5.9	0.6	8.6	−0.6	6.1	2.9
TOTAL	5.6	1.1	8.6	2.7	5.8	4.3
of which:						
Sub-Saharan Africa[a]	4.9	−0.5	9.1	−7.3	4.8	0.8
Severely indebted countries[a,b]	5.6	−2.3	8.4	−3.1	6.0	1.5

[a] Weighted averages.
[b] 17 developing countries, mostly in Latin America.

Source: *World Development Report, 1990*, World Bank, Washington, DC (World Development Indicators, Tables 2, 8, and 14).

ple, concluded that the decline in domestic investment in the period 1982–7 accounted for not more than one-third of the slowdown in the GDP growth rate compared with the years 1975–81.[15] For individual countries, the relationship between investment and GDP growth can vary substantially, depending on the structural characteristics of the economy, and on government policies, particularly those affecting domestic demand and import barriers. None the less, the World Bank figures in Table 2.6 indicate the existence of a loose positive association for broad groups of developing countries. Most of the low-income countries are heavily dependent on the primary commodity sector for their GDP growth, so that climatic variations as well as the availability of essential imported inputs, and changes in government policies, affect the outcome.

Of the three major commodity-dependent developing regions, only in Asia did GDP per capita continue to rise during 1980–8. For African commodity-exporters, GDP per capita was stagnant, while for Latin America there was a significant decline (Table 2.7). Over two-thirds of African countries, and four-fifths of Latin American, experienced declines in GDP per capita during the 1980s, but the proportion for Asia was less than one-third. For both Africa and Latin America, the 1980s have often been described as the 'lost decade' for

[15] IMF 1989*b*: 65–7.

Table 2.7. GDP growth rates of commodity-dependent countries, 1960–88 (% p.a.)

	Total GDP[a]			GDP per capita[a]		
	1960–70	1970–80	1980–8	1960–70	1970–80	1980–8
Africa	4.3	3.9	2.8	1.7	1.1	−0.1
Asia	4.5	4.7	5.0	2.1	2.4	2.9
Latin America	4.5	3.1	0.9	2.1	1.0	−1.2
TOTAL[b]	4.5	4.0	3.2	2.0	1.6	1.0

[a] Not including adjustments for changes in the terms of trade.
[b] Including developing countries in Europe and Oceania.

Source: UNCTAD 1990a: Table 6.2.

development. In this retrogression from previous decades of economic growth, the continuing low levels of real commodity prices have played a major role.

3. THE IMPACT ON HUMAN RESOURCES

The development of human resources, in terms of improved health, education, and skills, is an important end in itself, as well as constituting an essential factor in economic growth. Over the 1980s, however, there has been a marked deterioration in a large number of developing countries in both the quantity and quality of provision for the maintenance and improvement of human resources.

Children form one of the most vulnerable groups when economic conditions worsen. Country studies by UNICEF, for example, together with related analyses, have shown that during the 1980s child welfare deteriorated 'in at least 8 Latin American countries, 16 in sub-Saharan Africa, 3 in North Africa and the Middle East and 4 in South and East Asia (though the situation of children in most South-East Asian countries continued to improve in most cases)'.[16] Deterioration has occurred also in many countries in the nutritional status of children, in educational provision, and in infant and child mortality and morbidity rates.[17] Increasing child malnutrition and declining literacy levels are undermining the mental and physical capacity of the future labour force of many developing countries.[18]

The adult population of countries with falling per capita incomes have also generally been at risk, particularly so the poorer strata. Available evidence points to the likelihood that the number of people below a given poverty line has increased, while government expenditures on food subsidies, public health, and education have generally been cut.[19]

---

[16] G.A. Cornia, in UNICEF 1987: 34.
[17] Ibid.
[18] G.A. Cornia, R. Jolly, and F. Stewart, in UNICEF 1987: 287–8.
[19] G.A. Cornia, in UNICEF 1987: 27–8.

While much of this alarming deterioration in human resources development – a reversal of previous positive trends – has resulted from the sharp deterioration in the world economic environment, inadequate responses by governments of the developing countries concerned have also been to blame. The problems involved in protecting vulnerable groups in conditions of external and domestic financial stringency are now much better understood, and a number of countries have devised special protective programmes for this purpose. However, their success is likely to be heavily dependent on an amelioration in the external financial pressures faced by low- and middle-income developing countries, particularly those still heavily dependent on primary commodities. A substantial alleviation of these external pressures requires positive international policy co-ordination on a broad front, to include policies to deal with the continuing commodity crisis as well as with the debt overhang and the inadequacy of aid and other financial flows.

3
Raising Depressed Levels of Commodity Export Earnings

1. THE CASE FOR INTERNATIONAL ACTION

The dominant feature of the international commodity situation in the 1980s has been the persistence over a relatively prolonged period of abnormally low levels of commodity prices and real export earnings. This is in strong contrast to the experience of the 1970s, and for the longer period from 1962 to 1980, when the dominant feature was large short-term price fluctuations and related export earnings instability.

This reversal of previous experience raises the question whether the focus of international policies affecting commodity prices should now change. The logic of the present situation indicates that international policy in this area should now turn to consideration of possible mechanisms to deal with the persistence of depressed levels of commodity prices and export earnings, while continuing to address the short-term instability issue for those commodities for which it remains important. However, there has so far been no serious consideration in intergovernmental forums of possible measures to alleviate the problems caused by the prolonged period of depressed commodity prices. Indeed, the subject has been essentially taboo, in view of the strong opposition of the main developed countries to intervention in international commodity markets designed to raise the level of prices. This issue remains one of the most contentious in the entire dialogue between developed and developing countries on international economic policy.

As was seen in Chapter 2, the commodity price decline of the 1980s has involved a very large shift indeed in real income from developing to developed countries. To allow the commodity-exporting countries to expand their imports sufficiently to support increased levels of domestic activity, and to begin the necessary restructuring of their economies, a substantial increase in their foreign exchange availabilities is clearly required. Any reliable estimate of the magnitude of such a substantial increase would, of course, have to take into account the different economic situations and prospects of individual countries. Differences in import dependence, in debt service payments, and in the efficacy of domestic economic policies, in particular, would be important in this context. In many cases, also, allowance would have to be made for additional import requirements to replenish depleted stocks of essential foods, raw materials, and intermediate products.

Some guidance as to the possible orders of magnitude involved can however be derived from a comparison of the value of imports into the commodity-exporting countries as a group since 1980, and the value that would have obtained had import volume increased at the same annual rate as in the 1970s, i.e. at 3.9 per cent a year, instead of the actual rate of only 2.3 per cent a year. On this basis, the cost of imports of this group of countries would have been greater by an average of $20 billion a year ($195 billion, instead of the actual figure of $175 billion)[1] over the period 1981-8. At this rate, the cumulative shortfall in foreign exchange availabilities over these eight years was in the region of $160 billion.

However, the shortfall was increasing at a rapid pace as a result of the slow growth in actual imports. From a level of $12 billion a year during 1982 to 1984, the shortfall – on the basis used here – rose to an average of $33 billion in the years 1985 to 1988 (i.e. to almost treble the average for the early 1980s). On the same assumption concerning the required growth rate of imports, the shortfall would rise to some $60 billion in 1995 and about $100 billion in the year 2000 (at 1988 prices), compared with the position in those years if import volume continued to rise at the 1980-8 rate.

It could, of course, be argued that it would be over-optimistic to expect the trend rate of growth in import volume of the commodity-exporting countries in the 1980s, or in the 1990s, to be as high as in the 1970s, in view of the slowdown in growth in the Western industrial countries and the related contraction in the flow of financial resources to the developing countries. But even a somewhat lower import growth would still have involved a large increase above the actual level of foreign exchange availability in the 1980s.

This is, of course, a purely illustrative set of estimates of future levels of foreign exchange shortfalls, based on the assumption of the continuation of present policies, no major change in the commodity terms of trade, and the continuing inability of developing countries to expand their foreign exchange availabilities substantially over the 1990s. A recent more detailed WIDER research study of the external financing requirements of developing countries to achieve 'socially necessary' growth up to the year 2000 yielded somewhat lower estimates than those given above. This study indicates that to achieve this goal, the GDP of these countries as a group would have to grow by at least 5.5 per cent a year over the 1990s, and this would require an additional foreign exchange inflow of $40 billion in 1990, rising to $60 billion by the year 2000. For this purpose, 'socially necessary' growth was defined as meeting suitable basic needs objectives, reducing the prevailing backlog of unemployment to manageable levels, and achieving an improvement in income distribution.[2]

The WIDER study made no explicit provision for the cost of environmental

---

[1] Trade accounts basis. The calculation assumes that the higher growth rate in imports would not have significantly affected the terms of trade.

[2] Taylor 1990. These estimates were based on the findings of detailed studies for a sample of 17 developing countries.

protection measures which are needed in developing countries. The additional costs of such measures have been roughly estimated as in the region of $20 billion for 1990, rising to $65 billion for 1995, and to about $80 billion for the year 2000.[3] Moreover, the WIDER study could not have foreseen the oil price rise precipitated by the Gulf crisis of 1990, and the likelihood of a continuation of high oil prices in later years, which would add substantially to the foreign exchange requirements of oil-importing developing countries for a given growth in import volume.

On current economic trends and policies, there would appear to be little chance of a foreign exchange shortfall of even the WIDER estimates being met in the short- or medium-term. The virtual cessation of long-term commercial loans to most developing countries, the stagnation in aid and in private direct investment, and the continuing growth in total debt would seem to rule out the possibility of an expansion in net financial flows of the magnitude required.

The current international strategy to deal with the debt problem recognizes the need to combine the objectives of restoring financial viability of indebted countries with achieving satisfactory rates of economic growth. The 'Baker initiative' of 1985 comprised three main elements of the strategy, namely, new lending by commercial banks, increased and more effective structural adjustment loans by the World Bank and other development banks, and economic reforms in the debtor countries designed to increase the efficiency of resource use through increased reliance on market forces. However, it quickly became apparent that this approach suffered from some major weaknesses which prevented the attainment of its stated objectives. The key limitation was that the supply of new loans from the commercial banks which was envisaged in the strategy in fact failed to materialize (apart from a few exceptions). Though new initiatives were taken by the World Bank, for example, in its programme for sub-Saharan Africa, and by the IMF in its new contingency facility, overall the flows of official finance and of private investment have stagnated. Thus the total flow of financial resources has been far less than the minimum required to support a programme of stabilization with growth. In many cases, also, domestic reforms designed to shift resources into the export sector, in so far as they resulted in expanded exports of primary commodities, only added to the depressive forces on world commodity prices.[4]

A new initiative by the United States in 1989 – the Brady Plan – envisaged voluntary reductions by the creditor banks in debt service payments and/or in total debt, backed by financial support from the World Bank and the IMF. The new plan, in effect, attempts to put pressure on commercial bank creditors to write off a significant portion of existing debt, while diverting some proportion of international funds for the purchase of old debt or the financing of interest payments.

---

[3] Jayawardena 1990.
[4] See Maizels 1988 and Wattleworth 1988.

The concentration of international policy on the need for reducing the debt burden should result, if successful, in a significant amelioration of the external financial squeeze for many countries with a high debt-service ratio to exports and, to that extent, would alleviate the pressure to increase exports. However, for a great many other developing countries, especially those heavily dependent on commodity exports, the debt-reduction strategy, even if successful in meeting its immediate objectives, may not lead to increased economic growth in the absence of a complementary strategy designed to increase commodity export earnings. The total revenue of the commodity-exporting countries from merchandise exports accounted for about 75 per cent of their aggregate import bill in 1980, before the onset of the payments crisis, and the proportion rose to 80 per cent in 1986 and 1987, and to 82 per cent in 1988 (UNCTAD 1989a). Consequently, the current debt strategy is operating on only one part – for many countries, the minor part – of the payments problem.

In principle, there are several ways in which the international community could approach this issue of the inadequacy of commodity export earnings to support both immediate external stabilization and longer-term economic restructuring and growth. One approach would be to offset unforeseen and prolonged declines in real commodity export earnings by supplementary financing from international sources. This approach therefore would not involve intervention in the commodity markets themselves. A second approach, in principle, would be to apply the developed countries' systems of price support for agricultural products to their imports from developing countries. A third approach would be to evolve some appropriate form of supply management to balance world commodity supply and demand over a period of years at prices which were reasonably remunerative to the majority of producing countries, while being acceptable as fair by consuming countries. All three of these very different approaches, which are considered in greater detail below, have a long history of international negotiations, though only of limited effective action.

2. SUPPLEMENTARY FINANCING

A proposal to create a Supplementary Financing Facility, which would in effect underwrite the foreign exchange component of agreed five-year development plans of individual developing countries, was put forward by Dr Raúl Prebisch in his report to the first United Nations Conference on Trade and Development (UNCTAD) in 1964. Dr Prebisch argued that a deterioration in the terms of trade of developing countries impairs their capacity to import the capital equipment required for growth, so that such a deterioration undermines the achievement of the objectives for which international resources are supplied to them. He pointed out that while the IMF compensatory financing facility was available to tide countries over a period of temporary balance of payments difficulties resulting from export shortfalls, it was not designed to deal with the longer-term problems caused by a downward trend in the terms of trade (Prebisch 1964).

This argument received wide support at the 1964 Conference, where the delegations of Sweden and the United Kingdom jointly proposed—a proposal accepted by the Conference—a recommendation to the World Bank to study the feasibility of a scheme to provide longer-term assistance to developing countries in order to help them avoid disruption of their development programmes 'as a result of adverse movements in export proceeds which prove to be of a nature or duration which cannot adequately be dealt with by short-term balance of payments support'.[5]

In its study of this issue, the Bank staff concluded that the problem of adverse movements in the export proceeds of developing countries was indeed a genuine one, because of the resulting disruption to development programmes; that the existing international financial machinery did not meet the problem; and that a feasible scheme of supplementary financing could be worked out.[6] The scheme prepared by the IBRD staff provided for prior agreement between a member country and the agency administering the scheme, on export projections, development programmes and policies, and feasible domestic adjustments to offset export shortfalls. If a country kept within this agreement, a shortfall in exports below pre-agreed projections would provide a prima-facie case for assistance under the scheme, provided that such other finance as might be available, including from the IMF, was obtained, and that economies in foreign exchange expenditure would be effected in ways which would not disrupt the country's development programme (the so-called 'policy package'). A key assumption of the scheme was that the necessary finance would be additional to, and not a substitute for, existing aid programmes.[7]

An Intergovernmental Group on this subject, established in UNCTAD, examined the IBRD scheme in great detail. While the Group concluded that a scheme on the lines proposed could be viable, there was a consensus that it would be of little value if available resources were diverted from basic development finance for the purpose of supplementary financing.[8] Though UNCTAD then invited the Bank to consider elaborating arrangements for supplementary financing and, if appropriate, to consider introducing them,[9] the Bank decided to defer consideration of the scheme owing to the 'very limited support among potential donors for additional contributions for supplementary finance'.[10]

Moreover, the Bank's scheme would have implied an open-ended commitment for donor countries if the amount of supplementary financing were to depend purely on the export shortfalls from pre-agreed levels. In a period of general commodity price recession, claims on the proposed Facility could be very large indeed. For this reason, the Bank staff proposed that in the event of the aggregate

---

[5] UNCTAD 1964: i, Annex A.IV.18.
[6] IBRD 1965.
[7] For further discussion of the IBRD staff scheme, see UNCTAD 1967 and Dell 1967.
[8] UNCTAD 1967: para. 34.
[9] Resolution 60 (IX) of the Trade and Development Board.
[10] Letter from the President of IBRD to the Secretary-General of UNCTAD, dated 14 Aug. 1970.

level of export shortfalls eligible for financing in any one year being likely to exceed the financial resources available, provision would be made for a rationing scheme to be established.

Though the Bank scheme met with general approval by governments, it was subject to criticism, particularly by the Federal Republic of Germany, because of its complexity, its uncertain financial requirements, and the doubt as to whether recipient countries would be prepared to commit themselves to the 'policy package' unless they were assured that supplementary financing would cover the whole, or almost the whole, of a possible shortfall.[11] The Federal Republic therefore proposed

a much simpler scheme involving the establishment of a limited fund, claims on which would be reviewed by a Joint Committee representing the IMF and the Agency administering the scheme. The Joint Committee would have wide discretion in determining whether there was a shortfall in export proceeds and the Agency would have discretion to decide the amount and conditions of supplementary financing, taking into account the needs and performance of the country concerned and the availability of resources. (Dell 1967: 488)

However, this scheme did not attract majority approval, partly because it would have given too much discretion to the Agency, but also because the majority view was in favour of pre-agreed criteria for disbursements.

Meanwhile, the Bank was pressed further by UNCTAD to work out the details of a discretionary scheme.[12] In response, the Bank's President reiterated the need to defer consideration of the scheme, but added:

should a developing country, for reasons outside its control, experience an unexpected shortfall in its export earnings which threatens to disrupt . . . its development programme, the Bank Group would examine the case on its merits with a view to determining whether and how it could shape or modify its lending and other operations for that country in such a way as. to help the country to overcome the difficulties.[13]

This view was repeated in further communications from the Bank and, though representatives of developing countries questioned the validity of the Bank's position, the impetus for establishing a supplementary financing facility was soon lost in view of the opposition of the main Western countries to providing additional finance for this purpose. Following the sharp rise in oil prices in 1973/4, the focus of attention quickly turned to the need to expand the short-term financing facilities of the IMF to assist oil-importing developing countries, and the proposal for a supplementary financing scheme was quietly dropped.

It is interesting to speculate on the role that the proposed Supplementary Financing Facility, had it been established, might have played in the 1980s. Though the Facility was intended to apply to total foreign exchange shortfalls,

---

[11] See Dell 1967: 487–8.
[12] Declaration of the Trade and Development Board (A/8015/Rev. 1).
[13] Letter from the President of IBRD to the Secretary-General of UNCTAD, dated 4 May 1971.

whether arising in commodity trade or elsewhere, the overwhelming majority of claims on the Facility in the 1980s would have related to non-oil commodities, at least up to the downturn in oil prices in 1986. Thus the existence of such a Facility would have assisted commodity-exporting countries to withstand, to a greater or lesser extent, the severe payments difficulties caused by the prolonged period of depressed commodity prices.

However, the Facility was conceived essentially in relation to unfavourable world market changes which threatened to undermine the development programmes of a number of individual countries. At that time, during the 1960s, when the world economy was growing at what now seems a rapid rate, it was not expected that the Facility would need to support more than a limited number of development programmes. The total finance required to operate the scheme was estimated by the IBRD staff in 1965 at $300–$400 million a year for an initial experimental period of five years.[14] At 1980 prices (of manufactures), this amount would have been equivalent to some $0.9–$1.3 billion, and at 1990 prices to rather more, $1.2–$1.6 billion. It is evident that in conditions of a general collapse in commodity prices, such as occurred over the decade of the 1980s, a Facility on this scale would have had only a marginal, though none the less useful, role to play.

The original concept, of an international agency disposing of longer-term finance to support development programmes in danger of disruption as a result of adverse changes in the world economy, would seem to be even more relevant today than it was in the 1960s. A recent proposal on these lines has been made by Stoltenberg (1989),[15] who argued that the adjustment programmes of the 1980s had failed because nothing was done to protect developing countries against adverse developments in their external environment. He proposed that these adjustment programmes should be replaced by 'Development Contracts', which would provide the external resources to support a country's development plan to achieve a minimum socially necessary GDP growth rate up to the year 2000, 'having regard to its minimum development goals in areas such as basic needs, employment and income distribution'. The donor community would, on this proposal, not only agree to provide aid to underwrite the development plan, but would also be committed to providing some form of compensatory finance should export expectations underlying the plan, or the terms of trade, be undermined by developments outside the country's control (the Supplementary Financing element). As the *quid pro quo*, the developing country would undertake to maintain a domestic policy framework that would effectively support its development programme.

It is an open question, however, whether the developed countries would be prepared to establish such a system of Development Contracts in view of the large amount of additional finance likely to be required and, more importantly,

---

[14] IBRD 1965.
[15] Mr Thorvald Stoltenberg was at the time the Foreign Minister of Norway.

the consequent reduction in the present influence of the Bretton Woods institutions on national development policies.

3. PREFERENTIAL PRICES FOR COMMODITY EXPORTS FROM DEVELOPING COUNTRIES

Another approach designed *inter alia* to avoid depressed levels of commodity prices and export earnings has been in operation for many years for one important commodity exported by developing countries, namely sugar, for which preferential prices—substantially above world market levels—are fixed for certain trading channels.

The use of preferential pricing arose essentially as a means of economic support by certain developed countries for sugar-exporting developing countries with which they had political and cultural ties. The earliest such arrangement was that for British Colonial Territories under the inter-war Commonwealth Sugar Agreements. These Agreements lapsed following the United Kingdom's accession to the European Community, the special preferential arrangements for sugar being continued by a Sugar Protocol attached to successive Lomé Agreements between the Community and the associated African, Caribbean, and Pacific (ACP) countries. Under the Sugar Protocol, ACP sugar imported by the Community receives the same (high) price, up to a quota limit, as that paid for domestic sugar beet in the Community.

Another important preferential channel was opened in 1960, following the United States embargo on imports of Cuban sugar. Cuba then switched a substantial part of its sugar crop to exports to the Soviet Union at preferential prices which included a considerable subsidy element. A third preferential trading channel for sugar was established under the Caribbean Basin Initiative, launched by the United States in the early 1980s, which includes import quotas for sugar from designated countries in the Caribbean, thus allowing them to capture the difference between the world price and the higher United States domestic price.

During the 1980s a major divergence in trends emerged between the two, essentially insulated, sectors of the sugar market. The quantity of exports from developing countries to the free market contracted (by 20 per cent between 1980 and 1987), while exports in preferential channels expanded (by 25 per cent over the same period). At the same time, the over-supply of sugar on the world market resulted in a catastrophic fall in prices (by some 75 per cent from 1980 to 1987), the fall in unit value of sugar exported to the free market (some 60 per cent) also being a dramatic one. By contrast, the unit value of shipments to preferential markets in 1987 was higher (by over 10 per cent) than in 1980. As a consequence of these divergent movements, foreign exchange earnings from sugar exports to the free market fell sharply (by almost 70 per cent), while earnings from exports in preferential channels rose substantially (by almost 40 per cent), as can be seen from Table 3.1. The annual movements in quantities, unit values, and values are

Table 3.1. Sugar exports from developing countries to the free market and to preferential markets, 1980 and 1987

	To free market			To preferential markets		
	1980	1987	Change (%)	1980	1987	Change (%)
Quantity (million metric tonnes)	12.4	10.0	−20	4.9	6.2	25
Unit value ($ per metric tonne)	439	170	−61	882	976	11
Value ($ billion)	5.46	1.7	−69	4.34	6.02	39

Source: Appendix Table A.6.

given in Appendix Table A.6, while the movements in values are depicted in Fig. 3.1.

It is clear that the entire burden of the contraction in world trade in sugar in the 1980s fell on the countries exporting to the free market. For the seven years from 1980 to 1987, the cumulative shortfall from the 1980 level in export earnings of these countries from sales of sugar amounted to some $19 billion, equivalent to three times the corresponding 1980 value (see Appendix Table A.6). It could be argued, in principle, that had all developed countries operated preferential pricing systems for sugar, a substantial proportion of this loss of earnings would have been avoided.[16]

However, it would seem likely that an extension of the preferential pricing principle to all sugar exports from developing to developed countries would be strongly opposed by sugar beet producers in the latter countries in so far as it would involve a consequential reduction in their own production. Moreover, it could be argued that additional preferential arrangements, and their associated trade quotas, would only add to the fragmentation of the world market for sugar, which would be undesirable on resource allocation grounds, and which would be less efficient than the elimination of the systems of sugar price supports by the developed countries.

None the less, to the extent that the GATT Uruguay Round negotiations fail to reach agreement on the phasing out of systems of price and income support for agriculture in developed countries, there remains a 'second best' case for a wider use of the preferential pricing approach, not only for sugar, but also for a number of other agricultural exports of developing countries.

---

[16] Assuming that preferential prices would have applied only up to a certain quota level, as in the existing preferential schemes.

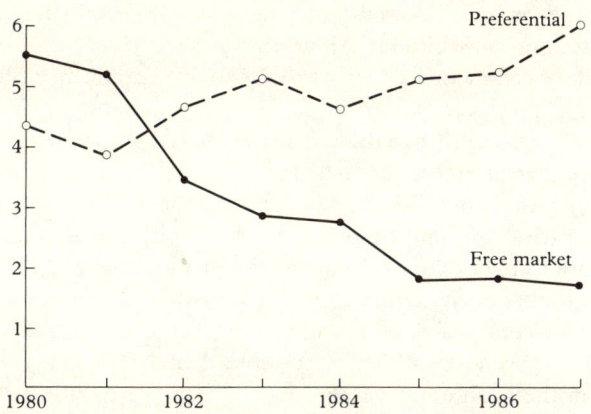

Fig. 3.1. *Sugar exports from developing countries to the free market and through preferential channels, 1980-7 ($ billion).* Sources: *see Appendix Table A.6*

4. SUPPLY MANAGEMENT

The third approach mentioned earlier which could be used to avoid a prolonged period of depressed commodity prices, or to raise prices from depressed levels, would be some form of supply management. Since this would necessarily involve market intervention to a greater or lesser degree, this approach has given rise to intense controversy between those who oppose market intervention in principle and those who see some benefits arising.

(*a*) Arguments against Market Intervention to Raise Depressed Levels of Prices and Export Earnings

A number of specific arguments have been advanced over the years, both by academics and by developed country representatives, against the use of agreements which can raise market prices by the regulation of supply. The most frequently advanced of such arguments have been that such agreements:

(i) would be unfair to importing countries;[17]
(ii) would be an inefficient means of transferring resources to developing countries;[18]
(iii) would distort commodity markets by encouraging unnecessary increases in production, thus entailing a misallocation of resources.[19]

As regards the first argument, it is of course the case that measures which raise prices will *ipso facto* increase the cost of imports of the commodity concerned

---

[17] See e.g. MacBean 1966: 301-2.
[18] MacBean 1966: 301 and 1978: 21-3; Pincus 1967.
[19] Rowe 1965: 215.

for the importing country (assuming that the price increase is not so great as to induce offsetting substitution). However, in the present context, raising depressed levels of commodity prices would be equivalent, in effect, to reducing the 'unfairness' to producers caused by the price depression itself. Thus, taking both phases of the price cycle together, there need not, in principle, be significant 'unfairness' to either producers or consumers.

Moreover, as past experience shows, an expansion in export earnings of developing countries resulting from higher commodity prices will be used in purchasing more from developed countries. These purchases should offset, to a greater or lesser extent, the higher cost of imports into developed countries of the commodity or commodities for which prices have been raised (though the extra cost will be borne by different enterprises and individuals from those benefiting from the additional exports). In any case, the question of equity in trade relations between developed and developing countries cannot be assessed purely in terms of narrow commercial advantage between importers and exporters of a particular commodity, but must be set in the wider context of development in the world economy as a whole.

Second, the suggestion that commodity agreements may be used to improve the price trend, even if only for a few selected 'problem' commodities in persistent over-supply, has often been criticized on the ground that this would involve a resource transfer by a method less efficient than that of direct aid. It has also often been claimed that donor governments are likely to reduce their aid budgets by an amount equivalent to any resource transfer through the operation of commodity agreements.

The question of the relative efficiency of aid against increased export receipts is virtually impossible to answer on an a priori basis. If by 'efficiency' is meant the contribution made to economic development, then the efficiency of direct aid will depend on the type of aid, the conditions attached, and the use made of it by the recipient government. Equally, the efficiency of price-raising agreements will depend, to a considerable extent, on the ability and willingness of governments of exporting countries to devote the additional foreign exchange to development purposes. Thus the efficiency of a price-raising agreement in contributing to the development process is likely to vary substantially among the different exporting countries, both because a given price increase will have very different implications for the export receipts of different countries, and because of the different ways in which the governments of these countries deal with the increased export receipts.

Moreover, additional export receipts resulting from a commodity agreement come with no 'strings' attached, either as to use or as to domestic policies, whereas aid is usually subject to restrictive conditions. Further, it could be argued that as aid from several large donor countries appears to be increasingly related to political factors,[20] its overall efficiency has been reduced relative to other means

---

[20] See Maizels and Nissanke 1984, and the references cited therein.

of promoting development. As regards the 'additionality' issue, it could be argued that since resource transfers through commodity agreements do not require budget appropriations, they are more likely than not to be additional to existing aid flows.

Third, it is often claimed that price-raising commodity agreements will inevitably result in a misallocation of resources by encouraging unnecessary increases in production.[21] There have, indeed, been many instances of prices set by governments at excessively high levels which have resulted in abnormally large increases in output. The high level of price support maintained by the European Community for domestic agricultural produce under the Common Agricultural Policy (CAP) is perhaps the most obvious example. This type of market intervention, practised to a greater or lesser extent by all the developed countries, is now generally acknowledged to involve huge distortions in the allocation of resources, with consequent real income losses. However, the type of market intervention envisaged here to deal with the adverse effects of continuing depressed levels of commodity prices is different from that under the CAP, since it would be based on the control of supply so as to bring prices up to 'more normal' levels.[22]

The Limitations of Neoclassical Theory

More generally, the argument that intervention in international commodity markets to stabilize, or influence, the trend of prices will necessarily distort the allocation of resources, thus involving a 'deadweight' loss and reducing global real income,[23] has had considerable influence with several developed-country governments, particularly those with a free market philosophy. This argument derives directly from neoclassical economic theory which, however, is based on a number of unrealistic assumptions.

The central assumptions are the existence of perfect competition, perfect foresight, perfect factor mobility and price flexibility, full employment, the absence of 'externalities', and the absence of increasing returns to scale (while the impact of free trade on the distribution of income between rich developed-country consumers and poor developing-country producers is ignored). On these assumptions, neoclassical theory demonstrates that the 'free play of market forces' will result in an equilibrium situation characterized by both an optimum allocation of resources and an optimum level of welfare or real income. Moreover, exogenous shocks will cause adjustments which will move the system towards a new equilibrium. Market 'imperfections', such as oligopoly or 'externalities', are then analysed as aberrations from the ideal world of perfect competition.

Given its assumptions, the neoclassical theory is a self-contained logical system. However, as has frequently been pointed out, those assumptions are so

---

[21] See Johnson 1967: ch. 5 for an early exposition of this argument.
[22] In recent years, the CAP has attempted to restrict output of particular agricultural products above agreed ceiling levels in order to limit the budgetary cost of farm support.
[23] This argument was deployed, for example, by Johnson 1977.

far removed from reality that the theory has little relation to actual economic change.[24] Moreover, as soon as some of the basic assumptions are modified, so as to reflect real-world phenomena, the theory is faced with major logical problems. As one eminent neoclassical theorist has explained, neoclassical general equilibrium theory faces logical limitations if there are increasing returns to scale which are large relative to the size of the economy (since this will lead to the emergence of large firms with monopoly power); if there is market power for individuals to exploit (since this will lead to individuals influencing equilibrium prices); if market information differs as between buyers and sellers (in which case certain contingent markets cannot logically exist); if there are public goods (for which the fundamental welfare theorems cannot hold); and if there are externalities, i.e. if one individual's actions affect the welfare of another.[25]

Even if all these assumptions are granted, it can be shown that, if demand elasticities are low, the efficiency or 'deadweight' loss resulting from price raising via supply regulation will be negligible relative to the net gain in welfare resulting from the redistribution of income from relatively rich consumers in developed countries to poor producers in developing countries.[26]

Neoclassical theory thus faces a dilemma — that as a logical system it is unrealistic, while as it moves towards reality it becomes subject to logical limitations. Some of these limitations arise in acute form where, as in many of the international commodity markets, large transnational enterprises use their oligopoly or oligopsony power not only to increase their profits but to extend their market power on a global scale, while for many commodities, the volume of trade as well as the price level are heavily influenced by the policies and actions of the governments of the larger developed countries.

The effects of market intervention in any particular commodity market will thus depend on a complex of factors: on the institutional structure of the market, on the type of intervention, on the regulatory mechanisms used and their flexibility in relation to changing market conditions, and on their effects on both current and longer-term demand and supply.

Moreover, most commodity markets are subject to major imperfections.[27] Particularly where market forces reflect an oligopolistic market structure, or are heavily influenced by national policies, decisions on investment, output, and prices can diverge substantially from those which would obtain in a perfectly competitive market, thus distorting both the allocation of resources and the division of benefit. Equally, the allocation of resources on a global scale is already

---

[24] See, in particular, Kaldor 1972 and 1975, Kornai 1971, and Leontief 1971.
[25] Hahn 1982.
[26] For a theoretical demonstration of this result, see Spraos 1983, ch. 8. An empirical demonstration can be seen in an econometric simulation of the effects of export quotas for coffee imposed in 1982 and 1983 under the International Coffee Agreement. The deadweight loss to all coffee exporters and importers is estimated at $167 million on average for the two years, as against a welfare gain of $1,932 million for all coffee exporters (Herrmann, Burger, and Smit 1980).
[27] See Helleiner 1979 for a perceptive analysis of such imperfections. See also Ch. 10 below for a more detailed discussion of market structures.

grossly distorted, by the results of government interventions both in domestic markets and in international trade flows. Consequently, it can hardly be claimed that intervention which raised prices, even by modest amounts, from depressed levels should be opposed on the grounds that it would necessarily result in a major misallocation of resources.[28]

The various arguments often advanced to justify the opposition of the main developed countries to proposals for supply management for international commodity markets are thus seen to have serious limitations. Indeed, in the light of the widespread supply management arrangements in force in all the developed countries, covering not only agricultural production but a wide range of manufactures such as textiles, clothing, footwear, steel, and automobiles, the opposition in principle to any form of supply management of the international commodity markets – apart from a few exceptions – is not convincing.

One alternative, and more credible, explanation of the opposition of the main developed countries to a supply management approach to the problem of depressed commodity prices is that these countries greatly benefit in the short term from continuing low prices for their imports of commodities, which have played a major role in reducing the rate of inflation in these countries[29] and, indirectly, in raising the level of industrial profitability. Thus in a period of depressed commodity prices, the industrialized countries have little, if any, incentive to enter into international commodity agreements involving supply management, since these are likely to raise prices or, at least, put a 'floor' under the market. In other words, these countries have generally taken a short-term view of their own commercial interests, so that they regard price-raising, even from unprecedentedly depressed levels, as an area in which their interests conflict with those of developing countries.

A further element influencing Northern attitudes to the problem of depressed commodity prices, and one which is perhaps more fundamental, is that the beginning of the 1980s coincided with a marked political shift in a number of the larger developed countries in favour of governments with strong views about the virtues of private enterprise and market solutions, and consequent reluctance to consider any proposals, however relevant, likely to promote interference with market forces.[30]

(*b*) Arguments in Favour of Market Intervention to Raise Depressed Levels of Prices and Export Earnings

A number of positive arguments can, however, be adduced in favour of some form of international action to raise commodity prices from the depressed levels

---

[28] For a non-neoclassical approach to an analysis of commodity markets, based on the concept of 'market power', see Labys 1980 and Maizels 1984.
[29] See Beckerman 1985 and Beckerman and Jenkinson 1986.
[30] The attitudes of developed-country governments to international commodity policies are explored further in Ch. 15.

of the 1980s and early 1990s. The central argument is that such action would be a major contribution to the alleviation of the severe foreign exchange constraint which continues to undermine the development process in virtually all commodity-dependent developing countries. This argument is particularly relevant for the poorer developing countries, including those in sub-Saharan Africa, many of which are heavily dependent on only one or two primary commodities for the bulk of their foreign exchange earnings.

As was seen in Chapter 2, the collapse in commodity prices was one of the factors, along with the sharp increase in debt service payments, and the contraction in commercial bank loans, which precipitated the continuing development crisis. So far, international discussions have focused primarily on the debt burden of heavily indebted countries and of sub-Saharan Africa. Many proposals have been put forward to reduce the debt 'overhang' simultaneously with reducing the exposure of the commercial banks of developed countries. Proposals have also been made for a substantial expansion in financial flows to developing countries from Japan,[31] and from other developed countries in balance of payments surplus.

Thus action to restore commodity prices to 'more normal' levels would complement and support actions being contemplated, or in progress, on the other external elements of the development crisis—the debt burden and the contraction in financial flows, in particular. What the target for 'more normal' price levels might be is, of course, open to argument, and would no doubt also vary from one commodity to another, even given agreement on the meaning of 'more normal'. But with commodity prices in the late 1980s and early 1990s at some 30–40 per cent below the 1980 level in real terms, any action which would substantially close this gap would make an important contribution to overcoming the development crisis.

A case for raising depressed commodity prices, at least for commodity exports from developing countries which compete with developed-country production and exports, can also be made in relation to the high levels of support provided by developed countries to their domestic commodity producers.[32] These supports, involving large budgetary expenditures as well as even larger additional costs to consumers, also result in increasing the depressive forces in world commodity markets. Though government concern has been focused essentially on the budgetary cost, the real cost to the international community arises from the enormous misallocation of global resources that is involved. A disproportionate part of the real cost falls on developing-country producers, who find their markets curtailed and their earnings reduced. International action to raise depressed commodity prices would, to some extent, help to redress this situation, which has arisen to a substantial extent as a result of the policies of the developed countries. Thus action to raise world market prices from depressed levels could

---

[31] Perhaps the best known of these proposals is the WIDER plan for an increase of $25 billion a year, over a five-year period, in financial flows from Japan to developing countries (WIDER 1987).
[32] See Ch. 12 for a detailed discussion of these supports and of their economic effects.

be considered as a form of partial compensation to developing countries for loss of markets or loss of export earnings.

Increased real foreign exchange earnings of developing countries would have beneficial effects for developed countries also. In the short term, to the extent that the foreign exchange constraint is alleviated, developing countries would be enabled to increase their purchases of goods from developed countries, as well as being more able to service their foreign debts. In the longer run, commodity-dependent countries would be given the incentive to expand their productive capacity and improve their productivity, so as more readily to meet any future expansion in demand for primary commodities in the developed countries.

The decline in gross domestic investment during the 1980s in many developing countries (as indicated in the previous chapter) is, however, likely to work in the opposite direction, bringing about a stagnation, or decline, in productive capacity over a range of important traded commodities. To this extent, the traditional boom-and-slump commodity price cycle is likely to be strengthened, with developed countries having to face shortages and high prices for essential raw materials in a future cyclical expansion.

The level of commodity prices is also of major importance with regard to two issues — environmental degradation and the rapid growth in the illicit production and use of narcotic drugs — which have in recent years become of major concern to the international community, and particularly to the developed countries. It is now generally recognized that production technologies and consumption patterns must be modified to minimize any adverse effects on the natural environment such as air and water pollution, global warming, deforestation, and land degradation. The underlying problem has been that the private costs of production and consumption have often fallen far short of the corresponding social costs, since the former have taken no account of the various externalities involved, such as environmental damage, including the depletion of natural resources. For developing countries exporting their main natural exhaustible resource, in particular, their export earnings may not cover the value of the depletion of their resource stock, in which case their net national product would be negative. Thus economic incentives have generally been seriously biased against 'environmentally friendly' activities. Moreover, it is now generally accepted that poverty in developing countries is a major cause of deforestation and other forms of environmental degradation in the Third World. In the context of a broad international strategy to promote 'sustainable' development, measures to promote levels of commodity prices which are more remunerative for developing-country producers would also be conducive to a more sustainable exploitation of natural resources.

Depressed levels of commodity prices have also played a part in the rapid growth over the past decade in the production and use of narcotic drugs. Production, and local consumption, of these drugs has been a longstanding tradition in several developing countries with tropical or semi-tropical climates. However, one important reason for the supply expansion appears to be the prolonged period of low prices obtainable for the traditional commodities produced by peasant farmers in such countries, where diversification into more profitable production of narcotics often appears as the only real alternative to hunger or starvation. A similar shift in production pattern can also occur when prices for traditional mineral products fall below marginal cost, and narcotic drugs provide virtually the sole alternative for the labour force involved.[33]

Attempts to reduce drug supply have not so far been very successful, in spite of the wider use of crop substitution programmes, the promotion of rural development and agro-industries in drug-producing areas, and related drug-eradication programmes.[34] The provision of some form of minimum price support for the traditional commodity exports of the countries mainly involved in drug production, by some form of international action, could be considered as one important element in a wider network of international co-operation designed to reduce demand by addicts in developed countries as well as supply by peasant farmers in developing countries.

Forms of Supply Management

The proposal made earlier that international action to raise commodity export earnings from depressed levels could comprise some form of supply management is not a new idea. Indeed, all the developed countries have operated supply management schemes for domestic agricultural production for a very long time. These schemes have evolved into very complex arrangements which cover price support for major products, often subsidies for essential farm inputs, subsidies for exports, deficiency payments, and, for certain commodities, arrangements for land to be taken out of production.

For the international commodity markets, the traditional approach has been much less complex. International commodity agreements (ICAs) have been negotiated which rely essentially on only one or two mechanisms – export quotas and/or buffer stocks – in order to reduce excessive fluctuations in market prices. The experience of ICAs over the post-war period, and the lessons to be learned, are considered later in this book.[35] Here it suffices to note that to the extent that export quotas, supported as necessary by buffer stocks, provide effective control over a given commodity market, these mechanisms could also be used to influence the price trend, in particular by raising prices from depressed levels.

However, in order to be effective in attaining this objective, ICAs would have to meet a number of stringent conditions, which have often been discussed in the literature on producer cartels such as OPEC. The key conditions are that: the demand for the commodity in question must be price-inelastic, so that any

---

[33] e.g. a sharp reduction in tin production in Bolivia after the collapse of the international tin agreement in Oct. 1985, and the resultant fall in tin prices by some 50%, was accompanied by a marked rise in the estimated volume of coca produced in that country (*Le Spectacle du Monde*, Paris (Nov. 1989)).

[34] See the review of such programmes in United Nations 1989: ch. 8.

[35] See Chs. 6, 7 and 8.

decrease in supply below what it would otherwise have been in absence of supply regulation will result in an increase in export earnings of the member countries; a high proportion of initial output must be under the control of member countries of the agreement; the member countries must retain a high degree of commitment to the agreement; and there must be significant entry costs for non-members.[36]

In principle, an agreement aimed at raising depressed price levels could be negotiated among all interested trading countries, whether exporters or importers, developing or developed. In practice, however, only one major agreement has ever been negotiated on this basis, namely, the International Coffee Agreement, 1962, which provided for the use of export quotas to raise world coffee prices above prevailing levels. This agreement was instigated by the United States in order to channel additional financial resources to Latin America, partly as a complement to the development programmes under the Alliance for Progress.

There have also been agreements involving developed countries designed to stabilize particular commodity markets or to raise particular commodity prices to levels more remunerative to producers. One example is the International Dairy Arrangement, negotiated under the auspices of GATT, which came into operation at the beginning of 1980. This arrangement establishes minimum export prices for a number of milk products, taking into account 'the current market situation, dairy prices in producing participants, and the need to ensure equitable prices to consumers, and the desirability of maintaining a minimum return to the most efficient producers in order to ensure stability of supply over the longer term' (GATT, 1987).[37] Further examples of action by developed countries to support prices received by commodity-exporting countries are the various preferential trade regimes for sugar which were discussed earlier.

Thus it would seem that developed countries are not averse, in principle, to participating in international supply management or price support schemes which benefit their own producers, or which support their own perceived foreign policy interests.

Agreements confined to developing countries only would, however, be very much more difficult to apply, other than to a limited range of commodities, than agreements which also involved the developed countries. This is mainly because for a large number of commodities developing countries supply only a part of the world market (cereals and sugar being obvious examples), while most industrial raw materials face competition from synthetics or other substitutes in their main end-uses. However, for the tropical beverage crops—cocoa, coffee, and tea—and for some tropical fruits and certain non-ferrous metals, viable supply management schemes operated by developing countries could be technically feasible. It would be important for such schemes to have a modest, and reasonable, price

---

[36] For a detailed discussion of these conditions see Spraos 1983.

[37] In addition to the EEC and eight other developed market-economy countries, four countries of Eastern Europe and three developing countries participate in this arrangement.

objective and not to aim at raising prices unduly as would a producers' cartel of the traditional type, in order to avoid retaliation by consuming countries.

An alternative form of supply management, which does not have a price objective, but which aims solely to reduce or eliminate a large stock 'overhang', could also be envisaged for commodities facing chronic structural over-supply.[38] To the extent that world stocks are reduced, the downward pressure on prices would be lessened, or even reversed. Such agreements should be easier to negotiate than those aiming at raising prices, and should not arouse opposition from consumers. The success of the main tin-producing countries in reducing world tin stocks by the use of export quotas is a recent example of this approach, which resulted in an appreciable rise in tin prices from the low level to which they had fallen following the collapse of the tin agreement in October 1985.

Supply management schemes of either type, even if effective, would be essentially short-term expedients to assist producer countries to finance a greater volume of essential imports for their economic development. But supply management cannot by itself deal with the underlying causes of over-supply on world commodity markets. A condition of persistent over-supply and depressed prices will eventually force marginal suppliers out of production, but for many countries there may be few alternative profitable activities. International financial support on a much larger scale than now available from the World Bank and regional Development Banks may be required to accelerate the diversification process in such countries, as well as in others facing stagnating or slow-growing demand for their traditional commodity exports. To the extent that supply management, by raising depressed prices, can assist in the financing of such diversification, it would also make an important contribution to the necessary longer-term restructuring of the economies of commodity-dependent countries.[39]

Market Solutions

The alternative to a supply management approach is to look for market solutions to the continuing commodity crisis. In the absence of measures to reduce abnormal stock overhangs or to raise prices from depressed levels for the majority of producers, market solutions will involve a prolonged period of hardship and economic distress for a large proportion of the world's primary producing population. Eventually, productive capacity will be sufficiently reduced to match the lower levels of global demand and prices may begin a new upward phase. But this will be at enormous cost in real income and in living standards in many developing countries. Moreover, the experience of past decades shows that the free play of market forces has been destabilizing for a wide range of primary commodities. Without some form of supply management, the underlying cycle of

---

[38] Supply management schemes by producing countries to reduce stock overhangs and promote the normal operation of market forces are discussed in some detail in Kanan *et al.* 1989.

[39] See Ch. 14 below for a more detailed discussion of the diversification issue.

glut, followed by shortage, followed by further glut, etc. will continue, or even be reinforced. A durable solution to the commodity problems of developing countries will be no nearer.

These problems are essentially similar—even if now more acute—to those experienced by primary producing countries during the Great Depression of the 1930s. In reviewing the inter-war experience, J.M. Keynes identified the main problems as violent short-term price fluctuations leading to the accumulation by producers of surplus stocks; periodic price slumps, during which producers were unable to secure a reasonable living; the difficulty of producers in curtailing production in such circumstances, leading to a deterioration in their terms of trade; the excess capacity created by government subsidies for high-cost production which aggravated the difficulties of producers, especially as consumption was also restricted; and the chronic surplus of commodities during the years of the Great Depression.[40]

Keynes envisaged a durable solution to these problems by general measures designed to control the trade cycle and to remove trade barriers, complemented by a series of regulation schemes for particular commodity markets. These schemes would have either or both of two distinct objectives:

(i) the 'moderation of excessive short-term fluctuations in prices about the long-term equilibrium price'; and
(ii) the 'maintenance of long-term equilibrium between supply and demand at a price level which provides to the majority of the producers a standard of life in reasonable relation to the standards of the countries in which they live'.[41]

Keynes's proposals to achieve the first objective are discussed further in Chapter 5. In the present context, it is Keynes's second objective which is relevant. If a situation of 'persisting disequilibrium in a particular commodity market failed to respond to reasonable changes in the world market price', then, he argued, 'other means may be necessary to attain this objective'. This would involve, he believed, measures 'to regulate the pace and violence of lasting changes and to mitigate the shock to producers who, through circumstances which they cannot control, find themselves losing their markets. Thus, measures to stabilize prices may need on occasion to be supplemented by measures to smooth the transition to the new conditions and to regulate output meanwhile, so as to safeguard the standards of life of primary producers, as well as to ease the pains of change and progress'.[42]

The need for such measures, to be taken by the international community, is even greater now than when Keynes was formulating his proposals for a

---

[40] Keynes 1943, in Moggridge (ed.) 1980: xxvii. 169. This was part of the final version of Keynes's memorandum, of which an earlier (fifth) draft, of Apr. 1942, was published in the *Journal of International Economics* (Aug. 1974).
[41] Ibid. 170.
[42] Ibid. 171. See also the related issue of 'indexation', discussed in Chapter 8.

new international economic framework. As indicated earlier, such international action must in any event be sharply distinguished from action by producers' cartels to raise prices in order to capture rents or monopoly profits.[43] The argument here is rather that it is in the longer-term interests of both developed and developing countries to evolve a coherent and mutually supporting set of measures to overcome the continuing development crisis. Raising persistently depressed levels of commodity prices and commodity export earnings should be a key element in such a strategy and should therefore be placed high on the agenda for international negotiation and positive action. This issue is taken up again in Chapter 15, where the elements of a possible new international commodity policy are further discussed.

[43] Raising depressed levels of commodity prices by means of an ICA would have direct benefits for developed countries if the alternative was an effective producer cartel (See Spraos 1983: ch. 8).

4
Instability, Stabilization Policy, and Economic Development

1. THE EFFECTS OF EXPORT INSTABILITY

Though the dominant feature of commodity markets since the early 1980s has been the depressed level of prices, rather than price instability, large short-term price fluctuations have remained of substantial significance for a number of important commodities (sugar being the outstanding example). For developing countries wholly or mainly dependent on such commodities for their export earnings, the effects of price fluctuations on their domestic economies will remain a major concern for economic policy. For this reason, it is necessary to consider the instability issue in depth, particularly as it has so far dominated the discussion of commodity problems and policies both in academic circles and in intergovernmental negotiations.

Over the earlier post-war decades, a widely accepted view was that instability of commodity prices and of export earnings was detrimental to economic development.[1] A number of distinct reasons were advanced in support of this view, and these can conveniently be grouped according to the effects which export instability was believed to have on the domestic income, prices, savings, and investment of commodity-dependent countries.[2]

Export instability is likely to affect the stability of total domestic incomes directly, since the export sector generally contributes a substantial proportion of total GDP in these countries. Moreover, there are likely to be multiplier effects on incomes in the non-export sectors as expenditures by the export sector on domestic goods and services fluctuate with export instability.

Many authors have argued that export instability is likely to increase instability in domestic prices and to lead to inflation.[3] In an export upswing, money incomes rise and, it is argued, there tends to be demand-pull inflationary pressure, but when the upswing ends, because consumer expenditures, as well as money wages, tend to be 'sticky', there are no offsetting deflationary effects on prices. Moreover, government expenditures tend to rise during an export

---

[1] In this chapter, no sharp distinction is drawn between instability in commodity prices and instability in export earnings. The relationship between these two aspects of instability is discussed in some detail in Ch. 9.

[2] Extended discussions of these adverse effects can be found in Myrdal 1956, MacBean 1966, Lim 1974, 1988, and, more recently, in Athukorala and Huynh 1987 and, particularly, in MacBean and Nguyen 1987.

[3] See Myrdal 1956 for an early discussion of the relation between export fluctuations and domestic prices.

upswing (since revenues are generally based to a large extent on taxes on foreign trade), but in the downswing many governments may indulge in deficit financing, to a greater or lesser extent, rather than making major cuts in expenditures, thus adding to inflationary pressure.

The effect of export instability on domestic saving has been a particularly contentious issue in the literature. The 'mainstream' view has been that export instability is likely to result in greater instability, and a lower level, of domestic saving than would otherwise occur. Since domestic savings usually provide the major part of the finance for new investment, the result of export instability would be to reduce the growth rate of domestic investment.

As regards fluctuations in savings, the argument has been that the export and government sectors both normally have higher marginal propensities to save than do other sectors,[4] so that export instability—which, as mentioned earlier, also increases the instability of government revenue—will increase the instability of total savings. Unless offset by compensatory capital inflows or by changes in monetary reserves, this will, in turn, increase variations in domestic investment. The mechanism by which export instability reduces the level of saving is different, since this depends on an asymmetry which, it is argued, distinguishes export upswings from downswings.[5] During an export upswing, the resultant rise in income is likely to be associated with a rise in real consumption, but during a subsequent export downswing, consumers may protect their living standards despite falling incomes by reducing their savings and, to that extent, the propensity to save is reduced over a complete cycle in export earnings.

Finally, export instability is believed to be detrimental to domestic investment, and thereby to the growth rate of GDP, for a variety of reasons in addition to the impact on savings.[6] First, export instability is likely to be associated with instability in imports, since for most developing countries export earnings constitute the main source of funds to purchase imports. Moreover, since a major proportion of imports into most developing countries consist of capital goods, intermediate products, and other essentials, fluctuations in total imports will be reflected also in fluctuations in these more specifically developmental goods. Such fluctuations, in turn, are likely to disrupt ongoing development projects, and generally reduce the opportunities for deployment of domestic resources.[7]

A second adverse effect on investment can operate via the government budget. Since tax revenues can be expected to increase during an export upswing, this will normally be accompanied by higher government expenditures, though some of the additional revenue may well be added to monetary reserves. In an export downswing, however, much of the earlier additions to expenditure (e.g. on social services) may well be in the nature of a political commitment, difficult to reduce,

---

[4] See MacBean 1966 and Maizels 1968b.
[5] See Radetzki 1970.
[6] A comprehensive discussion of the effects on investment is given in MacBean and Nguyen 1987.
[7] See, e.g. Helleiner 1972 and 1986.

so that expenditure cuts would fall mainly on government investment, unless there is resort to deficit financing.

A third effect is likely to be on private investment. Export instability can be expected to increase the general climate of business uncertainty in a developing country. This may lead to capital flight if savers prefer to invest their capital abroad. Otherwise, private investment may be channelled into domestic projects yielding short-term profits rather than into more risky ventures, even though the latter may reflect the country's comparative advantage.[8] There is also an important linkage between private and government investment in many developing countries. If export instability does, in fact, reduce the volume of government investment, as suggested above, this by itself could result in lower private investment in so far as the latter is dependent on e.g. adequate public transport, distribution, and other infrastructural facilities.

Fourth, there is an opportunity cost[9] of export instability to the extent that scarce skilled government officials are diverted to cope with recurrent foreign exchange crises resulting from a succession of export downswings, as well as with other consequent administrative problems. The continual disruption of successive development plans inevitably adds to problems of misallocation of resources and generally reduces the productivity of real capital assets.

A critique of the mainstream or conventional view that export instability is detrimental to economic growth was first formulated by Caine (1954). He based his case on two arguments, first in relation to the effect of export instability on investment and second, to its effect on saving. As regards investment, he argued that real investment may be greater when income and profits are high during an export earnings upswing than when they are evenly distributed over time. Furthermore, investment during an export boom may not be offset by disinvestment in the subsequent export slump, since heavy investment in the boom phase may require continuing supportive investment later. Caine adduced empirical data for the Malayan rubber industry to support this argument.

As regards the effect on saving, Caine argued that as greater export instability involves greater uncertainty, producers will find it necessary to keep larger monetary reserves to provide for contingencies. These increased funds, when channelled through the banking system, constitute additional savings for financing investment. This argument was later taken up by adherents of the 'Permanent Income' hypothesis suggested by Friedman,[10] who focused on the role of domestic savings in mediating between exports and investment. These authors make a distinction between permanent and transitory income (the latter defined as unforeseen income fluctuations), and argue that transitory income, being unexpected, is largely saved and not consumed, thus adding to funds available for investment. The conclusion of this school of thought is that export instability

---

[8] See Helleiner 1972.
[9] See exposition of this point by Lim 1974.
[10] See next section.

is not detrimental to economic growth or, in stronger terms, that export instability is conducive to faster economic growth—a conclusion diametrically opposed to that of the conventional approach discussed earlier.

However, the argument that fluctuations in transitory income lead to higher savings is not convincing. As MacBean and Nguyen (1987) point out, if savings are higher out of positive transitory income, then dissavings should also be higher out of negative transitory income, so that over a complete income cycle the effects on saving should even out. Moreover, the significance for economic growth of changes in savings depends on whether savings, rather than foreign exchange availability, constitute the dominant constraint on investment. Thus the transitory income and the conventional approaches may be said to be based on different implicit assumptions about the nature of the effective constraint on investment and growth.[11]

In the decades up to 1980, there was widespread interest among economists concerned with development issues in the significance of export instability for the economic development of commodity-exporting countries. Two distinct lines of analysis can be distinguished. One was essentially empirical, designed to test specific hypotheses concerning the effects of instability on growth. The second was purely theoretical, deriving normative policy prescriptions from basic economic theory.

2. THE EMPIRICAL EVIDENCE

A large number of statistical analyses have been made over the postwar period into the relationship between short-term instability in commodity exports and the growth rate of GDP (and also of other key variables such as domestic investment) in developing countries. These studies fall into two broad groups.[12] The first, and more numerous, group consists of cross-country regressions, or correlations, of domestic growth rates over selected periods on assumed explanatory variables, including some index of export instability. Second, there are a number of time-series studies for individual developing countries, in some cases a model of the world market for the commodity exported being integrated into a country model.

(a) Cross-Country Studies

The results of various cross-country studies seem, at first glance, to have been generally inconclusive. In a recent review by Behrman (1987) of 10 such studies, it appeared that five[13] showed that export instability had a negative effect on

---

[11] In terms of the two-gap model elaborated by Chenery and Strout 1966, the Permanent Income hypothesis implicitly assumes that developing countries are in a phase where the savings gap is dominant, while the conventional approach generally implicitly assumes a dominant foreign exchange constraint.

[12] See Behrman 1987 and MacBean and Nguyen 1987 for recent detailed reviews.

[13] Maizels 1968a, Glezakos 1973, Kenen and Voivodas 1972 (for 1956–67), Lancieri 1978, and Lahouel 1981.

growth, or on growth determinants, three[14] other studies suggested some positive effect, and an equal number[15] suggested no effect. These contradictory results can generally be attributed to the use of different country samples, different time periods, different model specifications, different methods of calculating instability, and the omission of one or more relevant variables.[16] On account of these differences, the results of the various studies are not strictly comparable.

In any case, most of these studies covered relatively few countries, often fewer than 30, which throws some doubt on the generality of their results. The major exception is the study of export instability by Lancieri (1978), covering 123 developing countries. An interesting result of Lancieri's analysis—which found a significant negative association between export instability and the growth rate of GDP—was that over the period covered, 1961-72, the degree of export instability was significantly higher for small and poor countries than for large and more economically advanced countries.[17] The exclusion, or inadequate representation, of small or poor developing countries from most of the other studies, because of lack of relevant data or for other reasons, may thus have seriously biased their results. This conclusion is consistent with the argument (Lim 1988) that the countries selected should be confined to 'those with large export sectors and a high degree of commodity concentration', since other developing countries 'cannot be affected in the ways postulated by theory'.

The use of time periods including years of abnormal conditions could also introduce bias. MacBean's (1966) analysis, which was the pioneering study in this field, with wide influence on a whole generation of economists and politicians interested in the export instability issue, covered the period 1946-59. As pointed out by Ady (1969), the late 1940s and early 1950s were characterized by widespread currency devaluations and by a persistent world dollar shortage, while a foreign-exchange constraint on growth did not become a general factor for most developing countries until later. Studies covering mainly the 1960s, when short-term export fluctuations were relatively small, were also likely to find less impact of instability on growth than studies focusing on other decades with greater export instability.

Differences in model specification can also be expected to influence the results. Lim (1978, 1988), for example, shows that small changes in model specification can significantly influence the results, while the relationships tested in several cross-country studies are misspecified. While most cross-country analyses assume, either explicitly or implicitly, that export instability will have an impact on domestic investment and hence on the growth rate of GDP, some studies—particularly Knudsen and Parnes (1975), and Yotopoulos and Nugent (1976)—

---

[14] MacBean 1966, Knudsen and Parnes 1975, and Lim 1980.
[15] Coppock 1962, Kenen and Voivodas 1972, and Moran 1983.
[16] See e.g. the reviews by Adams and Behrman 1982, Behrman 1987, and Stordel 1988.
[17] Lancieri's methodology has, however, been heavily criticized, e.g. by Lim 1988, and by MacBean and Nguyen 1987.

investigate the relationship between export instability and domestic savings, on the hypothesis that the transitory component of export income—the measure used to represent instability—is positively correlated with savings and hence with the GDP growth rate. However, the finding by Knudsen and Parnes that the hypothesis is proven rests on an invalid statistical procedure, viz. the inclusion of domestic income instability in addition to export instability in their instability measure.[18] Other studies of this issue have generally shown inconclusive or negative results.[19]

The cross-country studies also vary in the explanatory variables used, since these have generally been selected on an *ad hoc* basis, so that bias in the results could easily arise as a result of the omission of one or more relevant influences. Moreover, apart from a few exceptions,[20] these studies omit financial inflows as an influence on domestic investment, savings, and growth. This is, perhaps, surprising, since for countries constrained by foreign exchange, imports are financed to a greater or lesser extent by loans from the commercial banks, by capital inflows, and, on occasion, by drawing down monetary reserves, in addition to earnings from exports.

Thus if developing countries have adequate monetary reserves, or have ready access to foreign capital or finance and can offset fluctuations in export earnings, to a greater or lesser extent, by opposite changes in reserves or financial flows, the impact of export instability on imports, and thence on investment and GDP growth, would be minimized. The ready availability of loans from the Eurodollar market in the 1970s could well have been an example of this kind of effect. To test for this, linear and semi-log linear regressions on time were computed for the 1960s and 1970s for the purchasing power of exports and for import volume, separately, for the group of commodity-exporting developing countries. The results, confirming the hypothesis, showed that relatively large fluctuations in the purchasing power of exports had been very substantially smoothed out in terms of import volume during the 1970s, whereas in the 1960s there was relatively little instability in either series.[21]

One would therefore expect that for the 1970s the more 'creditworthy' developing countries may have succeeded, to a substantial extent, in avoiding fluctuations in their imports arising as a consequence of export instability, by arranging offsetting financial flows[22] or changes in their monetary reserves. Less 'credit-

---

[18] See e.g. Athukorala and Huynh 1987, and Stordel 1988 for a statistical refutation of the Knudsen and Parnes results.

[19] Gupta 1970 and Stordel 1988.

[20] MacBean 1966, Voivodas 1974, and MacBean and Nguyen 1987 discuss the influence of financial inflows in this context.

[21] For the linear regression, the $\bar{R}^2$ values were 0.494 for the purchasing power of exports and 0.853 for import volume for the 1970s; the comparable figures for the 1960s were 0.919 and 0.922, respectively. Virtually identical results to these were obtained for the semi-log linear regressions.

[22] The large financial inflows of the 1970s were, however, a major element in the debt crisis of the 1980s.

worthy' countries – often the poorer ones – could be expected to have less ability to arrange such offsetting finance.[23]

A study by Deméocq and Guillaumont (1985) explicitly investigated the effect of export instability on external financing, as well as on domestic savings and investment. Covering a sample of 58 non-oil-exporting developing countries, including 26 in sub-Saharan Africa, the analysis showed, for the 1970s, a significant and positive relationship between export instability and external indebtedness, but a negative relationship between export instability and domestic savings. These contrary effects for that decade appear to explain the somewhat contradictory results in earlier studies. Deméocq and Guillaumont also found a negative effect of export instability on the productivity of capital, which they explain by resource misallocation and bad planning of investment induced by export instability. As a result of these various influences of savings and investment, they conclude that the effect of export instability on growth rates is generally negative (Guillaumont 1987).

This conclusion would seem to be more applicable to the poorer developing countries with little access to external sources of finance than to others. As Helleiner (1986) argues, the principal external instability problem for such countries can plausibly be taken as import volume instability. Using single-equation regressions, he found that for a sample of 25 sub-Saharan African countries, there was a statistically significant negative relationship between import volume instability and the growth rate of GDP over the period 1960 to 1980. However, for an overlapping sample of 24 low-income countries (of which 18 were African), no such significant relationship emerged. These results indicate the importance of studying the intermediate links between export instability and the growth rate of a developing country. But they also reveal some of the weaknesses of the cross-country approach, in so far as the statistical results are sensitive to change in country coverage, time period, and whether the relationship studied has been correctly specified.

Moreover, all these cross-country studies suffer from another major defect, namely, that they implicitly assume that the countries covered have similar economic structures, so that a single regression equation can validly represent the relationship between export instability and economic growth for all countries.[24] Given that there are in fact considerable differences in economic structures among developing countries, it is inherently implausible to assume that a single relationship of this kind exists.

---

[23] The importance of offsetting financial flows and changes in monetary reserves in damping the effects of export fluctuations on the domestic economy is also stressed by MacBean and Nguyen 1987.

[24] This was one of the criticisms of MacBean's (1966) results made by the present author (Maizels 1968a); see also Rangarajan and Sundararajan 1976 on this point. MacBean and Nguyen 1987 have also stressed this defect, among others, in their recent assessment of the use of cross-country regressions to assess the impact of export instability on the domestic economy.

(b) Individual Country Studies

A small number of studies of individual developing countries, based on relationships between time series, generally using single-equation models, have also been made over the past few decades. MacBean (1966) was again the originator of this approach, with case studies of five developing countries. MacBean's results showed little or no sensitivity of domestic economic variables to export instability, which, he argued, confirmed the findings of his cross-country regressions. Lim's (1974) study of West Malaysia over the period 1960–70 showed a negative (but non-significant) association between GDP growth and export instability. However, Lim was doubtful of the significance of this or, indeed, any result derived from a single-equation model.

Other country time-series studies also gave rather contradictory results. An analysis for Ethiopia showed that changes in exports during the period 1961 to 1970 were positively and significantly correlated with changes in imports of capital goods and with domestic fixed-capital formation (Love 1975); but for Kenya, Uganda, and Tanzania short-term changes in real GDP were found to be not correlated, or positively correlated, with export fluctuations (Stein 1979). However, for Ghana, Zambia, and Zaire, export earnings instability was found to be negatively correlated with government revenue instability, so that export fluctuations for these countries had an adverse impact on government development programmes (Morrison 1979). A more recent time-series analysis, for 12 developing countries over the period from 1960 to the early 1980s, showed that export instability was positively related to instability in the volume of capital goods imports for eight countries, the relationship was negative for three countries, while for one country there was no statistically significant relationship; similarly, for six countries there was a positive relationship between export instability and instability in domestic investment. This study found little evidence of international reserves being used to offset the impact of export instability (Love 1989).

While such studies for individual countries based on single-equation regressions avoid some of the problems arising in the case of cross-country studies —particularly in avoiding the assumption of similarity in economic structures— many of them suffer from the defect of drawing conclusions from an oversimplified set of relationships, ignoring a number of dynamic elements of the economic growth process, including the role played by imports of capital goods and intermediate products in domestic investment.

A further difficulty can arise from the method used to calculate the export trend—a vital analytical issue, since instability is generally defined as deviations from the trend. While the method of trend calculation makes little difference in cross-country studies,[25] it can be significant in time-series analysis. A moving average trend, for example, will generally follow the price cycle, so that devia-

---

[25] See Stordel 1988: ch. 5, for a statistical demonstration of this conclusion.

tions will reflect mainly annual fluctuations within a given cyclical phase. Deviations from a linear or log-linear trend computed for, say, a decade or longer will, by contrast, capture much of the cyclical movement, in addition to annual variations, in the measurement of instability.[26] The results of different country studies may thus be non-comparable if they use different methods of trend calculation.

The difficulties of interpretation of the results of studies using single-equation time-series regressions can be largely overcome by the use of macroeconomic models of individual countries, which take account of their specific structural characteristics, including export instability. One of the earliest attempts to trace the impact of export fluctuations and export growth on the growth rate of GDP by use of such models was that by Rangarajan and Sundararajan (1976). They applied a simplified standard model to each of 10 developing countries, and simulated the effects of a steady rate of export volume growth on income to compare with the effects of actual, historical, export instability. For all these countries, export volume instability is shown to be positively correlated with instability in income. However, as regards the effects of export volume instability on income growth, no clear conclusion emerged, since for five countries income growth is shown to be reduced by export fluctuations, whereas it was increased in the other five.[27]

The standardized model used by Rangarajan and Sundararajan has, in any case, been criticized as not adequately taking into account the different structural characteristics of the various countries covered, or the special role of investment in creating new productive capacity;[28] and because the model used is 'so rudimentary' – for example, there is no allowance for supply constraints – that 'it is questionable what their results really show'.[29] In addition, the index of export instability which they use relates only to instability of export volume, so that an important element – instability of export prices – is omitted, and this by itself could easily result in major biases in the results.

A more sophisticated approach to testing hypotheses on export instability, based on integrating a detailed macroeconomic model for an individual developing country with a model of the world market for that country's major commodity export, was pioneered by a study on cocoa and the Ghanaian economy (Acquah 1972), reviewed by Behrman (1987). An integrated macroeconomic–commodity market model of this type can be used to simulate the dynamic effects through

---

[26] To illustrate this, linear and 5-year moving average trends were computed for real non-oil commodity prices (UNCTAD index) for the period 1955–70. The annual trend was the same in both cases (−1.9% p.a.), but the instability index (mean percentage deviation from trend) for the linear trend (6.62%) was about double that for the 5-year moving average trend (3.25%). However, a comparable calculation for the 1971–84 period showed relatively little difference in the instability indices, though that based on a linear trend (11.92%) was higher than for the moving average (10.80%).

[27] These results are also difficult to interpret because the period covered by the analysis is not stated. The model was also applied to one developed country (Australia).

[28] Athukorala and Huynh 1987: 28–9.

[29] Adams and Behrman 1982: 42.

the domestic economy of changes in particular parameters, including different degrees or duration of export instability.[30] This approach was followed by similar studies on Chile/copper (Lira 1974) and Venezuela/oil (Palma-Carillo 1976), and five studies at the University of Pennsylvania using a common methodology, viz. Brazil/coffee, Ivory Coast/coffee, Central America/coffee, Chile/copper, and Zambia/copper,[31] generally covering the period 1960 to 1977. In each case, export instability has been simulated by assuming that the price of the commodity concerned falls by 10 per cent in one period, the results then being combined with those resulting from a 10 per cent price increase in the subsequent period, with other variables constant. For all five countries, the net effect on investment and GDP is shown to be nil or marginal (except for investment in Chile) over a five-year cycle, a decline due to falling prices being wholly or mainly offset by a rise due to increasing prices.[32]

These models were also used to simulate the effects of sustained price increases or decreases (over 10 years) on the attainment of stated development goals of the countries concerned (Adams and Behrman 1982, ch. 8). The results showed that the total impact – including both the direct impact on the production sector and that induced in the rest of the economy – can be quite large. The indirect effects can also be larger than the direct ones because of under-utilized capacities, foreign exchange constraints, and expectations formation. The effects of sustained price changes of a major export commodity were shown to vary substantially across countries. For Zambia, for example, a sustained 10 per cent fall in copper prices would be associated with a 10 per cent fall in domestic investment, on average, for the first succeeding quinquennium. For Brazil, at the other extreme, a similar sustained fall in coffee prices would have only a relatively small negative impact on the domestic economy as a whole.

A separate study in this genre for Sri Lanka by Athukorala and Huynh (1987) is based on a detailed model for the period 1959 to 1977, taking into account the specific structural characteristics of the Sri Lankan economy, including the links of the export sector with domestic income and output. These links include the role of exports in generating foreign exchange to purchase imports of capital goods and intermediate products, the contribution of exports to government tax revenue, and the effects of exports on money supply. The impact of export fluctuations is derived by comparing the actual GDP growth rate with a simulated rate based on an assumed smooth growth rate of exports over the period. The results show that export instability had a serious adverse impact on imports of capital goods and thus on fixed investment and government revenue. A smooth growth of exports is simulated to increase annual growth rates, compared with actual outcomes, of real fixed investment by 13 per cent, government current

---

[30] See Adams and Behrman 1982 for a full discussion of this approach.
[31] By Adams and Priovolos 1981, Priovolos 1981, Siri 1980, Lasaga (1981), and Obidegwu and Nziramasanga (1981), respectively.
[32] See the summary of these simulations in Behrman 1987: Table 2, which also shows the impact on employment, prices, nominal income, and nominal non-wage income.

revenue by 10 per cent, and real GDP by 15 per cent. These results are in remarkable contrast to those (for Ceylon) given by Rangarajan and Sundararajan (1976), whose simulations show that the elimination of export instability would have resulted in negative GNP growth for that country. The omission of a terms of trade effect may well have been the reason for this result.

The mixed results given by the various time-series analyses for individual countries do not mean, however, that no valid generalizations can be made concerning the effects of export instability on the domestic economies of developing countries. Rather, it would seem that much of the confusion in results reflects differences in model specifications, the different degrees of commodity market instability in the different periods covered, differences in the relative weight of the export sector in the national economy, and other technical factors, such as the methods used to determine the underlying trend. A more pervasive influence on the econometric results, perhaps, has been the degree to which different studies related to countries which adopted policies, such as borrowing abroad, which offset to a greater or lesser extent the adverse effects of export instability.

Thus it would seem reasonable to conclude that for countries with relatively large export sectors in relation to the domestic economy, with no easy access to foreign loans, and possessing minimal monetary reserves, substantial export instability is likely to have serious adverse impacts on their domestic economies, in ways outlined earlier. For countries able to borrow adequate funds abroad to compensate for export shortfalls, these adverse effects can be avoided or minimized. Again, a given export fluctuation may have quite different impacts on the domestic economies of some countries than it has on others, as a result of structural differences, as well as differences in responses by enterprises and governments to the export fluctuation. Hence there can be no unique answer to the question as to whether export instability constrains economic growth, when this is put in a 'yes or no' context.

As MacBean and Nguyen (1987: 176–7) conclude, after a comprehensive assessment of the main empirical studies:

The difficulty of proving the detrimental effect of export instability on economic growth does not mean that we should abandon the view that risk and uncertainty, stop–go policies, disruption of imported capital goods or public investment programmes, and investment fluctuations have adverse effects on the level and efficiency of investment and hence growth rates. . . . Even in the absence of direct evidence confirming the detrimental effect of export instability on economic growth, a priori reasoning and indirect evidence still strongly suggest that those countries whose economies seem likely to be sensitive to export fluctuations should be encouraged and assisted to insulate their economies from the effects of export instability.

3. ECONOMIC THEORY AND MARKET STABILIZATION

Quite separately from the series of statistical studies reviewed above, theoretical economists concerned with economic development issues have engaged in a controversy concerning the significance of commodity price instability for economic growth in commodity-exporting developing countries. A dominant theme, espoused by the post-war school of neoclassical economists, e.g. Johnson (1967), has been that international measures to stabilize short-term fluctuations in commodity markets would not be in the interests of producing countries or of the world economy in general. The opposing school of thought—of which Keynes was a major proponent—argued in favour of market intervention, at least in appropriate circumstances, to minimize the adverse effects of excessive commodity market fluctuations.

Various arguments have been advanced by neoclassical economists over the post-war period against proposals for international action to reduce commodity market instability. The major ones have been that such action would have harmful effects both for producing countries and for the world economy as a whole; that such action is unnecessary, since its objective of reducing fluctuations in export earnings could be achieved more efficiently by other means; and that the use of market intervention to reduce price fluctuations will result in a misallocation of resources and thus in a reduction in global real income.

(a) Commodity Price Stabilization as 'Harmful'

One argument, which has had wide influence in the academic literature on commodity instability as well as among developed-country policy-makers, was first elaborated by Massell (1969), building on earlier analyses by Waugh (1944) and Oi (1961). This argument, which was later extended by many others, including Hueth and Schmitz (1972), Brook, Grilli, and Waelbroeck (1977), and McNicol (1978), was derived from a simple comparative static model of a commodity market based on a number of assumptions, viz. linear demand and supply functions; instantaneous reactions of demand and supply to price changes; parallel shifts in the demand and supply curves over two successive periods; and price stabilization at the mean of the prices in the two periods that would have obtained in the absence of price stabilization. On these assumptions, the following conclusions were reached regarding the operation of a price-stabilizing buffer stock:

(i) where the price fluctuation was due only to changes on the supply side, price stabilization would result in a destabilization of export revenues if demand is price elastic, and also if demand is inelastic but numerically larger than 0.5; and

(ii) where the price fluctuation was due only to changes on the demand side, the revenue fluctuation would be reduced, but only at the expense of a decline in total revenue over the two periods.

These results were often brought forward to throw doubt on the usefulness of international negotiations to establish International Commodity Agreements (ICAs) in general or, more particularly, ICAs for commodities where price fluctuations are normally the result of variations in supply (as for most agricultural products). The study by Brook, Grilli, and Waelbroeck (1977) even went so far as to identify the specific commodities (only four in number) for which price stabilization would bring a clear benefit to developing countries.

However, the analysis on which these results were based suffered from two major flaws, each of which is sufficient to invalidate all the strong conclusions that were drawn. The first flaw was the assumption that a buffer stock would maintain a *fixed* price. This was indeed a curious assumption, since the imposition of a fixed price has never been considered in the entire history of post-war international commodity negotiations. Where ICAs contain provisions for market intervention for price regulation they always specify a price *range* to be defended by one or more mechanisms, including a buffer stock in certain cases. The use of a price range is indeed an essential element of any stabilization exercise in order to allow sufficient flexibility to the operation of a buffer stock or other mechanism in the light of changes in market conditions, in exchange rates, or in other relevant factors.

The distinction between a fixed price and a price range is important in the present context, since the relationship between price and revenue stabilization differs significantly in the two cases. As Nguyen (1980) has conclusively shown, even assuming linear demand and supply functions, a buffer stock which maintains prices within an agreed (and market-related) range can stabilize export earnings even when price fluctuations are predominantly supply-induced, provided that demand is price inelastic. Since demand is, in fact, generally inelastic for the majority of commodities exported by developing countries, stabilization of prices within a suitable range will not lead to a destabilization of earnings. Nguyen also shows that price stabilization within a range has no effect on the long-term level of export earnings.

The second major flaw in the argument of Massell and his followers is that the assumptions underlying his model are not relevant to actual (or 'real world') commodity markets. In particular, the assumption of linear supply and demand functions with instantaneous reactions to price changes needs to be relaxed to allow for time lags, and for dynamic effects such as the influence on demand of a reduction in the amplitude of price fluctuations for natural raw materials competing with relatively stable-priced synthetic substitutes.

Thus the argument that price stabilization will destabilize export revenues for commodities with large supply fluctuations, and with demand elasticities between 0.5 and 1, is seen to be based on unrealistic assumptions. None the less, this argument is still raised on various occasions.

(b) Commodity Price Stabilization as 'Unnecessary'

A further argument against the use of intervention in international commodity markets to reduce excessive price fluctuations, which has also been influential, particularly with policy-makers of developed countries, is that such intervention is unnecessary, if the aim is to smooth the movement over time in the foreign-exchange availabilities of exporting countries (this aim following from the foreign-exchange-constrained growth model discussed earlier). Two separate, though related, strands of this argument have been put forward at various times.

(i) *The export earnings cycle.* The first strand rests on the cyclical character of commodity price movements, a price boom being followed by a price slump which, in turn, is followed by another price boom. It is thus conceivable, at least in principle, that a commodity-exporting country could accumulate monetary reserves in the price boom, which it could use later to offset the decline in export earnings in the succeeding price slump. This is the solution to the problem of short-term fluctuations in export earnings advocated by Caine (1958), who argued that this approach would work only if the real value of money put aside in a boom was not reduced by inflation before the succeeding slump. A similar argument was advanced by Johnson (1967), who suggested that the difficulties that 'fluctuations in export prices (and) earnings impose on governments of countries dependent on primary product exports attempting to plan their economic development and manage their domestic economies' could be avoided if 'domestic and investment policies [were based] on the normal or trend values of export prices or earnings, offsetting fluctuations around these values by alternating accumulations and decumulations of international reserves' (pp. 141–2).

A closely related argument has recently been advanced by Behrman (1987), who defines 'instability' as fluctuations around a secular trend, so that 'the expected magnitude of the downswing in the international primary commodity market just equals the expected magnitude of the upswing'. Once again, the implication is that commodity-exporting countries can, given appropriate domestic policies, accumulate sufficient monetary reserves during a commodity price boom to enable them to offset revenue losses during the succeeding price slump.

A major difficulty confronting governments of countries enjoying a commodity price boom is to decide, either explicitly or implicitly, on how long the boom is likely to last. In the case of a profound structural change in the market, as occurred after 1973 in the market for oil, the decisions of most oil-exporting countries appeared to assume implicitly that oil prices would remain high for a prolonged period. When oil prices fell in the 1980s, some countries were left with large foreign debts and acute balance of payments difficulties. Other price booms have usually been short-lived as, for example, the coffee boom of 1976–8, the sugar booms of 1974–5 and 1980–1, and the price boom for vegetable oils in 1983–4.

The typical response of producing countries to such price booms has been to use most of the additional export revenue to pay for additional imports, rather than to add to monetary reserves. Moreover, government revenues of developing countries, which usually rely heavily on tax revenue from the export sector, rose during these export booms, followed in many countries by increases in government expenditures. The end of the booms led to sharp increases in trade and fiscal deficits, declines in foreign capital inflows, and, in some cases, capital flight. Thus many of the countries which enjoyed export booms ended up worse off than before (World Bank 1988).

While governments need to act with fiscal prudence during export price booms, expecially since it is evident that such booms are usually of short duration, the argument that developing countries generally can accumulate reserves during a price boom needs further examination.

First, while monetary reserves could be held in the form of interest-bearing loans to other countries, as suggested by MacBean (1980), there is likely to be a significant opportunity cost involved in the form of essential imports, e.g. capital goods, forgone, with consequential adverse impact on domestic investment. The issue then revolves around the probable net economic (and political) benefit, if any, of adding to monetary reserves. Moreover, there are inevitably large differences among developing countries in the ability to use their reserves in this way. There may well be a net gain from such a policy for countries with satisfactory growth rates and payments positions, but a net loss for those chronically short of foreign exchange, and with negative growth resulting from 'import strangulation'.

A second difficulty with the Johnson argument is that since developing countries are normally in deficit in their foreign trade,[33] a general rise in prices that occurs concurrently with a commodity price boom will worsen their trade deficits, unless the improvement in their terms of trade more than offsets the increased cost of imports resulting from the effect of inflation.[34] A deterioration in the trade balance resulting from inflation in the world economy is thus likely to constrain the accumulation of monetary reserves during a commodity price boom.

This is exactly what happened during the commodity price boom of the 1970s. As Fig. 4.1 shows, non-oil commodity prices, in terms of current United States dollars, rose sharply in 1973 and 1974 and, apart from short-lived recessions in 1975 and 1978, continued their upward trend until 1980 (line A in Fig. 4.1). However, when commodity prices are expressed in terms of the prices of manufactured goods exported by developed countries—i.e. the commodity terms of trade—the upward trend disappears (line B). If, alternatively, the terms of

---

[33] The large trade surpluses which emerged in the 1980s for many heavily indebted developing countries, particularly in Latin America, can hardly be considered a normal feature for developing countries.

[34] The change in the terms of trade necessary to improve the trade balance when import prices are rising is given by the expression:

$$(P_x - 1)/(P_m - 1) > V_m/V_x$$

where V_m and V_x denote the value of imports and of exports, respectively, in the base year, and P_m and P_x are base-weighted indices of import and export prices. Alternatively, for current-weighted price indices P'_m and P'_x, the corresponding requirement is:

$$(1 - 1/P'_x)/(1 - 1/P'_m) > V'_m/V'_x$$

where V'_m and V'_x denote values in the current year, and all price indices are equal to unity in the base year.

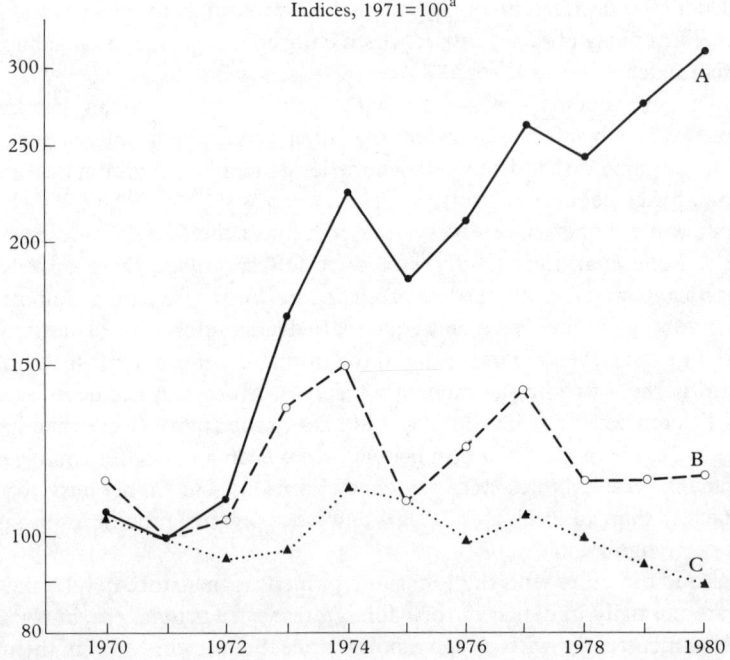

A = UNCTAD index of commodity prices in current US dollars; B = UNCTAD index deflated by UN index of unit value of exports of manufactures from developed market-economy countries; C = terms of trade index for commodity-dependent developing countries.

[a] Market prices of 39 major commodities, other than petroleum, exported by developing countries.

Fig. 4.1. *Commodity prices and terms of trade of commodity-dependent countries, 1970–80.* Sources: *UNCTAD* Monthly Commodity Price Bulletin, *1960–1984 Supplement, Geneva, July 1985; UNCTAD* Handbook of International Trade and Development Statistics, 1986 Supplement, *UN, New York, 1987*

trade are defined as the relative movement in the unit values of exports and imports of commodity-exporting countries, then the 'commodity price boom' becomes negative (line C). This reflects very largely the impact of the rise in import prices of both manufactured goods (resulting from the inflationary trend in developed countries during the 1970s) and of petroleum (resulting from OPEC actions).[35]

Thus the inflationary pressures in the developed countries, together with the two oil price 'shocks', effectively prevented the commodity-dependent countries as a group from accumulating reserves during the commodity price boom of the

---

[35] Other factors involved were that export unit values did not rise as fast as market prices during the commodity boom, while many commodity-exporting countries export some manufactures, the prices of which did not increase as fast as those of primary commodities.

1970s on a scale adequate to cope with the succeeding price slump. Over the whole decade of the 1970s, the cumulative net gain accruing to the commodity-dependent countries as a result of changes in their overall terms of trade was only a marginal one (in the region of $2–3 billion at 1980 prices), whereas the cumulative terms of trade loss suffered by these countries over the period 1980–8 was in the region of $155 billion, greater than their total merchandise export earnings ($123 billion) in 1980.[36]

A new factor which appeared in the 1980s and which, by itself, would represent a major limitation on the present relevance of the Caine–Johnson–Behrman argument is the sharp increase in the debt-service burden of commodity-exporting developing countries.[37] For the majority of these countries, this development has meant that commodity exports have become more a means of maintaining debt-service payments to foreign creditors than a means of economic development. Thus even if there had been a symmetry between 'excess' export earnings in the commodity price upswing of the 1970s and export earnings shortfalls in the 1980s, the Johnson–Behrman argument would be unrealistic in the light of the new element of 'excess' debt-service in the 1980s.[38]

There is also some doubt as to whether, even in a non-inflationary world economy, the gains to developing exporting countries in a commodity price boom are likely to equal the losses in the subsequent price slump. Avramović (1978) has argued that low-income developing countries do not have the financial resources to carry stocks, so that they are compelled to sell any surplus production even on a falling market. Thus their losses in a slump tend to be proportionately greater than those of developed-country exporters. Moreover, when prices are rising, developing countries generally cannot afford to hold on to supplies in order to sell later at higher prices, as developed-country exporters can, so that their gains in a price boom tend to be correspondingly lower, proportionately, than those of developed-country exporters.

At the same time, however, it is also the case that a number of developing countries which had enjoyed an unexpected export boom in the 1970s failed to utilize their revenue 'bonanzas' prudently. In most cases, government expenditure was correspondingly inflated on the implicit assumption that the boom would last indefinitely. This was the case particularly for many of the oil exporters, and for some of the coffee-exporting countries. The contraction in export revenues in the early 1980s, again unexpected, resulted for many of these countries in much sharper import cuts than would have been necessary had they arranged their finances so as to retain adequate monetary reserves.

---

[36] The cumulative terms of trade loss of $155 billion differs from that given in Ch. 2 (Table 2.2), since the former relates to all exports (including manufactures) from the commodity-dependent countries, whereas Table 2.2 relates to commodity exports from all developing countries, so that it does not take account—as does the $155 billion figure—of the fall in oil prices after 1985.

[37] Whereas in 1975 interest payments on foreign debts of this group of countries represented 9.6% of exports, by 1980 the proportion had risen to 16.1%, and by 1987 to 23.2%.

[38] As mentioned in Ch. 2, part of the rise in interest payments can be attributed to service of loans taken to offset the fall in export earnings resulting from the decline in commodity prices.

Apart from the such special cases, however, the argument that developing countries in general can offset the adverse effects of cyclical fluctuations in world commodity markets by operating a counter-cyclical monetary reserves policy would seem to be unrealistic.

(ii) *The role of compensatory financing*. The second strand in the argument that the stabilization of commodity prices is unnecessary is the claim that such stabilization is less efficient than the use of a central fund for compensating commodity-exporting developing countries for temporary shortfalls in their export earnings.

It is evident that even if market intervention is successful in reducing the amplitude of fluctuations in the total earnings of developing countries from the export of a particular commodity, this would not necessarily reduce the degree of fluctuation in export earnings from each individual country. As an UNCTAD Expert Group (1984*a*) report has shown, while fluctuations in total commodity export earnings of developing countries result mainly from price fluctuations, for many individual countries earnings fluctuations are due mainly to fluctuations in export volume.[39] The latter reflect, in turn, country-specific factors such as changes in output due to climatic variation, domestic price policies, political problems, or lagged responses to fluctuations in world market prices, as well as to variations in world demand. For this reason, a financing scheme which could compensate individual countries for shortfalls in their commodity export earnings would be able to reduce the instability of export earnings at the country level, an objective which schemes of market intervention may find more difficult to achieve.

Another advantage of the compensatory financing approach is that it can be applied to earnings shortfalls for any commodity, or for any group of commodities, whereas market intervention by means of buffer stocks or export quotas – the two traditional mechanisms of price stabilization – is unlikely to be successful, or even technically feasible, for more than a limited range of commodities. Moreover, a compensatory financing scheme, once established on a viable basis, can provide assurance of continuity, whereas an international price stabilization agreement often faces the possibility of breakdown, thus injecting an additional element of risk in the outlook for commodity export earnings.

These undoubted advantages of the compensatory financing approach have led a number of economists, as well as governments, to argue that efforts to negotiate new ICAs, or even to renegotiate existing ones, should be abandoned in favour of improving existing international compensatory financing schemes, or of introducing new ones. This argument, too, has a number of serious limitations. First, it assumes that the shortfalls in export earnings to be offset by compensatory finance are identical to the shortfalls which an ICA seeks to prevent or minimize. Based on the experience of the two compensatory financing

---

[39] See Ch. 9 for a detailed discussion of the relative importance of price and volume instability for individual countries.

schemes in operation—that of the IMF and the STABEX scheme of the European Community—the shortfalls for such schemes have been defined in relation to a moving short-term trend, usually of five years' duration. The 'floor' price defended by an ICA, however, will not necessarily be equal to the moving average centred on the year in question, so that it is unlikely that the corresponding export earnings shortfall will be close to that under the existing compensatory schemes. Much would depend on the willingness of the executive body of the ICA to shift the price range as market conditions change, and on the amount of financial and other resources at its disposal to defend the agreed price range. Thus the two approaches—compensatory financing and market intervention—are substitutes only to a limited extent.

Second, while an ICA's operations would influence export earnings of all producers of a commodity, it would seem highly unlikely that an international compensatory financing facility (CFF) would be endowed with financial resources adequate to offset commodity export earnings shortfalls for more than a limited number of developing countries. The finance required for full compensation is more likely to exceed that needed for a buffer stock, the more demand and supply are inelastic. Short-term elasticities are very low for many commodities, so that full compensation could involve very large amounts of finance. The IMF/CFF, in the peak year of its use, 1983, had drawings amounting to 2.6 billion SDR, but drawings under this facility declined sharply to 0.8 billion SDR in 1984. Since 1985, indeed, repayments of loans under the facility have rapidly increased, and there has been a net outflow of funds from developing countries.[40]

Third, the view that compensatory financing can substitute for the stabilization of commodity prices implicitly assumes that the economic impact of these two measures is closely similar. However, the economic impact is likely to be substantially different, at least in most cases. The difference arises essentially because compensatory payments must necessarily be made to the governments of the commodity-exporting countries concerned, and such payments may, or may not, be passed on, either wholly or in part, to the commodity sector suffering the export shortfall. Where Marketing Boards or *Caisses de Stabilisation* are in operation, the degree of 'pass-through' of compensatory payments is likely to depend on the price policies of these marketing bodies. By contrast, the successful support of a 'floor' price by an ICA has a direct, and stabilizing, impact on the export earnings of commodity producers, at least in the short term.

This differential impact can have important consequences for the traditional cycle of overproduction followed by underproduction of many agricultural commodities. A reduction of commodity price fluctuations can be expected to lead to a reduction in the amplitude of the production cycle whereas—as Ady (1980) has argued—compensatory payments would leave the production cycle untouched. Moreover, a compensatory scheme involving loans would require

---

[40] See Ch. 9 for a more detailed discussion of the IMF facility.

future debt-servicing obligations, an additional claim on scarce foreign exchange that would not arise if market intervention was successful in defending a 'floor' price.

In view of the different economic impacts of the two approaches, as well as the probable infeasibility of meeting temporary export earnings shortfalls from a compensatory payments scheme alone, it would seem desirable to pursue both avenues simultaneously. This would also have the important practical advantage of reducing the total amount of finance that would be required to meet temporary export earnings shortfalls of individual developing countries.

(c) Commodity Price Stabilization as a Mechanism for the 'Misallocation of Resources': The Case of Export Quotas[41]

(i) *The effect on the price trend.* Buffer stocks and export quotas have been the two principal mechanisms for the reduction of short-term commodity price fluctuations. There is an important difference between the two, in so far as buffer stocks cannot be expected to influence the underlying trend in prices (assuming the buffer stock has limited resources), while it is often argued that export quotas, by their restrictive influence on production, can (and do) raise the price trend, even though this was not the intention. For this reason, ICAs using export quotas have often been criticized by developed-country governments, which have shown a strong preference for the use of buffer stocks as the stabilizing mechanism when an existing ICA is renegotiated or a new ICA is being considered.[42]

Whether an export quota imposed within the framework of an ICA in order to protect an agreed 'floor' price in a period of over-supply will raise the trend of market prices will depend essentially on whether the quota results in a restriction of productive capacity. For minerals, where production may be controlled by large enterprises, it may be practicable to halt investment in new capacity, though a decision to this effect is likely to depend on the probable duration of the period of over-supply and the probable magnitude of the subsequent expansion in demand. For agricultural products, however, and particularly where peasant production predominates, the concept of 'capacity' is much more tenuous, since even if land is taken out of production when prices are low, it can in many cases be brought back again when prices rise.

There would thus not appear to be any a priori reason for expecting export quotas – especially if these are applied for a relatively short period – to raise the

---

[41] An extensive discussion of the arguments for and against the use of export quotas for short-term price stabilization can be found in Maizels 1982: chs. 3–5.

[42] On occasions, developed-country spokesmen decry both buffer stocks and export quotas, though attributing the same effects to both has no theoretical justification. A recent statement on these lines was that 'Experience with the tin agreement and other commodity agreements has shown that market intervention provisions such as buffer stocks and quota arrangements have severe defects: at best they are of doubtful benefit to producers and consumers and at worst they distort markets fundamentally and carry the risk of disastrous failure' (Statement by the United Kingdom Trade Minister to Parliament, 21 July 1988).

underlying trend of prices. For this to occur, producers would have to be convinced that there was a chronic situation of over-supply which would last for a number of years, thus providing an incentive to reduce existing capacity or, at least, not to expand capacity. In any event, if there were no export quota in a situation of over-supply, the market price would fall—almost by definition—below the 'floor' price which would have been defended by an export quota if such a quota had been in operation. It follows, then, that any reduction in productive capacity would be greater during a price slump of a given duration if there were no export quota than if such a quota were in force.

Consequently, in the upward phase of a price cycle, with demand expanding, producers would more easily be able to increase their supply after a quota period, than if there had been no quota and prices had fallen in the downward phase of the cycle to a level generally unremunerative to producers. Thus the main effect of an export quota used to defend the 'floor' price of an ICA may well be, in many cases, to reduce the amplitude of the price fluctuation rather than to raise the price trend. However, if productive capacity is, in fact, adversely affected as a result of an export quota, the price cycle itself is likely to be shortened, since the reduction in capacity would tend to raise prices sooner than they would otherwise rise once demand had begun to expand in the upward phase of the cycle.[43]

To recap, the main effects of an export quota imposed to defend the 'floor' price of an ICA may be to reduce the amplitude of the price cycle and to shorten its duration. These effects are more likely when the export quota does not lead to significant reductions in productive capacity. Where capacity is adversely affected, however, then an export quota would also be likely to raise the price trend. Which of these effects predominates will vary according to the characteristics of the commodity market concerned, and especially the decisions of producers affecting new investment.

(ii) *Defence of the 'ceiling' price.* A second criticism of export quotas is that while they may be effective in defending the 'floor' price of an ICA in a period of over-supply, they are much less useful in defending the 'ceiling' price in a period of shortage. Thus it could be argued that the use of export quotas would be unfair to commodity-importing countries. It is useful here to distinguish several broad groups of commodities.

First, there are temperate-zone foodstuffs, such as cereals and sugar, the production of which is heavily subsidized in developed countries. High levels of subsidy have resulted in large increases in production, a curtailment of demand, the accumulation of huge stocks, and an expansion of exports. The consequence has been that prices of these products in the world market have been reduced, and their volatility increased.[44] It can therefore reasonably be argued that agricultural protectionism in developed countries is inequitable to

---

[43] There is some evidence that the price cycle was shortened in the free market for sugar during periods when export quotas were in force.
[44] These effects are considered in some detail in Ch. 12.

commodity-exporting countries, and that any inequity to commodity importers resulting from the failure of an export quota to defend a price 'ceiling' would be merely a partial compensation for the economic losses imposed on exporters by agricultural protectionism.

A second group, industrial raw materials, faces substantial competition from synthetics and other substitutes.[45] Any ICA for such commodities would have to take into account the competitive position of the raw material concerned, so that any agreed 'ceiling' price would need to be in the region of the substitution-threshold price, or slightly below it, to be realistic. Consequently, in conditions of shortage, market forces are likely to operate so as to keep prices in the region of the ceiling price.

A third group consists of the tropical beverage crops: cocoa, coffee, and tea, the markets for which have been subject to wide price fluctuations, often accentuated—for cocoa and coffee—by speculative activity. ICAs which rely on export quotas to reduce the amplitude of these price fluctuations would need to be supported by an adequate system of international and/or nationally held stocks in order to provide an adequate 'cushion' in defence of an agreed ceiling price (while allowing export quotas to defend the 'floor' price), in order to make the ICA operation equitable to importing, as well as exporting, countries.

(iii) *The 'freezing' of production patterns.* An argument frequently deployed against the use of export quotas is that they tend to 'freeze' the existing pattern of production, thereby keeping high-cost producers in business and discriminating against more efficient producers. To this extent, there would be misallocation of resources and a loss in global real income. This has indeed been a major problem in the past for ICAs based wholly on export quotas (coffee and sugar), and no really adequate solution has yet emerged.

The difficulty arises because while it is in the collective interest of exporters to limit their aggregate export volume, it is in their individual interest to maximize their share of world exports of the commodity concerned. The allocation of quota shares, at least in the initial negotiations, tends to reflect very largely the relative bargaining strengths of the various exporting countries, rather than their relative export potential. Moreover, export potential depends to a greater or lesser extent on investment in new capacity, and this, in turn, is likely to be influenced by the quota allocation itself. Thus, unless there are effective provisions for quota reallocation during the lifetime of an agreement, there is a real danger that the export potential of small, or of new, exporting countries with weak bargaining power will be frustrated. An incentive would, therefore, exist for such countries either not to join an agreement, or to break away from it, unless acceptable quota allocation and reallocation arrangements were provided by the terms of the agreement.

Accommodating the interests of new exporting countries—some of which may have the capability of rapidly expanding their output to become large

---

[45] See Ch. 11 for a detailed review of this issue.

exporters—raises some difficult problems, since negotiations on market shares (which determine each country's basic quota) have necessarily to be based in large measure on historical performance. Since total exports are limited under a quota system, the share of new exporters can grow only at the expense of established exporting countries.[46] This is essentially a 'trade-off' situation, in which the established exporters will seek to offer small current quotas plus some degree of export growth in order to keep the new exporters in the agreement. The latter will seek larger current quotas than indicated by historical performance, together with provision for export growth corresponding to their production expansion programmes.

Quota negotiations would undoubtedly be greatly facilitated if some relevant principles could be devised for establishing initial quotas, and for periodic quota revisions, provided such principles were generally accepted by exporting countries. A proposal for an automatic system of establishing export quotas was indeed put forward over 25 years ago (Kaldor 1963). Under this proposal, the initial export quotas would be negotiated in the traditional manner. Each producing country would then impose a variable export duty, the height of the duty being set at a level that would limit domestic production to the total of domestic requirements plus the quantity of exports allowed by the quota. Once each country attains the export duty that keeps its domestic production in balance with its requirements, the level of that duty in relation to the f.o.b. price of the commodity gives a clear indication of the domestic cost of production in terms of international currency. It follows that a country which has to impose an export duty higher than average also has lower-than-average costs of production.

Professor Kaldor suggested that after an initial phase of, say, three or five years, during which the basic quotas would remain unchanged, there would be an annual redistribution of quotas in favour of countries whose net export duties are above average, at the expense of countries whose net export duties are below average. To guard against the imposition of excessive export duties to gain a quota increase, Professor Kaldor proposed that only countries making full use of existing quotas should be entitled to any quota increase. Since countries whose basic quotas are increased would be forced to reduce their export duties (in order to take up the additional quota), while countries whose quotas are reduced would be forced to increase their export duties (to avoid accumulating excessive stocks), there would be a gradual equalization of the level of export duties among various exporting countries.[47] This, in turn, implies that the scheme would tend to bring about the same distribution in the pattern of production and trade as would occur in a fully competitive market, but without the price fluctuations and uncertainties involved in the latter.

Professor Kaldor's proposal would, if fully implemented, reconcile the

---

[46] For a detailed consideration of conflicts of interest in commodity agreements, see Rangarajan 1978.

[47] To allow for the possibility of some countries providing subsidies to commodity producers, the export tax in Professor Kaldor's scheme should be interpreted as net of subsidy.

potential rigidities of an export quota scheme with the need for flexibility in production and trade patterns so as to reflect changes in relative productive efficiency. However, it would seem unrealistic to expect this type of scheme, even with modifications,[48] to be adopted by governments in the near future. For one thing, governments of many developing countries appear to be opposed in principle to the imposition of taxes on their exports, on the grounds, *inter alia*, that such taxes would be detrimental to an expansion in demand in consuming countries. A second consideration is that many governments are generally opposed to any automatic formula in the framework of ICAs, whether related to the price range, to the quota mechanism, or to any other aspect. The large established exporters, or the large importers, according to the issue in question, tend to prefer an open, non-automatic, system in which 'all relevant factors' can be discussed, since this maximizes their effective bargaining positions. While a modified Kaldor-type approach may be the most efficient solution in principle to the quota allocation problem, it is doubtful whether it could be successfully negotiated, at least in the medium-term future. Indeed, Kaldor himself later came to the view, following discussions with economists of underdeveloped countries, that his scheme was 'not one that is politically likely to be a "starter" in most producing countries' (Kaldor 1980).

Meanwhile, a more practical short-term approach would be to build on what has already been achieved. There is no doubt that the various quota-using agreements had made very considerable efforts to ensure some degree of flexibility in quota allocations, though clearly the flexibility achieved was greater in some cases than in others. One possible way forward in future negotiations might be to seek some appropriate indicator which would combine some of the main principles already in use, e.g. recent export performance, current levels of stocks, and the importance of the commodity in the export earnings of individual countries. Prior agreement by governments would, however, be needed that such an indicator would be a major determinant in the quota revision process.

---

[48] Apart from exemption of small exporting countries from quota cuts, such modifications would have to include allowance for changes in the effective exchange rates confronting exporters.

5
Commodity Markets and the World Economy

The discussion so far has focused on the effects of a prolonged period of depressed commodity prices, and of excessive short-term commodity price fluctuations, on the development of Third World countries. However, there are also important linkages between events in the commodity markets and the evolution of other sectors of the world economy, particularly the industrial and financial sectors, which impinge on the economies of the developed countries. It is important to identify these linkages and to trace any adverse impacts on the global economy, since if such impacts are likely to be important, this would provide a rationale for genuine international cooperation to pursue appropriate remedial policies.

In the analysis of the linkages between the various sectors of the world economy, their implications for economic growth and instability, and the remedial policies that should be pursued, Keynes and Kaldor were the outstanding innovators and protagonists. Virtually all the postwar academic discussion of the issues involved has related in one way or another to their basic analyses. Keynes's proposals for stabilizing the commodity markets included also a link with the international financial system, and are considered in further detail in Section 3 below. Kaldor's proposals for commodity stabilization, also involving an international currency link, arose in part from his analysis of the peculiar interconnections between the commodity markets and the industrial sector of the world economy (Hart, Kaldor, and Tinbergen 1964 and Kaldor 1976, 1983).

1. THE COMMODITY AND THE INDUSTRIAL SECTORS

First, Kaldor makes a clear distinction between the process of price formation in commodity markets and that in the markets for industrial goods. In the former, adjustment to changes in the balance of supply and demand is generally through changes in prices (i.e. commodities are traded in a market-clearing process), while for industrial products adjustment is through changes in output and stocks, and not through changes in prices. Industrial output prices are determined, instead, by percentage mark-ups over production costs. In other terminology, commodity markets are 'flexprice', while markets for industrial products are 'fixprice'.

This contrast in price formation has two major consequences. First, because industrial prices are 'sticky', adjustment in the world economy to an imbalance between the growth of primary production and the growth of industrial output falls entirely on the commodity markets, which exhibit large short-term fluctuations. Second, commodity price fluctuations tend to increase inflationary pressures and depress industrial output in the world economy, *irrespective* of whether commodity prices are rising or falling.[1] It is this latter 'stagflation' effect which is central to Kaldor's model.

In a phase of rising commodity prices, he argued that manufacturers would tend to raise the prices of their output so as to maintain their relative profit margins (implying also a rise in the absolute level of profits). This cost-push could be accentuated if the cost of living also rises and there is pressure from workers for wage increases. At the same time, demand for industrial goods in real terms would decline, since the rise in profits is not likely to be matched by a corresponding rise in spending by manufacturers. Moreover, Kaldor argued, governments would tend to introduce restrictive monetary or fiscal measures to reduce domestic demand in order to counter inflationary pressure. Thus rising commodity prices would lead to a more general inflation if monetary policies were accommodating or, if these policies were restrictive, to a decline in output and a rise in unemployment.

The adjustment process would, however, be very different in a period of falling commodity prices. In this case, the purchasing power of the commodity sector would be reduced, and consequently its demand for the products of the industrial sector would be curtailed. The fall in commodity prices would also lead to a fall in investment in the commodity sector, in both industrial and developing countries. In Kaldor's view, this reduction in demand was likely, on balance, to outweigh any additional demand arising in the industrial sector as a result of the fall in commodity prices.[2] Thus the net result of a large fall in commodity prices is likely to be a reduction in output in the industrial countries, other things being equal, rather than a fall in the general level of prices.

These asymmetrical effects of commodity price upswings and downswings result, on this analysis, in 'a highly inefficient regulator for securing continuing adjustment between the growth of availabilities and the growth in requirements for primary products in a manner conducive to the harmonious development of the world economy' (Kaldor 1976: 707). Instead of an expansion in supplies of primary commodities being used as a basis for an expansion of industrial production, the fall in commodity prices leads to a contraction in demand for industrial output. Similarly, a shortage in supplies of commodities leads to a rise in industrial prices and cost-push inflationary pressures, and probably to more restrictive monetary policies, leading to depressive effects on industrial activity.

There has clearly been a major asymmetry in government policies also – a key element in Kaldor's argument – over the past decade or two. Whereas in the

---

[1] For some recent appraisals of Kaldor's theory of the dynamics of the relationship between the commodity and industrial sectors see, in particular, Thirwall 1987, Spraos 1989, and Griffith-Jones 1989.
[2] Spraos 1989 shows that a net negative effect on the output of the industrial sector depends in principle on the sum of the reciprocal import-demand elasticities of the two sectors being less than -1. However, this is likely to be the case in practice.

1970s the sharp rise in oil prices prompted the imposition of restrictive measures, in the first half of the 1980s the large fall in commodity prices, which played a major role in the reduction in inflation,[3] did not lead the monetary authorities of developed countries to adopt less restrictive, let alone expansionary, monetary and fiscal policies. Together, these asymmetrical effects — both those arising from the processes of price formation and those arising from government policies — to the extent that they are operative, can cause large economic losses to the industrialized countries.[4]

The asymmetry between the effects of increasing, and of decreasing, commodity prices (the 'ratchet effect') has, however, been disputed. Two well-known studies are often quoted in this context. One (Goldstein 1977) covers the period from 1958 to 1973, before the rise of monetarist doctrine, and does not consider the probable impact of import price changes, via the balance of payments and domestic inflationary pressures, on government monetary and fiscal policies. The second study (Finger and De Rosa 1978) is based on a correlation test between indices of instability of primary commodity prices and the relative price trends of processed to crude forms for a sample of 20 commodities. This approach again fails to capture the Kaldor effect, since a sharp rise in commodity prices which provokes more restrictive monetary and fiscal policies will have general contractionary effects throughout the economy, rather than merely on the prices of processed forms of imported commodities.

The strength of the linkage between commodity price increases and inflation rates will depend not only on the structural characteristics of an economy, on the relative bargaining strength of wage-earners, and on government policies, but also on the relative weight of the commodities whose prices have increased in the aggregate of domestic output and consumption. It could be argued, for instance, that oil is a special case in view of its wide industrial and transport uses and its susceptibility to large price variation. The implication would be that for non-oil commodities the linkage could be much weaker.[5] This then becomes essentially an empirical issue.

There have been a number of empirical studies in this field. An early one (Popkin 1974), using a model differentiating between outputs at different stages of processing, concluded that for the United States nearly one-half of the increase in the consumer price index between 1973 and 1974 could be attributed to increases in primary commodity prices above their trend rates of growth. A later study for the United States (Nordhaus and Shoven 1977), based on an input-output model, concluded that about one-half of the increase in the wholesale price index from mid-1972 to mid-1974 could be accounted for by price increases for primary commodities and imports.

A more general study, by Bosworth and Lawrence (1982) calculated the contribution of primary commodity prices to inflation (defined as the price of GDP

---
[3] See the evidence in Beckerman 1985 and Beckerman and Jenkinson 1986.
[4] Behrman 1977 gives a statistical demonstration of the magnitudes that could be involved.
[5] MacBean 1978 uses a closely related argument.

plus imports) for the United States, West Germany, and Japan over the 1970s. The results showed wide differences among these countries, though in all three, price increases for primary commodities, including oil, were a strong inflationary force, particularly in 1974 and, for the United States, in 1979. Excluding oil, commodity prices made a significant contribution to inflation only in certain years (e.g. in 1973, when they contributed about one-third to the general rate of inflation in the United States), as a result of sharp increases in food prices.

A more recent study (Durand and Blöndal 1988) related indices of non-oil commodity prices to consumer price indices in seven major OECD countries, using quarterly data for the period 1960–87. The results of Granger-causation tests showed wide variations among these countries, and also among different commodity groups. These authors conclude that changes in the prices of certain non-oil commodities are significantly related to subsequent changes in aggregate OECD inflation rates,[6] though these relationships were found to be generally unstable over time, and subject to two-way inter–temporal causation. One limitation of this type of analysis is that it does not make specific allowance for the effect of changes in monetary and fiscal policies, or in 'real wage resistance', in influencing domestic inflation rates. It seems likely that such changes are one reason for the temporal instability in the relationships found in this study.

A further study using Granger-causality tests, by Labys and Maizels (1990), related commodity price indices to various domestic prices, industrial output, GDP, and money supply in six major industrial countries, using quarterly data for the period 1957–86. The results suggested a much stronger relationship than had been anticipated, between primary commodity prices and domestic prices, costs, and other economic variables, with a particularly strong relationship between commodity prices and prices of industrial shares.

The results of the tests for the impact of commodity price changes on domestic prices and wages were mixed, however, and this may possibly reflect an asymmetry in this relation as between commodity price booms and slumps. The tests for macroeconomic behaviour showed strong relationships running from commodity prices to real output, and to changes in interest rates, and, to a lesser extent, to adjustments in the money supply. This suggests that these industrial countries did, in fact, use monetary policy in some form to counter large swings in commodity prices. Strong relationships between commodity prices and wages and employment were found, as well as with exchange rates.

It is generally acknowledged that adverse economic effects occurred in the industrial countries as a result of the large shifts in oil prices. Fairly quickly after the first oil 'shock' of 1973–4, investment spending in the OECD area in 1975 was sharply reduced, stocks also being heavily cut back, while a substantial proportion of the additional income of the oil exporters was saved. This deflationary

---

[6] Significant relationships were found in this study between the OECD consumer price index and prior movements in the UNCTAD index for agricultural raw materials prices and in the metals and minerals price index of the Hamburg Institute für Weltwirtschaftforschung.

effect came on top of an incipient recession, and was combined with a sharp acceleration of inflation, with monetary policy being tightened in almost all OECD countries. The outcome was the most severe recession of the postwar period (OECD 1980: 121). The second oil 'shock' of 1979–80 also had severe deflationary effects. A simulation by the OECD secretariat in mid-1980 indicated that by 1981 the level of OECD real GNP was likely to be some 5.5 per cent below what it would have been had this oil price shock not occurred (OECD 1980: 123).

Similar calculations have not been done for movements in non-oil prices over the 1980s. However, some approximate guide to the impact-effect of the terms of trade loss by developing countries on the export sector of the OECD economies can be had by relating this loss to the value of total OECD exports of manufactures. In the two years 1987 and 1988, the terms of trade loss by developing countries on their exports of non-oil commodities, compared with 1980, averaged $36 billion a year (Appendix Table A.2), representing 3 per cent of annual OECD exports of manufactures (excluding processed foods and drink) in those years. This terms of trade loss was equivalent, very approximately, to the output of some 450,000 workers in the manufacturing export sectors of OECD countries, while the corresponding effect on total OECD employment would have been significantly greater than this as a result of multiplier effects. The net loss of jobs would, however, be less to the extent that the corresponding terms of trade gain by OECD countries allowed them to increase their own rates of economic growth.

2. THE COMMODITY AND THE FINANCIAL MARKETS

Commodity price instability can also have adverse effects on the economies of developed countries by exacerbating instabilities and uncertainties in the international economic system in general. Increased instability and uncertainty are likely to inhibit new investment, to lead to greater misallocation of resources (since prices become a less efficient indicator of the underlying trend in the demand/supply balance), and thus to a general reduction in the efficiency of resource use.

Since the early 1970s, the world economy has become much more unstable than in previous decades. It has experienced sharp shocks, particularly in the prices of key products such as petroleum, in interest rates, and in the exchange rates of major currencies. The degree of instability rose sharply in the 1973–80 period, particularly for petroleum prices (reflecting two very large price increases) and exchange rates, but also for non-oil commodity prices. The GDP deflator for industrial countries also became significantly more unstable in this period.

During the 1980s, instability has become less marked generally than in the 1973–80 period, the main exception being currency exchange rates where increased fluctuations reflected very largely the abnormally large appreciation of the US dollar from 1982 to 1985 and its subsequent equally large decline. Petroleum prices remained subject to wide fluctuation, but instability in non-oil commodity prices in the aggregate fell off to pre-1973 levels, though for a number of important commodities (particularly sugar, many vegetable oilseeds and oils, and certain non-ferrous metals) price instability remained high (Labys and Maizels 1990; UNCTAD 1987c).

Since the early 1970s, also, there has been an increased degree of interaction between the financial markets and those for primary commodities. One mechanism which links the two consists of shifts of speculative funds into, and out of, those commodity markets dealing in futures contracts (such as the terminal markets for cocoa, coffee, sugar, copper, rubber, lead, tin, and zinc). Over the past two decades, the volume of such speculative funds has expanded enormously. A broad indicator of this expansion is the net size of the Eurocurrency market, which amounted to $65 billion in 1970, grew to $255 billion by 1975, to $705 billion by 1980, and to some $1,450 billion by 1986 (Morgan Guaranty Trust Co 1987). These are very large amounts indeed in relation to the value of world trade in non-oil primary commodities (about $350 billion in 1986, of which about $100 billion from developing countries), though only a small proportion of Eurocurrency funds would normally be used for operations on the commodity terminal markets. However, in periods of heightened uncertainty about the future course of commodity prices, of currency exchange rates, or of inflation rates, very large amounts of funds can be switched, either for hedging or for speculative purposes, from other asset markets into commodities, or vice versa, thus greatly accentuating the commodity price cycle.[7]

A second link between the financial and commodity markets, mentioned in Chapter 1, arises through the influence of the rate of interest on the volume of commodity stocks held by private traders. Since 1980, there has been a period of abnormally high interest rates which, by greatly increasing the cost of holding stocks, has been an important factor—along with the slowdown in the growth rate of industrial production—in the reduction of stocks held by traders in developed countries to minimum working levels. Where such stocks had represented a substantial proportion of global stocks of particular commodities, the reduction in the private sector stock 'buffer' would have reduced the short-term price-elasticity of supply of such commodities so that a given shift in the imbalance between supply and demand would have been reflected in a greater price variation than previously. This seems to have been a significant 'once for all' effect during the price collapse of 1980-2. However, since then global stocks of virtually all the major commodities have risen, largely as a result of the production expansion in both developed and developing countries.

There are also linkages in the reverse direction, from changes in commodity prices to changes in key financial variables such as exchange rates and interest rates. One linkage mechanism here has already been mentioned, viz. the intro-

---

[7] See Labys and Thomas 1975 for a statistical demonstration of this effect.

duction of more restrictive domestic monetary policies consequent upon large increases in commodity prices, which necessarily involve higher interest rates and may well also affect exchange rates. Other mechanisms may also be at work. For example, shifts in current account balances resulting from commodity price changes – the petroleum case is, of course, the obvious example – may influence exchange rates because of country differences in portfolio preferences. Thus if increased demand for US dollars by oil-exporters, following a rise in the oil price, is less (more) than the decline in demand for dollars by oil-importers, there will be an excess supply of (demand for) dollars in the foreign exchange market, and the dollar will depreciate (appreciate). Moreover, those oil-exporting countries with large investments in developed countries will carefully consider the likely impact of their own output and pricing decisions on the financial markets and hence on their future investment incomes.[8]

For non-oil commodities, the linkages are likely to be different. Uncertainties about future commodity prices are likely to create uncertainties about future balance of payments positions of commodity-dependent countries, and thus also about the future exchange rates of these countries' currencies. In many cases, heightened uncertainties of this kind have been one factor leading to substantial capital flight, usually into the US dollar, thus giving added support to that currency's exchange rate.

The structural characteristics of the international commodity markets – the inelasticity of both supply and demand in the short term, the lag in the adjustment of supply to changes in demand, and the market-clearing nature of many of these markets – all work to ensure that commodity prices exhibit large short-term fluctuations. The various linkages with the financial markets mentioned above operate to accentuate, and not to mitigate, these fluctuations. At the same time, the accentuated commodity price instability tends to have an adverse 'feedback' for the industrialized countries in a recessionary period. In the short term, a contraction in real export earnings of developing countries will result in a reduction in exports to them from industrialized countries, while in the medium term the adverse effects of low commodity prices on productive capacity can precipitate a supply shortage, and a consequential commodity price boom, during a subsequent recovery period. Moreover, a prolonged period of depressed commodity prices, as in the 1980s, undermines the ability of commodity-exporting countries to service their foreign debts, and thus inevitably has an impact on the profitability of the private banking sector of the developed countries.

Thus the commodity sector has come increasingly to operate not only as a mechanism for the transmission of growth or recession from the industrial centres to the peripheral economies, but also as a major source of instability in the world economy as a whole. If petroleum is included in a broad definition of

---

[8] See the detailed analysis of the interactions between oil price changes and consequent changes in financial markets in Congressional Budget Office 1981.

commodities, then undoubtedly the unprecedentedly large swings in commodity prices since the early 1970s have injected severe and largely unexpected shocks into the international economy, with dramatically adverse effects on world trade, economic growth, and the debt problems of developing countries.

3. COMMODITY MARKETS AND WORLD ECONOMIC FLUCTUATIONS

The proposals put forward by Keynes during the Second World War to deal with excessive commodity price fluctuations—to which reference was made earlier—envisaged the establishment of a series of international buffer stocks for the principal commodities entering international trade.[9] The institutional and operational arrangements proposed for these buffer stocks are reviewed briefly in Chapter 6. However, in addition to their price-stabilizing functions, this system of buffer stocks could also be used, Keynes pointed out, as a mechanism which could make a 'large contribution to the cure of the trade cycle itself'.[10]

With unregulated commodity markets, Keynes argued, a decline in effective demand in the industrial countries 'causes a price collapse, which means a corresponding break in the level of incomes and of effective demand in the raw material producing centres, with a further adverse reaction, by repercussion, on effective demand in the industrial centres; and so, in the familiar way, the slump proceeds from bad to worse. And when the recovery comes, the rebound to excessive demand, through the stimulus of inflated prices, promotes, in the same evil manner, the excesses of the boom.'[11] By contrast, if the buffer stocks which Keynes had proposed were in a position to act as buyer of last resort when effective demand was falling in the industrial countries, then producers' incomes would retain some measure of stability so that the cycle might be inhibited at the start. Again, by releasing stocks when demand recovers, the buffer stocks can prevent the inflation of raw material prices which carries the seeds of an incipient boom.[12]

Keynes envisaged a triad of new international institutions to provide the framework for an expanding postwar global economy. One would be an International Clearing Union, to provide liquidity for countries facing temporary balance of payments difficulties; a second would be an International Investment Institution, to provide funds for longer-term postwar reconstruction;[13]

---

[9] These proposals were a development, in much greater detail, of an earlier plan (Keynes 1938) for the British government to offer storage facilities for raw materials produced in British Empire countries, in order to attenuate excessive commodity price fluctuations.

[10] Keynes 1942, fifth and sixth drafts. The section dealing with 'Buffer stocks as a measure contributory to the prevention of the trade cycle' was deleted from the final (1943) draft, but was attached as an Appendix (see Moggridge (ed.) 1980: xxvii 172).

[11] Keynes 1942, para. 16.

[12] Ibid.

[13] Successive drafts of Keynes's proposals for the Clearing Union and the International Investment Institution are given in Moggridge 1980: xxv.

and a third, an international body – called by Keynes the 'Commod Control' – to stabilize world commodity prices. The first two of these institutions were established at the Bretton Woods Conference of 1944, the first as the International Monetary Fund (a greatly emasculated form of Keynes's proposal) and the second as the International Bank for Reconstruction and Development. However, Keynes's proposals for an international body for commodity price stabilization were never seriously considered in the negotiations between the British and American governments on the postwar international economic institutions.[14]

The central feature of Keynes's commodity stabilization scheme was the establishment of a series of buffer stocks for the main traded commodities, these being subject to a co-ordinating body in the form of a General Council for Commodity Controls to deal with conflicting interests and to provide an adequate measure of conformity to a common pattern. The Council's General Executive would receive periodic reports from each of the Controls operating buffer stocks, 'to review their condition and, if necessary, to make recommendations as to the policy which they should follow. Such recommendations would have as their object the protection of the general interest, and especially the maintenance of a stable level of general prices and the control of the trade cycle.'[15] The General Executive, as the centrepiece of Keynes's scheme, would clearly have had an exceptionally important, even a decisive, influence on world commodity trade and the incomes of developing countries from their commodity exports.

Keynes's proposals for financing the individual buffer stocks were also innovative. While finance could be obtained through the General Executive by means of an international commodity loan, secured on the physical stocks held, and supplemented by a general levy on all the buffer stock commodities, Keynes pointed out the advantages that would derive if the fluctuating margin of finance were mediated through the General Executive's account with the International Clearing Union. The General Executive would then hold an increasing credit balance with the Clearing Union in times of general boom when the buffer stocks were being depleted, and an increasing debit balance in times of general slump when the buffer stocks were accumulating. This would, Keynes emphasized, introduce a stabilizing factor of major importance into the world economic system.[16]

This proposal for a link between commodity stabilization and the international financial system has some striking similarities with later proposals for combining

---

[14] Moggridge 1980: xxvii. One reason for the neglect of Keynes's commodity stabilization scheme was opposition by the UK Ministry of Agriculture (which wanted to see stricter quota regulations) and the Bank of England (which wanted greater scope for State trading).

[15] Ibid. 175. Keynes recognized the need for export quotas (in addition to buffer stocks) if a persisting disequilibrium failed to respond to reasonable changes in the market price, but he emphasized that quota regulation should not evolve into chronic restriction of output (see p. 59 above).

[16] Ibid. 184–5.

the stabilization of commodity markets with stabilization of the world economy. A major contribution here was again made by Kaldor. The 'stagflationary' effects of commodity price fluctuations which he had identified—which were discussed above—together with the defects of the international monetary system based on fixed exchange rates—discussed below—led Kaldor to support, and greatly elaborate, an earlier proposal to link international currency to a stock of commodities of importance in world trade, i.e. a commodity-reserve currency.[17]

The international monetary system established at Bretton Woods in 1944 was a gold exchange system, with the US dollar as the key reserve currency convertible into gold, and with other currencies having a fixed exchange rate with the dollar. The viability of the system depended both on the willingness of the United States to continue to supply increasing amounts of dollars as a reserve asset for other countries, and on continued confidence by these other countries in the convertibility of the dollar into gold. However, this system contained two major contradictions which, in time, were bound to undermine it.

One (the 'Triffin dilemma') arose because the US dollar, which was the effective *numéraire* in the system, was inevitably being weakened by continuing US balance of payments deficits. At some stage, other countries would not be willing to go on accumulating dollars, and then the system would break down (which it did in August 1971). The other contradiction was that the fixed exchange rate system made no allowance for secular shifts in rates of productivity growth as between the major trading nations, shifts which, when sufficiently large, were bound to exert irresistible pressure for changes in exchange rates.[18]

By creating a new type of international currency, backed by a commodity stock, Kaldor argued that the defects both of the existing international monetary system based on a single currency as the key reserve asset and of the existing linkage between the commodity markets and the industrial sector of the world economy would be overcome. The essence of the proposal, as set out in a paper[19] submitted to the first UNCTAD Conference in 1964, was that:

(i) The IMF would establish a new currency ('bancor') convertible into both gold and a fixed bundle of 30 or so principal commodities in world trade, which satisfy four criteria, viz. low storage costs, durability, having a well-defined price, and being free from price manipulation.

(ii) Bancor would be fully covered by gold and commodities, except for a fixed fiduciary issue.

(iii) Only the central banks of member countries would be entitled to hold bancor balances with the IMF, and these countries would accept bancor, as well as gold, in settlement of claims.

---

[17] A commodity-backed currency had been proposed independently by B. Graham 1937, 1944 and F.D. Graham 1942, and also, for the UK, by Grondona 1962, 1971.

[18] See the discussion in Griffith-Jones 1989.

[19] Hart, Kaldor, and Tinbergen 1964 and Hart 1966, 1976. According to Thirlwall 1987: 274, the proposal was 'Kaldor's brain-child, which he had been working on since April, 1963'.

It was suggested that the scheme could start with an initial distribution of bancor units, equivalent to a total of $30 billion, of which two-thirds would be for payment for the designated commodity bundles, with the remainder being used for purchases of gold and as the fiduciary issue.

Once a stock of commodities had been purchased under the scheme, the convertibility of bancor into both commodities and gold would ensure that the average price of the designated commodities in the bundle would be stabilized. This would be done by the purchase of units of the composite bundle of commodities when supply tended to outrun demand, and by the sale of these composite units in the reverse situation. Thus irrespective of changes in commodity prices in terms of any one, or more, currency, or currencies, the average price of the commodity bundle would be stabilized in terms of bancor and gold.

The scheme would have a more widely diffused benefit, since it would act, in effect, as a world income-stabilizing mechanism. In a situation of excess commodity supply, the incomes of primary producers would fall (if there is no market regulation), with the consequent stagflationary effects on world economic activity discussed earlier. By stabilizing commodity prices in terms of bancor, primary producers' incomes would be maintained, thus benefiting from an injection of liquidity into the system. Conversely, when there is a relative shortage of commodities, the IMF would sell the requisite amount of commodity units, thus withdrawing liquidity from the system, and thereby avoiding the inflationary effects of higher commodity prices.

Since this income-stabilizing objective was a major part of the scheme, it was necessary to design a mechanism to stabilize commodity prices *in general*, and not the prices of particular commodities. Hence the proposal to create units of designated commodities in fixed proportions. Clearly, the average price of a unit can be stable if changes in the prices of the component commodities are mutually offsetting. Providing the commodity bundle, or unit, comprised *all* the major internationally traded commodities, maintaining the stability of their average prices in terms of bancor would result in relatively little variation in the average bancor price of all traded commodities, even though prices of the minor commodities, not covered by the unit, continued to fluctuate.

Criticisms of the Proposal for a Commodity-Reserve Currency (CRC)

Though the proposal was not seriously considered at the UNCTAD Conference in 1964, it did arouse considerable interest (and a number of critiques) amongst economists concerned with international monetary, and/or international trade and development, issues. An early critique (Grubel 1965) was focused on the excessive cost of holding large stocks of commodities. However, it is not possible to make any reliable estimate of stock-holding costs in the absence of specific details, particularly of which commodities are to be held and at what prices the IMF would buy or sell commodity units, since the larger the difference between buying and selling prices, the smaller would the stock need to be. Moreover, as Bird (1987) argues, the IMF should make a profit on commodity transactions, which would reduce the net cost of the scheme, while the stabilization of prices would encourage private traders to reduce their own stocks, so that the net social cost would be lower than the net private cost. An additional factor is that effective stabilization of the general level of commodity prices can be expected to result in private speculators operating in a price-stabilizing way. Thus it can be argued that the scheme is likely to benefit the world economy in terms of more stable growth, higher levels of employment, and a lower rate of inflation than would otherwise obtain (Griffith-Jones 1989).

A second criticism (Grubel 1965) has been that the cost of stock-holding in the scheme could be avoided by the use of international fiat money (such as the SDR, which is a book-entry made in the IMF's accounts). However, there is an important difference inasmuch as under a CRC, the injections or withdrawals of liquidity are made automatically, while with the SDR, new issues are subject to the approval of the IMF Executive Governors. In the event, the IMF did not agree to any new issues of SDRs after 1981, owing to the opposition of the main Western countries, particularly the United States. Had a viable CRC been adopted during the 1970s, the commodity price recession of the 1980s would not have led to a drastic reduction in export earnings of commodity producers.

A third critique has been that operational difficulties will inevitably arise as a result of using one mechanism to achieve two objectives, viz. commodity price stability and adequate growth of international liquidity (Grubel 1965, Stewart and Sengupta 1982). If, for example, the commodity bundle included oil, and oil prices were raised by OPEC restrictions, there would have to be sales of commodity units from stock to keep the bancor price of a unit stable, thereby reducing international liquidity, even though an increase in liquidity would be warranted to offset the deflationary impact of the low absorption of oil-exporting countries. However, as Spraos (1989) points out, this kind of problem can readily be met simply by increasing the fiduciary issue of bancor, i.e. by using two instruments to achieve two objectives simultaneously. Though this would introduce an element of discretion in what is intended to be an automatic mechanism, there may be some way of devising an acceptable formula for increasing the fiduciary issue at appropriate times.

Other critiques can also be made. One is that stabilizing the general level of commodity prices could destabilize the prices of particular commodities which have contrary movements to the general level (Johnson 1967). This is more likely to arise when individual prices are driven mainly by supply fluctuations, and for such commodities there would be a case for compensatory financing as a supporting mechanism. Another critique would be that even if commodity prices are stabilized in terms of bancor, they may not be stabilized in terms of the prices of manufactured goods (Stewart and Sengupta 1984). This is not, however, a major issue since manufactures prices normally exhibit relatively small short-term fluctuations.

Kaldor himself, some years after the 1964 CRC proposal, had second thoughts on the issue, since the practical difficulties of implementing the scheme as proposed seemed to be insurmountable:

The enormous difficulties involved in operating a *composite* commodity reserve convinced me later that the most that one could hope for would be to stabilize the world prices of the most important basic commodities individually in terms of the international reserve currency unit, by means of open market interventions of international commodity corporations set up for the purpose, whose purchases and sales would thus automatically regulate the outstanding amount of the reserve currency as a counterpart of the net purchases or sales of commodities by the corporations. (Kaldor 1978: p. xviii)

The international reserve currency unit was envisaged as the SDR, so that 'a buffer stock scheme linked to the issue of SDRs would thus provide the world with a basic money unit which can be guaranteed to be stable in terms of basic commodities' (Kaldor 1983). Thus Kaldor came eventually to endorse the essential features of the Keynes plan of 1942.

Alternative Linkage Mechanisms between Commodity Prices and International Currency

Opposition by Western countries to any proposal for a commodity-backed currency has continued to be strong. It would appear, as Griffith-Jones (1989) suggests, that this opposition reflects the ideology of the governments of leading industrial countries towards 'free' markets and towards tight control of government-issued currency. Ideology, in this case, has been strengthened by what these governments perceive as their national interests in keeping commodity prices low as an anti-inflationary device.[20] In view of this opposition, and also of the existence of international fiat currency – the SDR – some alternatives to a CRC have been proposed.

One proposal has been simply that as the SDR already exists, policy should be focused on improving it and, to the extent possible, incorporating in it some of the features of a CRC (Stewart and Sengupta 1984). However, while an improved SDR would help mitigate the liquidity shortage of developing countries, it would not address the problem of commodity market instability – the central issue of the CRC proposal. Moreover, while it may be true, as Stewart and Sengupta argue, that commodity price stabilization has even less support among Western country governments than improving the SDR, it is also the case that their opposition to a new SDR issue remains strong. Hence, on present policies, abandoning the CRC route hardly guarantees success in terms of an improved SDR. Moreover, since the major Western countries remain opposed both to new SDR issues and to a CRC, there is even less likelihood that they would adopt a scheme involving both instruments than that they would accept either.[21]

---

[20] These motivations are discussed further in Ch. 15.

[21] I am indebted to Sidney Dell for this conclusion (private communication). He also pointed out that one of the reasons for the rejection of the SDR by the major Western countries is that it has no value other than the value resulting from the willingness of countries to accept it, whereas a CRC-linked SDR would have the intrinsic value of the commodity backing.

Another variant of the SDR route has been proposed by Bird (1987). The essential idea here is to divorce the liquidity-creation function from commodity stabilization. The former would be dealt with by the use of the SDR, as was the original intention, while the latter would be the concern of a Commodity Stabilization Agency (CSA), which could be the IMF. The CSA would, in effect, act as a multi-commodity buffer stock, financing purchases with SDRs or convertible currency, and receiving SDRs or convertible currency for commodity sales, so as to stabilize particular commodity prices (or export earnings). However, this proposal raises new problems, particularly its overlap with existing or future international commodity agreements, the functions of which may include short-term price stabilization. Moreover, stabilizing the prices of a number of individual commodities will not necessarily stabilize the general level of commodity prices, which was the centrepiece of the CRC scheme. In any event, the opposition of the main Western countries to the proposal seems likely to be as great, on their present policies, as it is towards the CRC.

Kaldor's theoretical analysis of the adverse effects of commodity price instability on the rate of growth, employment, and inflation in the world economy captures an essential defect in the working of unregulated markets, one which has detrimental effects not only for the economies of developing countries, but for the developed countries also. It would seem high time that the various proposals for bringing greater stability to commodity markets by means of a link to the international monetary system were given serious consideration by the world community.

II
INTERNATIONAL COMMODITY POLICY

6
The Post-war Background

1. EARLY POST-WAR DEVELOPMENTS AND THE HAVANA CHARTER

The wartime discussions and negotiations between the United States and Britain on post-war international economic institutions covered the whole range of commercial and financial policy, of which commodity policy was only a relatively small part. None the less, it is important to follow the post-war evolution of commercial policy in the broad sense, since this had significant implications for international commodity policy. In view of the great technological lead held by the United States, and its large expansion in productive capacity during the war, a free trade system was clearly the regime which would most benefit the American economy in the post-war world. In Britain, too, much thought was being given to the desirable character of the post-war international trading system. Both countries felt the need for international co-operation in the post-war world within an agreed framework of principles and rules to avoid the competitive currency devaluations and general raising of trade barriers which had greatly contributed to the world economic recession of the 1930s.[1]

The United States administration was strongly of the view that an expanding post-war world economy should be based on the principles of non-discrimination in trade and of multilateralism. These principles were expressed in general terms in the Atlantic Charter of 1941, and more specifically in the Mutual Aid Agreement of 1942 between the United States and the United Kingdom. Though the primary purpose of this agreement was to set out the principles governing the supply of Lend-Lease goods to Britain, it contained, in Article VII, provision for agreed action by the two countries 'open to participation by all other countries of like mind, directed to the expansion by appropriate international and domestic measures, of production, employment, and the exchange and consumption of goods, which are the material foundations of the liberty and welfare of all peoples; to the elimination of all forms of discriminatory treatment in international commerce, and to the reduction of tariffs and other trade barriers . . .' Though this provision was a declaration of principle and not a commitment for the adoption of specific policies, it did influence the ideas of policy-makers, and of economists, at least in North America, in the direction of a freer trading system.

The British agreement to the principles of free trade and non-discrimination

---

[1] A detailed review of the issues involved in the US–UK negotiations on the character of the post-war international economic system is given in Gardner 1980.

was, however, subject to some major reservations. First, the elimination of discrimination would mean the abolition of the system of Imperial Preference which fostered trade ties between Britain and the Commonwealth.[2] Second, the British government felt that some form of tariff protection for domestic industry would be needed in the post-war world to protect the economy from adverse effects of fluctuations in economic activity and prices in other countries. A third reservation was that some form of trade restriction might well be necessary in the post-war period to safeguard Britain's balance of payments.

Though the British interpretation of the principles in Article VII of the Mutual Aid Agreement thus differed from the American in some important respects, both were agreed on the need for a new international regime to govern international trade in the post-war world. Shortly after the end of the war, in November 1945, the two governments published 'Proposals for Consideration by an International Conference on Trade and Employment', which included proposals for the regulation of quantitative restrictions on trade, the reduction of tariff barriers, and the elimination of trade preferences. Further impetus to the preparation of a conference on the post-war trading regime was given by the first session of the UN Economic and Social Council (ECOSOC), which unanimously accepted a US proposal for a World Conference on Trade and Employment. The United States also published a *Suggested Charter for an International Trade Organization of the United Nations* in 1946 as a basis for discussion at the Conference.

The Conference, including its preparatory stage, lasted until 1948, with sessions in Geneva, London, and finally in Havana. Of the 56 participating countries, 20 were industrial (some of which were also metropolitan countries of many overseas colonies), while 32 participating countries would now be classified as 'developing'. The Havana Charter, which was annexed to the *Final Act* of the Conference, was wide-ranging in scope, covering not only the principles of trade policy and provisions for the negotiation of the reduction of trade barriers, but also measures relating to economic development, restrictive business practices, and private foreign investment, and an obligation for member States to maintain or expand domestic employment. The Charter was to be implemented under the aegis of a new United Nations body – the International Trade Organization (ITO).[3]

In its treatment of trade policy, the Charter was based essentially on the free market principles strongly espoused by the United States. This can be seen, in particular, in its treatment of intergovernmental commodity agreements. While recognizing that international trade in some commodities 'may be affected by special difficulties', the Charter approved the use of ICAs to prevent or

---

[2] The insertion of the phrase 'with respect for ... existing obligations' in the relevant paragraph of the Atlantic Charter in effect safeguarded the system of Commonwealth Preferences (see Kock 1969 for a review of the policy discussions involved).

[3] Havana Charter 1948 in UN 1948. See Wilcox 1949 and Rossen 1981 for succinct summaries and critical appraisals of each of the main elements of the Havana Charter.

alleviate such difficulties only if 'adjustments between production and consumption cannot be effected by normal market forces alone as rapidly as the circumstances require'.[4] Thus the use of market regulatory mechanisms was regarded as being appropriate only in exceptional circumstances, defined as the development of a 'burdensome surplus' of a commodity, or 'widespread unemployment or under-employment', which could not be corrected in good time by normal market forces.[5]

The Charter also specified the principles for operating ICAs in such exceptional circumstances. These agreements should, *inter alia*, assure adequate supplies at prices 'fair to consumers and providing a reasonable return to producers, having regard to the desirability of securing long-term equilibrium between the forces of supply and demand';[6] importing countries should have equal voting rights with exporting countries;[7] and such agreements should not last more than five years, with provision for renewal for a further period (or periods) of five years.[8] The limitation on the duration of an agreement focused its operation on short-term problems, such as those arising from temporary surpluses, while the reference to long-term market equilibrium implicitly ruled out any attempt by an ICA to raise prices above the market trend.

However, while the commodity policy chapter of the Havana Charter was essentially an expression of free market principles, in a number of other important policy areas compromises had to be made with those countries which supported the need for government planning. As a result, many exceptions to the principles of free trade and non-discrimination were allowed. The underdeveloped participating countries, for example, succeeded in inserting a special section in the Charter proclaiming that economic development was a primary objective of the proposed international trade regime, while underdeveloped countries were allowed to impose quantitative restrictions on imports to protect their domestic industries. Moreover, while the United States had envisaged clauses designed to protect private investment in underdeveloped countries, the latter succeeded in including in the Charter the right of host countries to regulate such investment. The Charter also provided for measures to eliminate restrictive business practices, though such measures were generally opposed by the advocates of free market principles.[9]

Because of these various compromises with the principles of free trade and non-discrimination, and the inclusion of important elements of planning, the Havana Charter was strongly opposed by the United States business community and, mainly for this reason, the Charter was not submitted to the US Congress for ratification. The other signatory countries, which were waiting for US ratification, also decided not to ratify.

[4] Havana Charter 1948, Article 57(*a*).
[5] Ibid. Article 62.
[6] Ibid. Articles 63(*a*) and 57(*c*).
[7] Ibid. Article 63(*b*).
[8] Ibid. Article 65.1.
[9] See Gardner 1980 for a detailed discussion of these issues.

Though the Havana Charter did not come into operation, one of its sections did become operational in the form of the General Agreement on Tariffs and Trade (GATT), negotiated in 1947 among the members of the Preparatory Committee on the Havana Charter. It was signed in 1947 and ratified in early 1948. The aims of GATT were, however, much more limited than those of the Havana Charter, since the General Agreement was confined to a fairly restricted field, aimed at liberalizing trade through the exchange of tariff concessions on the basis of the principle of non-discrimination. The failure to ratify the Havana Charter together with the establishment of GATT had two important consequences for the management of the world economy. In the first place, the absence of the International Trade Organization envisaged in the Havana Charter meant that a range of important issues, many relevant to the trade of developing countries and of state-trading countries, including those relating to 'burdensome surpluses' on the commodity markets, were not subject to regular international discussion and surveillance. Second, the creation of GATT as a separate organization to deal with tariff negotiations and commercial policy meant that no provision was made in the post-war structure of international economic institutions for any comprehensive or integrated consideration of the increasingly interdependent spheres of trade, money, and finance.[10]

The Havana Charter, however, remained an important influence on the general trend of international commodity policy. In 1947, ECOSOC had accepted the principles of the Charter for regulating international commodity markets, and had set up an Interim Co-ordinating Committee for International Commodity Arrangements (ICCICA) to be responsible for convening commodity study groups, for making recommendations regarding calling conferences to negotiate commodity agreements, and for co-ordinating the activities of study groups and councils administering commodity agreements. The central principles on which such commodity agreements were to be based were: that such schemes would be adopted only to deal with severe market disruption; that they were to aim at price stabilization, and not price increases; and that importing and exporting countries would share equally in the control of the schemes.[11] A number of commodity stabilization agreements, for coffee, sugar, tin, and wheat, were concluded under the aegis of ICCICA.[12]

The general approach to international commodity problems embodied in the Havana Charter and in the operations of ICCICA implicitly assumed that the

---

[10] As Rossen 1981 put it, 'The main implication of the failure [to ratify the Havana Charter] is the continued absence of a comprehensive international trade organization based on an operational Charter. In contrast to the practices prevailing in national administrations and also within the OEEC (later OECD) and the CMEA, the General Agreement treats commercial policies as an area separate from other fields of economic policy' (p. 11).

[11] ECOSOC resolution 30(IV). A useful survey of the issues involved is given in Finlayson and Zacher 1981.

[12] For a detailed review of these early post-war agreements, see 'The Stabilization of International Commodity Markets', prepared by the UN secretariat for UNCTAD, in UNCTAD 1964: iii. 81–93; also Law 1975, Rangarajan 1978 and Gordon-Ashworth 1984.

free working of commodity markets would normally provide an optimum allocation of the world's resources, and that the upward trend in demand in the developed countries for primary commodity exports from the developing countries would provide the required motive force for the economic growth of the latter group of countries. However, neither of these assumptions was soundly based. In fact, over the period between the Havana Conference and the early 1960s, there was a substantial downward trend in the terms of trade of commodity-exporting countries, superimposed on increased short-term instability in commodity prices and revenues, particularly during the sharp price cycle associated with the war in Korea. As a result, a large number of developing countries failed to fulfil their development plans.[13]

2. THE EMERGENCE OF UNCTAD

The 1950s and 1960s were notable also for the emergence of a large number of former colonies to independent statehood, many of which began to witness their efforts at development planning being undermined by adverse changes in world commodity markets. Moreover, there was a growing belief in many of the newly independent countries that much of the external constraints on the development process arose from the nature of the international trade regime itself—i.e. the rules governing trade and financial flows—overseen by GATT and the Bretton Woods institutions. The free trade philosophy on which these institutions were essentially based appeared to be geared to the development of the industrialized countries rather than to effective support for the development process. This perception on the part of a growing number of politically independent developing countries, together with adverse trends in their foreign trade during the 1950s and early 1960s, were the main factors behind the pressure by these countries for the convening of the first UNCTAD Conference in 1964, though the socialist countries had also been pressing since 1956 for an international trade organization.[14]

The debates at that conference were heavily influenced by the arguments put forward by Dr Prebisch, its Secretary-General. In his report to the Conference,[15] he identified the principal cause of the external payments constraint on the development process as arising from a secular tendency of the terms of trade of primary commodity-exporting countries to deteriorate, a tendency which was accentuated by the protectionist policies of developed countries in the area of

---

[13] As a result of the terms of trade deterioration and the sluggish growth in world demand for primary commodities exported by developing countries, there was 'a serious deterioration in export earnings' of these countries, from a growth rate of 4.2% p.a. in the period 1950–5 to 2.9% p.a. in 1955–60, while the growth rate of per capita income fell off from 2.5 to 1.8% p.a. (Frank 1968: 45–6).

[14] For a detailed and authoritative review of events leading to the establishment of UNCTAD, see Cordovez 1967.

[15] Prebisch 1964: 5–64.

agricultural trade.[16] Prebisch had argued for many years that the deteriorating trends in developing countries' external trade were 'not casual or accidental, but were deeply ingrained in the world trading system itself' (Dell 1985a).

Dr Prebisch's report to UNCTAD I was an important milestone in the evolution of international commodity policy, not only for its analysis of the commodity problems of developing countries but also because it placed these problems firmly in the context of those countries' development needs. Moreover, instead of reliance on the free play of market forces to stimulate development, the logic of Prebisch's argument pointed to the need for positive action by governments, on a common basis, designed deliberately to improve the long-term rate of growth of commodity export earnings and to reduce short-term fluctuations in those earnings, while taking into account the interests of consumers in importing countries. It is this link between commodity policy and development, established by Prebisch, which has profoundly influenced all subsequent commodity analysis and related policy proposals debated in UNCTAD, as well as in other international forums.

The opposition of the Western industrial countries to this new approach to trade policy, including international commodity policy, linking it directly to the development needs of Third World countries, was strongly expressed at UNCTAD I. This opposition was generally based on the fear by the larger developed countries that the UNCTAD approach might undermine the *laissez-faire* principles of the trade policy provisions of the Havana Charter, and of the GATT, principles which had served the developed countries well throughout the post-war period. Thus while the Final Act of UNCTAD I set out the principles of a new global strategy for development, major reservations were entered by the Western industrial countries on critical issues. On commodity policy, for example, 12 of these countries opposed the recommendation on the stabilization of primary commodity prices (Special Principle 7), while most of the remainder abstained. The majority of these countries abstained on the recommendation on modification in domestic support policies for primary production by developed countries (Special Principle 5), while the United States opposed the recommendation on the regulation of surplus disposal for primary commodities produced by developed countries (Special Principle 8).[17]

A comparison of the UNCTAD I principles with the provisions of the trade policy sections of the Havana Charter reveals an underlying conflict of approach. While the UNCTAD resolution explicitly linked international action to ensure

---

[16] Prebisch's original thesis (1950) of the tendency of the terms of trade of developing countries to deteriorate was published at approximately the same time as a similar thesis by Singer (1950). A recent analysis by Spraos, including an extension of the Prebisch–Singer thesis to the double factorial terms of trade, has demonstrated that the latter terms of trade—more fundamental than the usual definition of the ratio of export to import prices—will deteriorate for developing countries if the demand for their commodity exports is inelastic with respect to both income and price (which is generally the case in practice), and if they export a high proportion of their commodity production (which is applicable to many such commodities). (See Spraos 1983, especially ch. 5.)

[17] UNCTAD 1964: i. 23.

the stabilization and growth of the commodity export earnings of developing countries to their need for accelerated economic and social development, the Havana Charter—as already mentioned—viewed interventions in international commodity markets as exceptions to the 'rules of the game', and thus as necessary evils to be adopted only in carefully prescribed circumstances and on a temporary basis. The adoption of many of the new UNCTAD principles was thus viewed by the Western industrial countries as unwarranted interference with the free play of market forces, which would inevitably lead to a misallocation of resources and a decline in global economic welfare. Even measures designed to reduce excessive fluctuations in commodity prices—which later came to be accepted as desirable by most developed-country governments—were opposed as a matter of principle.

There was also a conflict between developed and developing countries at the 1964 UNCTAD meeting as to whether a permanent body should be established to carry forward the work of the Conference and to oversee the implementation of its recommendations. The Western countries argued strongly that a permanent body was unnecessary since the existing international institutions could deal adequately with trade, finance, and development issues. However, the developing countries succeeded in having the Conference recommend the establishment of UNCTAD as a permanent body, a recommendation accepted by the General Assembly at the end of 1964.

In its resolution establishing UNCTAD, the General Assembly *inter alia* transferred to UNCTAD the functions performed by ICCICA, so that UNCTAD became the sole agency responsible for negotiating international commodity agreements, as well as for formulating international commodity policy in relation to development and for co-ordinating the activities of intergovernmental commodity groups and of councils administering commodity agreements.[18]

An interesting statistical analysis by Ansari (1978) of the voting record at UNCTAD I of each of the 'Group B' countries[19] reveals that indicators of 'economic power' were highly correlated with the degree of opposition to UNCTAD principles. His results showed that the higher the GNP of any Group B country, the greater its voting power in the IMF and IBRD, the greater the aid it gave as a percentage of GNP, and the greater its direct private investment in developing countries, the greater the probability that it would oppose the new UNCTAD principles. It is reasonable to deduce from this analysis that the Group B countries were well satisfied with the existing international economic system and with the Bretton Woods institutions and the GATT, all effectively

---

[18] GA resolution 1995(XIX), para. 23(*a*). The co-ordination function was interpreted in practice as reporting on their activities by the various commodity bodies, including the FAO intergovernmental groups, to the regular sessions of the UNCTAD Committee on Commodities and to the relevant committee of the conference sessions.

[19] i.e., the developed market-economy countries, so called because of their inclusion in a 'List B' for the purpose of election to membership of UNCTAD bodies.

under their control, and that they were strongly opposed to any substantive changes in them.

This conclusion is supported by a recent review by Edmund Dell, the former British Secretary of State for Trade, 1976–8, of the issues involved in the UNCTAD proposal for a Common Fund (which is considered in more detail in Chapter 7). In this review, Dell comments that UNCTAD was 'a forum created to enable developing countries to state their grievances and command an audience among developed countries. It was not generally regarded by the developed countries as a reliable repository of executive power. In so far as there was any executive power over international economic relations, the developed countries wished to keep it in their own hands.'[20]

It is necessary at this stage to consider more deeply the principal considerations behind the strong opposition by the Western industrial countries to the UNCTAD approach to trade and development issues, since without an understanding of the underlying reasons for this opposition, it would not be possible fully to comprehend the later evolution of the North–South dialogue, both in UNCTAD and in other international forums, and more specifically the vicissitudes of negotiations on international commodity issues.

The particular reason for the opposition to the UNCTAD approach to international commodity policy has already been mentioned, i.e., it was regarded as a threat to the *laissez-faire* principles embodied in GATT, by opening the way for a possibly widespread use of regulatory mechanisms in international commodity markets. Regulation of these markets, if linked to the development needs of Third World countries, could, it was feared, lead to higher prices for developed commodity-importing countries, and even to restricted scope for the large transnational commodity trading and financing enterprises of developed countries. Moreover, the UNCTAD recommendation calling for a modification in domestic support policies for primary production was seen as unjustified interference in well-established internal farm-support policies of the developed countries.

It could be argued, with Sidney Dell, that while the opposition of these countries at UNCTAD I to intervention in international commodity markets 'could be understood in terms of their short-term interests, it was less clear that it was rational in a longer run perspective, since rising real income in the developing countries was clearly in harmony with the interests of the developed countries from many points of view, including the larger markets for their exports that a prosperous Third World would imply'.[21] The opposition to modifying domestic agricultural support policies of developed market-economy countries was also understandable in view of the political pressures exerted by farming interests in these countries, but here too, it could be argued that such support policies, by reducing the export opportunities and the level of prices in world commodity

[20] E. Dell 1987.
[21] S. Dell 1985*a*: 17.

markets, also restricted the ability of developing countries to purchase additional goods from the developed countries. Moreover, the subsidization of high-cost agricultural production in developed countries was resulting in a major misallocation of resources on a global scale.[22]

The opposition by the Western countries to the UNCTAD approach to international commodity policy was complemented, and strengthened, by two further factors of a more general nature. The first was that in spite of strenuous efforts by these countries to obtain a veto, or at least a blocking vote, in UNCTAD decisions, and place the new organization under the authority of ECOSOC,[23] the final decision provided for one State – one vote, thus giving a voting majority to the developing countries, though with allowance for a conciliation procedure to evolve compromise solutions where necessary.[24] Though the conciliation procedure has, in fact, been dormant, there has been a tacit, informal, understanding that UNCTAD decisions should, so far as possible, be based on compromise solutions agreed among the different groups of member countries. None the less, it was evident that, for the first time, a major organization concerned with international economic policy had emerged which was not fully under the control of the larger Western industrial countries.

A second, and related, aspect of the emergence of UNCTAD was the wide scope of its mandate, covering virtually all aspects of international economic relations – trade, monetary issues, financial flows as well as certain other 'invisibles' such as shipping and insurance. Though the convergence of these major, and closely interdependent, policy issues within a single forum provided the potential for the discussion, and eventual evolution, of a coherent international development strategy, this potential has been largely frustrated by the fear on the part of the Western industrial countries that an organization not under their control could establish policies directly impinging upon the activities of GATT and of the Bretton Woods institutions.

For these general reasons, the strategy of the Western industrial countries, and particularly of the larger ones, has been to confine UNCTAD activities so far as possible to deliberative functions, thus ensuring that practical operations are allowed only in exceptional cases and where they appear to be unavoidable. In the fields of international monetary and financial policy, for example, UNCTAD as an organization makes 'recommendations' on desirable policy changes to the Bretton Woods institutions, which alone are allowed to take firm or definite decisions on the issues involved. A partial exception, in this policy area, was the decision at the 1978 Ministerial session of the UNCTAD Trade and Development Board under which creditor countries agreed to grant relief to

---

[22] See Ch. 12 for a more detailed discussion. In 1987, budgetary subsidies to agriculture in developed market-economy countries exceeded the total value of all agricultural exports from developing countries.
[23] For a detailed discussion of the negotiations on this issue, see Cordovez 1967.
[24] UNCTAD 1964: i, Annex A.v.1.

low-income developing countries on their bilateral official debt,[25] though the United States – the largest creditor nation – declined to provide debt relief under the UNCTAD resolution.[26]

Again, in the field of trade policy, the general strategy of the industrial countries is to assert the primacy of GATT, which is responsible for organizing periodic 'Rounds' of trade negotiations, for enforcing existing GATT principles and rules governing the conduct of international trade by its member countries, and for evolving new principles and rules to meet the needs of a changing world trading environment. Though the need for improved access to the markets of developed countries for developing country exports has been discussed at length in UNCTAD bodies, both during UNCTAD I in 1966 and since, serious negotiations within UNCTAD on market access have been avoided by the developed countries, which have 'remained unwilling to see any of GATT's authority devolve upon UNCTAD, where their influence is much weaker'.[27]

The negotiation of the Generalized System of Preferences (GSP) in UNCTAD was another specific departure from the Western conception of this organization as merely a debating forum.[28] The acceptance and implementation of the GSP was secured in the face of strong initial opposition by Western countries, especially the United States, to its departure from the GATT principle of non-discrimination, and its reliance on positive discrimination in favour of developing countries (in the form of tariff preferences). However, the Western countries, in eventually accepting the GSP concept, insisted that it could not be regarded as creating a new permanent legal system; rather, it was accepted only through the granting of a waiver from GATT obligations.[29]

In the commodities field, it is UNCTAD – as mentioned earlier – and not GATT that has responsibility for organizing negotiations for new, or renewed, international commodity agreements. An early attempt, however, was made to bypass UNCTAD when negotiations were organized in 1967 in the framework of the GATT Kennedy Round to create freer access to world markets for cereals, meat, and butter – together accounting for a substantial part of world trade in agricultural products. Though an agreement was reached in GATT in relation to cereals for human consumption, it was eventually agreed to submit the results to a full international conference for the renegotiation of the International Wheat Agreement, the conference to be convened jointly by the International Wheat

---

[25] UNCTAD Board resolution 165(S-IX). Under this resolution, 33 low-income countries had by mid-1987 benefited from debt relief measures provided by 15 developed countries, the nominal value of these measures being estimated at about $4 billion (see UNCTAD 1987a: 193).

[26] See the discussion in Haji 1985, and references there cited.

[27] Finlayson and Zacher 1988: 46.

[28] Other legal instruments negotiated in UNCTAD, and embodying the principle of preferences for developing countries, include the Convention on a Code of Conduct for Liner Conferences, 1974, and the Set of Multilaterally Agreed Equitable Principles and Rules for the Control of Restrictive Business Practices, 1980, though the latter has no binding force.

[29] For a detailed discussion of the legal status of the GSP, see Berthoud 1985 and Krishnamurti 1985.

Council and UNCTAD.[30] A more recent example of the preference of the Western industrial countries for commodity negotiations within the framework of GATT is the International Dairy Arrangement, to which reference was made in Chapter 3.

This general strategy of the Western industrial countries has the incidental unfortunate effect that new policy proposals for pressing international economic problems which are first put forward in UNCTAD often do not receive serious consideration by these countries, even though such proposals may be economically advantageous and technically viable. As the late Professor Kaldor commented, in relation to the UNCTAD proposal for a Common Fund for commodities:

since [this] scheme originated with the 'developing' countries (members of UNCTAD), it had the same cool reception which Keynes's ideas received from the British establishment during the War. Nobody seems to have understood that, while the proposal was promoted by the developing countries, its adoption was in the vital interest of the 'developed' or industrialized countries, since it is a pre-condition for securing adequate long-term investment necessary for sustained industrial growth. (Kaldor 1983)

As will be seen in the following chapters, it is this general strategy of the West (in a sense, the 'hidden agenda' of UNCTAD meetings) which sets the context within which the international community has attempted, with limited success, to evolve a viable international commodity policy. Over the past decade, the negotiations to this end have focused on UNCTAD's Integrated Programme for Commodities, including its central feature, the Common Fund.

---

[30] The association of UNCTAD with this conference was achieved only after a formal protest from Dr Prebisch about the GATT procedure in this matter (see Krishnamurti 1985: 68).

7
The Integrated Programme for Commodities and the Common Fund

1. THE COMMODITY-BY-COMMODITY APPROACH

The decade following the establishment of UNCTAD in 1964 was one of frustration and stalemate in efforts to evolve an international policy to deal with the commodity problems of developing countries. Throughout the period from the mid-1950s to the early 1970s commodity prices in real terms had been on a downward trend, and price fluctuations for many commodities were still regarded by the developing countries as excessive and injurious to their interests. In addition, a range of commodities – particularly those competing with temperate-zone foods – faced substantial barriers in exports to developed-country markets, the markets for natural raw materials were being eroded by competition from synthetics and other substitutes, while for commodities in persistent oversupply there seemed to be an urgent need for international support for diversification programmes in developing countries.

The difficulties faced by the commodity-exporting developing countries prompted the UNCTAD secretariat to propose, at UNCTAD II in 1968, that a comprehensive programme of measures should be considered to deal with the various interrelated aspects of the commodity problem.[1] Though the particular characteristics of individual commodity markets may require the use of different combinations of policies in each, there was, it was argued, a need for an overall review of progress in the commodity trade of developing countries. Moreover, the effectiveness of a comprehensive set of policies to deal with the commodity problem would be enhanced if they were consciously related to the economic development needs of the developing countries. A further argument advanced in favour of a comprehensive approach was that rational action in any one commodity market could be taken only when the probable effects on other commodity markets were fully taken into account.[2]

More specific elements of the secretariat's proposal included policy options for reducing excessive short-term fluctuations in commodity prices and in the commodity export earnings of developing countries, including a proposal to create a central fund to assist the financing of international buffer stocks;[3] for promoting the consumption of primary commodities in developed countries; for

---
[1] See 'The Development of an International Commodity Policy' (TD/8/Supp. 1) in UNCTAD 1968, iii.
[2] Ibid. para. 28.
[3] Ibid. para. 218.

improving the competitive position of natural products exported by developing countries *vis-à-vis* their synthetic substitutes; for expanding commodity exports to socialist countries and to other developing countries; and for encouraging appropriate diversification away from the production of commodities in persistent oversupply.

However, at UNCTAD II the Western industrial countries avoided any serious discussion of the proposal for a comprehensive commodity policy or of its analytical basis. It was evident that such a policy, if made operational, would greatly enhance UNCTAD's role in the management of the world economy while, at the same time, reducing the influence of market forces as determinants of commodity price movements. There was also the danger, in the Western view, that intervention in the 'free play of market forces' – which was inherent in the UNCTAD secretariat's approach – would result in higher prices for their essential imports of raw materials. For these reasons, the major Western countries were strongly opposed to the UNCTAD secretariat proposal.

The strategy adopted by the Western countries was simple and – from their viewpoint – effective. First, they insisted that progress could be made, not by discussing general principles or the need for a comprehensive approach, but only by considering the problems of each commodity separately. By rejecting the need for an overall framework, the Western countries were, in effect, also denying the need for linking international commodity policy to the development of Third World countries. Second, the Western countries also insisted that the problems of individual commodities should be considered in the various specialized international commodity Study Groups – which functioned either in FAO or autonomously – and not in the UNCTAD framework.

This strategy was successful, since the developing countries agreed to proceed on this basis, and UNCTAD II identified a range of 'problem' commodities, 19 in all, for consideration by the specialized commodity Study Groups.[4] No results of any significance, however, emerged from this procedure. New international agreements on sugar and cocoa were concluded in 1968 and 1972, respectively, but both were the result of long periods of negotiation, rather than of the Conference resolution. For some commodities, the Study Groups gave little or no priority to the UNCTAD II resolution; there was generally inadequate technical preparation; in several Study Groups progress was limited mainly by conflicts of interest among developing countries regarding market shares, while conflicts of view concerning the nature of the problems confronting particular commodities often resulted in abortive meetings.[5] By shifting the discussion of the problems of individual commodities outside the UNCTAD framework the Western countries had ensured that the programme lacked an overall focus, and that the problems considered were viewed entirely in terms of the commercial interests of the countries trading in particular commodities,

---

[4] UNCTAD resolution 16(II) in UNCTAD 1968, i.
[5] For a detailed review of the fate of the UNCTAD II programme, see UNCTAD 1973: ii. 61–6.

rather than as part of a common endeavour to evolve an effective commodity policy to assist Third World development.

A similar strategy was adopted at the next major review of commodity policy, at UNCTAD III in 1972. At that meeting, the developing countries expressed their concern at the lack of progress in the consultations on individual commodities, and stressed the need for action on a wide front, including measures to reduce excessive commodity price fluctuations, to provide financial assistance for diversification, to improve the market position of raw materials facing competition from synthetics and substitutes, and to increase access to the markets of developed countries. However, the Conference was able to reach agreement only on a further series of commodity-by-commodity consultations.[6] Though such consultations were held in the following two years in respect of 15 commodities, once again little of significance emerged in the form of agreed measures to be taken, for much the same reasons that explained the fate of the earlier UNCTAD II effort.

2. THE INTEGRATED PROGRAMME FOR COMMODITIES (IPC)

The success of the strategy of the Western industrial countries up to the mid-1970s was heavily dependent on the acquiescence of the developing countries in the commodity-by-commodity approach, with consultations being conducted in separate, and essentially independent, bodies with no time limits or common objectives. This strategy, however, faced a sudden major challenge as a result of the OPEC success in raising oil prices sharply in 1973 and 1974.

The OPEC action inevitably involved a dramatic change in North–South economic relations. It also had major repercussions on the negotiating situation for other primary commodities. For one thing, it greatly encouraged developing countries to pursue the possibilities of organizing producer associations with the aim, *inter alia*, of improving their market power and thereby attaining higher prices or, at least, defending agreed minimum prices. From 1973 to 1975 a number of associations of commodity-exporting countries were established, and existing ones strengthened, covering, *inter alia*, bananas, bauxite, coffee, and iron ore. At the same time, sudden shortages of many minerals and metals, and of certain agricultural products—cereals, vegetable oils, and some tropical products—led to an intense debate in the developed countries on whether, and to what extent, their essential raw material imports from developing countries were becoming dominated by producer cartels. An early, and influential, analysis of the new situation (Bergsten 1973) concluded that there was a real possibility that the developing countries could back their policies by their economic leverage in key commodity markets, and that the United States, which had so far ignored Third World demands, would now need to change its policy so as to promote co-operation with developing countries.

---

[6] UNCTAD resolution 83(III) in UNCTAD 1973, i.

It was against this background that the United Nations General Assembly held a special session on 'Problems of Raw Materials and Development' in May 1974, which resolved on a 'Programme of Action on the Establishment of a New International Economic Order'. This resolution called, *inter alia*, for the 'preparation of an overall integrated programme for a comprehensive range of commodities of export interest to developing countries'.[7] In response to this resolution, the UNCTAD secretariat put forward an outline of an overall integrated programme in August 1974, and the issue came under intensive debate in UNCTAD bodies throughout 1975 and the early months of 1976.

As Gamani Corea, the then UNCTAD Secretary-General, explained in his report[8] to the UNCTAD IV meeting in 1976, the proposed integrated programme would differ in several ways from earlier efforts which had been such conspicuous failures:

it would cover a wide range of commodities on which negotiations would proceed simultaneously, so that individual countries could secure an overall balance of advantage from several different commodity agreements;

it would use a variety of measures, including some which had not previously been employed to a significant extent;

the individual commodity negotiations would take place on the basis of common general objectives and within a common time frame;

the negotiation of individual commodity agreements would be substantially assisted by the creation of a new international financial institution, the Common Fund.[9]

The proposal envisaged negotiations on 17 commodities of particular interest to developing countries, of which 10 commodities, accounting for some three-quarters of the value of exports of all 17, appeared suitable for market regulation by means of buffer stocks. The total financing requirement for these 10 commodities was estimated at $6 billion, of which $3 billion would be needed initially, with the rest available on call. Since the buffer stock operations were regarded as essentially a self-financing process, it was proposed to obtain only one-third of the total finance as capital from governments, the remainder being borrowed from commercial sources.[10]

As a result of the intensive prior debates on these proposals, the negotiations at UNCTAD IV itself were essentially political, strong pressure being exerted by the Group of 77 – the negotiating arm of the developing countries in UNCTAD – which saw the Integrated Programme as a key element of a New International Economic Order and as an important test case of the willingness of the developed market-economy countries to co-operate with them in practical measures towards that objective.

---

[7] General Assembly resolution 3202(S-VI).
[8] Corea 1976: para. 54.
[9] Ibid. paras. 65–6.
[10] Ibid. para. 64.

The resolution, which was adopted without dissent at UNCTAD IV, was very wide-ranging in character, envisaging the negotiation of agreements or arrangements for 18 specified commodities,[11] with the aim of avoiding excessive price fluctuations and achieving price levels 'remunerative' to producers and 'equitable' to consumers, as well as pursuing longer-term objectives such as increased export earnings for developing countries, improvement in market access and reliability of supply, diversification of production, improved competitiveness of natural products competing with synthetics, and improvement in market structures and in the marketing, distribution, and transport system for commodity exports of developing countries. The resolution also called for the negotiation of a Common Fund as a central financing facility for the Programme as a whole.[12]

Since this financing proposal was central to the concept of an 'integrated' programme and, moreover, since it gave rise to a serious clash of perceived interests in the later negotiations, it is necessary to consider in some depth the views and concerns of the principal protagonists on this issue.

3. THE STRUGGLE FOR A COMMON FUND[13]

Dr Corea had stressed in his report that the essential purpose of the proposed Fund would be the provision of the finance needed for the creation and operation of buffer stocks that might be established under commodity agreements to be negotiated under the Programme. Thus, it was not the intention that the Fund would itself buy and sell commodities; that function would be left to the specialized bodies to be set up under the commodity agreements. A further function envisaged was that where no such agreements yet existed, the Fund would be empowered to intervene under agreed conditions in particular commodity markets in exceptional emergency situations.[14]

The establishment of a Common Fund was seen by Dr Corea as having a number of advantages compared with the previous commodity-by-commodity approach. First, it would achieve financial economies as compared with the establishment of separate funds for each commodity. Second, the availability of a ready source of finance could provide an impetus to the successful negotiation of agreements for individual commodities. The developed commodity-importing

---

[11] Provision was made, however, for additional commodities to be subsequently included in the Programme.

[12] Conference resolution 93(IV), in UNCTAD 1977.

[13] For a detailed and authoritative review and appraisal of the complex negotiations involved, see Dr Corea's own account (Corea, forthcoming: chs. 6 and 7).

[14] Corea 1976, para. 65. It is of some interest to note that the concept of a Common Fund had considerable affinity not only to the earlier idea of a central fund advanced at UNCTAD II, but also to the financing functions envisaged by J.M. Keynes for his proposed International Clearing Union, and to the supervisory functions he envisaged for a central organization to take a broad view of the changing situation in all the international commodity markets (see Keynes, 1942, 1943). The Keynes proposals are discussed in more detail in O'Neill 1977: 14–16.

countries had traditionally taken the view that the finance of buffer stocks in the context of a commodity agreement should be borne by the developing producing countries alone, and this must have deterred the latter from pressing for the establishment of such stocks. Third, it would be the sole operational body that could take an overall view of global commodity problems, and could thus inject a new dynamism into the approach to these problems. Finally, he argued, the Common Fund would provide a suitable investment outlet for the financial surpluses of the OPEC countries; such investments would enjoy reasonable rates of return, their security would be backed by collateral in the form of commodity stocks, and the OPEC countries would thereby be supporting a programme of benefit to other developing countries.[15]

The proposal to establish a Common Fund as a new international financial institution with its own substantial capital structure was strongly opposed by the majority of the Western industrial countries, and particularly by the larger ones, the United States, the Federal Republic of Germany, and the United Kingdom. These countries advanced several objections to the Common Fund proposal, the main ones being the following:[16]

(i) *It would involve an advance financial commitment which might encourage the establishment of unnecessary buffer stocks.*[17]

This argument was not very convincing, since it was well known that negotiations for establishing international buffer stocks had always been difficult and time-consuming. Since developed importing countries would be participating fully in negotiations to establish appropriate market regulatory mechanisms for individual commodities – which might include buffer stocks along with other possible mechanisms – it appeared highly unlikely that these countries would agree to establish buffer stocks that were unnecessary.

(ii) *A Common Fund is unnecessary since an international commodity agreement would always provide the finance to establish its own buffer stock if such a stock were required.*[18]

This argument, too, was a weak one at the time that it was advanced. As already mentioned, the industrial countries had consistently refused to contribute to financing international buffer stocks, except on a voluntary basis,[19] so that, for example, the burden of financing the tin buffer stock by direct government contributions had fallen almost entirely on developing exporting countries.[20] The financing asymmetry was a major reason for the small size of the tin buffer stock and for its consequent limited ability to defend the agreed price 'ceiling'.

A closely related argument was that if a buffer stock was to be set up, a number

---

[15] Corea 1976, para. 66.
[16] These various objections are discussed at some length in Vastine 1977. See also E. Dell 1987.
[17] Vastine 1977: 462.
[18] E. Dell 1987.
[19] Only France and the Netherlands had made such voluntary contributions before UNCTAD IV.
[20] The cocoa buffer stock – the only other operative international buffer stock – was financed by a levy on cocoa exports.

of alternative means for financing the stock were already available – such as direct government contributions, borrowing from commercial banks, trade levies, and the International Monetary Fund – so that it was unnecessary to consider the establishment of a new institution, the Common Fund, for this purpose.[21] However, the UNCTAD proposal had envisaged that buffer stock financing would involve sources other than direct government contributions, while the mediation of a central financing institution would reduce borrowing costs – a point generally acknowledged as valid – and would also provide an important overview function of all the various international commodity markets, a function that would otherwise be forgone.

(iii) *It would be more logical to negotiate international agreements with buffer stocks before establishing a fund to help finance them.*

There was a major difference of view, as between developed and developing countries, on the reasons for the slow progress in negotiating individual commodity agreements. The developed countries argued that the major constraint had been the competitive interests of the proposed members of a commodity agreement, particularly as regards the allocation of market shares for exporting countries.[22] By contrast, the UNCTAD proposal, as indicated above, was based on the argument that the lack of an assured source of finance had been a major reason for limited progress in establishing buffer stocks.[23] The simultaneous negotiation of a number of separate buffer stocks, as envisaged in the Integrated Programme, would clearly require much larger financial support than had hitherto been necessary, and the prior existence of a central financing facility could thus reasonably be assumed to act as a catalyst in these negotiations.

A number of other arguments were also put forward by Western leaders, some more fanciful than serious. For example, the leader of the United Kingdom delegation at UNCTAD IV, Edmund Dell, apparently believed that the existence of a Common Fund would actually hinder negotiations on individual commodities, and that the Common Fund might itself indulge in speculation on the commodity markets.[24] However, it was unlikely that such views would gain general acceptance.

These various arguments were thus not accepted by the developing countries, which continued to press strongly at the UNCTAD IV meeting for the establishment of the proposed Common Fund. In this they were supported by a number of smaller West European countries – Finland, the Netherlands, Norway, Portugal, and Sweden – while France also accepted the need for a central fund, though one based on 'pooling' the financial resources of the individual commodity agreements rather than being itself a 'source' of finance. The consequent divergence of policies among the Western industrial countries, together with the political pressure exerted by the developing countries, which included support from OPEC countries, resulted in a compromise formula being

[21] Vastine 1977: 462.   [22] E. Dell 1987: 27.   [23] Corea 1976: para. 66.   [24] E. Dell 1987.

adopted to negotiate the establishment of a Common Fund. These negotiations proved to be extremely complex and protracted, but an Agreement was eventually signed in June 1980, four years after the UNCTAD IV resolution, on the objectives, functions, capital structure, mode of operation, and organizational and management structure of the Common Fund.[25]

While the Western industrial countries expressed objections, or reservations, in respect of several aspects of the Common Fund proposals, they also had more fundamental concerns. In the first place, the proposed new international financial institution would be setting what might be a precedent in so far as it would be the first non-aid financial institution not firmly under the control of the major Western countries. Secondly, such an institution with a large sum of money at its disposal, by promoting the negotiation of additional agreements, as well as intervening in the markets for some commodities facing emergencies, would greatly diminish the scope for the 'free play of market forces' to which Western countries were committed as a matter of principle. Finally, the new financial institution might well develop important leverage over the operations of individual buffer stocks, and thus, to this extent, could endanger the autonomy of the councils operating international commodity agreements.

Of the specific issues in the negotiations, four were of particular significance. These were whether the Common Fund should itself be empowered to intervene in commodity markets in situations of emergency; whether it should be a 'source' or a 'pool' of finance; whether it should engage in financing other than for stock operations; and whether the developing countries could obtain a much greater share in decision-making in the Common Fund than they had in the Bretton Woods institutions.[26]

(i) *Market intervention in emergency situations.* The rationale behind the proposal for a Common Fund which would not be tied solely to those commodity markets where ICAs existed was elaborated by Avramović (1978).[27] His argument was that the lack of adequate finance available to commodity producers in developing countries meant that in times of surplus, they could not hold back their output but were forced into distress sales on a falling world market, in sharp contrast with producers in developed countries who could finance their own stocks and sell only when prices recovered from low levels. Thus what was needed was an international source of finance to support market prices in situations of oversupply, either by means of ICA mechanisms, or — where there were no ICAs — by the financing of international stocks in developing producing countries. This central finance was envisaged as helping these countries 'to overcome

---

[25] UNCTAD 1981*a*. A useful summary of this Agreement on the Common Fund is given by Chadha 1980, while Corea, forthcoming, provides a detailed (and fascinating) account of the various arguments and issues involved. Tait and Sfeir 1982 discuss some of the legal aspects of the proposals.
[26] This Section draws heavily on the analysis in Corea, forthcoming.
[27] Dragoslav Avramović was closely involved in the elaboration of the Common Fund proposal as Adviser to the UNCTAD Secretary-General.

the initial shocks in commodity markets and to give them breathing space in which to organize themselves and start applying policies aimed at adjusting supply, if market disturbances prove to be more than temporary'.[28] Thus this stock-financing function was conceived as one essential element in a broad package of measures, including supply management and diversification, as appropriate to the particular commodities concerned.

However, the concept of a new institution actively financing commodity stocks, both international and national, would undoubtedly have been strongly opposed by the Western developed countries for the reasons indicated above. Yet this possible function of the Common Fund was not, in fact, seriously discussed during the negotiations, as a result of its prior rejection by the Group of 77, who had stated in their Ministerial Declaration of 1976 that the Common Fund should finance stabilization measures only in the framework of international commodity agreements.[29]

In the later stages of the negotiations, the UNCTAD secretariat's proposal that provision should be made to enable the fund in emergency situations to finance stocking activities for commodities not covered by ICAs was given support by the Group of 77 but, as Dr Corea states (forthcoming: 97), it was 'not pushed very hard presumably because the chances of its being accepted by the other groups were judged to be negligible'. Thus the original concept of a fund with power to act effectively and promptly to support commodity prices in conditions of market weakness, even where no ICA was in existence, was in effect rejected. As Dr Corea put it, such a concept 'would have established an entirely new régime for regulation of commodity markets and made the Common Fund an immensely significant and powerful institution on the world economic scene' (ibid. 73). It was, no doubt, for this very reason that it would have been opposed by the Western developed countries.

(ii) *The fund as a 'source' or a 'pool' of finance.* For the reasons already indicated, the Western developed countries were opposed to the concept of a strong fund with substantial capital of its own, able to borrow additional funds from commercial banks and providing an assured source of financing for the stock operations of existing or new ICAs. Moreover, their argument that a central fund for the financing of buffer stocks of individual ICAs was unnecessary because each ICA could raise its own finance was clearly on weak ground, as mentioned earlier, in view of their own traditional refusal to agree that they should make mandatory contributions to ICA stocking operations. This difficulty was overcome in the course of the negotiations by the Western developed countries announcing their acceptance of mandatory contributions from both

---

[28] Avramović 1978: 387.

[29] According to Corea, forthcoming, this decision reflected the concern by a number of producing countries that this proposed function 'might lead to interference by outside countries, that were neither producers nor consumers of particular products, in decisions pertaining to these products', and that, more generally, the developing countries at that early stage had no clear perception of the role of the Common Fund (p. 74).

producing and consuming member countries of an international commodity agreement, on the basis of equal shares of the cost of financing buffer stocks.

This change in policy enabled the Western developed countries to present a credible alternative to the original 'source' concept. Since they were now committed to the principle of stock financing, this enabled them, at various stages in the negotiations, to propose (1) that member governments of an ICA should meet the full cost of an agreed buffer stock (either through capital subscriptions or by guarantees, or some combination of the two); and (2) that the individual ICAs should make cash deposits with the Fund, which would thus become a 'pool' of finance provided by ICAs rather than, as in the 'source' concept, being endowed with its own capital for financing ICA stock operations. This reversal in the relationship of the Fund and the ICAs would clearly have reduced the importance attached by the developing countries to the proposed new financing institution, and was not acceptable to them.

The deadlock on this issue was broken by an initiative of the UNCTAD secretariat.[30] The financing requirements originally proposed amounted in total to $6 billion, of which one-third (or $2 billion) would be raised by direct contributions from governments, the remainder being raised, as and when necessary, by borrowing. Since the Western countries had proposed that ICAs should meet the full costs of their own stock operations, Dr Corea, the UNCTAD Secretary-General, proposed that the capital of the Common Fund could be scaled down to $500 million – for working capital and administrative expenses – leaving the Fund still able to borrow from private capital markets any additional funds required for the financing of stock operations of ICAs. This borrowing power would be possible because, as proposed by the Western countries, the ICAs would make cash deposits with the Fund and provide the Fund with stock warrants as collateral, while the Fund would also have government guarantees in the form of callable capital.

This proposal formed the basis for the eventual 1980 Articles of Agreement of the Common Fund, which provided for some $400 million of direct government contributions. This relatively small sum has often been contrasted with the original proposal for a capital of $6 billion to indicate that the Fund will have far less scope for financing commodity market stabilization than was originally envisaged or, indeed, was required. However, the two figures are not comparable, since the Agreement provides for the Fund borrowing in the capital markets to meet any additional sums required for financing stock operations over and above the sums deposited with it by the individual ICAs. The real difference between the Fund as originally proposed and that agreed in 1980 is that now the price-stabilization function of the Fund is wholly dependent on the conclusion of new, or renewed, ICAs (and, moreover, on whether or not their respective Councils choose to conclude financing agreements with the Fund).

(iii) *Financing purposes other than stocking.* A major impasse in the

---

[30] Described in some detail in Corea, forthcoming: 91–3.

negotiations in the UNCTAD Conference on the Establishment of a Common Fund also arose as a result of a proposal that the Common Fund should finance development measures other than stocking (e.g. research and development, productivity improvement, and promotion of consumption) on concessional terms. This idea had been advanced by some Western interests as an alternative to a Fund devoted to commodity market stabilization. However, it gained strong support from African countries, as well as from countries exporting commodities not in the list of those proposed for market stabilization. As a result, the developing countries united in a call for a Fund with two 'windows', the first for stabilization financing, and the second for 'other measures'.

The proposal for a second window initially met strong opposition from the larger Western developed countries, and particularly from the United States. Their view was that financing on concessional terms would be unacceptable duplication with the activities of the World Bank and the regional Development Banks. Though several smaller developed countries – the Nordic countries and the Netherlands – were willing to accept the second window idea, the clash of views between the developing countries, particularly the African group, and the larger developed countries led to a temporary suspension of the negotiations. The issue was eventually settled by a compromise whereby a second window was to be established by voluntary contributions from member governments, with a modest target of $280 million, with provision for the transfer of at least $70 million to the second window from government capital contributions to the first window for market stabilization.

It is, perhaps, ironic that the second window, which was not part of the original concept of the Common Fund, seems likely to become its more important operational arm, since the first window will be dependent for its activation on the establishment of new ICAs based on buffer stocks. The meagre results of the parallel negotiations on individual commodities, discussed further in Chapter 8, together with the inhibiting effects of the collapse of the tin agreement in 1985, and of the coffee agreement in 1989, make it appear highly unlikely that the first window will become the dynamic catalyst it was intended to be, at least until the major developed countries modify their present ideological objections to international market-regulation schemes.

(iv) *Decision-making in the Common Fund.* Though the developing countries had hoped to obtain a majority of votes in the Fund, so that they would gain effective control over decision-making, a compromise solution became inevitable in view of the fact that the greater part of government contributions would come from Western developed countries. The formula finally adopted was that the developing-country group obtain 47 per cent of the total votes; Group B (Western developed countries), 42 per cent; Group D (socialist countries of Eastern Europe), 8 per cent; and China, 3 per cent.

The Western countries will thus retain power to block decisions with 'significant financial implications' (such as increases in the Fund's capital), which require a three-fourths majority, or 'other important' decisions (such as projects to be financed by the second window), which require a two-thirds majority. As Finlayson and Zacher (1988: 63) put it, 'it would be wrong to conclude that the developing countries have achieved a decisive decision-making position in the fund. The developed countries as a whole, and indeed just five of the most powerful, have an effective veto power. The North still holds the reins firmly in its hands.'

There is little doubt that the larger developed countries viewed the original Common Fund proposals as a potential threat to their present dominance of world commodity markets, and that this threat was successfully nullified by their negotiating stance in UNCTAD. The unwillingness of the OPEC countries, which had huge payments surpluses at the time, to make a major contribution to the required capital of the Fund, while understandable, was also an important reason for the various compromises which the developing countries found themselves having to make.

The Common Fund was established as an autonomous international institution only in 1989, almost a decade after the conclusion of the negotiations on its Articles of Agreement. These Articles had stipulated that the Agreement would enter into force only when two conditions were met: that not less than 90 countries ratified the Agreement; and that the countries ratifying should together account for two-thirds of the Fund's directly contributed capital. Ratifications were, however, very slow in coming, due, in part, to the normally slow process in many countries of obtaining parliamentary approval. A more pervasive influence was probably the dramatic collapse in commodity prices, together with the increasing difficulties of negotiating new price-stabilizing ICAs as well as renegotiating old ones (an issue discussed in Chapter 8). It was only in 1986, after repeated requests by UNCTAD to governments which had not ratified, that the number of ratifications reached 90, satisfying the first condition stipulated in the Agreement.

The main obstacle to the establishment of the Common Fund, however, was non-ratification by both the United States and the Soviet Union, since without either country the 'two-thirds of contributed capital' condition could not be met. By 1985, the United States had announced its decision not to ratify, at which point the chances of the Fund coming into being appeared small indeed. The breakthrough came at the UNCTAD VII Conference in Geneva in 1987, when the Soviet Union announced its decision to ratify the Agreement. By 1988, with further ratifications by several small countries, the second condition was met.

The first annual meeting of the Governing Council of the Common Fund was held in July 1989, at which date the total resources committed to the Fund by its 104 member States amounted to approximately $547 million, of which about $317 million represented subscriptions to the directly contributed capital, and about $230 million were voluntary contributions pledged to the Second Account. The new Common Fund has the potential to evolve and develop over time, particularly if it builds on its position as the only intergovernmental institution with a specific focus on the problems of the international commodity markets. How this might best be achieved is taken up in Chapter 15, as one element in a more comprehensive international commodity policy that could be evolved in the future.

8
Negotiations on Individual Commodities

1. THE DUAL PRICE OBJECTIVE

The UNCTAD resolution on the Integrated Programme for Commodities, as mentioned in Chapter 7, called for negotiations on 18 different commodities, of which 10 were regarded as 'core' commodities suitable for some form of market regulation to achieve a wide range of objectives.[1] The 'core' commodities in total accounted in 1976 – the date of the IPC resolution – for almost one-half of the value of all primary commodity exports from developing countries, the corresponding proportion for all 18 commodities being two-thirds. Hence, the Programme envisaged tackling many of the urgent problems faced by developing countries in world commodity markets over a very substantial and relatively important range of commodities. Moreover, the IPC commodities selected were those in which developing countries were large net exporters. Thus developing countries stood to gain directly from measures adopted under the Programme which would improve their terms of trade, expand their real export earnings, or otherwise promote their development efforts.

It is, perhaps, not widely appreciated that the IPC resolution had broad objectives covering both short-term and longer-term issues, and both price and non-price aspects of the 'commodity problem'. The price objectives were formulated as:

1. To achieve stable conditions in commodity trade, including avoidance of excessive price fluctuations, at levels which would:
   (a) be remunerative and just to producers and equitable to consumers;
   (b) take account of world inflation and changes in the world economic and monetary situations;
   (c) promote equilibrium between supply and demand within expanding world commodity trade.
2. To improve and sustain the real income of individual developing countries through increased export earnings, and to protect them from fluctuations in export earnings, especially from commodities.[2]

While this formulation is explicit in its reference to the objective of reducing fluctuations in commodity prices, and in export earnings of developing

---

[1] The 10 'core' commodities were cocoa, coffee, sugar, tea, cotton, hard fibres, jute, natural rubber, copper, and tin. The remaining commodities listed in the resolution were bananas, bovine meat, vegetable oils and oilseeds, non-coniferous timber, bauxite, iron ore, manganese ore, and phosphate rock.

[2] UNCTAD resolution 93(IV), in UNCTAD 1977.

countries, it also implicitly includes a price-raising objective. For example, though the concept of 'remunerative', 'just', and 'equitable' prices can have no precise meaning, it clearly implies that measures may be required, as appropriate to the conditions of particular commodity markets, to raise prices from levels regarded by producers as depressed, though not to raise them above levels regarded by consumers as excessive. In other words, the concept was included as a loose framework within which bargaining could take place to find some common agreement on an acceptable range of prices. Again, the implication of the phrase 'to improve ... real income ... through increased export earnings' is also that action may be required to raise the level of commodity prices where such action is deemed appropriate and feasible.

Thus the IPC was aiming at a dual objective as regards pricing issues: to reduce excessive short-term fluctuations in commodity prices and in commodity export earnings; and to raise commodity prices, where feasible and appropriate, to benefit producers, while taking the interests of consumers into account. These two issues, which need separate consideration, were the focus of intense debate and contention in the negotiations relating to commodities, and form the subject-matter of the present chapter. The other main objectives of the IPC – improving market access and reliability of supply, diversifying production and expanding primary product processing in developing countries, improving the competitiveness of natural products competing with synthetics and substitutes, improving market structures, and enhancing the participation of developing countries in the marketing, distribution, and transport of their commodity exports – are considered in Part IV below.

2. PRICE-RAISING AND 'INDEXATION'

Though price-raising had been included, even if implicitly, in the 1976 IPC resolution, in fact this objective was never seriously considered in the subsequent negotiations on individual commodities, which were concerned very largely with specific issues arising in particular markets rather than with broad policy objectives. There was, however, a sharp difference of view, as between developed and developing countries, on the broad objective of price-raising, which centred around the concept of 'indexation'. This controversy had its origins well before the formulation of the IPC programme but, none the less, was related to it.

Pressure by the developing countries for international measures to improve the trend of primary commodity prices was accentuated following the collapse of the Bretton Woods system of fixed exchange rates in 1971 and the subsequent rise in inflationary pressures in the Western industrial countries. From 1971 to 1974 the dollar prices of manufactured goods exported by these countries rose by some 50 per cent (or by an average of 14 per cent a year), and though many developing countries enjoyed even faster growth in the prices of their commodity exports, many others faced real losses as a result of worsening terms of trade.

One approach to meeting the problem of a deterioration in the terms of trade of commodity-exporting developing countries gained prominence in this period following an agreement made in 1971 between OPEC and the international petroleum companies, under which posted prices were to be increased by 2.5 per cent to take account of the effects of inflation on the prices of imports into OPEC member countries. This linking of commodity prices with the prices of imports, most of which were from developed countries, came to be known as 'indexation'.

The indexation issue was considered at UNCTAD III in 1972 on the basis of a secretariat analysis,[3] but no consensus was reached. The issue was, however, pursued by the Group of 77, and at the 1973 session of the General Assembly a resolution was adopted[4] calling for a study on indexation. In the following year, the sixth Special Session of the General Assembly, in its resolution on a New International Economic Order, called for 'efforts to ... work for a link between the prices of exports of developing countries and the prices of their imports from developed countries',[5] and the possibility of creating such a link was taken up as part of the UNCTAD discussions leading up to the IPC resolution of 1976.

In principle, there are two alternative approaches to creating a link between export and import prices of commodity-exporting countries. One approach, usually known as 'direct indexation', makes use of market stabilization mechanisms, such as buffer stocks or export quotas, as traditionally used in international commodity agreements, which aim to stabilize the market price of a particular commodity within a specified range. If an indexation principle were applied, then the price range would have to be adjusted upwards in line with increases in the prices of imports of the countries exporting the commodity in question.[6] Clearly, the ability to make such upward adjustments depends on the body operating the agreement exercising effective control over supplies coming on the market, while such adjustments would not be viable if consumers had readily available alternatives (e.g. synthetic substitutes, in the case of natural raw materials). However, for a limited group of commodities, particularly where production is wholly or mainly in developing countries, indexation would be technically feasible.

A second approach, known as 'indirect indexation', would not involve intervention in commodity markets, but would instead compensate exporting countries for foreign exchange losses incurred as a result of adverse movements in their terms of trade. Indirect indexation was envisaged as a possible mechanism for

---

[3] UNCTAD 1973: ii, 'Pricing Policy ...'.
[4] Resolution 3083(XXVIII).
[5] Resolution 3202(S-VI), Part I, para. 1(d).
[6] A number of variants can be imagined: e.g. linking to prices of manufactures in which the commodity is used; to changes in the cost of production of the commodity; or to changes in the exchange rate of the currency, or currencies, in which trade in the commodity is denominated. For further discussion, see UNCTAD 1973: ii, 'Pricing Policy ...'.

those commodities for which direct indexation was not feasible.[7]

The indexation concept, however, met with strong and determined opposition from Western industrial countries, partly on the grounds that it would inevitably lead to further global inflationary pressure, and partly that (in its direct form) it would interfere with the free play of market forces. The advocates of indexation, on the other hand, pointed out that indexation could not be a significant cause of inflation in developed countries, but was rather an element which would strengthen the motivation for controlling inflation in these countries; it should instead be viewed, it was argued, as a protection for developing countries against the adverse effects of that inflation. As regards the free play of market forces, indexation was simply the extension to the international sphere of the 'income parity' concept which lay behind the domestic agricultural support programmes operated by most of the developed market-economy countries themselves.[8]

Other objections were also raised against the concept of indexation of commodity prices including, in particular, that it would benefit developed country producers more than those in developing countries.[9] However, this unintended effect could be largely avoided if indexation was interpreted as relating only to commodities supplied wholly or mainly by developing countries.

The general economic background at the time of the controversy on indexation was one of high inflationary pressures, and developing countries were looking for some new international mechanism to protect their terms of trade and external payments positions. Thus the possibility of indexation involving a reduction in commodity prices in a recession period was never raised as an issue, though it would clearly have become one in the 1980s, had some form of indexation been adopted. In any event, a *general* indexation of commodity prices was an unrealistic goal, since it implied the successful negotiation of a wide range of effective price-regulating commodity agreements, a highly unlikely outcome given the opposition of Western countries to any possibility of price-raising mechanisms. However, the alternative of indirect indexation was never pursued, and the indexation concept was not included in the IPC resolution of 1976. Thus general indexation as a means of offsetting a terms of trade deterioration was thereafter not a 'live' issue in the context of international commodity policy.

None the less, the idea of establishing some form of link between commodity prices and the prices of imports of developing countries was not entirely lost, since the IPC resolution called for 'negotiated price ranges, which would be periodically reviewed and appropriately revised, taking into account, *inter alia*, movements in prices of imported manufactured goods, exchange rates, production costs and world inflation, and levels of production and consumption'.[10] However, it is unlikely that this precept had any significant influence on the

---

[7] For a detailed discussion of these varieties of indexation, and of their implications, see UNCTAD 1974a and Cuddy 1976.
[8] Corea 1976: 24–5.
[9] See e.g. Rangarajan 1978: 239.
[10] Resolution 93(IV), Part III, para. 2(c).

bargaining outcomes over price ranges negotiated in the framework of individual commodity agreements.

Before leaving the indexation issue, two related developments are worthy of note. The first concerns the partial success of a number of Caribbean bauxite-producing countries in indexing the prices they receive for their bauxite exports to the price of aluminium ingots in the North American market. While this is an isolated example, it does indicate that, given the appropriate conditions, indexation can be effective in increasing the benefits of trade for countries exporting a specific commodity. The other development of interest is the extension by the IMF of its Compensatory Financing Facility in 1981 to cover the increased costs of cereal imports resulting from price rises on the world market. This is, in effect, an application of the principle of indirect indexation, albeit on a limited scale, and with compensation on a repayable basis.

3. THE POST-WAR STABILIZATION EXPERIENCE: TECHNICAL LIMITATIONS OF THE ICAs

All the post-war ICAs have included a wide range of objectives, both short term and long term, though the combination of stated objectives has differed considerably among the five ICAs with economic provisions. Only two objectives – ensuring price stability (or reducing excessive price fluctuations) and promoting increased consumption – have been included in all five ICAs (see Table 8.1).

However, the central objective of all these ICAs was the short term price stabilization function. This is shown by the fact that by far the greater part of the time of the governing Councils and of the secretariats of the agreements has been devoted to this issue; that the mechanisms at the disposal of the Councils relate wholly or mainly to price stabilization; and that breakdowns in agreements have been almost entirely due to disputes relating to price targets and/or to the instruments used to achieve them. The success or failure of the various ICAs has thus to be judged in terms of the degree to which they have managed to reduce market instability.

Such a judgement cannot, however, be made in terms of whether or not prices have remained within an agreed range, because price movements are influenced by changes in market conditions as well as by the operations of ICAs; and also because the price range itself can be, and often has been, shifted to reflect changes in market conditions. Nor can a comparison validly be made between price fluctuations during the life of an ICA with those immediately preceding, or following, if no agreements were then in force, because changes in market conditions would once again affect the comparison. The only valid method for making a quantitative assessment of the degree of success of ICAs in price stabilization would be a comparison of actual market price fluctuations during the life of an ICA and an econometric simulation of prices which assumed no market intervention. Such stimulations, however, have not been made, except for one or two

Table 8.1. Objectives and instruments of selected International Commodity Agreements

	Cocoa[a]	Coffee[b]	Sugar[c]	Natural rubber[d]	Tin[e]
A. *Price and earnings objectives*					
1. Price stability	★	★	★	★	★
2. Earnings stability and growth	★	★	★		★
B. *Longer-term development objectives*					
1. Market access and supply reliability	★	★	★	★	
2. Diversification and industrialization	★		★		
3. Competitiveness of natural products			★	★	★
4. Market structure and marketing, distribution, and transportation			★	★	
5. Increased consumption	★	★	★	★	★
C. *Other objectives*					
1. Alleviation of serious economic difficulties	★	★		★	★
2. Prevention of unemployment or under-employment		★			★
D. *Instruments*[f]					
1. Buffer stock	★			★	★
2. Export quotas		★	★		★

[a] 1980 Agreement; earlier agreements provided for a combination of buffer stock and export quotas (as well as for disposals for non-traditional uses if necessary).
[b] 1976 and 1983 Agreements.
[c] 1977 Agreement. This also provided for holding of national stocks under the control of the International Sugar Organization. The 1984 Agreement contained no provisions relating to price stabilization.
[d] 1979 Agreement.
[e] 1975 and 1980 Agreements.
[f] For attaining price and earnings objectives.

Source: Relevant Agreements.

commodities (e.g. Smith and Schink 1976 for the tin market; Herrmann, Burger, and Smit 1990 for the coffee and rubber markets).

Useful qualitative assessments of the successes and failures of the various post-war ICAs can, however, be derived from an historical description of their stabilization efforts in periods of very different market conditions, as in the 1970s and 1980s. Though all the ICAs suffered from technical difficulties and limitations of one kind or another, there were also underlying problems reflecting differences of perceived national or ideological interest.[11] The principal technical problems that impeded the successful operation of the post-war ICAs at one time or another related to the price range to be defended; the mechanisms used for that defence; the financial resources allotted for that purpose; and, in the case of export quotas, the allocation of market shares.

(a) The Price Range

Two related issues are involved, viz. the need to set the initial range at a realistic level, and the need to provide for appropriate adjustment to the range as market conditions change.

Of the many post-war ICAs, there are several which began with unrealistic price objectives. Perhaps the classic case is that of cocoa, for which negotiations on an agreement began in the mid-1950s, were suspended, and were taken up on a new basis in 1965 after the establishment of UNCTAD. After seven years of intermittent negotiating conferences, an agreement was finally concluded in 1972, to enter into force provisionally in October 1973. The long period of negotiation tended to make the positions taken by importing and exporting countries more, rather than less, rigid on a number of issues. In particular, the price range adopted (23–32 US cents per lb.), though it was no doubt appropriate for the late 1960s, or the early 1970s, was quite inappropriate for the changed economic situation from 1973, when market prices were rising rapidly. In 1973, cocoa prices averaged 51 cents per lb., rising to 71 cents per lb. in 1974, but falling to 56.5 cents per lb. in 1975, when a new agreement was negotiated. In the 1975 cocoa Agreement, the price range was increased to 39–55 cents per lb., and there was a further increase, to 65–81 cents per lb., as from the second year of the Agreement. However, even these higher price ranges remained far below market levels (93 cents in 1976, 172 cents in 1977, and about 150 cents in both 1978 and 1979), thus rendering the Agreement inoperative.

Even where the initial price range is realistic, it will need to be adjusted to accord with changes in market conditions. This has often involved difficult and protracted negotiations, and in several instances precipitated suspension of the price stabilization functions of the agreements concerned. These particular difficulties might be largely overcome if future agreements made provision for some kind of semi-automatic formula for adjusting the price range objective. Such a formula might include indicators of the various elements generally agreed as relevant, such as current market trends, changes in commercial stocks and in the holdings of the buffer stock (where one exists), as well as forecasts of world supply and demand. Problems created by fluctuations in exchange rates of the currency in which the price range is expressed – as occurred

---

[11] For more detailed reviews and analysis see, in particular, Gordon-Ashworth 1984, UNCTAD 1985a, and Gilbert 1987.

for the tin Agreement in 1985 – can largely be avoided by expressing the price range in terms of a combination of currencies as, for example, the SDR (as adopted in the 1980 cocoa Agreement).

Whatever the formula used, it is unlikely that governments would accept it as fully automatic; they would usually wish to retain some freedom of action in the light of more general considerations. This would be of particular importance when market prices are on a definite upward or downward trend; in the former case, consuming countries are likely to resist any quick increase in the price range, while in the latter case, producing countries will tend to resist a price range reduction (this issue is discussed further later on). However, a semi-automatic formula would go a long way in assisting the negotiating process, at least by giving a strong indication of the direction and desirable magnitude of the price range adjustment that appeared to be required.

(b) The Mechanisms of Price Stabilization

The five Agreements have used either a buffer stock or an export quota system, or a combination of the two, in order to keep market prices within an agreed range (Table 8.1). The mechanism or mechanisms selected, to be successful, must reflect the central problems of the commodity market concerned. For example, for commodities characterized by persistent structural surplus, any attempt to defend a floor price by means of a buffer stock alone will inevitably fail unless governments are prepared to provide virtually unlimited financial resources. This was the fundamental limitation of the 1980 cocoa Agreement, which undermined its credibility and led to destabilizing speculation.[12] In such cases, an export quota system, or a joint export quota/buffer stock scheme, would be more appropriate in dealing with persistent market imbalances, provided that the quotas did not freeze existing (or past) patterns of production;[13] that producing countries could obtain financial assistance for appropriate diversification; and that national policies did not undermine the objectives of the agreement.

The national policies of the major trading nations have never seriously entered into negotiations on individual commodity agreements. Yet in certain cases, these policies have been a major factor in the difficulties encountered in reducing price instability. The clearest case is the international sugar Agreement, which aimed to reduce price fluctuations in the residual world sugar market mainly by means of export quotas. However, high support prices for domestic producers in developed countries led to very large surpluses, especially in the European Community, which was not a member of the 1977 sugar Agreement, and to correspondingly large additions to supplies on the world market. Throughout the 1980s, there was severe downward pressure on world sugar prices due largely to overproduction of subsidized sugar in developed countries, but also to the

---

[12] See UNCTAD 1985a: para. 73.
[13] See the discussion of this issue in Ch. 4, Sect. 3.

rapid expansion in the use of sugar substitutes, encouraged in part by the high domestic sugar prices maintained within the United States as part of its farm support policies. Sugar prices fell sharply in 1981 to below the floor price of the Agreement, which lost control of the market in early 1982, since when its economic provisions have lapsed.[14]

Another case where national policies have been of vital importance related to the tin market. Before its collapse in 1985, the international tin Agreement aimed to maintain prices within an agreed range by means of a buffer stock, supported as necessary by export quotas. However, the tin Agreement's buffer stock was considerably smaller than the surplus tin held in the United States strategic stockpile. Thus the possibility existed that stockpile sales could in certain situations (e.g. when prices were near the floor of the price range) frustrate the objectives of the Agreement. However, informal understandings were reached between the two organizations concerned – the International Tin Council and the US General Services Administration – that the latter's operations would not be such as to disrupt the market.

There would seem to be a good case, therefore, for future negotiations to establish price-stabilizing ICAs to consider national policies, to the extent that these affect the price objectives of an agreement, and to make appropriate recommendations or arrive at suitable understandings to ensure that national policies do not frustrate or undermine the ICA's objectives.

A closely related issue affecting the efficacy of stabilization mechanisms relates to the country coverage of an agreement. As already indicated, the European Community did not join the 1977 sugar Agreement, which left it free to move from a net importer in 1976 to the largest net exporter to the free market in 1980 and subsequent years. Again, a major factor undermining the efficacy of the tin buffer stock in the 1980s was the growing production of tin in non-member countries (Brazil and China), while the decision not to join the 1980 cocoa Agreement by the United States, the major consumer, and the Ivory Coast, the major producer, substantially contributed to the difficulties faced by the Agreement in attempting to stabilize market prices. A major difficulty was that the cocoa buffer stock's resources were kept considerably below the maximum envisaged, since participating countries were unwilling to make good the shortfall of finance arising from the non-participation of the United States and the Ivory Coast.

An efficient mechanism for market stabilization by an ICA thus depends, among other things, on support by the major trading nations, both in their national policies and in their participation in the relevant agreement.

(c) Financial Requirements for Market Stabilization

The finance required to support ICA price-stabilization relates, apart from administrative expenses, essentially to the cost of operating a buffer stock. Given

[14] Sugar prices on the free market reached the floor price of the lapsed 1977 Agreement in the second half of 1989.

the price-elasticities of supply and demand, the amount of a commodity which a buffer stock will need to purchase to defend a given price range will depend on the relationship between the amplitude of the fluctuation in market prices that would occur in the absence of buffer stock intervention and the price ranges to be defended. For a given amplitude of fluctuation in market prices, the wider the price range to be defended, the smaller will be the stock, and the corresponding financial resources, that will be required. There is thus a trade-off between the amount of finance required and the degree to which price fluctuations are reduced.[15]

The degree to which the operative ICAs aimed to attenuate market price fluctuations in the late 1970s and the first half of the 1980s is summarized in Table 8.2, which also shows comparable data for the two informal price-stabilization arrangements, for jute and sisal, under the auspices of FAO. The periods covered differ somewhat from one ICA to another, partly because of the different periods covered by the Agreements, but mainly because the market price cycles have diverged.

Over the more recent cycle, from the early- to the mid-1980s, the coffee, sugar and tin target price ranges were the most ambitious in relation to the amplitude of fluctuation in the corresponding market prices; in each case, the price range was targeted at only about one-third of the market price cycle. For both coffee and sugar, the ratio of the price range to market price cycle in this period was significantly lower than in the preceding cycle from the late 1970s to the early 1980s, either because prices became more unstable (sugar) or because the target price range was narrowed (coffee). The targets for cocoa and rubber, at the other extreme, aimed at a price range of about 80 per cent of the market price cycle. For cocoa, this was a substantial rise compared with the ratio for the preceding price cycle, as it became clear by the time of the negotiations for the 1980 Agreement that the range in the 1975 Agreement was unrealistically narrow in view of the increased instability in the cocoa market.

Given the structural parameters of the market for a particular commodity (i.e. the relevant price elasticities and the anticipated amplitude of market price fluctuation), the setting of a target price range involves an implicit decision concerning the size of the buffer stock necessary to defend the 'floor' and 'ceiling' prices.[16] However, in no case so far have the negotiators attempted to relate the

---

[15] Assuming that supply and demand are functions both of price and of autonomous shifts due to non-price factors, and that the price-elasticities are constant, the quantity of stocks required by a buffer stock to defend the 'floor' of a target price range (B_f) can be expressed as:

$$B_f = \bar{Q}\{(e_s - e_d)\ (\pi - \mu)\}$$

where $\bar{Q}$ is the quantity sold in the world market at the mean price of the relevant price cycle; e_s and e_d are, respectively, the price-elasticities of supply and demand; π is the proportionate decline in the market price from the cyclical mean to the nadir; and μ is the proportionate deviation of the 'floor' price from the mid-point of the price range. For a description of the underlying model, see Maizels 1982: Appendix I.

[16] See formula in the previous footnote.

Table 8.2. Commodity agreement price ranges in relation to amplitude of market price cycles, late 1970s to mid-1980s

	Late 1970s to early 1980s			Early 1980s to mid-1980s		
	ICA price range[a] (%)	Market price cycle[b] (%)	Ratio[c]	ICA price range[a] (%)	Market price cycle[b] (%)	Ratio[c]
Formal agreements						
Cocoa	±11	±42	0.26	±23	±27	0.85
Coffee	±15	±34	0.44	±12	±35	0.33
Sugar	±29	±73	0.40	±28	±87	0.32
Natural rubber	±29	±47	0.62	±29	±37	0.78
Tin	±11	±42	0.26	±13	±36	0.36
Informal arrangements						
Jute	±10	±30	0.33	±10	±60	0.16
Sisal	±9	±31	0.29	±7	±26	0.27

[a] Ceiling or floor price as percentage of mid-point of range.
[b] Peak or nadir as percentage of mid-point of price cycle.
[c] Ratio of ICA price range to market price cycle.

Sources: UNCTAD *Monthly Commodity Price Bulletin* (various issues); FAO *Commodity Review and Outlook* (various issues).

resources made available to a buffer stock established under a commodity agreement to the degree to which that stock is required to diminish the amplitude of market price fluctuation.

This seems one explanation of the divergence between price-stabilization aims and the inadequacy of the supporting financial resources made available (e.g. in both the cocoa and tin Agreements). The fact that the divergence has always been in one direction, i.e. a paucity of resources, indicates also a general unwillingness of governments to commit adequate resources for stabilization purposes (prompted, for many developing countries, by a chronic shortage of foreign exchange). For more effective use of the buffer stock mechanism in future agreements, it would seem necessary to make much more careful, and more soundly based, quantitative estimates of the optimum size of a proposed buffer stock – preferably by the use of an econometric model – and to establish an assured source of finance, either in contributions from member governments, or by a levy on trade in the commodity (or both), fully adequate to meet the likely costs of the agreed degree of market stabilization. The financial cost of operating a buffer stock would, in any event, be considerably reduced if the stock were supplemented by export quota provisions to defend an agreed floor price. In view of the general reluctance of governments to make direct budgetary contributions to the finance of buffer stocks, an alternative source of funds, such as a small levy on trade in the commodity concerned—levies having been used in both the sugar and the cocoa ICAs—could usefully be deployed as a supplement, or even an alternative, to budgetary contributions.

(d) Market Share Allocation

A major operational difficulty for ICAs which rely wholly or mainly on export regulation for price stabilization has been the allocation of export quotas among producing countries. Disputes over quota allocation have often been the cause of suspension of negotiations for the renewal of ICAs, as well as of numerous breakdowns in existing, or past, agreements. The collapse of the coffee Agreement in July 1989, in large part the result of a quota allocation dispute, is only the most recent example of the importance of this issue.

The need for adequate flexibility in quota sharing to take into account both changes in the pattern of world demand (e.g. for different grades or varieties) and changes in comparative advantage among exporting countries is likely to be even greater in future ICAs using export quotas, especially for commodities in persistent surplus on the world market. The suggestion made in Chapter 4 that an appropriate indicator might be devised to show the direction, and preferably also the amount, of quota revision required could assist in achieving the flexibility that is needed.

4. THE POLITICAL ECONOMY OF INTERNATIONAL COMMODITY NEGOTIATIONS

While these various technical issues have often been important, and sometimes crucial, to the success of the post-war ICAs in reducing excessive price instability, it would be wrong to consider them as inherent defects which must necessarily undermine the usefulness of the ICA approach. Rather, useful lessons should be drawn from the experience so far, so that in any future negotiations these, and other, technical limitations can be avoided or minimized. Moreover, much of the difficulties experienced by the five ICAs during the 1980s emanated from a more general cause. These agreements were all designed in a world economic environment much less hostile than in the 1980s. The dramatic commodity price collapse of the early 1980s had no counterpart in earlier postwar decades, and none of the ICAs was equipped to cope with a price recession of unprecedented magnitude and duration.

The operational difficulties of the ICAs may have had some adverse impact also on the progress of the IPC negotiations on other commodities, though this was unlikely to have been a major factor since progress had been extremely limited even in the later 1970s, when only one new ICA—for natural rubber—had been established. Rather, the more fundamental constraint appears to have been the belief of the Western developed countries in the virtues of market forces and, consequently, their negative attitude to intervention in the international commodity markets.[17] A number of specific policies derived from this general ideological stance.[18]

First, on the insistence of the larger developed countries, particularly the United States, the 1979 natural rubber Agreement together with the renegotiated 1980 cocoa Agreement were limited to using only buffer stocks for stabilization purposes. The cocoa Agreement had previously relied on both buffer stocks and export quotas, while for natural rubber the developing countries had also pressed for the use of export quotas. The opposition by Western countries to export quotas was based on the view that export quotas are likely to raise the price trend and also lead to a misallocation of resources,[19] while neither of these adverse effects would arise if buffer stocks were used as the stabilization mechanism. However, by excluding the use of export quotas, the efficacy of both these ICAs in defending a given price floor was considerably reduced, as was seen during the price collapse of 1980–2.

If ICAs were indeed to be confined to the use of buffer stocks as the sole price-stabilization mechanism, then the need for the Common Fund to assist in their financing would be all the more necessary. As Corea has argued, the long delay in bringing the Common Fund into operation may well have been an additional factor in reducing the interest of developing countries in negotiating new ICAs.[20]

Second, the Western developed countries have consistently steered the negotiations on new ICAs away from price stabilization and towards 'development' measures, such as productivity improvement, cost reduction, and market promotion, aspects which should yield direct benefits not only to developing exporting countries, but also to developed importing countries in terms of greater certainty of future supplies, at lower cost, than would otherwise be the case. Agreements on jute and jute products (1983) and on tropical timber (1984) are both devoted solely to such development measures, thus excluding any price-stabilization function. However, agreements which ignore the immediate export difficulties of developing countries are unlikely to retain their full support. Recent discussions (October 1989) on a renewal of the jute Agreement, for example, were marked by proposals by the leading exporters, Bangladesh and India, for the introduction of a price support mechanism and the use of a buffer stock when the Agreement is renegotiated.[21] The difficulties of developing countries in negotiating agreements with pricing provisions may also have reduced their interest in establishing new ICAs (as suggested by Corea, forthcoming).

A third notable trend has been the insistence of Western developed countries

---

[17] On this issue, see the related discussion in Ch. 3.
[18] See also Maizels 1985, and Corea, forthcoming: ch. 7 on recent trends in international commodity negotiations.
[19] See Ch. 4, Sect. 3(c) for a critique of this view.
[20] Corea, forthcoming.
[21] The International Jute Agreement was, however, extended in 1989 for a second five-year term without a price support mechanism.

during the 1980s on reducing the agreed price range defended by an ICA when market prices fall below the 'floor' level. In a sense, this is to be expected, in the same way as, when market prices are on an upward trend—as in the 1970s—developing exporting countries would normally insist on the agreed range being increased. However, in the financial crises of the 1980s in the commodity-dependent countries, due in substantial measure to the collapse in commodity prices, it is wholly understandable for these countries to wish to use the mechanisms of market stabilization (buffer stocks and/or export quotas) as a legitimate defence of their attenuated export earnings. Thus a dichotomy of views has developed which has made the smooth operation of stabilization mechanisms extremely difficult in a situation of continuing depressed price levels. Moreover, the fact that the ICAs could not be used as 'safety nets', in defence of an agreed floor price, must also have been a factor inhibiting the interest of many developing countries in negotiating for new agreements.[22]

The difficulties experienced by the various operative ICAs were reflected also in the negotiations for new ICAs within the framework of the Integrated Programme. The period following the 1976 Nairobi Conference was one of continuous and intensive consultations and negotiations on the problems of the non-ICA commodities listed in the IPC resolution. Over the seven years from 1977 to 1984, some 115 separate meetings were held in UNCTAD on 16 such commodities.[23] Yet the results obtained were disappointing and limited, only one new ICA being concluded, that for natural rubber. In this case, the producing countries had evolved a credible 'fallback' position in case no agreement could be reached with the consuming countries, namely, a producer-only buffer stock/export quota scheme. This alternative persuaded the consuming countries to negotiate seriously, though they successfully insisted, as already mentioned, on a price-stabilization scheme based only on a buffer stock. The failure of producing countries to arrive at similar 'fallback' schemes for other commodities was, no doubt, one important reason for the very limited results of the UNCTAD negotiations on individual commodities.

As a result of these trends, the central objective of the Integrated Programme, i.e. the stabilization of prices of a wide range of commodities and the improvement of the real export income of commodity-dependent countries, has been effectively undermined. At the same time, the lack of progress in establishing new ICAs, together with the lapsing, or collapse, of several of the traditional agreements, will inevitably reduce the significance of the first window of the Common Fund. It would indeed appear that the analysis of the voting at UNCTAD I, quoted earlier,[24] still holds good as regards the commodity negotiations of the past decade: viz. that the Western developed countries are well satisfied with the existing organization of commodity markets and have no

---

[22] See also Corea, forthcoming.
[23] Ibid.
[24] See Ch. 6, Sect. 2.

wish to make significant institutional or structural changes. Indeed, though the strengthening of the commodity sector of the economies of developing countries by the mechanisms envisaged in the IPC for the stabilization of prices and export earnings would bring benefits to developed as well as to developing countries, this consideration seems to be outweighed by the fear felt by the developed countries that their present predominant role in world commodity markets would thereby be substantially reduced.

It remains true, nevertheless, that the original conception of the Integrated Programme was a viable one, given adequate financial resources and a strong political commitment by governments. The Programme would have involved the negotiation and establishment of a series of ICAs using appropriate price-stabilization mechanisms and would have made a significant contribution towards the attenuation of the commodity price recession of the 1980s. This, in turn, would have enhanced the ability of commodity-exporting countries to service their foreign debts, and would have helped many countries to avoid drastic degrees of domestic economic contraction.

9
Compensatory Finance

1. THE ORIGIN OF FLUCTUATIONS IN COMMODITY EXPORT EARNINGS

It was often argued by mainstream economists, as well as by many developed-country representatives in the period following the IPC resolution that compensatory financing of temporary shortfalls in the export earnings of developing countries was a more efficient method of stabilizing these earnings than market intervention designed to reduce commodity price fluctuations. The implication of this argument was that efforts to negotiate new ICAs under the Integrated Programme should be abandoned in favour of improving existing compensatory financing arrangements. As pointed out earlier, however, the two approaches should be viewed as complementary rather than competitive.[1] None the less, the difficulties which arose in the negotiations on individual commodities in the IPC framework tended to divert the attention of policy-makers increasingly to the compensatory financing issue.

A key empirical question which arises in any comparison of the relative merits of these two approaches is the extent to which export earnings fluctuations of individual countries can be attributed to fluctuations in commodity prices on world markets, rather than to fluctuations in the volume of commodity supplies from each country. Much light on this issue is thrown by a detailed analysis at the country level, made by an UNCTAD Group of Experts, relating to unit value, volume and value instability over the two decades 1962 to 1981 for the major commodity exports[2] of developing countries, the results of which are summarized in Table 9.1. Over this period, of the 174 country/commodity cases covered, 101 (or almost three-fifths) had greater unit value (i.e. price) instability than volume instability.[3] In other words, for the majority of the developing countries covered by the analysis, price fluctuations – which market intervention aims to reduce – were indeed the main cause of fluctuations in their commodity export earnings.

However, for a substantial minority of cases (73, or two-fifths of the total) the main element of export earnings instability arose from instability in export volume. While market intervention to reduce price fluctuations would not

---

[1] See Ch. 4, Sect. 3(c)(ii) for the arguments involved.
[2] The commodities included accounted for 57% of the value of all primary commodities (except petroleum) exported by developing countries in 1980.
[3] The greater relative importance of unit value instability was particularly marked for tropical beverage crops, and mineral, ores, and metals. By contrast, volume instability was more important for vegetable oilseeds and oils, and for agricultural raw materials.

Table 9.1. Relationship between export instability indices of unit value (I_{uv}), volume (I_{vol}) and value (I_{val}), for individual countries and selected commodities, 1962–81

	No. of countries[a] in which $I_{uv} > I_{vol}$	No. of countries[a] in which $I_{vol} > I_{uv}$			Total no. of countries[a]
		Total	Countries in which $I_{val} > I_{vol}$	Countries in which $I_{vol} > I_{val}$	
Food[b]	18	17	12	5	35
Tropical beverages[c]	40	5	1	4	45
Vegetable oilseeds and oils[d]	5	12	8	4	17
Agricultural raw materials[e]	16	31	17	14	47
Mineral ores and metals[f]	22	8	3	5	30
TOTAL	101	73	41	32	174

[a] Large exporters of the individual commodities covered, plus other countries where the commodity concerned represented at least 5% of total export earnings. Individual countries are counted more than once if they export more than one commodity covered by the table.
[b] Bovine meat, sugar, bananas.
[c] Coffee, cocoa, tea.
[d] Groundnuts, groundnut oil, palm oil, coconut oil.
[e] Cotton, sisal, jute, natural rubber, tropical timber.
[f] Bauxite, copper, iron ore, manganese ore, phosphate rock, tin.

Source: Based on UNCTAD 1984a: Table X.

necessarily reduce export earnings fluctuations in these cases, where supply is responsive in the short term to changes in prices, measures which reduced price fluctuations could reduce fluctuations in volume and hence in export earnings also. In this connection, a useful distinction can be made between situations where the value instability exceeded the volume instability, and those where the reverse was the case. The former situation was found for 41 cases (nearly three-fifths of the 73 cases where volume instability was dominant), the excess in value instability indicating that volume instability had been reinforced by unit value instability. For these cases, therefore, market intervention which reduced unit value instability would thereby also reduce the instability of export earnings, particularly for commodities with significant short term elasticities of supply.

Thus, to the extent that the countries and commodities included in the analysis are reasonably representative, it can be concluded that market intervention which succeeded in reducing price fluctuations at the world level would also reduce export earnings fluctuations for the majority of exporting countries, either directly, because price fluctuations are the principal element in earnings fluctuations, or indirectly, because they reinforce the impact of volume fluctuations. However, as already mentioned, for a number of reasons successful market intervention is unlikely to be practicable for more than a limited range of commodities. For the latter, the reduction in world price fluctuations resulting from market intervention would greatly reduce the amount of compensatory financing of export earnings shortfalls, if the two schemes were to be in operation simultaneously.

2. DEFINITION OF AN EXPORT EARNINGS SHORTFALL

A major issue in considering the elements of a scheme of compensatory financing is the definition of a 'shortfall'. The concept of a shortfall implies that receipts from exports are lower than some norm, however defined. Clearly, the amount of 'shortfall' in any given period can vary greatly, depending on the definition of the norm. There are four main aspects to be considered here.

First, should the norm reflect a longer-term counterfactual situation (e.g. export earnings now if the preceding 10-year trend had continued), or a purely short-term trend value? Since commodity export earnings of developing countries were on a marked upward trend (in nominal terms) in the 1970s, but fell sharply from 1980 to 1982, followed by a succession of years with stagnating values, the longer-term counterfactual position would indicate a much larger shortfall since 1980 than would a norm based on recent short-term movements.

One could also postulate alternative counterfactual situations that would yield much larger shortfalls than even the 10-year trend ending in each shortfall year. For example, it might be argued that the relevant shortfall from the viewpoint of maintaining the momentum of development would be the gap between actual export earnings and what these earnings would have been had the pre-1980 upward trend continued. An approximate calculation on this basis shows an annual average shortfall in commodity export earnings of some $35 billion for the period 1981–4, as against $15 billion gross shortfall derived from the use of a 10-year trend.[4] However, the former figure could be criticized as unrealistic, in so far as it takes no account of the changes in the world economy – particularly the slowdown in growth of the industrialized countries – that have taken place since 1980.

The alternative approach is to argue that since compensation is intended to offset temporary shortfalls in export earnings, the norm should be the short-term trend value for any given year. This is the approach used by both the existing

---

[4] See UNCTAD 1987b: para. 14.

international compensatory financing schemes currently in operation, which are considered in more detail below. Alternative calculations based on short-term trends show much smaller shortfalls than those mentioned above for longer-term counterfactual situations. For example, for the same period, 1981–4, the average annual shortfall in commodity export earnings was $4.8 billion for a 4-year arithmetic average norm,[5] and $3.5 and $2.9 billion respectively, for 5-year and 3-year geometric average norms.[6]

Thus, on this 'short-term' definition of an export shortfall, the major part of the foreign exchange difficulties of commodity-exporting developing countries in the 1980s falls outside the scope of compensatory financing schemes. Rather, these difficulties can be attributed essentially to a downward, or stagnant, *trend* in export earnings, for which other remedial mechanisms would need to be sought.[7]

A second issue is whether shortfalls should be calculated on a gross or net basis. Gross shortfalls would relate to the aggregate of shortfalls for individual commodities, or commodity groups, ignoring commodities which have no shortfalls, or which have 'overages' (i.e. where actual export earnings for a particular period are above the norm used). For the net shortfall calculation, however, the shortfalls and overages of individual commodities would be offset against each other.

The argument in favour of using the net method is that export shortfalls are an integral part of a country's overall balance of payments situation, which is affected by the net value of exports, irrespective of the absolute size of individual commodity shortfalls or overages. Proponents of the gross concept, however, argue that compensation on a net basis may well be too small to allow adequate funds to reach those particular commodity sectors which have suffered an export shortfall. While it is open to governments, at least in principle, to tax sectors enjoying overages so as to subsidize those sectors with shortfalls, in practice it is highly doubtful whether most developing countries would have the administrative apparatus adequate to carry out such internal income transfers (apart from the political and social tensions that may be aroused by such action).

The compensation of net shortfalls would, by definition, involve smaller funds than similar compensation of gross shortfalls. Calculations for the period 1980–1984, for example, indicate that for all developing countries the total of net shortfalls was some 60 per cent of the corresponding gross total, for both the 4-year arithmetic average and the 3-year geometric average norms, and only slightly less (56 per cent) for the 5-year geometric average.[8] It is therefore, perhaps, no coincidence that this is one reason why industrialized countries

---

[5] Ending in the year prior to the year of shortfall calculation.

[6] Ending in the year of shortfall calculation. See UNCTAD 1984a for details.

[7] The need for a mechanism to offset adverse trends in export earnings was the rationale behind the proposal by Raúl Prebisch for a Supplementary Financing facility (see discussion in Ch. 3).

[8] UNCTAD 1984a: Table 1. The ratio of net to gross shortfalls for the 10-year trend, however, was as high as 87%.

generally favour the net concept, while the developing countries support the gross concept.

A third issue relates to the range of commodities for which shortfalls should be compensated. Clearly, petroleum would have to be excluded in any case if the amount of financing is to be kept to reasonable proportions. The main question is whether compensation should relate to total export shortfalls, or only to commodity export shortfalls. The argument in favour of using total exports as the criterion is the analogue of that for using net, rather than gross, commodity shortfalls, namely, that it is the total of export earnings which is relevant to a country's balance of payments situation, rather than export earnings from commodities alone. Thus, a shortfall for commodities, if exactly offset by an overage for, say, manufactures would leave total exports unchanged, so that there would be no justification in this case for balance of payments support.

This argument, however, does not dispose of the case for compensation based on commodity shortfalls alone. Where there are offsetting movements in commodities and manufactures, to take the above example, then by denying the exporting country any balance of payments support, the commodity sector which has suffered the export shortfall is also denied any relief, given that, as indicated earlier, governments of most developing countries will not be willing, or able, to tax domestic manufacturing industry in order to provide financial support, even on a temporary basis, to the commodity sector. On this argument, therefore, compensation for commodity shortfalls should be viewed in the context of the particular problems of commodity producers, rather than just as a pure external payments problem.[9]

A fourth major consideration relates to the unit of value in which shortfalls are to be compensated. Clearly, there would be some exchange rate risk involved if compensation were calculated in a single currency. In practice, both the current schemes use currency 'baskets' (the IMF using the SDR, while the European Community scheme is based on the ECU), which minimize the exchange rate risk. A more fundamental issue, as regards the unit of value, is whether compensation should relate to the current money value, or the real value, of export shortfalls. Both the IMF and EC schemes are based on current money values, so that in a period of inflation, when the prices of developing countries' imports are rising, the real value of a given amount of compensation will be declining. The reverse situation would apply in a period of falling import prices.

Thus, it is evident that the magnitude of an export shortfall will depend heavily on decisions by policy-makers in regard to all of these four issues. Decisions to use short-term norms, net shortfalls, and monetary units, in particular, will involve very substantially smaller shortfalls especially in an inflationary period than would the use of longer-term norms, gross shortfalls, and real values. In

---

[9] Of the two compensatory financing schemes currently in operation, one (the IMF facility) is based on shortfalls in total exports, while the other (the European Community's STABEX) is based on shortfalls in a selected list of commodities (see Sect. 4 below).

addition, the amount of shortfall is usually restricted by the use of 'thresholds' which operate to exclude small trade flows or small changes in shortfalls. All these decisions, which have technical and administrative aspects, are heavily influenced by broader economic and political considerations.

3. THE EFFECTS OF EXPORT EARNINGS SHORTFALLS ON ECONOMIC DEVELOPMENT

Since shortfalls arise from fluctuations in exports around a trend, however defined, the impact of export shortfalls on the economies of developing countries is closely related to that of export instability generally, which was discussed in Chapter 4. Following that earlier argument, the effects of export shortfalls can be divided into those relating to the domestic macro-economy; to the particular producing sector suffering the shortfall; and to the world economy in general.

As regards the domestic economy, an export shortfall will adversely affect the actual or potential rate of economic growth through its impact on the capacity to import. Since domestic investment in developing countries has a relatively high import-content, an export shortfall, if sufficiently large or prolonged, can be expected to lead to reduced levels of imports and investment, and consequently to reduced employment and income, unless the shortfall is made good by foreign loans (including compensatory financing) and/or by additional capital inflows. Indirect effects can also be substantial and adverse. Government revenue in developing countries is generally highly dependent on taxes on foreign trade, and export shortfalls often lead to pressure on governments to increase budgetary deficits, which also tends to accentuate inflationary pressures.

Much would depend, of course, on the magnitude and duration of an export shortfall and the extent to which it can be offset. It may also depend on whether the export trend itself is a favourable or unfavourable one. Countries whose principal export is on a downward trend (in terms of foreign exchange earnings) may find it much more difficult to borrow from the international banking system or to attract new private investment to help offset an export shortfall than countries whose main export is on an upward trend.

Since in many developing countries the export sector—particularly where estate agriculture or large-scale mining is important—provides a considerable proportion of domestic saving, a substantial or prolonged export shortfall is likely also to reduce the level of saving. In such cases, lower savings add to the contractionary impact of a fall in imports and investment. As mentioned earlier, proponents of the 'rational expectations' school advance the contrary thesis that higher export instability will lead to higher rates of domestic savings which, in turn, will promote higher levels of investment and growth in the economy. However, statistical tests for a sample of developing countries have shown that this assumption was not valid over the two decades up to 1983,[10] and it seems very doubtful as a proposition of general applicability.[11]

The adverse impact of a substantial or prolonged export shortfall on the commodity producers themselves could be much more severe, relatively, than that on the domestic economy as a whole. If not offset by internal transfer payments (e.g. by Marketing Boards or *caisses de stabilisation*), the loss of income involved in an export shortfall could, in many cases, seriously damage living standards of producers, reduce their savings potential, and cut expenditure on maintenance of productive capacity. Moreover, the empirical evidence indicates that a continuous succession of shortfalls and overages can greatly exacerbate uncertainties, and tends to perpetuate further cycles in production and thus in market prices.

Finally, as already discussed in Chapter 5, commodity market instability adversely affects the stability of the world economy as a whole. Successive periods of shortage and glut, reflecting the disjuncture between cycles in world demand and supply, also affect the security of supply of essential commodities for consuming countries. Moreover, commodity market instability, by destabilizing the demand of developing countries for the manufactured and other exports of the industrialized countries, also accentuates uncertainty and increases instability in the export sectors of these countries, and could well add to their inflationary pressures.[12]

Some indication of the likely global effects of a scheme of compensatory financing for shortfalls in the commodity export earnings of developing countries is given by an econometric exercise carried out by Professor Klein and Dr Bollino of the University of Pennsylvania. Their results showed that there would be significant positive, though modest, effects on the global economy in terms of growth rate, employment, and trade, without significant increases in inflation and interest rates, while there would be a net positive effect also for the developed countries.[13]

While the effect of export instability and export shortfalls on the economies of developing countries has remained a contentious issue in the academic literature, governments of both developed and developing countries have long been agreed that export shortfalls have a damaging effect on the economies of develop-

---

[10] See Ch. 4.

[11] The expectation that the size of export shortfalls is negatively associated with the growth rate of GDP is supported by the results of a cross-country regression (for 24 developing countries), with the annual average percentage change for 1980-4 in real per capita GDP (Y/N) as the dependent variable, and the annual average for 1980-3 of export earnings shortfall as a percentage of domestic investment (XS/I) as the explanatory variable (data from UNCTAD 1987b: Table 6). The results are:

$$Y/N = 0.176 - 0.155(XS/I) \quad (\bar{R}^2 = 0.304)$$
$$(-3.32)$$

with t value in brackets. The low value of $\bar{R}^2$ was to be expected, since it reflects country differences in population growth rates and in incremental capital-output ratios, as well as in the relationship between export shortfalls and GDP growth.

[12] See Ch. 5 for a fuller discussion.

[13] The results of the econometric simulations are summarized in UNCTAD 1984a: Annex VI.

ing countries, and that international arrangements for offsetting compensatory finance are necessary.

4. INTERNATIONAL COMPENSATORY FINANCING POLICIES

Hopes for a smooth expansion of international trade and economic growth in the immediate post-war years appeared to be dashed by the economic upheaval caused by the Korean War of the early 1950s. Sharp increases in the prices of key raw materials, reflecting mainly increases in demand for military uses, particularly in the United States, together with purchases for that country's strategic stocks,[14] were followed by equally drastic price declines as the war came to an end. In the meantime, many world commodity markets had been severely disrupted, with adverse effects on the stability of the foreign exchange earnings of a wide range of developing countries.

The export instability problem came under intensive discussion at the United Nations, which established an Expert Group in 1951 to consider appropriate measures to improve international economic stability.[15] This was followed, in 1953, by a second Expert Group on the issue.[16] Both these Expert Groups recommended the establishment of a compensatory financing scheme in the form of countercyclical lending by the IMF designed to offset pressures on the balances of payments of member countries resulting from fluctuations in the import demand of other members. One of the experts in the 1953 group, F.G. Olano, proposed the establishment of a system of mutual insurance whereby compensatory payments would be made out of an appropriate fund to countries experiencing 'unjust, unfair and inequitable' terms of trade.[17]

As Sidney Dell pointed out, these ideas were further developed by UN economists and subsequent Expert and Intergovernmental Groups, into a scheme for compensatory financing of export fluctuations. Then in May 1962 the UN Commission on International Commodity Trade (CICT) invited the IMF to present a report as to whether and in what way the Fund might undertake such a responsibility. It was as a result of this initiative on the part of the UN that the IMF established its Compensatory Financing Facility (CFF) in February 1963. Moreover, after it was established, the new Fund Facility was liberalized several times as a result of recommendations arising in UNCTAD.[18]

The IMF Compensatory Financing Facility

This Facility allows a member country to make a compensatory drawing provided that three conditions are met, viz. that an export earnings shortfall is of

---

[14] Demand for armaments production in the United States and Western Europe and for the strategic stockpile is estimated to have risen, as a proportion of world supplies, from 5-7% in 1950 to 27-31% in 1951 for aluminium; from 12-13 to 15-19% for copper; and from 9-10 to 15-18% for zinc. Comparable percentages for lead and tin, however, show declines from 1950 to 1951 (Economic Commission for Europe 1951: 82).
[15] United Nations 1951.   [16] United Nations 1953.
[17] Ibid. Appendix D.   [18] S. Dell 1985b.

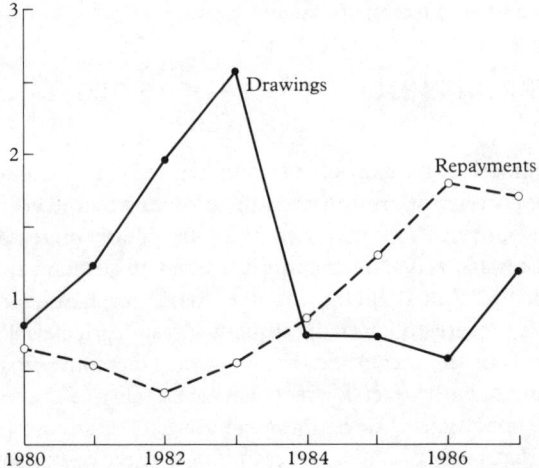

Fig 9.1. *Drawings and repayments of developing countries with the IMF Compensatory Financing Facility, 1980–7 (SDR billion).* Sources: *UNCTAD 1984a and 1987b*

a short-term nature and caused largely by circumstances beyond the country's control; that the member country has a balance of payments need for financial support; and that the country is willing to co-operate with the Fund to find, where required, appropriate solutions for its balance of payments difficulties. The maximum amount of outstanding drawings was originally set at 25 per cent of quota, but this was progressively raised to 50 per cent in 1966, 75 per cent in 1975, and 100 per cent in 1979.[19] In 1984, the drawing limit was reduced to 83 per cent of quota, the quotas themselves being generally increased at the same time.

As a result of the sharp squeeze on the external financial position of developing countries in the early 1980s, their drawings on the CFF rose substantially, from 1.0 billion SDR in 1980 to 1.2 billion in 1981, 1.5 billion in 1982, and, in the peak year 1983, to 2.6 billion (see Fig. 9.1).

In 1983, the Fund changed the conditions of drawing on the CFF in a drastic manner. Previously, countries drawing the first 50 per cent of quota under the Facility were not required to discuss with the Fund the appropriateness of their policies to deal with their balance of payments difficulties, but only to co-operate with the Fund 'where required'. After the 1983 decision, however, all drawings on the Facility were made conditional on the drawing country being ready to receive an IMF mission and 'to discuss, in good faith, the appropriateness of the member's policies' and to take action that gives 'a reasonable assur-

---

[19] In 1979, also, member countries were given the option of including earnings from tourism and workers' remittances in the calculation of export earnings.

ance that policies corrective of the member's balance of payments problems will be adopted'.[20] Thus even early tranches of drawings under the CFF became subject to strict conditionality, thereby depriving the IMF of the major part of its low-conditional resources.[21]

Following this new policy, there was a sharp fall in compensatory payments by the Fund to developing countries from 2.57 billion SDR in 1983 to 0.75 billion in 1984, though part of this decline no doubt reflected the recovery in import demand in some of the industrial countries.[22] Compensatory payments to developing countries remained slightly below the 1984 level in 1985, fell to under 0.6 billion SDR in 1986, but then rose to almost 1.2 billion SDR in 1987, followed by a further decline to 0.7 billion SDR in 1988 and to 0.35 billion SDR in 1989. Meanwhile, repayments of the loans under the IMF Facility had been rapidly increasing, and after 1985 there was a substantial net flow of funds from developing countries to the IMF under the CFF, totalling some 2 billion SDR over the three years 1985–7.

In 1988, the CFF was incorporated into a new Compensatory and Contingency Financing Facility (CCFF), though the basic provisions of the CFF were retained. Where an export shortfall (or, since 1981, an excess in cost of cereal imports) is the only source of balance of payments difficulty, the member country may continue to draw compensatory finance up to 83 per cent of quota (subject to a limit of 105 per cent of quota for drawings related to both export shortfall and cereal import costs). However, where balance of payments difficulties have arisen from external factors beyond the control of a member country, then – if contingency mechanisms have been involved at the country's request – financing is provided to cover part of the net effect on the balance of payments of unfavourable deviations in key variables such as export earnings, import prices, and international interest rates. The underlying purpose of the Contingency Facility is to maintain the momentum of adjustment programmes in the face of unfavourable external economic changes.[23] In all cases, the strict conditionality introduced in 1983 is retained, though greater flexibility has been allowed in its application.

The recent history of the IMF–CFF indicates that it has ceased to act as a countercyclical source of balance of payments support, which was the original intention behind the creation of this Facility. Instead, it has in recent years been operating in a procyclical manner, and has been fully integrated into the IMF system of conditionality.[24]

---

[20] See UNCTAD 1984a: Annex VII, p. 10.
[21] According to Dell, the Fund management had been applying the new conditionality policy for some time before the formal decision by the Executive Board in Sept. 1983 (S. Dell 1985b: 246).
[22] Ibid. 246.
[23] *IMF Survey: Supplement on the Fund* (Aug. 1989): 11–12.
[24] An analysis of IMF conditionality and of the effects of IMF-supported stabilization policies falls outside the scope of the present book. For an authoritative analysis see Killick 1984, Williamson 1983, and Taylor 1988.

The STABEX Scheme of the European Community

The STABEX scheme of compensatory financing was evolved by the European Community essentially as an alternative approach to the UNCTAD proposal for a Common Fund to finance market intervention by commodity agreements. STABEX provided the Community with an important initiative on commodity stabilization without commitment to financial disbursements for buffer stocks.[25]

STABEX differs from the IMF-CFF in several major respects. First, it is a regional arrangement, being established in the framework of the successive Lomé Conventions linking the European Community to a large number of developing countries in Africa, the Caribbean, and the Pacific (ACP countries).[26] Compensation is therefore related to shortfalls in earnings from exports to the European Community only, whereas the IMF scheme relates to exports to all countries. Second, the STABEX scheme relates to gross shortfalls for a selected list of agricultural products only,[27] whereas the IMF scheme relates to overall shortfalls for all exports, so that, in effect, it is on a net basis. Third, STABEX compensation is now, under Lomé IV, entirely in the form of grants,[28] whereas IMF compensation is in the form of loans subject to strict terms of repayment, including interest charges. Finally, STABEX compensation has been only mildly conditional under earlier Lomé Agreements, since while the use of the funds transferred was left open for the recipient government to decide, that decision had to conform to the general guidelines that financial flows should be maintained in the sector suffering the shortfall, while some or all of the funds could be used in other sectors to promote the diversification of the economy.[29] Under Lomé IV, conditionality has become a little stricter to ensure that STABEX funds are used in the affected sector.[30] This is, however, in sharp contrast to current IMF practice which, as already noted, insists on the right to propose changes in domestic economic policies before compensatory payments can be made.

The total fund available for STABEX compensation is, however, relatively small. The allocation for Lomé III, at 925 million ECU (roughly the same, in real terms, as the smaller allocations for Lomé I and II) represented 185 million ECU (or about $180 million) a year, to be shared among some 50 potential recipient countries. Under Lomé IV, the funding has been raised to 1.5 billion ECU over five years. In 1985, the EEC announced its intention to introduce a further

---

[25] Hewitt 1987. See also Guillaumont 1987.

[26] Four Lomé Conventions have been negotiated so far, Lomé I, II, III, and IV, covering the periods 1975–9, 1980–4, 1985–9, and 1990–9, respectively. Almost 70 ACP countries are signatories to Lomé IV, which has a renewable 5-year financial protocol.

[27] Iron ore was included under Lomé I and II, but not under Lomé III and IV.

[28] The least-developed ACP countries (which include more countries than those in the UN list) were exempt from repayment under earlier Lomé Agreements, while other ACP countries were required to repay only if the market recovered, and if other conditions were met; in practice, relatively little repayment was made.

[29] *Stabex: User's Guide*, Brussels, Commission of the European Communities, 1985.

stabilization scheme for the agricultural export earnings of those least-developed countries which are not in the ACP group. This new scheme, which began operation in 1987, has been allocated 50 million ECU over five years, Bangladesh being expected to be the principal beneficiary. However, disbursements under this scheme are not additional to the aid already allocated under the European Community budget to Asian and Latin American developing countries.

The importance of STABEX lies not so much in its effectiveness in offsetting export shortfalls (though it has been important in this respect for a few countries), but rather in the example it sets of an international mechanism for the rapid disbursement of funds to offset export shortfalls, with low conditionality.

Alternative or Additional Compensatory Financing Proposals

A considerable number of different proposals have been made by governments to improve the availability of compensatory finance.[31] An early proposal was one made in 1975 by the United States at the seventh Special Session of the UN General Assembly. This was to establish a new 'development security facility' to stabilize overall export earnings, as a replacement for the IMF-CFF. It was proposed that the new facility would 'give loans to sustain development programmes in the face of export fluctuations of up to $2.5 billion and possibly more in a single year, with a potential total in outstanding loans of $10 billion'.[32] However, this proposal was not pursued.

Of the other governmental proposals, that by the Federal Republic of Germany is the most articulated.[33] First published in 1978 and revised in 1985, its main features include: coverage of all developing countries (though the scheme could be confined to countries with a minimum of 50 per cent dependence on commodity exports); coverage of all non-fuel commodities on a net shortfall basis; fluctuations in export earnings below 10 per cent (2.5 per cent for the least developed countries) to be excluded; compensation of 70-80 per cent of shortfalls (100 per cent for least-developed) in the form of credits; repayments in up to 8-10 years, or earlier if export earnings had recovered; interest charges at slightly less than market rate, with concessionary rate for the least-developed; and establishment of a revolving fund (one-third as government contributions, the rest as loans) to finance the scheme.[34]

This proposal combines some features of both the IMF-CFF and STABEX. The overall net shortfall criterion is similar in concept to that of the CFF, but the German scheme is clearly aimed at commodity stabilization rather than short-term balance of payments support. Moreover, it reflects the STABEX approach

---

[30] Lomé IV Convention, reproduced in the *ACP-EEC Courier*, 120 (Mar.-Apr. 1990).
[31] Annex VIII of UNCTAD 1984*a* lists proposals by 10 countries (9 developed and 1 developing).
[32] GA 7th Special Session, verbatim record, 1 Sept. 1975.
[33] Most of the other proposals are confined to the least-developed and/or the poorest countries, or those heavily dependent on exports of commodities.
[34] A detailed discussion of the German proposals is given in Kebschull 1985; see also Hewitt 1987.

also in so far as there would be no strict conditionality on the use of compensatory funds. The German proposal has not, however, gained general support among other industrialized countries, one objection (by Canada) being that the benefits of the scheme would accrue largely to relatively few countries.

More recently, in early 1988, the Swiss government announced its intention to inaugurate a STABEX-type scheme for export earnings shortfalls of developing countries in their exports of agricultural commodities to Switzerland. Though Switzerland is a minor market for developing countries, this announcement implicitly acknowledges the need for a wider application of the principle of shortfall compensation.

The UNCTAD Proposal for an Additional Compensatory Financing Facility

As mentioned earlier, the UNCTAD Integrated Programme, adopted in 1976, contained specific provision for compensatory financing as one of several mechanisms to strengthen and stabilize international commodity markets.[35] The need for more adequate compensatory financing was discussed in greater depth at the 1983 UNCTAD VI session, which called for a detailed study on this issue.[36] An Expert Group, set up in 1984, proposed the establishment of a new facility, complementary to the IMF–CFF and STABEX, which the Group had found inadequate both in amount of funds available, and in a failure to reduce the instability of commodity supply.

Since the analysis of commodity instability made by the Expert Group had shown that commodity supply instability was a major cause of export earnings fluctuations,[37] and therefore of shortfalls, the key proposal of the experts was that a new facility was required in order to finance measures aimed at reducing the instability of commodity supply in the producing countries. The proposed facility would cover all developing countries; would relate only to shortfalls in commodity export earnings; would compensate for shortfalls in *real* terms (unlike the two existing schemes); and would make compensatory payments conditional on the adoption of measures by the recipient country to reduce supply instability in a manner that is also consistent with stability in the world commodity economy.[38]

The Expert Group also made recommendations on the institutional aspects of a new commodity-specific compensatory facility. It advised against the establishment of a new institution, and agreed that the Common Fund, when it came into operation, would be a suitable location for the new facility. However, if the Common Fund did not become operational within a reasonable period of time, the experts recommended that a separate facility for this purpose within the World Bank should be considered.[39]

[35] See Chapter 7.
[36] Resolution 157(VI) in UNCTAD 1984*i*.
[37] See Sect. 1 of this chapter.
[38] UNCTAD 1984*a*: para. 89. The experts also made proposals regarding the financing of such a new facility, terms of repayment, concessions to the least-developed countries, etc.
[39] Ibid. paras. 118–23.

The proposed link between compensatory finance and the adoption of supply stabilization measures by developing countries is an innovation which distinguishes the Expert Group proposal sharply from the objectives of either the IMF–CFF or STABEX. The latter operate to *offset*, to a greater or lesser extent, the *effects* of instability, whereas the Expert Group's scheme would operate, to the extent it is successful, by *reducing one of the primary causes* of instability itself. The two approaches are essentially complementary and could be regarded as mutually supporting, in so far as a reduction in supply instability, by reducing the incidence of export earnings shortfalls, would require a lower level of offsetting compensatory finance from the conventional schemes. However, measures to reduce the sources of supply instability[40] are likely also to have an enduring influence in moderating supply variations over the longer term, whereas the conventional compensation approach deals purely with the temporary manifestations of instability.

Even before the Expert Group began its work, a sharp division of views had emerged among the industrialized countries as regards the need for an additional compensatory financing facility. Many of these countries – France, the Federal Republic of Germany, Finland, Norway, and Switzerland – were in favour of examining this need in depth, including the need for concessional terms for the least-developed countries. However, other developed countries, particularly the United States and Canada, were strongly opposed.

The principal argument advanced by the latter countries was that a new low-conditionality financing facility would allow developing countries with export shortfalls to avoid drawing on the high-conditionality financing that might be available from the IMF, and thus delay the necessary corrections to domestic economic policies. The Canadian statement added that a commodity-specific scheme would reduce the incentive for diversification and further processing, and would discourage commodity producers in developing countries from responding adequately to market signals.[41]

This line of argument, however, implicitly rejects the distinction between payments difficulties arising from falls in export earnings below a short-term trend (with which the IMF–CFF was originally designed to deal), and the longer-term need for diversification and restructuring of the economy (with which bilateral and multilateral channels of development finance are particularly concerned). By insisting on strict conditionality on both counts, involving major shifts in domestic economic and social policies, this argument has led in many developing countries to excessive reductions in living standards and in domestic

---

[40] The source of supply instability identified by the Expert Group included producers' responses regarding future production to current prices and income fluctuations; variations in the costs and availabilities of production inputs; and the incidence of disease and other natural occurrences. (See statement by Dr Arjun Sengupta in UNCTAD 1985c, para. 20.)

[41] These arguments were included in their comments on UNCTAD Resolution 157 (VI) (see UNCTAD 1984a: Annex IX).

investments.[42] Such changes generally tend to make the necessary longer-term structural shifts more, rather than less, difficult.

A related argument put forward was that the establishment of a new facility would duplicate the activities of existing institutions and would thus dilute their effectiveness. The analysis of the operations of the IMF–CFF and of STABEX made by the UNCTAD Expert Group showed, however, that the existing compensatory facilities, apart from being inadequate in amount, do not, in fact, address the causes of supply instability. Moreover, supply adjustment schemes to be financed by the proposed new facility were not necessarily related to long-term adjustment issues such as are addressed by World Bank structural adjustment lending.[43] Thus, a new commodity-specific facility would fill an important gap in existing arrangements.

The argument that a new facility would dilute the effectiveness of existing institutions is to a large extent another version of the first argument about conditionality. However, it also implies that a new compensatory financing scheme – especially if it were lodged in UNCTAD's Common Fund – could undermine the IMF's present role in overseeing policy changes in developing countries, and as the focal point of the international monetary system. In other words, this line of thought gives priority to the financial disciplines and domestic policy changes required by strict IMF and World Bank conditionality over the need for financing of measures designed to reduce short-term supply instability in the commodity sectors of developing countries.

The Expert Group's report provoked considerable comment by a number of countries, revealing a division of views both among developed countries and among developing countries. Of the former group, both Japan and the United Kingdom expressed opposition to the idea of an additional commodity-specific scheme, the German Federal Republic advanced its own scheme (which was referred to earlier), while the Nordic countries generally approved the proposal, though they felt that more analysis of the scheme was required, particularly of the interplay between supply and demand factors. The interrelationships between supply and demand were also cited by a number of developing countries as a reason why the proposal for a community-specific scheme aimed only at reducing the instability of supply was incomplete and not likely to be effective. Moreover, some governments felt that some part of supply instability was simply a reflection of instability in demand, and that the Expert Group had not taken sufficiently into account the interrelationships of supply, demand, and prices.

The Expert Group's report was discussed in detail by an Intergovernmental Group of Experts, convened in 1986, which issued its final report in 1989. This latter Group, which benefited from contributions from the IMF, the World Bank, and the European Community, reached agreement that virtually all developing countries had experienced sizeable shortfalls in their commodity

---

[42] See e.g. the WIDER studies reviewed in Taylor 1988.
[43] Sengupta, in UNCTAD 1985c, para. 17.

export earnings, which had a severe negative impact on economic and social development; that there was a significant difference between their total shortfalls and the compensatory finance available from the existing schemes; and that compensatory financing could be commodity-related and thereby contribute to rehabilitation and diversification of the commodity sector. It also recommended that developed countries, other than the European Community and Switzerland, be invited to consider the possibility of introducing commodity-related compensatory financing schemes.[44]

However, when this report was considered at the Trade and Development Board in March 1990, strong opposition to the proposal for a new facility was again expressed by the United States and Canada. Both countries maintained that export earnings shortfalls were a balance of payments and macro-economic issue, and not a purely sectoral one, and that accordingly any compensatory financing facility was a matter for the IMF and not UNCTAD.[45] This general opposition to the concept of a commodity-related scheme, as well as to the possibility of compensatory financing being undertaken by an agency outside the IMF, was endorsed by a number of other developed countries, including Australia and the United Kingdom. Though the developing countries, together with China and some smaller developed countries, supported the conclusions of the Intergovernmental Group, a consensus decision was ultimately arrived at to keep the issue 'under review in UNCTAD'.[46]

Thus, the larger developed countries in effect ensured the continuing predominance of the IMF in the area of compensatory financing, and avoided the danger, as it seemed to them, of creating a new financial facility which could undermine the effectiveness of the IMF and which, if it was established as a third window in the Common Fund, would thereby enhance the role of the latter in the management of the global economy.

Commodity Risk Management

An alternative approach to offsetting short-term shortfalls in foreign exchange earnings from commodity exports has been developed in recent years, using new kinds of financial instruments involving options, swaps, and commodity-based bonds, as well as more traditional futures and forward contracts. These instruments now allow for hedging against commodity price falls beyond one year. The World Bank began a programme in 1989 to assist developing countries in using international financial markets to manage the risks inherent in their commodity export trade.[47] Hedging activity of this type should prove a useful addition to the compensatory schemes of the IMF and European Community, though none of these approaches deals (or deals adequately) with the underlying causes of supply instability in the main international commodity markets.

---

[44] UNCTAD 1989b, Annex II.   [45] UNCTAD 1990d: Suppl. 1A.
[46] Ibid. Suppl. 1.   [47] World Bank 1989b: 12.

III
LONGER-TERM ISSUES

10
The Structure and Control of International Commodity Markets

1. THE MAIN ENTERPRISES AND THEIR TRADING CHANNELS

In many of the major primary commodity markets, particularly those for minerals and metals, the dominant economic forces are large transnational corporations (TNCs) of Western industrial countries, often operating on a global scale. Many of these TNCs act as oligopsonists in their purchases of commodities from developing countries or, as vertically integrated entities, control both the production and trade of developing (and often of developed) countries in particular commodities. At the same time, governments – both of developed and of developing countries – have been playing an increasing role in influencing the general terms and conditions of international commodity trade.

For such commodity markets, a realistic analysis must therefore take large enterprises, typically the transnationals, as the 'representative firm', rather than the atomistic firm of neoclassical theory, which cannot by itself influence market prices.[1] The principal channels in which commodities are traded internationally are shown in Table 10.1, which distinguishes the role of the TNCs and, for a number of commodities, state trading enterprises. The main trading channels are (i) 'arm's length' trade, i.e. sales between independent enterprises at market-determined prices; (ii) sales under long-term contracts (which normally contain provisions for prices to be adjusted with changes in market conditions); and (iii) shipments between different parts of the same transnational (intra-TNC trade), or between affiliated enterprises (related-party trade).

For many commodities, the bulk of world trade is handled by a small number of multi-commodity trading corporations, which are interposed between the producers in exporting countries and the consumers in importing countries. These powerful trading conglomerate transnationals are generally in a position to influence market prices by the volume of their operations on the spot and futures markets. In some commodities, state or parastatal agencies participate directly in international trading (though in a number of cases TNCs manage nationalized productive enterprises, or market their output under contract), while governments of many developing countries are also generally involved in regulating and monitoring the terms and conditions of private long-term contracts between domestic firms and TNCs, particularly in the minerals and metals sector.

---

[1] This section is based on the discussion in Maizels 1984.

Table 10.1. The principal channels of trade in commodities exported by developing to developed countries.

Developing Countries	Developed countries		
	TNCs	Other non-government enterprises	Governments
TNCs (branches, subsidiaries, and affiliates)	Intra-firm and related party trade	Arm's length trade	(i) Long-term supply contracts (ii) Arm's length trade
Other non-government enterprises	(i) Long-term supply contracts (ii) Arm's length trade	Arm's length trade	Arm's length trade
Governments (including state trading enterprises)	(i) Barter and countertrade deals (ii) Long-term supply contracts (iii) Sales under management or marketing contracts	Arm's length trade	[Agreements or arrangements affecting trade flows, e.g. international commodity agreements, market access arrangements]

The relative importance of the major trading channels varies among the different commodity markets, and there has also been substantial change over the past few decades. Reliable estimates are, however, available for only a few commodities. For iron ore, a study for the late 1960s showed that roughly 40 per cent of world trade was intra-firm, another 40 per cent was covered by long-term contracts (of up to 20 years), and the remaining 20 per cent was sold on an 'arm's length' basis.[2] The market for bauxite/alumina/aluminium is even more dominated by large TNCs, which are vertically integrated from bauxite mining in developing countries to smelting and fabrication of aluminium products in developed countries, the six largest of these TNCs controlling over one-half of world capacity in the industry outside the former socialist countries.[3]

TNC dominance is also found in a number of agricultural products. In sisal,

[2] Bosson and Varon 1977.
[3] Labys 1980.

for example, while free market sales account for about two-thirds of world trade, over half the total (or 70 per cent of the free market) is handled by four or five large trading corporations.[4] In bananas, almost 70 per cent of total world trade is in the hands of only three transnationals,[5] in cocoa one transnational accounts for a quarter of world trade, while in diamonds—perhaps the extreme case—one transnational controls the marketing of 80 per cent of the world's rough diamonds. Data for the United States reveal that for a range of important commodities—cotton, rubber, bananas, bauxite—two-thirds or more of total imports from developing countries consist of 'related party' trade,[6] while for some other commodities—tea, iron ore, manganese, and certain tropical timbers—the 'related party' share was over 20 per cent.

On the other hand, there are many commodities—particularly those of agricultural origin—where market conditions, at least on the supply side, apparently approximate to those assumed by theory based on fully competitive markets, i.e. there are a large number of sellers, no one of whom can influence the price by his own actions. This appears on the surface especially true for commodities sold by an auction system (e.g. tea and tobacco). More detailed studies, however, have revealed that auction prices may be substantially influenced by the (possibly collusive) actions of a limited number of large-scale buyers.[7] For commodities with terminal markets, prices are influenced—and often manipulated—by transactions in futures contracts (often reflecting speculative activity) as well as by the supply/demand balance for the physical product. All commodity markets are sensitive to expectations about future trends in supply and demand, thus allowing traders or speculators with 'inside' knowledge to reap disproportionate gains.[8]

The channels and terms of international commodity trade are also subject to change or modification as a result of government actions or intergovernmental agreements. International commodity agreements, even if directed solely to price stabilization, may also in certain circumstances significantly influence the price trend,[9] and thereby the division of benefit between exporters and importers. But the major influence of government action up to the present has arisen from measures which change the terms or conditions of market access for the commodity exports of developing countries. The sugar policy of the European Community is perhaps the outstanding example of this, preferential access for the associated ACP countries being combined in this case with severely restricted access for other developing countries and greatly expanded domestic sugar production. The European Community has in recent years become the largest sugar

---

[4] UNCTAD 1981*b*.
[5] UNCTAD 1974*b*.
[6] Helleiner 1979.
[7] UNCTAD 1975.
[8] Cocoa is rather a special case, since the largest trading corporation is also the source of the most authoritative forecast of the current crop.
[9] See the discussion in Ch. 4, Sect. 3(*c*)(i); also Maizels 1982.

exporting area, surplus sugar being sold on the world market at subsidized prices. As a result of the protection of domestic sugar production in the developed countries, the world market has become subject to wide price fluctuations and with a significantly lower average return for developing-country producers than would have obtained in the absence of the market access restriction.[10]

The relative importance of different trading channels is associated in a general manner with the market structure for a given traded commodity. In this context, market structure denotes the institutional organization of supply and demand, with particular reference to the resultant degree of competition or monopoly on each side of the market. Market structure, in turn, is a central determinant of the process of price formation and of the division of the benefits of trade.

Where there is a high degree of concentration (one or a few entities) on both sides of the market, then price will reflect the relative bargaining strengths of buyer and seller within limits set by the underlying cost and demand conditions. Where, however, foreign trade is between different firms, or subsidiaries, of the same TNC, the recorded export price then becomes an internal transfer price, which is open to manipulation in the interests of maximizing the TNC's global profits. The actual situation in particular cases can, however, be a complex one, with the recorded export price being only one among several instruments used to attain the TNC's profit objectives. If, for example, a TNC subsidiary in a developing country imports equipment, intermediate products, or specialist services from its parent company, it can reduce its declared profits by overvaluing such imports, by undervaluing its commodity exports, or by some combination of the two.

One major incentive for the manipulation of foreign trade prices in the intra-firm transactions of a TNC arises because of differences in tax rates (import duties, corporation and profit taxes, etc.) in the different countries in which it operates. For any given set of tax rates (and tax allowances) in those countries there is a corresponding pattern of declared profits that will minimize the TNC's global tax payments. Once the desired level of declared profits has been determined for the operations of a TNC subsidiary in a developing country, appropriate adjustments can be made in its transfer prices to arrive at this desired level. A different incentive for the manipulation of transfer prices would arise if a TNC wished to repatriate part, or all, of its capital investment in a subsidiary in a developing country while avoiding official restrictions on capital outflow. This could be done by undervaluing exports from the subsidiary, and overvaluing its imports, thereby accumulating credits abroad.

To the extent that tax rates on TNC operations in developing countries tend to be higher than in 'home' (developed) countries, and TNC investment remains susceptible to possible nationalization or other uncertainties, there would be powerful incentives for the undervaluation of exports from developing countries,

---

[10] See Ch. 12 for further discussion of the impact of agricultural protection on world prices, and Appendix Table A.6 for trends in sugar prices since 1980.

thus minimizing the relevant tax receipts of these countries.[11] However, where developing-country tax rates are low, TNCs would have an incentive to overvalue their exports so as to minimize their tax payments in their home countries.

Transfer pricing manipulation appears to have been particularly widespread in the 1950s and 1960s. According to one estimate, for example, Jamaica lost approximately $84 million in tax revenue as a result of artificially low transfer prices for bauxite shipped to parent corporations in North America during the period 1953–66.[12] Transfer pricing abuses also appear to have been widespread in intra-firm transactions of chemicals and pharmaceutical transnationals. One study in the late 1970s showed that imports into India of a selection of chemical intermediates were overpriced by between 124 and 147 per cent.[13]

It is important to distinguish between TNC involvement in commodity production and processing in developing countries, and their involvement in downstream activities in the international marketing, transport, and distribution of developing-country produce, since changes in market structures have been very different in these two sectors.

At the production and processing stages, TNC involvement has been substantially reduced over the past decade or two as a result of a considerable expansion of state ownership or control of domestic capacity, particularly in the minerals sector. In petroleum, the 'seven majors' dominated crude production before 1972, but the situation changed dramatically thereafter. While TNCs accounted for about 95 per cent of world crude petroleum output (outside the socialist countries) in 1970, the proportion had fallen to 45 per cent by 1979 (the share of the seven majors falling even more sharply from 61 to 25 per cent).[14]

Among non-fuel minerals, the proportion of mine production controlled by TNCs had fallen by the early 1980s to some 40 per cent for bauxite and 27 per cent for copper; and to 22 per cent for iron ore exports from developing countries.[15] For manganese ore, the greater part of exports entering international trade is produced by TNCs, though about one-half of output is produced by state enterprises.[16] For the metal-processing industries, the TNC shares in the early 1980s were between 40 and 50 per cent for aluminium, copper, and tin,[17] having been substantially reduced from the position a decade earlier.

---

[11] One method of avoiding this result, and of expanding tax revenues from TNC operations, would be to relate tax not to the value of commodity production or exports, but to the value of the final product on consumer markets. This method has been in use for a number of years by Jamaica in taxing the production of bauxite by TNCs in that country. Another method would be the use of the unitary system of taxation, under which profits realized in the host country would be deemed to be the same fraction of worldwide profits of a TNC as sales in (including exports from) the host country are of worldwide sales.

[12] Girvan 1987: 731.

[13] *Economic and Political Weekly*, Bombay (30 Oct. 1976), quoted in Clairmonte and Cavanagh 1981: 149.

[14] UNCTAD 1985: Table v.1.

[15] Girvan 1987: Table 1.

[16] UNCTAD 1984b.

[17] Girvan 1987: Table 1.

Among agricultural commodities, the greater part of Central American production of bananas is owned by three United States TNCs, while in some other areas, notably in the Philippines, the TNCs have utilized purchasing contracts with local producers which, in effect, allows the TNCs full control over banana-growing operations.[18] Similar purchase contracts in other developing countries have been adopted for some other agricultural produce, such as tobacco. United Kingdom TNCs still retain an important share in tea production, particularly in India and Kenya, while over one-quarter of sisal production is in the hands of TNCs.[19] However, where foreign-owned plantations have been affected by land re-distribution or nationalization, joint ventures between TNCs and domestic enterprises have become widespread. One example is the sugar industry, where TNC ownership has been reduced to only about 2 per cent of all commercial sugar-cane mills in developing countries.[20]

The role of TNCs has, however, remained dominant in the downstream marketing, transport, and distribution system. The evidence for the late 1970s and early 1980s shows a very high corporate concentration of sales for a number of important commodities. Among foods and beverages, a small number of TNCs account for 85 per cent or more of world trade in grains, coffee, and cocoa, while of the agricultural raw materials a similar high concentration in trade is found for timber, cotton, tobacco, and jute among agricultural raw materials, and for copper, iron ore, and bauxite among non-fuel minerals (see Table 10.2).

Thus over the past decade or two the erosion of the control by TNCs over commodity production in developing countries has been accompanied by the maintenance, and often reinforcement, of their presence in the marketing and distribution system. Producer countries have generally been unable to enhance their participation in the marketing and distribution of their commodity exports, let alone succeed in some form of regulation of TNC downstream activities. This inability has been the main reason for the relatively small share of the final prices paid by consumers in developed countries which accrues to the developing exporting countries.[21] For raw cotton and tobacco, for example, the grower's price in about 1980 represented only 4–8 and 6 per cent, respectively, of the final product price (cotton clothing or cigarettes). For bananas, producing countries received about 14 per cent of the retail price, while for jute goods the proportion was 11–24 per cent. For packeted tea, the grower's share of the United Kingdom retail price (in 1977) was 47 per cent, but for tea-bags sold in the United States (1978), the grower's share was only 15 per cent.[22]

While developing countries have been unable to make significant inroads into the existing marketing and distribution networks, which remain very largely in the hands of the TNCs, they have devoted their efforts, with some success, to

---

[18] Girvan 1987: 717. See also UNCTAD 1974b.
[19] UNCTAD 1984d and e.
[20] Girvan 1987: 716–17.
[21] On this point, see the discussion in UNCTC 1985: 150.
[22] Girvan 1987: Table 6.

Table 10.2. Estimated shares of commodity trade controlled by largest TNCs, 1983

	Value of exports ($ billion)		Proportion marketed by 3-6 largest TNCs[b] (%)
	Developing countries	World[a]	
Foods and beverages			
Wheat	1.8	17.9	85–90
Coarse grains	2.5	14.3	85–90[c]
Sugar[d]	8.1	10.8	60
Coffee	8.7	9.4	85–90
Rice	1.7	3.6	70
Cocoa beans	1.8	2.0	85
Tea	1.5	2.0	80
Bananas	1.3	1.4	70–5
Agricultural raw materials			
Non-coniferous timber	6.1	8.9	90[e]
Cotton	2.7	6.5	85–90
Hides and skins	0.4	4.2	25
Tobacco	1.9	4.2	85–90
Natural rubber	3.2	3.3	70–5
Jute and jute products	0.7	0.9	85–90[f]
Minerals, ores, and metals			
Mineral fuels	227.2	378.6	75
Copper	5.1	8.4	80–5
Iron ore	2.6	6.5	90–5
Bauxite and alumina	1.6	3.5	80–5[g]
Tin	1.8	2.2	75–80
Phosphate rock	0.9	1.6	50–60

[a] Including re-exports.
[b] In a few cases, up to 15 TNCs account for the bulk of the market.
[c] Maize (corn) only.
[d] Raw and refined.
[e] All forest products.
[f] Raw jute.
[g] Bauxite.

Source: Clairmonte and Cavanagh 1988.

increasing their bargaining position as host countries in negotiations with TNCs engaged in local production or processing, particularly in the mining sector.

2. THE ELEMENTS OF BARGAINING POWER

With the increasing importance of TNCs in the world economy, and in the economies of developing countries, the role of 'market power', as expressed in the relative bargaining strengths of the TNCs and host country governments or enterprises, has become a central feature of the process of price determination, and of the division of benefit, in a wide range of commodities exported by developing countries.

This is particularly the case for minerals, where TNC operations in developing countries are typically conducted under the terms of contracts with governments. In such cases, the 'price' of the mineral export is not simply the f.o.b. or transfer price, but is rather to be interpreted as including royalty and other tax payments on production or export. Thus, for the TNC, the relevant 'price', in the sense of net unit return, is the product price less the sum of the extraction cost and royalty/tax payments, whereas for the host country, it is the retained unit value, consisting of royalty/tax receipts plus payments to domestic factors.[23]

The relationship between the initial net return to the TNC and that to the host country can be substantially altered by subsequent renegotiation of the terms and conditions of TNC operations, or by unilateral action by the host government – for example, by increasing the royalty or tax on profits. Alternatively, the host government can buy part of the equity of a TNC subsidiary, or even majority, or full, control. However, where the international marketing of minerals is contracted out (there are several examples of the marketing of minerals produced by newly nationalized mines being contracted out to the same TNCs that had previously owned the mines), there could be heavy losses for the nationalized enterprise if mineral prices are stagnant or declining while TNC marketing fees remain high.

When one turns from price (or net return) to the wider concept of the 'gains from trade', there is a considerable variety of indirect effects of TNC operations to be taken into account, including 'backward-linkage' effects on the domestic economy, 'income spread' effects, etc. Here again there may be scope for bargaining, since the host country government can try to ensure that a new TNC investment will have maximum linkage effects and minimum leakages to the foreign sector.

Given that bargaining power plays a major role in price formation and the division of benefit in a range of primary commodity markets, it is useful to hypothesize the general form of the relationship involved. The curve in Figure 10.1 illustrates what seems to be a reasonable first hypothesis, assuming for the moment that the 'proportion of the benefits of trade retained by the developing country' and the 'relative bargaining power of the developing country and TNCs' can each be accurately assessed on a scale from 0 to 100. The intercept a on the vertical axis represents an extreme situation where domestic interests in a developing country have zero bargaining power, so that the terms and conditions of TNC operations in that country are determined solely by the TNC concerned. In this situation, local costs would represent little more than subsistence wage levels plus local materials used. Government taxes borne by the TNC are also

---

[23] See Brodsky and Sampson 1980 for an exposition of the concept of retained value.

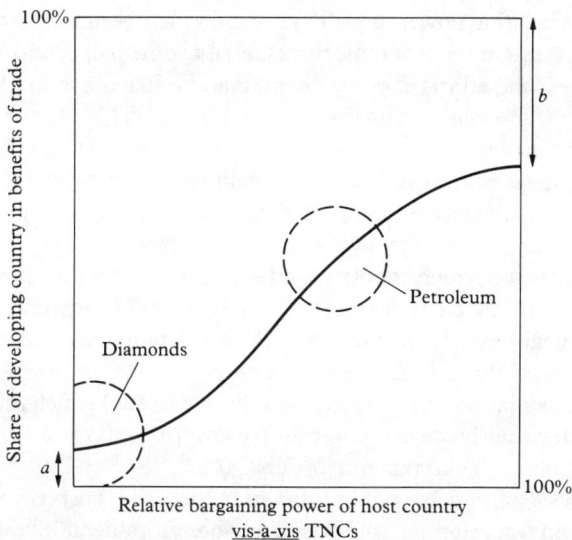

Fig. 10.1. *Hypothetical relationship between bargaining power and the division of the benefits of trade*

likely to be minimal, government expenditures being devoted largely to the provision of the necessary infrastructural facilities. Diamond purchases in African countries by the De Beers organization would seem to approximate to this situation, as would mining operations by TNCs in Namibia under South Africa's rule. An analogous situation would arise in politically independent developing countries where transnational corporations arrange contract prices through corrupt intermediaries; in such cases, the payment of bribes is, in effect, in exchange for the virtual elimination of the bargaining position of the host countries.[24]

At the other extreme, intercept *b* represents the minimum profit accruing to a TNC operating in a developing country (measured as a proportion of the benefits of trade) which will allow it to continue its operations.[25] It is difficult to envisage a situation in which TNCs have zero bargaining power, but there could well be situations in which individual TNCs have very little bargaining power *vis-à-vis* a group of developing countries with closely co-ordinated production policies.

Certainly, the OPEC countries still retain considerable bargaining strength *vis-à-vis* the petroleum TNCs, provided that they maintain a unified strategy. Action by OPEC during the 1970s shifted the position of petroleum in Figure 10.1 from a position on the lower part of the curve before 1973 to a considerably more favourable position for the producing countries in terms of their share of the

---

[24] It is not suggested that corruption in foreign trade is confined to developing countries.
[25] The two intercepts, *a* and *b*, need not, or course, be equal.

benefit. The bargaining power of OPEC has, however, been very largely eroded since 1980 as a result of the economic recession, the growth of production by non-OPEC countries, and efforts at energy conservation. Bauxite is another example of a commodity whose position on the curve in Figure 10.1 has been shifted quite substantially by action on the part of host country governments.

What, then, determines the relative bargaining strengths of the two sides? Clearly, there are many factors involved, their relative importance no doubt varying substantially from one commodity to another, as well as varying over time, and depending also on which countries and which TNCs are involved. However, it is useful for analytical purposes to group the elements of bargaining power into three broad categories, viz. factors specific to the individual commodity concerned, those specific to the host country—including, in particular, its macroeconomic situation and prospects—and those (if any) which relate to international action, either by developing-country governments (or other entities) or by developed-country governments (or TNCs).[26]

In his analysis of the bargaining situation between host governments in mineral-exporting developing countries and foreign mineral-investing TNCs, Labys[27] distinguishes nine relevant factors, all of which relate to the characteristics of the particular commodity market structure in question. These nine factors, which are listed first in the right-hand panel of Figure 10.2, relate essentially to the bargain struck between host governments and TNCs on the terms and conditions of new investment in mining, and on the bases for revisions of existing mining contracts.[28]

The degree of dependence of a country on the export of a particular commodity is relevant, since the higher the dependence, the more vulnerable is the government of that country in bargaining with a foreign enterprise. If a new mine involves a large initial capital investment, in relation to a country's financial resources available for investment, this by itself will tend to strengthen the bargaining position of the foreign investing enterprise. However, once a large investment is made by a TNC, the balance of bargaining power will shift, thus allowing the host country to extract more favourable terms.[29] When the technology involved is complex and changeable, it may be available only from one, or relatively few, TNCs which gives the latter an important bargaining lever. On the other hand, it may be possible for a host government to play one TNC off against another in order to obtain more favourable terms. When the

---

[26] A broadly similar, though more comprehensive, conceptual framework to that presented here has been developed by the United Nations Centre on Transnational Corporations jointly with the United Nations regional Economic Commissions. The UN schema covers political factors in host countries (such as the political philosophy of the government), the world political order (including decolonization), and the world economic and information orders, in addition to the more specifically commodity-related aspects considered here. The UN schema is also elucidated by Girvan 1987.
[27] Labys 1980.
[28] The following discussion of these nine factors is based essentially on Labys 1980.
[29] In extreme cases, this could precipitate a repatriation by a TNC of its original investment.

Commodity Market Structure and Control

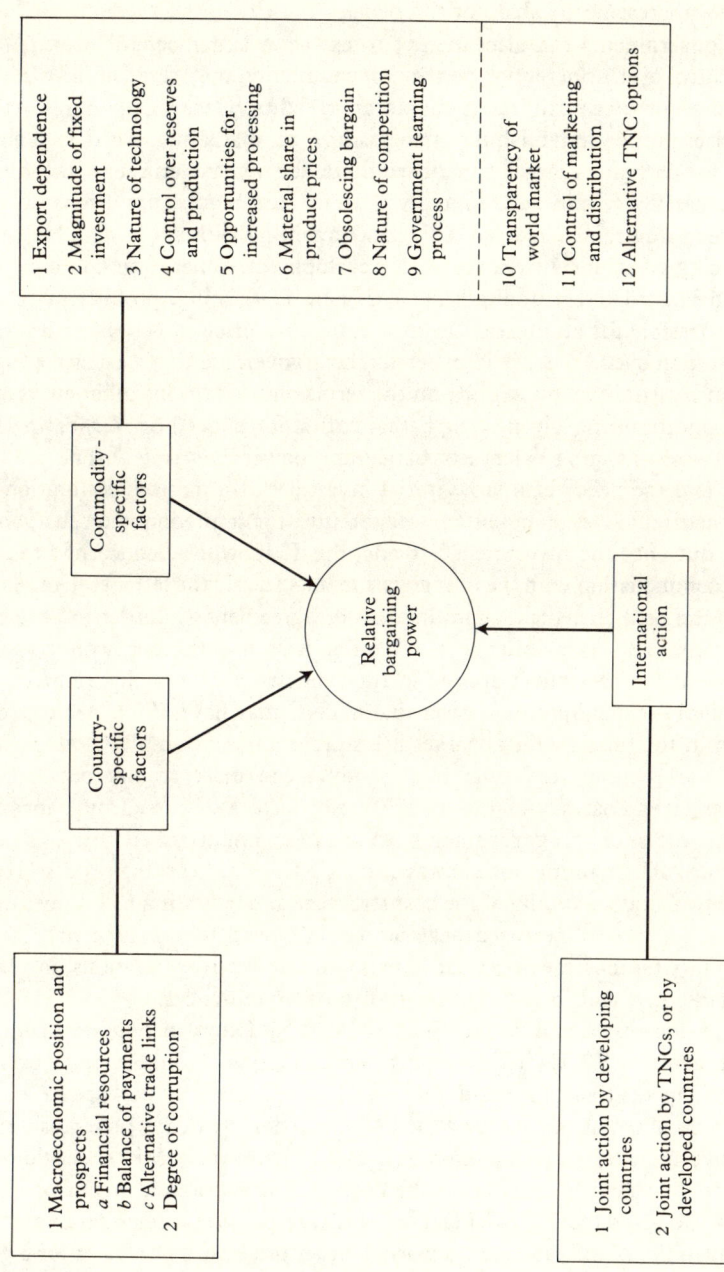

Fig. 10.2. *The elements of bargaining power between TNCs and governments and enterprises of developing countries*

technology involved is simple, stable, and diffused, the host country has a better chance of increasing its share of the benefit.

Host governments can also attempt to extract a larger benefit by extending their control over mineral reserves and/or production by foreign enterprises, for example, by restricting the latter's exploration rights, by taking up shares in these enterprises, or by establishing state trading or marketing entities. Another avenue for deriving a larger benefit would be for host governments to promote local processing of minerals. In appropriate circumstances, provisions for such local processing can be evolved, either in bargaining with a mining TNC, or by introducing fiscal incentives for such development. Where the commodity in question is a relatively unimportant cost item in the final product price, it is usually possible for an increase in the commodity price to be passed on to the final user. In such cases, it is easier for host governments to extract a higher 'price' in bargaining with a TNC on the terms and conditions of a new project.

The concept of the 'obsolescing bargain', first introduced by Vernon in 1971, relates to the changing balance of bargaining power over time.[30] The presence of risk, and the need for a large initial investment (in mining exploration and infrastructure), gives a potential foreign investor a predominant bargaining power. But once the investment is made, the TNC will be concerned to come to an accommodation with the host government – should the latter seek to renegotiate the original terms and conditions of the agreement – in order to protect its investment. The bargaining strength of a host government would also be increased if new suppliers appear in the domestic market, thus reducing the oligopolistic or monopolistic power that a TNC may have. The degree of competition in the final product market is also relevant, since a TNC which has a strong market position for its final product can more readily pass on cost increases to end-users. Finally – in the list of factors discussed by Labys – the learning process of host governments can also be an important element in shifting the balance of bargaining power away from TNCs. The 'learning process' relates to improved understanding of the cost-structure and operating techniques of the industry, as well as increased negotiating skills, and this in turn provides an opportunity for increased host participation in productive operations, in control over marketing, and in the regulation of profit remittances.

In addition to these nine factors elaborated by Labys in relation to mining developments by TNCs in developing countries, there would seem to be some further elements that can usefully be identified, particularly perhaps in relation to contractual arrangements between TNCs and domestic enterprises (as distinct from governments) in developing countries. In Figure 10.2, three such additional elements are listed. First, there is the degree of 'transparency' in the operation of the world market for a particular commodity, especially as regards the differential availability of information on world market prices and prospects for a given

---

[30] Vernon 1971.

commodity. Very often, domestic producers in a developing country do not know what the final prices to consumers in developed countries are, let alone being equipped to estimate the probable future trends of prices. In such situations an oligopsonistic TNC has considerable room for manoeuvre in setting a buying price favourable to itself.

Asymmetry also often exists in the availability of information to a host government and to an interested foreign corporation in regard to the dimensions and quality of local resources, reflecting the technical, research, and marketing expertise of the foreign interests concerned. Equally, when a developing country wishes to invest in commodity processing plants, there is often a lack of knowledge about the relevant market structures—which often limit access of processed commodities to major markets—as well as about the costs and benefits of alternative technological options. Some developing countries have, however, created some countervailing power by establishing Technology Information Centres which provide relevant information to domestic enterprises.

Second, the nature of competition in the international marketing and distribution system for commodity exports of developing countries can also influence relative bargaining strengths. Where international marketing channels are virtually in the control of a few TNCs, the domestic enterprise in a developing country has little alternative but to sell its output through the established channels. In some cases, however, the established channels can be bypassed, at least to some extent, for example by selling direct to retail stores or other end-users in developed countries, thus reducing the bargaining strength of TNC marketing and distribution entities. Third, TNC bargaining strength in a particular developing country will depend *inter alia* on the TNC's alternative options for concluding contracts in other countries. These options may be very limited in some cases, for example, where the particular country possesses a mineral deposit of higher-grade ore than can be found elsewhere, or where alternative locations involve more political risks. But where viable alternatives exist, and can be demonstrated, the threat of diverting investment can give the TNC a predominating bargaining strength.

Where governments of host countries are active participants in the bargaining process, the various commodity-specific factors discussed above are by no means the only ones to be considered. The general economic position and prospects of the host country will also be relevant.[31] Three elements of the general economic position seem particularly relevant (see top left-hand panel in Figure 10.2). These are the financial resources available to the host country, the current and prospective balance of payments positions, and the possibility of establishing alternative trade links. Countries which have little or no monetary reserves, and which find it difficult to raise loans on world capital markets, may thereby find themselves in a generally weak bargaining position, which could well offset any bargaining

---

[31] The political stability of the host country government could also be an important influence on that government's bargaining position, but political factors are not considered in the present context.

advantage they might have in a particular commodity setting. In such a situation, a host country government would find it extremely difficult to refuse a TNC offer which would increase the country's net export income, even though the major share of the benefit would accrue to the TNC. On the other hand, those (relatively few) developing countries with ample financial resources would not suffer from this disability in their negotiations with TNCs (which normally also have large financial resources).

Equally, countries which are in heavy deficit on their current payments account, due for example to a serious deterioration in the terms of trade and/or to a significant increase in the proportion of their export earnings which has to be devoted to servicing their external debt, may also find their general bargaining power seriously undermined, particularly if the prospects are for continuing external deficits. Countries which have adjusted relatively successfully to the external 'shocks' of recent years and have continued their economic expansion without incurring major current account deficits can adopt a generally more active bargaining stance in negotiations with TNCs.

Another macroeconomic element to be considered is the possibility of a developing country establishing new trading links through, for example, the conclusion of bilateral trade agreements, or adherence to a regional economic grouping, thus opening the way for bypassing traditional dependence on one or a few industrialized countries. Trade agreements between a number of Asian and African developing countries and socialist countries, for example, may well have improved the bargaining position of the developing countries concerned in negotiations with TNCs.

As already indicated, the bargaining power of a government in its dealings with a TNC can be dramatically weakened, or even reduced to zero, by means of bribery and corruption. Many TNCs regard bribes paid as a necessary marketing cost, and budget accordingly. Well-known cases in recent years include bribes paid in both developed and developing countries. Where bribes have become an essential part of the system, recorded prices of international transactions can be seriously at variance with actual or effective prices, while the division of benefit can be significantly shifted in favour of the bribe-giver (i.e. the TNC) or, in some cases, in favour of the bribe-taker.

The third category of factors distinguished earlier as influencing the bargaining situation, viz. international action, relates to joint measures by governments of developing countries, or joint action by interested TNCs or by their home country governments. Joint action by governments of developing countries would include measures to regulate supplies coming on the world market by means of a cartel-type arrangement; common fiscal policies, such as agreements among host governments to impose a uniform tax or royalty on TNC production or export of a given commodity; the pooling of import purchases (e.g. of fertilizers or tractors) from TNCs for commodity production; or the establishment of regional technology transfer centres to advise small developing countries in their negotiations with TNCs.

Joint action by TNCs to influence a bargaining situation is likely to arise only in extreme cases where competing TNCs all feel themselves threatened, for example, by nationalization without their claims for 'fair and adequate' compensation being met. In some cases, their home country governments may also intervene to put political and/or economic pressure on host governments not to nationalize the TNC interests in question, or to pay compensation in full, or, more generally, to modify existing or proposed policies so as to favour their home TNCs or to protect their interests.

The balance of bargaining power is thus a complex phenomenon, the elements of which are likely to change in relative influence over time. In commodity markets substantially dominated by oligopoly/oligopsony, the division of benefit will be heavily influenced by the relative bargaining strengths of TNCs and host governments. The mechanism by which the benefit is distributed is the negotiated 'price', which, in many situations, must be interpreted in terms of net unit return.

Moreover, such a 'price' is essentially a long-run concept. It represents the intended division of benefit over the period of a contract, or over a period long enough to amortize the capital investment of a TNC in a specific project in a developing country. In practice, market prices – and thus the TNC's net unit return – will fluctuate in the short term as a result of shifts in the supply/demand balance on the world market. An analysis which focuses solely on shifts in supply and demand, and thus on changes in market prices, will not, however, reveal the underlying relationships between the TNCs and producers in developing countries. For that, it is necessary to place the supply/demand analysis in the context of the structures of control and decision-making which govern the production, trade, and marketing of a given commodity, and to show how these structures influence the price outcome and the division of benefit between developed and developing countries.

3. STRATEGIES OF HOST COUNTRIES AND TNCs

The main objective of developing countries in which the TNCs operate commodity producing or processing enterprises has generally been to increase their share of the benefits of TNC operations. Though host country governments have been particularly concerned with their receipts from taxation (on production or export, and on profits), they have also increasingly come to emphasize the need for training and upgrading of local skills in processing activities and, in many cases, have agreed minimum proportions of processed output to be exported, and of inputs to be purchased in local markets.

Apart from increasing state requirements in relation to TNC operations, particularly as regards new mining and metal-processing projects, many developing countries have pursued policies of nationalization, either wholly or in part, of the local subsidiaries of TNCs which, in their view, control key sectors of their economies. The main wave of nationalization, in the 1960s and early 1970s, was fairly widespread in the mining sector (including copper, bauxite, and tin), but was also of importance in estate cash crop agriculture (including tea, sisal, and cotton).

Thus by the late 1970s the dominant role of the TNCs in commodity production in developing countries had been substantially reduced, while host country governments were increasingly regulating the conditions under which TNC operations were taking place. According to estimates by Radetzki (1985), roughly one-half of the non-fuel mineral industries in developing countries were government-owned by the mid-1980s. In addition, for many important commodities, the period after the successful OPEC action of 1973 saw the establishment of a number of associations of producer countries aiming to strengthen their bargaining power *vis-à-vis* the TNCs.

These actions by developing countries, however, were only partially successful in achieving their objectives, particularly that of obtaining a substantial increase in their tax receipts from TNC operations. There were two main reasons for this. First, and no doubt the principal factor, was the sharp fall in commodity prices in the first half of the 1980s, so that even if host countries increased their share of the profits of TNCs, this would have been more than offset by the overall reduction in profits. Second, the TNCs themselves responded to the changing role of the State in developing countries by changing their own strategies.[32]

As summarized by Girvan, these strategies differ as between primary production proper and the 'downstream' activities of international marketing and distribution.[33] He notes two main strategy trends in the primary sector. First, there has been a modification of the traditional forms of TNC operation by means of joint ventures, partnerships, and a variety of non-equity arrangements, such as the provision of management, marketing, and technical services. In the minerals and metals sector, these new contractual forms have generally led to a more equitable division of the costs and benefits of investment as between host country and the foreign investing enterprise.[34]

Second, TNCs have tended to diversify their sources of supply, including redirecting their investments towards politically 'safe' producing countries, including developed countries, to the extent possible. The pattern of TNC investment by region has, in fact, changed substantially over the past decade, the share of investment in developing countries being sharply reduced (in spite of the more accommodating attitudes of most host governments). The principal reason for this switch, as regards the commodity sector, was the decline in world commodity prices and the gloomy outlook for world demand for most primary commodities. For minerals and metals, the considerable expansion in productive capacity that occurred in the early 1980s – a result of relatively high prices in the late 1970s – and the concurrent contraction in demand for metals left these com-

---

[32] For a more detailed analysis of the changes in TNC strategies, see Girvan 1987 and Clairmonte and Cavanagh 1981, 1988.
[33] Girvan 1987: 716. Girvan also gives specific examples of each of the trends cited.
[34] See UNCTC 1988: 10.

modity markets with a substantial stock overhang for a number of years, a situation which also militated against renewed investment in mines or processing plants. The financial difficulties of many state mining enterprises in the 1980s have tended to result in their launching new mining projects as joint ventures with one or several TNCs, with the government holding an important equity position, though not necessarily a majority one (Radetzki 1985).

As regards downstream activities, several new responses by the TNCs to the changing situation can be observed. TNCs involved in the mining sector have strengthened the barriers to entry in processing through horizontal integration and joint ventures with other TNCs for large-scale projects. In some agricultural raw materials and minerals, there have been attempts at forward vertical integration to capture rents accruing at final product stages. In the food, beverages, and tobacco sector, and in some metal products, such as aluminium, TNCs have invested heavily in product diversification, product differentiation, and innovation in marketing strategy to capture economic rents in the markets for final and semi-finished goods. Finally, in some commodity sectors (food and beverages, some minerals) TNCs have formed conglomerates by a succession of mergers and acquisitions, providing a stronger financial base and enabling them to 'cross-subsidize' to support aggressive marketing so as to increase their market share.[35]

4. INTERNATIONAL NEGOTIATIONS RELATED TO COMMODITY MARKET STRUCTURES

Discussions of possible international action to improve market structures in favour of developing countries have proceeded in United Nations bodies for almost two decades. One major approach was to negotiate a Code of Conduct for TNCs, a negotiation which proved extremely contentious, complex, and time-consuming. This Code is intended to be comprehensive, covering the whole range of relations between governments and TNCs, including legal and quasi-political aspects as well as purely economic ones.[36] By 1990, almost a decade and a half after negotiations began in 1976, under the auspices of the UN Commission on Transnational Corporations, the draft Code had still not been fully agreed. Two key issues remain unresolved, viz. the applicability of the Code to enterprises of socialist countries, and the recognition of the force of international law in relation to matters covered by the Code.[37] As regards the first issue, an agreement was reached *ad referendum* in 1987, which provides that the Code applies to all enterprises operating across national boundaries and in any field of activity, irrespective of whether they are in private, state, or mixed ownership. This is, however, contingent on the resolution of all other major outstanding issues in the Code.

---

[35] For a more detailed discussion of cross-subsidization and other techniques used to increase market share, see Clairmonte and Cavanagh 1981.

[36] See the discussion of this draft Code in UNCTC 1985: 80–9 and UNCTC 1988: 350–63.

[37] See the detailed discussion in Dell 1990: 88–90, on which the present summary of the position on the Code is based.

Lack of progress on the second issue reflects disagreement on whether the Code should acknowledge the obligations of States under customary international law. A number of industrial countries argued that agreement on clauses in the Code relating to nationalization and compensation, dispute settlement, etc. would be much easier if a general provision were included which recognized the applicability of international law. Some developing countries, however, could not accept that customary international law might prevail over domestic law, while others did not agree that international law included generally accepted provisions regarding nationalization, compensation, and related matters. Dell (1990) felt that the impasse on this issue reflects 'the lack of a clear overall political decision rather than the difficulty of the particular issue in itself', and suggests that a compromise could be devised which would be acceptable to both points of view and thus clear the way for the adoption of the Code as a whole.

Though the draft Code remains to be finalized, the negotiations have resulted in consensus on a substantial number of specific provisions or of broad principles relating to the 'ground rules' for TNC operations in developing countries.[38] To this extent, the draft Code can be considered a useful reference point which can be taken into account by developing countries in formulating their policies regarding TNC activities.

A negotiation within UNCTAD on the more specific issue of restrictive business practices did, however, lead to agreement on a set of principles and rules for the control of such practices.[39] These principles and rules, which are not mandatory, are intended to apply to market practices in both manufactures and commodities, and whether domestic or international. The relevant restrictive practices in the commodities area would include the use of market sharing arrangements between dominant TNCs in supplying a particular commodity, which restrict market access by independent enterprises; price-setting or differential pricing by geographical area or other criteria; and restrictions on TNC subsidiaries or associated firms in developing countries in exporting, or in exporting to particular markets. Restrictive practices can also arise from the market operations of dominant trading firms which influence market trends by providing a major source of market information.[40] However, it seems doubtful whether these principles and rules have had any significant effect on the working of the commodity markets. The first review Conference, in 1985, was unable to agree on an evaluation of results, and a further review Conference is to convene late in 1990.

Restrictive practices of TNCs are only one element in the difficulties faced by

---

[38] These include, *inter alia*, principles for dispute settlement, for standards of corporate conduct (including the principle that TNCs are to operate in conformity with the broad economic goals and development objectives and priorities of host States), and for the elimination of transfer pricing practices which have detrimental economic effects. The draft Code also prescribes standards regarding consumer protection and environmental protection (UNCTC 1988).

[39] The Set of Multilaterally Agreed Equitable Principles and Rules for the Control of Restrictive Business Practices (adopted by the UN General Assembly in Resolution 35/63, dated 5 Dec. 1980).

[40] See UNCTAD 1981*c*: para. 47.

developing countries in their efforts to expand their commodity processing activities—and their processed commodity exports—and to enhance their participation in the marketing and distribution system, both of which would help to raise their share of the benefits derived from commodity trade. A broader attack on the problem was launched at UNCTAD V in 1979, in a resolution calling for the establishment of 'frameworks of international co-operation' to consider appropriate measures that might be taken to promote commodity processing in developing countries and to enhance their participation in the marketing and distribution system.[41]

In developing the proposed frameworks, the 1979 resolution envisaged that certain specific elements would be taken into account, viz. (i) improvement in market transparency, including action where appropriate to improve the functioning of commodity exchanges; (ii) increased technical and financial support for the development of national marketing and distribution systems of developing countries; (iii) contracts, practices, and arrangements governing the marketing of commodities listed in the 1976 resolution on the Integrated Programme for Commodities; and (iv) elimination of barriers to fair competition between marketing enterprises of developed and developing countries.

As part of the development of intergovernmental consideration of these issues, the UNCTAD secretariat has made a large number of proposals for policy changes.[42] To improve market transparency, it is proposed *inter alia* that each developed country should establish a body to report periodically on the short-term and long-term prospects of individual industries, covering developments both in the private sector and in relevant policy changes by governments.[43] A related proposal is that developed countries should consider offering incentives to private and state corporations to provide more information. However, Western countries have not accepted these ideas, mainly on the ground that much of the relevant market information is inevitably confidential to trading firms.

Proposals to improve the operation of commodity exchanges (or 'terminal' markets), and to make them more transparent, include suggestions that developing countries should be represented on the governing boards of the exchanges; that there should be better information available on the rules and regulations involved; that better training facilities should be provided for developing-country nationals as regards use of these exchanges; and that assistance should be provided for establishing similar exchanges in interested developing countries.[44] There would indeed be advantages in developing countries becoming involved in the operation of the existing commodity exchanges. They would benefit from greater insights into the working of the markets of interest to them, as well as gaining access to up-to-date information and market forecasts. In any event, developing countries could arrange to follow market trends, and probable future

---

[41] See UNCTAD 1981: i, Resolution 124(v).
[42] Summarized in UNCTAD 1984*f*: Ch. 6.
[43] Ibid.: 7–8.
[44] Ibid. paras. 29–60.

changes, without buying a 'seat' at the commodity exchanges.

Increased technical and financial support by the international community for the establishment of marketing enterprises by developing countries is proposed, together with the creation of a new international training institute in this field.[45] Assistance for developing countries on the negotiation of contracts (e.g. with TNCs), including the monitoring of contracts and the elaboration of model contracts, is also proposed.[46]

As regards the more pervasive difficulties caused by the asymmetry in market power between developing-country enterprises and TNCs, which result in barriers to fair competition, it is proposed that new codes of conduct should be negotiated to prevent abuses of market power and to promote truthful advertising by TNCs.[47]

Though these various proposals are still under consideration in UNCTAD bodies, the reactions so far by Western countries indicate that they would oppose any new institutional arrangement, especially in the form of codes of conduct, which might restrict the freedom of action of their TNCs. Joint action by developed and developing countries on the lines envisaged in the UNCTAD resolution would help to improve the share of the benefits of commodity trade accruing to developing countries by strengthening their international marketing enterprises. However, the overall impact is not likely to be a major one while downstream activities continue to be so dominated by large transnational entities.

5. POLICY OPTIONS FOR DEVELOPING COUNTRIES

During the 1980s, against a background of acute foreign exchange shortage, many developing countries relaxed their previous conditions for TNC operations in order to attract additional foreign direct investment. An expansion in foreign capital inflows would offset, to a greater or lesser extent, the falling-off in commercial bank lending, and it would normally be accompanied by the introduction of modern technology and by an assurance of export markets in the home countries of the TNCs involved. These benefits could, however, be substantially offset by financial outflows, either in payments for imports of capital goods and intermediate products and for royalties or other services, or as remittances of profits. For this reason, many developing countries are now having some misgivings about the value of financial and other incentives on offer to foreign direct investment, such as extended tax holidays and the provision of infrastructural facilities and a suitable labour force, often in special free-trade zones.

Moreover, there are other policy options which developing countries could consider. For example, there would seem to be scope for useful action by producing countries on several of the issues listed in Figure 10.2 above, such as control

---

[45] Ibid. Ch. 5.   [46] Ibid. Ch. 3.
[47] Ibid. Ch. 4. The proposals also include the application to commodities of existing agreed codes, such as the one relating to restrictive business practices.

over reserves and production; the government learning process; and increased cooperation among national state trading organizations to improve their common bargaining position.

There are a number of instances over the past two decades of governments of mineral-exporting countries improving their bargaining position by exercising greater control over reserves and production. For example, exploration rights held by TNCs have on occasion been withdrawn, while there have been important instances, particularly in copper, of governments taking partial or full control of TNC operations. The purchase of UK rubber estates by the Malaysian government is another example of this type of action. Action by developing countries to create or expand processing facilities could be envisaged as part of a 'package' deal with TNCs. One example, quoted by Labys,[48] was the refusal of Jamaica in the mid-1960s to grant new bauxite concessions unless the TNCs involved agreed to build local alumina plants. As regards the obsolescing bargain, there has been a marked trend for governments to insist on renegotiation of mineral contracts some time after the initial investment by TNCs, the governments using such devices as increased corporate taxes, and increased participation in equity, to negotiate better terms.

Governments of developing countries can accelerate the learning process in a number of ways, e.g. by providing technical and managerial training in required skills, as well as by incorporating provisions for in-house training of local personnel in contracts with TNCs and their subsidiaries. Governments can also establish specialized institutes to study the technical, economic, and marketing problems of particular commodities, so that they are fully aware of these problems when negotiating with TNCs.

For some commodities, where international marketing and distribution channels are dominated by TNCs, there may be possibilities for developing producing countries, acting in concert, to establish alternative sales outlets, for example, by promoting their own brand names (which would be possible in tea, and probably in coffee) and selling through their own marketing companies. In other suitable cases, contracts could be arranged directly with mail order firms or retail stores in developed countries.

A further possibility is for cooperation among state trading organizations of producer countries to offset the present dominance of the TNCs in the global marketing and distribution system. One recent suggestion to this end is that the importation of certain manufactured products from the industrialized countries could be centralized, and tied to commodity exports to those countries at stable, and more remunerative, prices.[49] This arrangement, which would involve a form of countertrade, would depend for its viability largely on the alternative marketing options available to the TNCs, as well as on the alternative sources of supply of manufactures for the developing countries.

Increased control of marketing channels can also cover the important case of

---

[48] Labys 1980.   [49] Kuwayama 1988: 106.

joint action by developing countries, e.g. through Producer Associations, to regulate total supplies of a commodity coming on the world market. Such regulation, if successful — and, as was discussed in Chapter 3, certain preconditions must be satisfied for this to be the case — can substantially shift the division of benefit in favour of developing producing countries. Alternatively, in suitable circumstances, governments can successfully impose a uniform export tax (as for bananas), or royalty (as for bauxite), to increase their net return.

Finally, among the macroeconomic factors influencing the bargaining situation, there is one which has been deployed effectively by some developing countries, viz. the opening of quite new trade channels (with China or with Eastern Europe, in particular) which effectively bypass the TNCs or, at least, may significantly reduce the latter's bargaining power in negotiations with the developing countries concerned.[50]

These and related measures involving common policies and joint action by commodity-producing countries, which introduce new institutional forces in the market, can result in significant shifts in the balance of bargaining power in a number of commodity markets in favour of developing countries and, to that extent, they would tend to result in a reduction in the disproportionate share of the benefits of trade which is now captured by oligopolistic TNCs. The potential for such joint action is considered further in Chapter 15 in the context of a wider strategy for strengthening the commodity sector of developing countries' economies.

---

[50] See Ch. 13 for a more detailed discussion of new trade channels.

11
Technological Change and the Challenge of Synthetics

1. TECHNOLOGY AND COMMODITY MARKETS

The development and wide diffusion of new technologies, first and foremost in the industrialized countries and later—and on a smaller scale—in developing countries, have already had major repercussions on the markets for primary commodities, and hence on the economic position and prospects of commodity-exporting countries. These repercussions arise because new technologies have substantial impacts both on world supply of, and world demand for, commodities and thereby also on commodity prices and commodity export earnings of developing countries.

Technological innovations have a number of distinct effects on the supply of primary commodities. First, the efficiency of resource use of productive enterprises is likely to be generally enhanced with the assimilation of new technologies, either by the enterprise itself or by its suppliers of inputs or purchasers of its output. Second, a more specific influence on commodity supply would arise since new technological processes normally result in increased output of given products per unit of resources used. Third, new techniques can bring into production inputs which otherwise would remain unused, e.g. by new methods of extracting low-grade mineral ores or by expanding the use of land through irrigation. Fourth, new technologies can result in improved quality of existing varieties of a commodity, as well as the evolution of new and improved varieties. Since quality improvement adds additional value to production, this is an important element in the expansion of commodity output.

Technological innovations which expand commodity supply can, however, also add significantly to private and social costs. In the case of the 'Green Revolution' of the 1960s and 1970s, for example, there were high private costs in the form of fertilizers and irrigation, which confined the benefits of the increased grain output mainly to the larger farmers able to purchase these necessary inputs. The clearest example of high social cost arises where new technologies result in pollution and environmental degradation. With the rapid growth in recent years of awareness of the dangers to the global environment that may be caused by economic growth patterns in individual countries—patterns often associated with technological change—there has been growing recognition, as mentioned in Chapter 3, of the need for new national and international policies for environmental protection. To the extent that such policies shift the cost of environmental protection back to the producer (the 'polluter pays' principle), the fall in production costs associated with the introduction of new technology will be correspondingly less. However, to the extent that such policies also encourage the development of 'environmentally friendly' technologies, they will eventually help to reduce the social costs of technological change.

Technological innovation also has a major negative impact on the demand for primary commodities. This arises in several ways: through the development of new industrial materials, particularly synthetics and the new engineering materials (including metal super-alloys, ceramics, and composites), which displace older traditional materials; through changes in final products which use less materials; and through changes in industrial structures. These various changes, all closely linked to technological innovation, have substantially reduced the level of consumption of natural raw materials per unit of GDP in the industrial countries.

This underlying adverse trend in the demand for commodities has led some analysts to suggest that commodity consumption is becoming divorced from the economic growth process in the industrial countries and that consequently the economies of these countries are becoming 'dematerialized'. A second school of thought lays stress on the overlapping cyclical changes in consumption of different commodities, implying that total materials consumption represents a sequence of such cycles rather than a declining trend, a concept known as 'transmaterialization'. It is useful to consider these and related hypotheses further before reviewing actual post-war trends.

2. DEMATERIALIZATION AND TRANSMATERIALIZATION

In the early 1970s there was much concern in the industrialized countries about possible future shortages of critical raw materials which could arise from the exhaustion of known physical reserves if economic growth continued at rapid rates. Studies by the Club of Rome (Meadows *et al.* 1972) attempted to quantify this problem and to draw conclusions relating to sustainable growth rates.

Following the sharp rise in petroleum prices in 1973–4, however, concern was directed more to supply restrictions that then seemed likely to occur as a result of the operation of producer cartels (Bergsten 1973). In the 1980s, by contrast, it has seemed to many analysts that the new technologies associated with the electronics revolution, the development of newer synthetic and composite materials, and the emergence of biotechnology on a commercial scale have largely divorced the industrial sector from its former close dependence on inputs of traditional raw materials, both agricultural and mineral (Drucker 1986). On this view, the industrialized economies are becoming 'dematerialized'.

Demand for these traditional materials appears to have been affected on several levels. First, such materials have been displaced in many specific uses by new materials, particularly synthetic materials, which possess more desirable technical properties or – in some cases – have a significant cost advantage. The substitution of polypropylene for jute and sisal and the more recent displacement of copper by optical fibres in telecommunications are both important examples of this process.

Second, the demand for traditional materials has been affected by broader structural changes in the economies of the industrialized countries. A major feature of the changes in economic structures over the past decade has been the relatively rapid expansion of the 'high-tech' industries, particularly the electronic, information, and associated sectors, which generally use much less material inputs per unit of output than the older 'heavy' industries, which have grown less rapidly, or have stagnated.[1]

Third, new technologies have resulted in changes in many traditional end-products, or even in their obsolescence as, for example, in the development of bulk handling equipment for the storage and transport of grain, thus obviating the need for jute sacks. Again, the spread of electronic devices has facilitated the downsizing of products, thus saving on materials usage. Another feature of industrial change in the 1980s has been the strong impetus to economizing in the use of raw materials to reduce costs in a more competitive environment than in previous decades.

The dematerialization thesis would indeed appear to have been in operation, to a greater or lesser extent, among the agricultural raw materials. Jute and sisal have already been mentioned as having been largely displaced by synthetic substitutes. Other examples of substantial inroads made by synthetics include the substitution of polypropylene and nylon for abaca in cordage; polyurethane, PVC, and polypropylene for coir in upholstery and matting; and polyurethane, PVC, and poromerics in footwear (FAO 1983-4).

However, producers of some of the agricultural raw materials have taken steps to improve the competitive position of their products. Cotton and wool, for example, have both established their positions as relatively high-priced 'quality' fibres, catering to the upper end of the consumer market, while cotton and, to a lesser extent, wool have increased their market through blends and finishes involving synthetic fibres. In the case of natural rubber, improvements in the form of technically specified and uniform-quality standards, together with productivity increases, have helped to maintain the product's market position where it competes mainly on price with synthetic rubber. In other important end-uses, however, such as for radial tyres and surgical uses, natural rubber has decisive technical advantages over synthetic rubber. Thus the dematerialization thesis would seem to be too sweeping a generalization to be a useful description of the complex relationship between materials consumption and industrial production.

---

[1] It is often argued that the decline in the share of manufacturing industry in GDP has also contributed to a reduction in the growth rate of demand for traditional raw materials because, it is argued, the consumption of these materials per unit of output is relatively small in the growing services sector. But, as Vogely 1976 and Auty 1985 indicate, there is no firm evidence for this view. Indeed, government services—which include expenditure on armaments—may well be more resource-intensive than many manufacturing industries.

A more credible hypothesis about how this relationship changes over time is provided by the product life-cycle theory, first proposed by Dean (1950).[2] This suggests that, for mineral commodities, production, consumption, and prices follow a well-defined life cycle. In an initial phase, after the discovery of a mineral or the beginning of a major use for it, consumption increases rapidly as its properties become more widely known, and its sale is promoted through research and dissemination of information. Then follows a mature phase, as the commodity becomes more widely used, and production growth slows down. A third ('gerontic') phase comes next, during which production continues at a high level, but with little growth. Finally, there is a long and erratic phase of production decline, reflecting mainly the difficulty of expanding supply (as in the case of tin in recent decades).

This hypothesis seems to be a good description of the history of a number of minerals and metals, each of which has come slowly into commercial use, then enjoyed rapid expansion before being displaced by a newly exploited mineral or synthetic. However, the life-cycle theory has come under sharp criticism, particularly by Humphreys (1982). He argues that, if there is a life cycle, it would be related to general economic conditions, so that a given metal could be gerontic in highly industrialized countries, while still youthful or mature in developing countries. Again, there could be occasions when a reverse movement, e.g. from decline to youthful phases, might occur as a result of quite new mineral discoveries. Moreover, in examining specific cases of production decline, such as the phasing-out of mercury production (asbestos would be another example), it appears that these were not related to the depletion of resources.

The idea of cyclical change in the consumption of materials was taken up by Labys and Waddell (1989) in their paper on transmaterialization. They argue that as the needs of an economy change, industries replace old materials by newer, technologically more advanced, materials. They distinguish five groups of minerals and metals, each of which has passed through a life cycle at different periods over the present century. Each group shows a peak of 'intensity of use' (defined as consumption per unit of GDP in the United States) from 1937 up to 1974 for the first to fourth groups; the fifth group, by definition, has not yet peaked (see Table 11.1). On this analysis, Labys and Waddell argue that transmaterialization represents a sequence of replacement cycles, rather than a long-term trend.

None the less, the existence of such cycles does not preclude the operation of a long-term trend. This is essentially an empirical issue, not a theoretical one, since it depends on the extent to which the increase in value of the materials entering later cycles offsets the loss in value of the materials which are being phased out. Some guidance on this issue can be gained by examining post-war trends in materials consumption per unit of industrial production in the industrialized countries.

[2] For a more detailed review of the life-cycle theory, see Humphreys 1982 and the references cited therein.

Table 11.1. Peak years in life cycles of selected minerals and metals

Period	Peak year for intensity of use	Selected minerals and metals
I. 1900–50	Before 1939	Arsenic, copper, iron ore, lead, tin, zinc
II. 1925–70	Soon after 1945	Asbestos, bismuth, molybdenum, nickel
III. 1935–75	1956–70	Chromium, ilmenite, lithium, manganese, vanadium
IV. 1945–85	After 1970	Aluminium, barite, cobalt, phosphate rock, rutile
V. 1955–	–	Gallium, germanium, hafrium, platinum group metals, rare earth metals, titanium, yttrium.[a]

[a] Labys and Waddell also included polyethylene in this group.

Source: Labys and Waddell 1989.

3. POST-WAR TRENDS IN RAW MATERIALS CONSUMPTION

From the end of the war up to the early 1970s, the economies of the Western industrial countries grew at unprecedented rates, and for a prolonged period – some 25 years. Rapid growth was accompanied by marked changes in demand patterns, in industrial structures and international trade, and in the output of synthetic materials.

An early analysis of materials consumption, by Rowlatt and Blackaby (1959), showed that over the period from 1950–2 to 1955–7, substantial substitution of synthetic for natural materials had taken place in the main OECD countries. Consumption of cotton and wool, for example, had risen by 9 per cent over this period, whereas consumption of manmade fibres had risen by 54 per cent. Again, natural rubber consumption grew by 15 per cent, as against a rise of 44 per cent for synthetic rubber. For plastics, the rise was much faster – almost 100 per cent. However, for all the 16 major materials covered – agricultural, metal, and synthetic – the volume of consumption had risen in aggregate at virtually the same rate as manufacturing output (just under 30 per cent in each case). Moreover, the approximate constancy of the ratio of total materials consumption to manufacturing output held good for each industrial country separately. For the 1950s, then, the life-cycle sequence of different materials did not involve a downward trend in overall materials consumption per unit of final output.

The results of a similar analysis for later periods, covering 20 major industrial

Table 11.2. Consumption of the major industrial raw materials in developed market-economy countries, 1963-5 to 1984-6

	Consumption[a] ($ billion at 1978-80 prices[b])				Growth rates (% p.a.)		
	1963-5	1971-3	1978-80	1984-6	1963-5 to 1971-3	1971-3 to 1978-80	1978-80 to 1984-6
Agricultural raw materials[c]	24.8	25.9	23.6	23.5	0.6	-1.3	-0.1
Minerals and metals[d]	32.6	48.0	54.4	52.7	5.0	1.8	-0.5
Total natural materials	57.4	73.9	78.0	76.2	3.2	0.8	-0.4
Synthetic materials[e]	21.9	53.2	63.8	72.7	11.6	2.6	2.3
TOTAL	79.3	127.1	141.8	148.9	6.1	1.6	0.8
Memo item: OECD industrial production					5.5	3.0	1.5

[a] Annual averages for each period.
[b] Quantities consumed valued at world export unit values, average of years 1978-80.
[c] Cotton, wool, sisal, jute, rubber, non-coniferous timber, tobacco.
[d] Aluminium, copper, iron ore, lead, manganese ore, nickel, tin, tungsten, zinc and phosphate rock.
[e] Synthetic fibres, synthetic rubber, and plastic materials.

Sources: UNCTAD *Commodity Yearbook* (various issues); *Production Yearbook* (various issues), FAO, Rome; *Textile Organon* (various issues); United Nations *Yearbook of International Trade Statistics* (various issues).

Table 11.3. Materials consumption per unit of industrial production in developed market-economy countries: 1963–5 to 1984–6 (growth rates, % p.a.)

	Natural materials			Synthetic materials	Total
	Agricultural	Minerals and metals	Total		
1963–5 to 1971–3	−4.2	−0.5	−2.2	5.9	0.5
1971–3 to 1978–80	−4.2	−1.2	−2.2	−0.4	−1.4
1978–80 to 1984–6	−1.5	−2.0	−1.8	0.7	−0.6
1971–3 to 1984–6	−3.0	−1.6	−2.0	−0.1	−1.1

Source: Table 11.2.

materials, are summarized in Table 11.2. Several relevant conclusions emerge. First, the inroads made by synthetic materials into the markets for traditional materials have continued to grow over the entire period since the early 1960s. Second, the displacement of natural materials has so far adversely affected agricultural materials to a far greater extent than minerals and metals. Third, for both groups of natural materials taken together, the ratio of consumption growth to industrial production growth fell off sharply in the 1980s; whereas the consumption growth rate had been some 50–60 per cent of that for industrial growth in the two earlier periods, in the latest period, consumption growth became negative.

A similar picture is shown in Table 11.3, which gives the annual rates of change in the ratio of materials consumption to industrial production. Changes in this ratio are the result of all the various influences discussed earlier, which can usefully be considered in two categories, viz. the substitution of synthetic for natural materials, and all the other relevant factors, such as the influence of new technologies on materials usage, downsizing of final products, structural changes within manufacturing industry, etc. Two results of interest emerge. First, while in the 1960s and 1970s the rate of displacement of agricultural materials in total industrial production was easily the largest adverse change, in the 1980s the rate of displacement per unit of output was greatly reduced, whereas the corresponding rate for minerals and metals almost doubled, and exceeded that for agricultural materials for the first time. Over the whole period from the early 1970s, however, the main substitution appears to have remained in relation to agricultural materials.

Second, the overall consumption of all 20 materials (natural and synthetic) per unit of industrial output fell off significantly, by some 1.5 per cent a year, on average, between the early and late 1970s, whereas in the 1980s the rate of decline was much reduced, to only about 0.5 per cent a year. Examination of the annual series for the minerals and metals group, which accounts for over two-thirds of the total value of consumption of the natural raw materials covered, shows that a break occurred after 1973. Total metal consumption per unit of output, which had varied only marginally from year to year up to 1974, thereafter showed a significant downward trend.[3] This would indicate that efforts by manufacturing industry to economize on energy, following the sharp rise in petroleum prices in 1973-4, which was associated also with increasing use of lighter materials, downsizing, and greater use of synthetic substitutes, must have played a major role. None the less, the consumption of synthetic materials per unit of industrial output declined marginally in the 1970s, and this, too, was probably a result of the rise in the cost of petroleum feedstock.

The decline in the natural materials content of industrial output, in so far as it represents a long-term trend, poses a difficult dilemma for the development strategies of countries heavily dependent on exports of these materials. An underlying issue is whether, and to what extent, the relative stagnation in the consumption of natural materials in the developed countries reflects the latter's economic slowdown, which could be reversed in the future, rather than technological innovation, which is likely to continue or intensify. This issue has recently been analysed by Tilton (1989) in relation to the consumption of six major metals, by relating changes in consumption to changes in real income, and in the intensity of use[4] of these metals, in the OECD area. He showed that over the period from 1973 to 1985, the stagnation or, for some metals, declines in consumption reflected both the slowdown in economic growth, compared with the 1960-73 period, and a decline in the intensity of metal use. The decline in the intensity of use, as Tilton states, can be attributed to two causal factors: changes in the material composition of products, and changes in the product composition of income. Both these factors have shifted over the period since 1973 in a manner tending to depress the level of metal consumption, though the intensity of use method of analysis does not yield a quantitative assessment of the relative importance of these two factors.

In the present analysis, which covers both the main minerals and metals, and also the principal agricultural raw materials, further light on the factors influencing the consumption of industrial materials is derived from a decomposition analysis, the results of which are summarized in Table 11.4. (For the decomposition formula, see the Annexe to this Chapter.)

In the first of our periods, from the early 1960s to the early 1970s, the volume of consumption of the natural materials included in the present analysis rose by 3.2 per cent a year. Had natural materials consumption risen at the same rate as

---

[3] Semi-logarithmic regressions of metals consumption per unit of industrial output in developed market-economy countries, with time as independent variable, show a decline of 0.32% p.a. for the period 1960-73 ($\bar{R}^2 = 0.333$), as against a decline of 1.67% p.a. for 1974-86 ($\bar{R}^2 = 0.856$). A definite break after 1973 in the total consumption of six major metals in OECD countries has also been demonstrated by Tilton 1989.

[4] 'Intensity of use' was defined as the ratio of metal use to national income, so that a change in metal consumption is necessarily equal to the product of the change in intensity of use and the change in income.

Table 11.4. Major influences on the growth of consumption of natural raw materials in developed market-economy countries, 1963–5 to 1984–6

	1963–5 to 1971–3		1971–3 to 1978–80		1978–80 to 1984–6	
	Value change[a] ($ billion)	Growth rate (% p.a.)	Value change[a] ($ billion)	Growth rate (% p.a.)	Value change[a] ($ billion)	Growth rate (% p.a.)
1. Potential growth[b]	27.6	5.0	35.5	5.8	14.8	2.9
2. Recession effect[c]	5.1[d]	0.8[d]	−18.5	−2.8	−7.8	−1.4
3. Actual industrial growth (=1+2)	32.7	5.8	17.0	3.0	7.0	1.5
4. Substitution of synthetic for natural materials	−17.9	−2.9	−4.8	−0.9	−5.7	−1.2
5. Change in materials content of industrial output	1.7	0.3	−8.1	−1.6	−3.1	−0.7
TOTAL CHANGE	16.5	3.2	4.1	0.8	−1.8	−0.4

[a] Values at 1978–80 prices.
[b] Assuming that actual industrial production had grown at same annual rate as over the previous period shown. For the change from 1963–5 to 1971–3, the previous period is taken as from 1953–5.
[c] Difference between actual industrial production growth rate and that in previous period.
[d] These figures are positive, since industrial production in this period grew at a faster rate than in the preceding decade (5.8 as against 5.0% p.a.).

Source: Table 11.2. For method of computation, see Annexe.

industrial production, consumption would have increased by almost 6 per cent a year. However, the large-scale displacement of most agricultural materials by synthetics resulted in a loss in the consumption of natural materials equivalent to some 3 per cent a year. In this period, as mentioned earlier, changes in the overall materials content of industrial production were marginal.

In the second period, covering most of the 1970s, the major feature was the slowdown in the industrial growth rate, which contributed the equivalent of a loss of nearly 3 per cent a year in natural materials consumption. In addition, both changes in the materials content of industrial production and continuing displacement by synthetic materials were significant, together accounting for an additional loss of 2.5 per cent a year in natural materials consumption. Total natural materials consumption continued to grow, but by under 1 per cent a year. Finally, in the 1980s, the further slowdown in the industrial growth rate remained the single most important influence. The negative effect of synthetic materials competition increased, compared with the 1970s, but the reverse was true for changes in the materials content of output.

These calculations, however, underestimate the degree of displacement of natural by synthetic materials, particularly for the period since 1978–80. An outstanding feature of technological innovation in the 1980s has been the development of a range of research-intensive new materials, including ceramic and composite mixtures, with technically superior properties to more traditional materials. Comprehensive data on the consumption of these new materials — which include optical fibres, ceramics, and high-performance engineering materials among numerous others — are not readily available; although they amount to far less in tonnage terms than the traditional materials which they displace, their high value-added makes them a significant element in the overall picture. To the extent that Table 11.4 underestimates the adverse impact of synthetic materials on the consumption of natural materials, the adverse impact of changes in the materials content of industrial output is thereby overestimated (by definition: see formula in the Annexe). Taking both elements of technological change together, the evolution of new types of high-tech materials, not included specifically in Table 11.4, does not therefore affect the overall quantitative results.

The retardation in the growth rate of natural materials attributable to technological change in this broad sense (i.e. the sum of items 4 and 5 in Table 11.4) appears to have declined moderately since the early 1960s. During the first period (see Table 11.4), this retardation represented a loss of 2.6 per cent a year, the corresponding rates of loss being 2.5 and 1.9 per cent a year for the two succeeding periods, respectively. It might well happen that the retardation will accelerate in the 1990s when new technologies now in the experimental stage come into commercial application.

Assuming for illustrative purposes a loss in natural materials consumption in the 1990s of between 2 and 3 per cent a year as a result of further technological change, then total industrial production in the OECD area would have to rise by similar percentages to prevent any further decline in natural materials consumption. To regain the 1960s situation of a 3 per cent annual average growth rate in natural materials consumption, industrial output in the Western developed countries would have to grow by 5–6 per cent a year, as against an average rate of not quite 2 per cent a year from 1978–80 to 1986–8.

4. THE IMPACT ON DEVELOPING COUNTRIES

Changes in the volume of imports of agricultural raw materials have closely mirrored the corresponding changes in consumption in the developed countries. Synthetic materials substitution has been greatest for sisal and jute, imports of which had been reduced by the mid-1980s to only a fraction of previous levels. Of the other major agricultural raw materials, only for natural rubber and tobacco were both consumption and imports from developing countries higher than in the early 1970s. For the minerals and metals group, imports from developing countries rose in volume terms at a faster rate than consumption after the early 1970s, reflecting a marked shift, particularly for aluminium and copper, to lower-cost sources of supply in the developing countries. Corresponding shifts also occurred in the 1980s for lead, nickel, and, to a lesser extent, zinc (Table 11.5).

For both groups of raw materials, export earnings of developing countries fell substantially during the first half of the 1980s as a result of the sharp fall in prices. The decline in earnings from agricultural raw materials from 1978–80 to 1984–6 was due entirely to the price fall, export volume in these two periods being virtually unchanged. For the minerals and metals, however, export volume in the later period had risen by over 10 per cent, but this was more than offset by the loss in earnings due to lower prices.

The developing countries hardest hit by the displacement of their traditional exports by synthetics have been those, such as Tanzania (sisal) and Bangladesh (jute), where consumption has been most reduced since the early 1970s. However, the slowdown in the growth rate of consumption of the major metals in the 1980s, together with the sharp falls in their prices—at least until 1987—brought major foreign exchange difficulties to producing countries, particularly those with high production costs, such as Bolivia (tin) and Zambia (copper). In these and other cases, the adverse changes in the world market for their staple exports have created unemployment in their export sectors and confronted these countries with the need to reduce production costs or to diversify their economies away from their traditional specialized exports.

5. THE SEARCH FOR AN EFFECTIVE INTERNATIONAL POLICY

By the time of the first UNCTAD Conference in 1964, the traditional markets for virtually the entire range of agricultural raw materials had already been

Table 11.5. Consumption and trade in industrial raw materials, 1971–3 to 1984–6

	Developed market-economies					Developing countries		
	Consumption		Imports from developing countries			Total exports		
	1978–80	1984–6	1978–80	1984–6		1978–80 ($ billion)	1984–6 ($ billion)	Change (%)
	(volume indices, 1971–3 = 100)							
Agricultural raw materials	91	91	97	87		16.40	13.74	−16
Cotton	79	89	72	72		3.05	2.55	−16
Wool	88	96	92	73		0.39	0.36	−8
Sisal	36	25	38	25		0.11	0.07	−41
Jute	48	22	39	14		0.91[a]	0.76[a]	−16
Natural rubber	108	118	106	121		3.74	2.98	−20
Tropical timber	91	74	108	81		6.70	5.29	−21
Tobacco	110	104	131	126		1.50	1.75	17
Minerals, ores, and metals	112	108	132	137		15.59	14.35	−8
Bauxite, alumina, and aluminium	126	131	174	159		2.37	3.25	37
Copper	111	108	161	164		5.16	4.44	−14
Lead	127	116	97	148		0.49	0.23[b]	−53
Nickel	115	119	151	133		1.01	0.92[b]	−9

Technological Change

Tin	87	75	92	77	2.48	1.39	−44
Tungsten	108	85	..	..	0.14	0.05	−64
Zinc	95	94	93	114	..	..	..
Iron ore	99	80	91	95	2.55	2.88	13
Manganese ore	94	74	79	63	0.29	0.23	−21
Phosphate rock	133	124	..	..	1.10	0.96	−13
Synthetic materials	120	137	..	..	..	..	..
Synthetic fibres	109	102	..	..	..	..	..
Synthetic rubber	111	104	..	..	..	..	..
Plastic materials	125	153	..	..	..	..	..

[a] Including jute manufactures.
[b] 1984–5 average.

Source: As for Table 11.2.

substantially affected by rapidly growing competition from synthetic substitutes. The problem and possible remedial international measures were considered in depth at that conference. A Recommendation was adopted without dissent calling for a series of special measures to protect the competitive position of natural materials, and for the establishment of a permanent intergovernmental group on this issue.[5]

Of the many special measures envisaged, three were perhaps the most fundamental. First, action was recommended for raising productivity and improving quality of natural materials, and intensifying technical and market research on their end-uses.[6] Second, the Recommendation called for increased access to developed-country markets for natural and semi-processed products facing competition from synthetics, with progressive reduction in the relevant trade barriers with a view to their final elimination.[7] Third, to assist developing countries to adjust their productive structures so as to reduce the impact of the expansion of synthetic materials on their long-term export prospects, the Recommendation envisaged the introduction of appropriate financial measures.[8]

As envisaged in the Recommendation, a Permanent Group on Synthetics and Substitutes was established, and began its work in 1967. The Group made intensive studies of the competitive position of natural and synthetic materials in each of the industries most affected, and elaborated a series of detailed policy recommendations to governments. In the case of natural rubber and cotton, these recommendations were focused essentially on research and development (R & D) to improve productivity, methods of processing, and quality, and to develop new end-uses, together with complementary measures to improve marketing. For both products, the need for greater international financial support for these proposals was stressed.[9]

In the early 1970s, the Permanent Group also initiated surveys of the global R & D effort relating to natural materials facing competition from synthetics and substitutes (covering jute, hard fibres, and hides and skins, as well as rubber and cotton). One interesting finding was that expenditure on R & D for some natural raw materials represented only some 0.5 per cent of the global value of output, whereas for their synthetic competitors, the corresponding proportion was far greater. The specific R & D needs for individual materials were considered also at the technical level by the relevant FAO Intergovernmental Groups and by an UNCTAD Expert Group for hides, skins, and leather.

The UNCTAD Expert Group's report, published in 1971,[10] stressed the inadequacy of the current R & D efforts, as well as the lack of international co-

---

[5] UNCTAD 1964: Final Act, Annex A.II.7. [6] Ibid. paras. 1(i), (ii), and (iii).
[7] Ibid. para. 1(vii).   [8] Ibid. para. 1(x).
[9] The detailed proposals originated with the relevant specialized intergovernmental bodies – the International Rubber Study Group, the International Cotton Advisory Committee, and the International Institute for Cotton – which worked closely with the UNCTAD Permanent Group on these issues.
[10] UNCTAD 1971a.

ordination of national research activities, and proposed a figure of about $20 million, equivalent to 1 per cent of the average annual value of world production[11] of hides and skins in 1965–7, as the minimum amount needed annually for research, development, and promotion for leather. The report also called for national measures to remedy a shortage of scientists working in this field, and for an appropriate body to provide international co-ordination of the R & D programme.[12]

As a result of these various technical studies, it was apparent that far more extensive R & D, and promotion, efforts would be essential if natural materials were not to be displaced by synthetics at an even greater rate than in the 1960s.

This issue was taken further at UNCTAD III, held in 1972. A resolution, also adopted without dissent,[13] called for the development of comprehensive programmes on R & D and for increased international technical and financial assistance for R & D and promotion; urged producing countries to co-operate to prepare and implement long-term strategies to expand consumption in developing countries; and urged all countries concerned to provide relevant information on synthetics to facilitate study of the problems facing natural products. The resolution also drew attention to the relevance of environmental pollution to the competitive position of natural and synthetic materials.

In regard to technical and financial assistance, the resolution requested the Consultative Group on Agricultural Research, sponsored jointly by FAO, IBRD, and UNDP, to give urgent consideration to the need for such assistance. However, the Consultative Group decided that its overriding purpose was to finance research and development relating to food production. A later suggestion by the UNCTAD Secretary-General that the Consultative Group might consider establishing a special technical committee to advise it on problems of research relating to agricultural raw materials was turned down. Though the possibility of the Consultative Group financing research into raw materials was left open, in fact the Consultative Group's finance has continued to be devoted solely to research to promote food production.[14]

In the event, some new international R & D programmes were begun, e.g. for cotton, financed mainly by existing international financial sources, such as IBRD and UNDP, while one developed country – the Netherlands – announced its intention of using part of its development aid to assist R & D for commodities facing competition from synthetics and substitutes. No major international action was, however, forthcoming in regard to the preparation and implementation of long-term strategies for countries exporting natural raw materials. Such strategies would need to cover not only R & D to improve productivity and to develop new end-uses, but also the promotion of consumption, and measures, such as buffer stocks, to reduce excessive short-term price fluctuations.

---

[11] Excluding China.   [12] Ibid. paras. 17 and 18.
[13] UNCTAD 1973: Resolution 50(III).
[14] A summary of the correspondence between UNCTAD and the Consultative Group is given in UNCTAD 1974c.

The recommendation on pollution was brought to the attention of the UN Conference on Human Environment (1972), which recommended that measures should be taken by Governments and the competent international organizations with a view to promoting 'international trade in natural products and commodities which compete with synthetic products that have a greater capacity for pollution'.[15]

A number of policy options to follow up the UNCTAD Conference recommendations were on the agenda of the 1974 session of the Permanent Group, but no decisions on any of these were possible in the time available. Unfortunately, this session was to be the last of the series, since international consideration of commodity issues in subsequent years was almost entirely concentrated on the Integrated Programme for Commodities (IPC). Though this Programme did make provision for measures to improve the competitive position of natural products facing competition from synthetics,[16] and the issue was considered for the main commodities concerned, the focus of the IPC negotiations was essentially on the price stabilization issue. By 1987, there had been no meeting of the Permanent Group for over a decade, its mandate then being subsumed in that of the UNCTAD Committee on Commodities, the Permanent Group itself being abolished.

Though this effort at international co-operation to improve the competitive position of natural products *vis-à-vis* synthetic materials yielded only limited practical results, there were a number of positive features. First, the Permanent Group provided a useful forum in which representatives of producing interests of both natural and competing synthetic materials could explore their common, as well as their conflicting, interests (for example, in regard to the expansion of productive capacity). Second, it succeeded in preventing the processed forms of certain raw materials (particularly, the new types of technically specified natural rubber) being treated as manufactures by developed countries, thus ensuring their entry into these countries at zero or low rates of duty. Third, it rapidly evolved a general consensus among both developed- and developing-country representatives that a far greater R & D programme was required to improve the competitive position of natural raw materials.

At the same time, the effectiveness of the effort was seriously undermined by a number of factors. One was the unwillingness of the synthetic materials industry, and of the Western industrial countries, to provide regular and detailed information relating to output, trade, prices, and productive capacity of synthetics on the grounds that such information was either not available or was commercially confidential. This made it virtually impossible to take a reasoned view of future prospects for costs, prices, and market shares of individual competing materials. A second limitation was the reluctance of the Western countries to discuss their own barriers to trade in crude, semi-processed, and processed

---

[15] *Report of the UN Conference on Human Environment*, 1973, recommendation 103(*f*)(ii).
[16] UNCTAD Resolution 93(IV), para. I.5.

natural materials in an UNCTAD forum, on the grounds that this was a matter for discussion in the GATT.

However, perhaps the most important limitation was that the Permanent Group itself had no means of financing the expanded R & D programmes which it had agreed were essential. The IBRD Consultative Group on Agricultural Research, as mentioned earlier, continued to devote its efforts, most successfully, to R & D related to food production. In practice, finance for R & D for agricultural raw materials has continued essentially on an *ad hoc* basis of bilateral or multilateral aid, without any internationally agreed strategy.

As shown earlier, the competitive position of natural raw materials continues to be eroded by the expansion of synthetic substitutes, both on price and technical grounds. The need for an adequate and internationally coordinated R & D programme to improve the competitive position of natural materials would seem now to be even more justified than at the time of the Permanent Group's reports two decades ago. Their insistence on assured and adequate international financial support would remain an essential feature of any new strategy in this field.

A movement in this direction could now be forthcoming with the ratification of the Common Fund. As mentioned in Chapter 7, the second Account of this new financial institution will support commodity development measures aimed at improving the structure of commodity markets and at enhancing the long-term competitiveness of natural raw materials by measures such as R & D, improvements in productivity and quality, the promotion of local processing, and the development of new end-uses. A considerable number of programmes and projects already prepared by the relevant international commodity bodies for submission to the second Account of the Common Fund relate mostly to R & D, processing, and market promotion.[17]

The Common Fund, as the only international organization concerned solely with commodity issues, should be in a position to develop a global strategy, in consultation with other concerned agencies such as UNCTAD, FAO, and the World Bank, to strengthen the world commodity economy, including measures to improve the competitive position of natural products facing competition from synthetics. A new international endeavour in this area should draw on the legacy of studies and policy proposals left by the Permanent Group, relating to each of the principal natural materials.

In addition, a new concern needs to be addressed, namely, the cost of environmental damage caused in the production and use of a number of synthetic materials and in the disposal of synthetic waste. Governments are now taking measures to reduce, and eventually prohibit, the production of chlorofluorocarbons (CFCs) which have already seriously damaged the earth's ozone layer. The

---

[17] The list of project proposals is given in UNCTAD 1985*b*. The total cost was estimated at almost $520 million, as against the financial resources target of about $350 million for the second Account of the Common Fund (though, as mentioned earlier, somewhat less than this amount was available when the Fund became operational). The adequacy of the resources of the second Account will be reviewed before the end of its third year of operation.

extent of environmental pollution and degradation resulting from the use of synthetic materials of all kinds now needs to be carefully examined, and the policy implications widely disseminated. The hidden costs to the world community of the displacement of natural materials by synthetics could then more readily be assessed.[18]

The potential role of the Common Fund, and the environmental aspects of the commodity issue are taken up again in Chapter 15.

ANNEXE

Decomposition of the Change in Consumption of Natural Raw Materials

Decomposing a change in consumption into different elements is basically an index number problem, since different weighting can lead to different results. For the calculations presented in Table 11.4, base weighting has been used for each linkage of periods, the detailed formulae involved being given below.

Let C_i = consumption of natural material i
$\sum_{i=1}^{n} C_i$ = total consumption of natural materials
$\sum_{i=1}^{n} C_i^*$ = total consumption of materials, natural and synthetic
r, r^* = annual growth rate of $\sum_{i=1}^{n} C_i$ and $\sum_{i=1}^{n} C_i^*$, respectively
p = annual growth rate of industrial output
0, 1 = subscripts for base and current periods, respectively

Then, the change in consumption of natural materials from base to current periods is:

$$\Delta \sum_{i=1}^{n} C_i = \sum_{i=1}^{n} C_{i0} \{ (1+r)^t - 1 \} \tag{1}$$

where t = number of years from base to current periods.

Equation (1) can be written as:

$$\Delta \sum_{i=1}^{n} C_i = \sum_{i=1}^{n} C_{i0} \{ (1+p)^t - 1 \}$$
$$+ \sum_{i=1}^{n} C_{i0} \{ (1+r^*)^t - (1+p)^t \} \tag{2}$$
$$+ \sum_{i=1}^{n} C_{i0} \{ (1+r)^t - (1+r^*)^t \}$$

where the first term on the right-hand side represents the influence of the rise in industrial output (other things being equal); the second term represents the effect of changes in the materials content of industrial output; and the third term indicates the effect of the substitution of synthetic for natural materials.

To place the change in consumption of natural raw materials in historical perspective, it is useful to consider the extent to which such consumption would have increased in the 1970s and 1980s had there been no slowdown in the growth rate of industrial output. This can be done by subdividing the first term on the right-hand side of equation (2) into two elements:

---

[18] See also the discussion in Ch. 3, Sect. 4(b) on environmental degradation and narcotic drugs.

$$\sum_{i=1}^{n} C_{i0}\{(1+p)^t - 1\} = \sum_{i=1}^{n} C_{i0}\{(1+p_{-1})^t - 1\} \qquad (3)$$
$$+ \sum_{i=1}^{n} C_{i0}\{(1+p)^t - (1+p_{-1})^t\}$$

where p_{-1} denotes the annual growth rate of industrial output in the preceding period. The first term on the right-hand side of equation (3) represents the notional growth in consumption of natural raw materials if the growth rate of industrial output of the preceding period had been maintained in the current period (the 'potential growth effect'). The second term then represents the change in natural materials consumption attributable to the difference in industrial growth rates between the two periods (the 'recession effect').

Somewhat different results would be arrived at using different weights. For example, had current period weights been used, equation (2) would be amended to:

$$\Delta \sum_{i=1}^{n} C_i = \sum_{i=1}^{n} C_{i1}\{1 - 1/(1+p)^t\}$$
$$+ \sum_{i=1}^{n} C_{i1}\{1/(1+p)^t - 1/(1+r^*)^t\} \qquad (4)$$
$$+ \sum_{i=1}^{n} C_{i1}\{1/(1+r^*)^t - 1/(1+r)^t\}$$

For the 1971–3 to 1978–80 link, these three elements had growth rates, using equation (4), of 2.6, −0.7, and −1.4 per cent a year, respectively, as against 3.0, −0.9, and −1.6 per cent on base weighting (as in Table 11.4). For the 1978–80 to 1984–6 link, the corresponding percentages were 1.3, −1.2, and −0.6 on later period weights, as against 1.5, −1.2, and −0.7 on base weighting. The differences between these results do not affect the argument in the text.

12
Protectionist Barriers to Commodity Trade

1. THE EXTENT OF PROTECTION

All developed countries protect their domestic agriculture, to a greater or lesser extent, against import competition. By contrast, a large number of developing countries impose taxes, mostly implicit, arising from protection given to local manufacturing or service industries, which increase input costs for the agricultural sector. The subsidization of high-cost agriculture, and of the associated processing activities (the agro-industries) in developed countries has been at high, and increasing, levels over the post-war period, with substantially adverse economic impact on lower-cost producers, including those in developing countries.

The primary purpose of agricultural subsidization policies in developed countries is to maintain the incomes of the farm population at stable levels deemed reasonable in relation to those of the rest of the population. A number of subsidiary, or derivative, objectives may also be pursued, such as improving the rural environment, accelerating technological change, enhancing productivity, or providing special assistance to older farmers or to those wishing to leave farming altogether. The main objective is attained either by direct means (such as deficiency or other payments to farmers), or indirectly by manipulating the market mechanism so as to increase the prices received by farmers for their output, and/or by reducing the prices they pay for essential inputs, such as fertilizers, water, transport, or insurance, or by some combination of both direct and indirect methods. The subsidization of agriculture involves an indirect subsidy to domestic agro-industries, which also benefit from direct protectionist barriers against lower-cost competing imports.

The particular combination of protective mechanisms used varies considerably across countries and across products.[1] The Common Agricultural Policy of the European Community, for example, combines a variable import levy with a guaranteed price for domestic output for an important range of products (most cereals, sugar, milk, beef and veal, pigmeat, sheepmeat, and certain fruits and vegetables). Certain other products (eggs, poultry, flowers, and some fruits and vegetables) are protected only by import barriers, while for a third group (durum wheat, olive oil, and tobacco) additional aid is provided along the lines of deficiency payments to cover the difference between market prices and higher target prices. Exports from the Community are subsidized by the difference between domestic and world prices. High and sustained levels of domestic farm prices led

---

[1] For more detailed descriptions of the mechanisms in use, see OECD 1990.

in the 1980s to sharp increases in output and the accumulation of large excess stocks of a number of agricultural commodities.

It led also to a continual rise in spending from the Community's resources which, by 1984, threatened to undermine the entire Community budget. A first step in containing CAP expenditures was taken in that year by the imposition of production quotas for the dairy sector, which resulted in a cut of about one-quarter in milk production in two years. For other CAP commodities, 'budget stabilizers' were agreed by the Community in 1988, involving reduced prices, the imposition of production quotas (for milk), the introduction of a maximum guaranteed quantity (for cereals and oilseeds) which, if exceeded, would result in cuts in farm-gate prices, and a new tax (or 'co-responsibility levy') on cereals sold by farmers. Partly as a result of this new emphasis on containing budgetary expenditures for agricultural support, these have roughly stabilized, after having risen rapidly between 1982 and 1987.

The United States also applies different combinations of mechanisms to suit particular commodity markets. For grains, for example, deficiency payments are combined with 'Payment in Kind' entitlements, and with loans to farmers by the Commodity Credit Corporation (CCC), the CCC loan rate operating as a guaranteed floor price. For dairy products, price supports are maintained by import tariffs and quotas, and by government purchases, while for sugar and milk there are import restrictions to back up price supports for domestic production, with the Government ready to acquire stocks to maintain prices. A notable feature of the United States support system for agriculture consists of a 'set-aside' programme, under which farmers must take a proportion of their acreage out of production to be eligible for government support. United States agricultural exports are subsidized under several programmes in order to maintain or increase their share of the world market.

Agricultural income support in Japan is provided largely by price support schemes backed by import quotas and tariffs. In addition, there are deficiency payments on milk and on soyabeans used for human consumption, while supply controls are used to divert resources from rice to other crops, some of which also receive high rates of assistance.

Import restrictions, which are an integral part of wider systems of income support for the farm sector, usually comprise a variety of non-tariff barriers to imports, in addition to traditional tariffs – non-tariff barriers having become much more widespread, and providing generally greater barriers to trade, than tariffs. A major reason for the shift to non-tariff barriers was that the floating of currencies following the breakdown of the Bretton Woods fixed exchange rate system greatly reduced the protectionist effect of tariffs.

The pervasiveness of non-tariff barriers to commodity trade can be seen from Table 12.1, which shows the percentage of import items which are subject to specified barriers by the industrial countries. Imports of raw materials and of the beverage crops – cocoa, coffee, and tea – face few non-tariff barriers. At the other extreme, 70 per cent of imports of sugar, and over one-half of imports of meat

Table 12.1. Frequency of application of various non-tariff barriers to imports of agricultural products into industrial countries, 1984 (%)[a]

	Tariff quotas and seasonal tariffs	Quantitative restrictions	Minimum price policies		Total[b]
			Variable levies	All	
Sugar[c]	–	22	58	58	70
Dairy products	7	30	26	29	55
Meat[d]	12	41	24	26	52
Beverages[e]	19	23	1	18	42
Fruits and vegetables	16	19	1	5	33
Cereals	2	11	22	22	29
Other food	1	16	13	14	27
Raw materials	–	8	0	0	8
Cocoa, coffee, tea	0	4	3	3	7
Total, agricultural products	8	17	8	12	30
Manufactures	2	7	–	1	9

[a] Number of items subject to non-tariff barriers shown as a percentage of the total number of items.

[b] Total is less than sum of previous columns if imports subject to more than one barrier. Commodities listed in order of total percentages.

[c] Including sugar confectionery.

[d] Including live animals.

[e] Mainly wine and fruit juice; excludes cocoa, coffee, and tea.

Source: Adapted from Table 6.2, World Bank 1986.

and dairy products, face at least one non-tariff barrier. Variable levies are fairly widespread for these three commodity groups which are also subject, for many items, to quantitative restrictions. Beverages (mainly wine and fruit juice) and fruits and vegetables, on the other hand, are subject to few variable levies, but are effectively controlled by seasonal tariffs, tariff quotas, and quantitative restrictions. As Table 12.1 also shows, primary agricultural imports into developed countries are generally far more subject to non-tariff barriers than are imports of manufactured goods.

In view of the diverse mechanisms employed to maintain farm incomes, comparisons of the degree of protection or of income support among countries or among different products can, at best, be only approximate. One approach often used has been to relate farm output at domestic prices to the same output valued at world market prices, the difference between the two capturing the effects of both tariffs and non-tariff barriers. Calculations on this basis for the period

Table 12.2. Net producer subsidy equivalents[a] in the agricultural sector of OECD countries, 1979–85 and 1986–9 (%)[b]

	1979–85 (av.)	1986	1987	1988[c]	1989[d]
Major importers					
European Community	35	50	48	43	38
United States	26	42	40	35	27
Japan	64	75	76	75	72
Other European countries					
Austria	29	49	51	49	44
Finland	57	68	73	74	72
Norway	71	76	76	76	74
Sweden	42	60	58	52	47
Switzerland	67	80	82	80	75
Oceania					
Australia	11	16	11	10	10
New Zealand	23	33	14	7	5
TOTAL	34	51	49	45	39

[a] Value of transfers to farmers generated by agricultural policy, both by consumers (via price supports), and by taxpayers (via direct budgetary payments or in other ways). The figures are net of the additional cost of feed to livestock producers resulting from price supports for feed.
[b] Net PSE expressed as percentage of total value of production at domestic prices.
[c] Estimates.
[d] Provisional.

Source: OECD 1990, Table IV.1. For 1979–85, the figures relate to EC-10, and from 1986 to EC-12.

1980–2, for seven major agricultural commodities,[2] showed rates of support ranging from 16 per cent in the United States to 54 per cent in the European Community, 84 per cent for other countries in Western Europe,[3] and 144 per cent for Japan.

More recently, a wider concept of 'Producer Subsidy Equivalent' (PSE) has been introduced by the OECD to include all public expenditures (e.g. on research, training, extension, and related items as well as on price and income support), plus the additional costs to consumers in the form of higher prices arising from government policies. The OECD calculations on this basis, which are summarized in Table 12.2 for the countries for which the detailed calculations have been made, cover individual products accounting for about 75 per cent

---

[2] Wheat, coarse grains, rice, beef and lamb, pork and poultry, dairy products, and sugar (Tyers and Anderson 1986, quoted in World Bank 1986: 112–13).
[3] Austria, Finland, Norway, Sweden, and Switzerland.

of the value of agricultural output in the European Community, the corresponding percentages being 69 for the United States, 65 for Japan, and 75–85 for the other countries listed.

There is clearly a wide dispersion in the levels of agricultural support among the OECD countries, with Japan and the smaller countries of Western Europe having high support levels, Australia and New Zealand having low levels, and the European Community and the United States occupying intermediate positions. In both the European Community and the United States, support levels were falling in the later 1980s, reflecting both reductions in guaranteed prices for individual farm products and, in the case of the Community, increases in world prices which substantially reduced the cost of export subsidies. Little change occurred in support levels in Japan, where roughly three-quarters of income from farm produce is still derived from government policies. By 1989, average support levels in the countries covered by the OECD calculations had been substantially reduced from a high point in 1986, but were still higher than the average for the first half of the decade.

Processed Commodities

In addition to barriers to trade in primary agricultural products, the second major area of commodity protectionism relates to the processed forms of both agricultural and mineral commodities. In all developed countries, both tariff and non-tariff barriers (NTBs) generally escalate with the degree of processing to which a product has been subjected. The escalation is most marked in NTBs on imports of agricultural raw materials, such barriers being few or non-existent for primary forms, but generally widespread for the processed forms (see Table 12.3). For the food group, of the nine commodities listed, six show increases in NTB frequency rates, of which four (fruit, oils, cocoa, and tobacco) show increases of over 10 percentage points from primary to processed forms.[4] For minerals and metals, NTBs are generally non-existent for ores, but for intermediate forms and finished metals NTB frequencies are substantial for steel, aluminium, and zinc.

There is also a clear escalation in the average tariff rate as the degree of processing increases. The extent of tariff escalation is particularly marked for meat, cocoa, and tobacco in the foods, beverages, etc. group, and for cotton, wool, sisal, and leather among agricultural raw materials, and for aluminium, lead, and tin among metals. The degree of escalation in trade barriers is, however, understated for many commodities by the use of nominal tariff rates, or by the nominal tariff-equivalents of non-tariff barriers, since for these commodities the price-elasticity of demand is significantly greater for the processed, than for the raw, forms.[5]

[4] Sugar is the main exception, the NTB frequency rate being higher for unrefined than for refined sugar.

[5] e.g. estimates of the price-elasticity of demand in the European Community show a rise from -0.34 for soyabeans to -0.57 for soyabean oil; from -0.47 for cocoa beans to -0.66 for cocoa butter and -0.84 for chocolate; and from -0.07 for green coffee beans to -0.18 for roasted coffee beans and to -1.03 for coffee extracts. On the other hand, for both raw tobacco and cigarettes, the estimated elasticities are the same (-0.24) (UNCTAD/UNDP/WIDER 1990, Annex II).

Table 12.3. Escalation of trade barriers in industrial countries by stage of processing

	Average tariff rates (%)[a]		NTB frequency rates (%)[b]	
	Primary[c]	Processed[d]	Primary[c]	Processed[d]
Food, beverages, and tobacco				
Meat	7	22	49	43
Fish	4	6	35	31
Vegetables	9	12	39	48
Fruit	5	14	20	54
Sugar	14	10	78	56
Oilseeds and oils	3	8	33	56
Cocoa	1	9	–	14
Coffee	7	9	11	17
Tobacco	56	82	11	22
Agricultural raw materials				
Cotton	1	6–11	6	44–61
Wool	2	2–22	–	44–72
Jute	3	5–8	–	33–44
Sisal	–	7	–	56
Rubber	2	3–7	–	6–14
Leather	–	4–10	–	13–26
Wood	2	7	6	9–12
Paper	–	1–6	6	0–8
Minerals and metals				
Iron and Steel	3	6	10	23
Copper	2	5	3	3
Aluminium	6	10	39	16
Lead	4	7	6	6
Zinc	3	5	22	9
Tin	–	4	–	–
Phosphates	–[e]	2–6	–[e]	0–6

[a] Post-Tokyo Round rates.
[b] Percentage of 4-digit CCCN items affected by non-tariff barriers.
[c] Intermediate for minerals and metals.
[d] For raw materials, where a percentage range is shown, the lower figure usually relates to simply-processed intermediate products, the higher figure to the finished goods stage.
[e] Natural phosphates.

Sources: UNCTAD 1984g: Table D.9.

Table 12.4. Tariff rate averages for selected processing chains in developing countries, 1981

	No. of processing chains	Tariff on processed, as proportion of tariff on primary, forms (%)[a]		
		Unweighted	Actual trade weights	Potential trade weights[b]
Foods[c]	6	146	181	625
Agricultural raw materials[d]	5	183	377	1,198
Minerals and metals[e]	7	189	723	1,197
Petroleum	1	197	251	421
TOTAL	19	174	436	976

[a] Unweighted averages of rates for individual processing chains.
[b] See footnote 7 for explanation.
[c] Meat, fish, fruit, vegetables, vegetable oils, coffee, cocoa, sugar.
[d] Leather, rubber, wood, wool, cotton (excluding finished manufactures).
[e] Iron and steel, copper, aluminium, lead, zinc, tin, phosphates.

Source: Adapted from Laird and Yeats 1987: Table 1.

Consequently, a given nominal tariff, or tariff-equivalent, will keep out a higher proportion of potential imports of processed, than of primary, commodities. Differences in demand elasticities can, however, be allowed for by relating the value of potential imports kept out by a tariff, or tariff-equivalent, to the total value of imports that would have come in to a country in the absence of trade barriers.[6] This measure of the height of a trade barrier clearly indicates that imports of processed commodities are subject to a double constraint.[7]

---

[6] This is one of two measures of the height of a trade barrier first proposed by the present author (see Maizels 1963: 142); they have recently been applied in an analysis of tariff escalation in developing countries (Laird and Yeats 1987).

[7] Using as weights the proportion of potential imports which is kept out by a tariff (or the tariff-equivalent of a quantitative restriction), the average height of tariffs for a given group of commodities would be:

$$D = \sum_{i=1}^{n} p_i q_i \{\eta_i \cdot t_i / (1 + t_i)\} / \sum_{i=1}^{n} p_i q_i \{1 + \eta_i \cdot t_i / (1 + t_i)\}$$

where p_i and q_i represent the duty-free import price, and the actual import quantity, of commodity i, respectively; η_i is the import price-elasticity of demand for i with respect to the duty-paid price, and t_i is the corresponding tariff or tariff-equivalent rate. For a single commodity i, the height of the tariff, in terms of $p_i q_i$ as the *numéraire*, would then be:

$$D_i = \eta_i \cdot t_i / (1 + t_i + \eta_i \cdot t_i)$$

so that the height of the tariff will increase if either η_i or t_i, or both, increase with the degree of processing.

When allowance is made for differences in demand elasticities, the degree of tariff escalation is seen to be far greater than is indicated by nominal rates. As shown by Table 12.4, which relates to tariffs of developing countries, the height of tariffs on processed commodities, when allowance is made for differences in demand elasticities, is far greater, in relation to tariffs on primary forms, than is the escalation shown by nominal tariff rates. Though comparable calculations have not yet been made for developed countries, a similar relationship between tariff escalation with, and without, allowance for differences in demand elasticities must be expected.

The degree of protection afforded to processing industries is measured by the rate of effective protection, i.e. the degree to which protection allows the value added in production to exceed that which would obtain in free trade conditions. Effective protection rates are thus not direct measures of trade barriers, but show the extent to which productive resources may be directed away from sectors where exporting countries have a comparative advantage.[8] An analysis of (pre-Tokyo Round) tariffs, and tariff-equivalents of some NTBs, on imports of selected processed agricultural products entering the European Community, Japan, and the United States showed that the rates of effective protection were generally several times the nominal rates, with the divergence being particularly high for vegetable oils, for which effective rates range up to eight times the nominal.[9] The sharp discrimination by developed countries against imports of processed commodities as a result of tariff and NTB escalation has been, and remains, a major reason for the slow growth of exports of processed commodities from developing countries.[10]

Tropical products. Though the tropical beverage crops—cocoa, coffee, and tea—and tropical fruits and other tropical products (e.g. spices) not produced in developed countries are not subject to protectionist trade barriers, many developed countries impose excise duties or internal sales taxes on these products. While such taxes are imposed purely for revenue purposes, they have the incidental effect of reducing domestic consumption, and thus world demand, so that both export prices and export volumes of developing countries are reduced. Moreover, many developed countries employ escalating tariff rates on the processed forms, e.g. on processed cocoa and chocolate products, and on processed coffee. As long ago as 1958, the Haberler Report pointed out forcefully that fiscal charges imposed on cocoa, coffee, tea, and tobacco by some Western European countries were so high as 'to justify the presumption that consumption and imports are being substantially restrained'.[11] Though this issue has since been raised many times in international forums, no significant reductions in these internal taxes have yet been made.

---

[8] For a more detailed discussion, see Yeats 1979 and Corden 1985.
[9] Yeats 1981.
[10] This issue is discussed in more detail in Ch. 14.
[11] GATT 1958: 105.

The GATT Tokyo Round negotiations included the objective of special priority treatment for the liberalization of trade in tropical products, and though a considerable number of concessions were negotiated, these related mainly to spices and tropical nuts. In the Uruguay Round, tropical products were again to receive special treatment, and detailed proposals by the European Community have been under consideration since late 1987. These include proposals to abolish or reduce tariffs on unprocessed goods, and to reduce significantly those on processed forms, to phase out quotas still in force (except for bananas), and to phase out revenue duties.[12] These proposals were, however, made conditional on a number of specified criteria being met, viz. that other countries should also make concessions; that countries benefiting most from the proposed measures should offer adequate reciprocity; and that developing countries with a dominant supply position should make a proportional reduction in measures, such as export duties, which limit their commodity exports. It was not clear, at the time of writing, what the outcome of this part of the Uruguay Round negotiations would be.

One alternative to the abolition of revenue taxes on tropical products which has never been considered in GATT negotiations would be an arrangement whereby some proportion of the tax revenue is remitted to the producing countries. Since the price-elasticity of demand for many of the products concerned is relatively small, the tax revenue is necessarily very much larger than the foreign exchange loss suffered by producing countries so that this loss could be fully offset, in principle, by a remission of only a proportion of the tax revenue.

2. BENEFITS AND COSTS OF AGRICULTURAL PROTECTION

While agricultural support has generally one major specific objective, i.e. to maintain the real incomes of the farm population, who are the immediate beneficiaries of the system, the costs are spread widely over the economy as a whole. Moreover, the benefits do not accrue uniformly to the farm population. In the European Community, in particular, the distribution of benefit is heavily skewed in favour of large farms, since income support is generally related to output.[13] Since farmland is virtually in fixed supply, the increase in demand for such land resulting from subsidization of agriculture results in a rise in land prices and land rents, whereas the rate of return on farm capital is geared to the general profit rate of the economy.[14] Agricultural support thus benefits mainly the large farms and the owners of farmland.

---

[12] For a detailed discussion of the treatment of tropical products in the Uruguay Round, see Koekkoek 1989 and Cobban 1988.

[13] It is estimated that about 75% of the Community's budgetary support for agriculture goes to the top 25% of farms, in terms of size (Bureau of Agricultural Economics 1985).

[14] For the US, it has been estimated that each $1 billion permanent rise in government payments generated an increase of about $1 in returns per acre, and a $15 rise in the price of land per acre (World Bank 1986: 124).

The costs of agricultural support are more diverse, comprising not merely the payments out of government budgets – the burden of which falls on taxpayers – and the extra cost of food and other agricultural produce which consumers have to meet, but also the 'deadweight' losses to the economies of the countries concerned arising from the distortion in the use of resources as a result of high levels of support to agriculture.

During the 1980s, budgetary supports rose sharply. For the commodities and countries covered by the PSE calculations in Table 12.2, the net total PSE increased from an annual average of $99 billion in the period 1979 to 1985 to a peak of $173 billion in 1987, before declining to an estimated $163 billion in 1988 and $141 billion (provisional) in 1989 (OECD 1990), still substantially higher than the level of the early 1980s. About three-quarters of the increase of over $40 billion between 1979–85 levels and 1989 was accounted for by the European Community and Japan.

The additional cost to consumers of high support prices has also been very large. The OECD has assessed this by the use of 'Consumer Subsidy Equivalents' (CSEs), which measure the implicit aggregate tax on consumers generated by agricultural policy. For the commodities and countries covered by the calcula-

Table 12.5. Total transfers associated with agricultural policies in OECD countries, 1986–9 ($ billion)

	EC-12	United States	Japan	Others[a]	Total
Transfers from taxpayers					
1986	32	59	14	11	116
1987	38	50	18	13	119
1988	46	49	19	11	125
1989	44	46	16	11	117
Transfers from consumers					
1986	72	30	49	18	169
1987	78	30	55	22	185
1988	64	26	61	21	172
1989	54	22	52	19	147
Total transfers[b]					
1986	103	88	54	28	273
1987	116	80	63	31	290
1988	109	74	66	31	280
1989	98	67	58	28	251

[a] See Table 12.2 for countries included.
[b] Transfers from taxpayers and consumers less budget revenues arising from price distortions (on imported agricultural products).

Source: OECD 1990: Table IV.8.

tion, the aggregate CSE rose from $68 billion, on average, during the period 1979 to 1985, to a peak of $132 billion in 1987, before declining to $122 billion in 1988 and $104 billion (provisional) in 1989.

Allowing for commodities not covered by the PSE/CSE calculations, and for additional budgetary costs not directly attributable to the policies covered by the PSE calculations, the total monetary transfers to the agricultural sector reached a peak of $290 billion in 1987, before falling to $280 billion in 1988 and $251 (provisional) in 1989 (see Table 12.5). In the European Community, and even more so in Japan, the greater part of the transfer comes from higher prices for agricultural products paid by consumers, whereas in the United States some two-thirds of the total comes from Federal and State budgets.

The 'deadweight' losses to the economies of developed countries arising from distortions in resource use as between agriculture and other sectors are also likely to be significant. Since other sectors use resources more efficiently than does agriculture, high agricultural subsidies, by attracting resources, will result in a less efficient economy as a whole. Real income losses are also likely to arise within the agricultural sector itself as a result of large differences in the rates of support for various products.

Recent research has also shown that the high level of agricultural support in the European Community, by acting as an implicit tax on the manufacturing sector, has been a major factor in the decline of the Community's share of world manufacturing production and exports, and in the rise in the import share of its consumption of manufactured goods. As a result, the rate of economic growth has been depressed, and the level of unemployment in the Community has been raised, compared with the levels that would have obtained in the absence of agricultural subsidization.[15]

For developing countries, the adverse impact of developed countries' protection of their agriculture is also severe. By raising prices in developed countries, agricultural support reduces domestic consumption and encourages domestic (high-cost) production. This reduces market outlets for (lower-cost) producers elsewhere, while developed country surpluses are exported under subsidy, thus adding to supply on the world market. Two consequences follow: world prices are reduced, and they become more unstable than they otherwise would be. Both consequences involve economic losses for low-cost commodity exporters, both developed (such as Australia and New Zealand) and developing.

Estimates of the increase in world prices that would ensue from developed country trade liberalization for agricultural products vary considerably among commodities, and according to the particular mechanisms of liberalization that are pursued. An UNCTAD/UNDP/WIDER study (1990) estimates the increase in world prices of a sample of important commodities that would ensue as a result of four alternative liberalization policies, which were selected so as to reflect broadly the policy proposals under consideration in the GATT Uruguay Round

---

[15] Stoeckel and Breckling 1988.

of trade negotiations. First, the study assumed a situation of complete agricultural liberalization, i.e. the reduction of PSE and CSE levels to zero, and the elimination of all tariffs and quotas, as well as of revenue duties on tropical products. This corresponds to the 'zero option' proposals which had been put forward by the United States.

A second alternative considered was a reduction in producer price support by 20 per cent, corresponding largely to the proposal of the European Community, which envisaged a reduction in the level of farm support for certain products without a fundamental change in the nature of market intervention. A third alternative was the elimination of export subsidies, corresponding to the minimum proposal of the Cairns Group;[16] while the fourth was an autonomous increase in imports of each product by 10 per cent into each of five developed-country markets (the European Community, United States, Japan, Canada, and Australia), an approach which corresponds to the minimum access proposal supported by a variety of countries.

The results of the price calculations, using a partial equilibrium comparative static model, based on published supply and demand elasticities, are summarized in Table 12.6. It is clear that the pattern of price changes will differ very sharply according to the particular mechanisms of trade liberalization that are adopted. While considerable caution must be exercised in assessing the individual price changes shown,[17] the broad picture can be taken as generally valid.

The greatest divergence in price effects arises as between a policy of complete liberalization, under which food prices are likely to rise substantially (with some increases for processed coffee and cocoa, but little or no price increase for other commodities), and one of a 10 per cent autonomous increase in imports, where the prices of tropical products (particularly coffee and cocoa but also copra and tobacco) would be the main beneficiaries. Either of the two other policies would raise prices of wheat, rice and meat by some 10–18 per cent, while sugar prices would rise by more than 10 per cent, given a 20 per cent cut in producer support prices.[18]

Taking the increase in world agricultural prices following a complete liberalization of agricultural trade by developed countries as 10 per cent, the consequent increase in the real income of developing countries has been estimated as almost $26 billion at 1985 prices.[19] This figure includes not only the gain from the improvement in export earnings, but also the real income gain from greater

---

[16] The Cairns Group consists of 14 agricultural exporting countries: Australia, New Zealand, Canada, 5 countries in Latin America, 4 in South-East Asia, Fiji, and Hungary.

[17] The model used provides essentially a static picture of the likely price changes, assuming that factors other than assistance to agriculture are held constant. Moreover, in practice, dynamic effects would also influence prices (e.g. the interaction between the grains and livestock sectors). The use of data for the period 1983–5 also limits the applicability of the results for the early 1990s.

[18] The price effects of complete liberalization, as shown in Table 12.6, are generally consistent with the comparable results of earlier studies (see e.g. Anderson and Tyers 1986b and Zietz and Valdés 1986).

[19] Loo and Tower 1988.

Table 12.6. Estimated change in world prices of agricultural products under alternative liberalization policies (% increase[a])

	Complete liberalization	20% reduction in producer support price	Elimination of export subsidies	10% increase in imports
Foods				
Wheat	20	8	12	*
Maize	15	*	*	*
Rice	43	18	9	*
Sorghum	12	*	0	*
Beef and Veal	13	13	11	*
Sugar	27	11	*	*
Vegetable oilseeds and oils				
Soyabeans	*	0	0	*
Soyabean oil	*	*	0	0
Groundnuts	*	*	0	5
Groundnut oil	*	*	9	*
Copra	0	0	0	10
Palm oil	*	0	0	*
Tropical beverages				
Tea	*	*	0	8
Coffee: green	*	*	0	30
roasted	8	0	0	39
extracts	8	*	0	*
Cocoa: beans	*	0	0	20
butter	*	*	0	9
powder	5	*	0	*
chocolate	9	*	0	*
Industrial Materials				
Cotton	*	*	0	9
Tobacco: leaves	*	*	0	12
cigarettes	*	*	0	0
cigars	*	*	0	*

[a] An asterisk denotes a price increase of under 5%.

Source: UNCTAD/UNDP/WIDER 1990: Table 1.

efficiency of resource use and from a less distorted system of taxation (assumed to be made possible by a rise in tax revenue).

One general effect of agricultural liberalization in developed countries, in whatever form, would be increased real incomes in the net commodity-exporting countries, and a tendency to redistribute income to labour in the agricultural sector, an important effect on equity grounds as rural real wages are generally lower in these countries than are real wages in other sectors. Moreover, a similar exercise for different groups of developing countries shows that the greatest relative benefit from an assumed 10 per cent increase in world agricultural prices would accrue to low-income countries (other than India and China).

Some developing countries would, however, be net losers from a general rise in world prices of agricultural products, in so far as they are net importers — particularly of cereals — and would thus face a foreign exchange loss, or be forced to reduce food imports. However, there might well be an offset, to a greater or lesser extent, in so far as higher food prices eventually result in an increase in domestic food production in such countries. It has also been argued that the efficiency gains in resource use in net food-importing countries, combined with gains from a reduction in tax rates, would outweigh the terms of trade loss. However, there would be net income losses, in the short term at least, for the net food-importing countries from a rise in world food prices, if domestic policies are not such as to yield the offsets mentioned above.

To the extent that there would be a net gain to developing countries as a result of agricultural trade liberalization (an issue considered in more detail in the next section), this would in turn have positive 'feedback' effects on the economies of developed countries. Any rise in export earnings of developing countries resulting from a substantial reduction, if not elimination, of agricultural support in developed countries would quickly lead to expanded demand for developed country manufactures, technology, and associated services. Agricultural liberalization would thus not only release resources for these other sectors in developed countries, but would also promote increased demand for their products in the markets of developing countries, as was argued in Chapter 3. Similarly, a rise in developing countries' export earnings would ease their debt servicing difficulties, thus making them more creditworthy on international capital markets and allowing them greater possibilities for repaying existing debt.

A substantial reduction, or complete elimination, of agricultural subsidies would also significantly reduce commodity price fluctuations on world markets. The variable import levies imposed by the European Community on a range of important agricultural products have a particularly marked effect on world price instability. One recent econometric study indicates that agricultural trade liberalization by developed countries would significantly reduce price instability: the coefficient of price variation would be reduced, according to this study, by 33 per cent for wheat, by 10 per cent for coarse grains, by 19 per cent for rice, and by 15 per cent for sugar.[20]

3. NATIONAL AND INTERNATIONAL POLICIES AFFECTING AGRICULTURE: THE PROSPECTS FOR LIBERALIZATION

The systems of farm support in developed countries are long established and well entrenched. They have also remained outside the rules of the General Agreement

---

[20] Tyers and Anderson 1986.

on Tariffs and Trade (GATT), since when the GATT was established neither the United States nor the other main industrial countries wished to dismantle their agricultural support programmes.[21] Thus, as one authority on this subject remarks:

[The] GATT rules were written to fit the agricultural programmes then in existence, especially in the United States. Since then the rules have been adopted or interpreted to fit various other national agricultural policies. So instead of developing domestic agricultural policies to fit the rules of international trade, we have tried to develop rules to fit the policies.[22]

The two main mechanisms of agricultural policy, as indicated earlier, are subsidies (direct or indirect) to farmers and the associated restrictions—mainly NTBs—on competing imports. In both respects, the GATT rules relating to trade treat agriculture very differently from other industries. While export subsidies on goods other than primary commodities are prohibited under GATT (Article XVI: 4), export subsidies for primary commodities are allowed, provided that such subsidies do not result in the exporting country gaining 'more than an equitable share of world trade' in the product concerned (Article XVI: 3). As the recent history of agricultural 'trade wars' between the United States and the European Community has clearly shown, the GATT export subsidy provision for primary products has remained ineffective, essentially because of the ambiguity of the term 'equitable share'.

Similarly, the GATT rules prohibit the use of quantitative restrictions on trade, with certain exceptions (Article XI). One major exception relates to agricultural or fishery products, since for these, governments are allowed (under Article XI: 2) to use quantitative restrictions in several different circumstances, including where domestic price support or production control is in force. Thus the use of NTBs to restrict agricultural imports is, in effect, condoned by GATT. In addition, the United States obtained in 1955 a special waiver under Article XI which allowed the right to impose quantitative restrictions on imports of any agricultural product that materially interfered with the operation of any of its domestic agricultural programmes, even if such programmes did not involve domestic price support or production control.[23]

GATT rules can also be bypassed where the imports of particular agricultural products are channelled through state or quasi-state trading agencies. These agencies play an important role in world trade in certain products, particularly grains.[24] Such agencies can limit imports by restricting their purchases on the world market, thus avoiding the need to impose import quotas. Similarly, by sell-

---

[21] See discussion on this point in Hathaway 1987.
[22] Ibid. 104.
[23] The GATT waiver is still in effect and is used to restrict the imports of sugar, peanuts, and dairy products (see Hathaway 1987: 108–11).
[24] State trading agencies handle some 90% of world trade in wheat, and about 70% of trade in coarse grains (ibid. 111).

ing abroad at prices below domestic prices, state trading agencies can, in effect, provide an export subsidy.

The various negotiating 'Rounds' of GATT, up to the Tokyo Round of the late 1970s, all failed to tackle the problem of agricultural protectionism. However, the growing budgetary cost of farm support programmes, and the associated unprecedented size of unwanted food stocks during the early- and mid-1980s, particularly in the European Community, prompted governments to seek ways of cutting the growing burden of farm support. In September 1986, a new GATT Round – the Uruguay Round – was launched which aims, among other things, 'to develop a more open, viable and durable multilateral trading system'.[25] In the field of agriculture, the Declaration launching the Round called for greater liberalization of trade and for bringing all measures affecting import access and export competition under strengthened and operationally effective GATT rules.

This objective would appear to be difficult, if not impossible, to achieve given the time frame of the Uruguay Round – some four years of negotiations – the complexity of existing farm support and trade restriction systems, and the evident conflicts of interest among the major countries involved – particularly the United States and the European Community – in their efforts to increase their market shares for the principal temperate-zone foods.

An interesting analysis by Honma and Hayami has shown that the greater part of the variation among developed countries in nominal rates of protection of agriculture over selected years from 1955 to 1980 can be attributed to three factors, viz. the relative comparative advantage of each country in agriculture, the relative share of agriculture in the national economy, and the international terms of trade between agricultural and manufactured products.[26] All three of these factors were found to be inversely related to the nominal rate of protection, the relationship for the degree of comparative advantage being highly significant statistically. The other two factors also proved to be significantly associated with nominal protection rates, though the influence of each appears to be less than that of relative comparative advantage.

The close negative association between nominal protection rates and comparative advantage in agriculture in developed countries implies that this could be a major constraint on a general movement towards liberalization of this sector. Since there is wide variation in productive efficiency, there is likely to be strenuous opposition by the less-efficient producing countries to any significant reduction in current levels of agricultural support, if traditional policies are continued in the future.

---

[25] GATT, ministerial decision of 20 Sept. 1986.
[26] Honma and Hayami 1986. These three factors accounted for 80% of the variance in nominal rates of protection, defined as $(\sum_{i=1}^{n} A_d - \sum_{i=1}^{n} A_w)/\sum_{i=1}^{n} A_w$, where $\sum_{i=1}^{n} A_d$ is the value of total agricultural output at domestic prices, and $\sum_{i=1}^{n} A_w$ is the corresponding value at world (or border) prices. The full analysis was based on a pooled regression of data for 10 industrial countries and 6 separate years from 1955 to 1980.

An underlying question here is why governments are generally so determined to maintain protection and income support for the farm sector. If there is indeed an inverse relationship between the degree of protection and the relative size of the agricultural labour force in the working population, as was found by Honma and Hayami, then it might be supposed that countries where agriculture employs only a small proportion of the workforce would have less incentive to maintain or increase agricultural protection than would countries where agriculture is a relatively large employer. Honma and Hayami argue, however, that the inverse relationship operates because as the agricultural sector contracts relatively, it becomes easier for farmers to organize political lobbying while, at the same time, the relatively contracting agricultural sector reduces the resistance of the non-agricultural population against agricultural protectionism.[27]

This argument is, however, not entirely convincing for two reasons. First, while there may be an inverse relation between agricultural protection rates and the relative importance of the farm sector in the economy, if measured over time as well as across countries (as in the pooled regression of Honma and Hayami), the relationship for any one year is strongly positive.[28] Second, as was mentioned earlier, the beneficiaries of farm support and related policies have been essentially the larger, and more efficient, farms, the agro-processing industries, and the owners of land. The landowning class has traditionally wielded great political power in almost all developed countries, either directly or indirectly through coalitions with sympathetic political parties and groupings. Since landowners stand to lose financially – probably very substantially – by significant reductions in agricultural support programmes, it must be expected that they would give strong political backing to resistance by farmers and by the associated processing interests to proposals for reducing protection for agriculture and domestic food processing. If this interpretation is somewhere near the truth, the prospects for a genuine movement towards agricultural liberalization would seem to depend on the development of political countervailing power. An important element here could be a much wider appreciation of the hidden costs of agricultural protection, particularly those borne by consumers and exporters in developed countries, and by the more efficient agricultural producers, including those in developing countries.

---

[27] Ibid. 127.

[28] A linear regression for the year 1980, for example, covering the same 10 countries used by Honma and Hayami, gave the following result:

$$NRP = 3.90 + 5.36\ (AG) - 6.61\ (EC) + 46.55\ (NON)$$
$$(0.16)\quad (2.16)\quad\ \ (-0.35)\quad\quad (2.00)$$
$$(\bar{R}^2 = 0.494)$$

where NRP = nominal rate of protection; AG = proportion of economically active population in agriculture; EC = dummy for member country of European Community ($=1$), others ($=0$); NON = dummy for country not member of a military alliance ($=1$), others ($=0$). The coefficients for the relative size of agriculture, and for non-alliance countries (Sweden and Switzerland), are both positive and statistically significant (t values in brackets). The corresponding regression for 1975 also showed a significant positive coefficient for AG, viz. 3.54 (2.18), with $\bar{R}^2 = 0.456$.

Table 12.7. Estimated net foreign exchange and welfare impact on developing countries of alternative policies for liberalization of agricultural trade: regional summary ($ billion at 1985–7 average prices)

Policy	Africa	Asia[a]	Latin America[b]	Total
1. *Complete liberalization*				
Foreign exchange earnings	−0.48	0.57	1.55	1.64
Welfare	−0.81	−0.41	0.67	−0.55
2. *Reduction of 20% in producer price support*				
Foreign exchange earnings	−0.25	0.16	0.53	0.44
Welfare change	−0.38	−0.22	0.20	−0.40
3. *Elimination of export subsidies*				
Foreign exchange earnings	−0.26	−0.09	0.26	−0.08
Welfare change	−0.36	−0.33	0.04	−0.65
4. *Increase of 10% in developed-country imports[c]*				
Foreign exchange earnings	1.88	0.89	3.64	6.41
Welfare change	1.27	0.42	2.86	4.54

[a] Including the Pacific islands.
[b] Including the Caribbean.
[c] Imports into the European Community, United States, Japan, Australia and Canada.

Source: UNCTAD/UNDP/WIDER 1990: Table 2.

There is now a new political impetus in favour of reducing farm support levels, both in the United States and in the European Community. However, much of this impetus, particularly within the European Community, derives from the excessive budgetary cost of farm support programmes (i.e. the visible, rather than overall, cost). None the less, the possibility of some real progress towards agricultural liberalization appears to be opening within the framework of the Uruguay Round negotiations.

Some guidance as to the likely effects of agricultural liberalization in the developed countries on the economies of developing countries can be derived from the estimates in Table 12.7 of the impact on the net foreign exchange earnings and welfare[29] of the latter countries of the four alternative liberalization policies assumed in the UNCTAD/UNDP/WIDER study. The regional results[30] indicate that:

when the agricultural sector is completely liberalized, or the level of assistance is reduced by 20 per cent in the five major agricultural trading countries, the resulting increase in

---

[29] The welfare impact is defined as the sum of the consumer surplus, the producer surplus, and the change in government tariff and tax revenue for individual products.
[30] The regional totals should be treated with caution, since the gains of one country cannot be used to offset the losses of another.

world prices would lead to a net loss of foreign exchange (i.e. a higher import bill) for the African region, but to net foreign exchange gains for Latin America and the Caribbean, and for the Asian and Pacific regions. The corresponding welfare changes would be positive for Latin America and the Caribbean, but negative for Africa, Asia and the Pacific. When only export subsidies are eliminated, the African region would again be a net loser both of foreign exchange and welfare, as would also Asian and Pacific countries. Latin America and the Caribbean, by contrast, would gain on both accounts. Only under the scenario of an exogenous increase of 10 per cent in the volume of imports in each of the five countries do all of the developing regions experience net gains in foreign exchange earnings, gains which are far larger than the corresponding gains — where they occur — under the alternative scenarios.

As regards tropical products in particular, the elimination of tariffs and internal taxes, and of domestic support where relevant, improves the net export earnings of all developing regions. The results indicate that an exogenous increase in the volume of imports of the five major agricultural trading countries yields by far the greatest gain in both foreign exchange and welfare for all developing regions.[31]

The rise in world food prices which would result from agricultural liberalization in the developed countries could be beneficial to developing countries in the long term, provided that the higher prices are passed on to producers in food-deficit countries and that they are supported by improved infrastructure, credit facilities, extension services, etc. However, in the short term, higher world food prices could seriously damage the balance of payments position of food-deficit countries, and lead to food shortage situations. This suggests, as argued in the UNCTAD/UNDP/WIDER study, that a balanced outcome of the Uruguay Round would need to include trade and other measures designed to offset the short term losses likely to be suffered by food-deficit countries.

The outcome of the Uruguay Round negotiations may depend heavily on the willingness of governments to reduce the present excessive levels of agricultural protection and farm support. However, even if governments wish to retain these support levels, they should consider changing the mechanisms of support in order to minimize any adverse effects on international trade. One possibility would be to convert existing NTBs, including import levies, into equivalent *ad valorem* tariffs, thus bringing agricultural protection within the GATT rules. The use of bound tariffs would have the effect of making domestic agricultural production and consumption levels responsive to changes in world markets, instead of being isolated from them. This would also allow more efficient producers a larger share of developed-country markets, particularly when world prices are relatively low. It would also significantly reduce world commodity price instability for the products affected. A related proposal would be to transform existing NTBs into tariff quotas, which do not restrict imports quantitatively, but impose an additional rate of duty on imports in excess of a specified level.

A further possibility would be gradually to reduce existing farm support pro-

---

[31] UNCTAD/UNDP/WIDER 1990: 5–7.

grammes, and to provide partial compensation to farmers by direct government payments for revenue losses on farm sales. This would increase the transparency of farm support programmes, and would also result in lower domestic prices for agricultural products in developed countries, thus encouraging greater consumption while discouraging high-cost domestic production. Other possibilities should also be considered, including the wider use of deficiency payments, instead of more protective mechanisms such as import levies. Deficiency payments do not involve any market intervention, payments to farmers being based on the difference between the market price and a higher guaranteed level. A switch to deficiency payments from existing interventionist support programmes may, however, be too drastic for most governments to accept, at least in the short term.

A reduction in the level of agricultural support could also be varied by commodity or commodity group. If reductions in support levels were greater, or made more quickly, for commodities for which developing countries were the major exporters (e.g. sugar, vegetable oilseeds, and oils) than for commodities for which they are large net importers (particularly cereals), this would bring them substantial foreign exchange gains. However, the interests of the major developed countries may be focused on their own export specialities, such as cereals, meat, and dairy products.

These various possible mechanisms could be used, in alternative combinations, to reduce the adverse impact of support policies on international trade, even if governments insist on maintaining present support levels. An international agreement to phase out agricultural support, including export subsidies, over a period of years would, however, be much more beneficial for future world economic growth and for promoting the development of Third World countries than merely changing the support mechanisms. Equally, measures to increase the volume of agricultural imports into developed countries would be of significantly greater benefit to net commodity-exporting countries than would reductions in domestic support prices or the elimination of export subsidies. Measures to reduce the escalation of barriers to trade in processed commodities are also long overdue. Though this issue has been aired on many occasions over the past two or three decades in various international forums, no remedial action has so far been taken by national governments. The international community is now at a crossroads as regards agricultural policy, since national policies—which have created largely 'managed' domestic markets—have proved to be incompatible with sustained growth in the international commodity markets, as well as acting as a major constraint on the rational use of global resources and on world economic growth.

13
New Trade Directions: South–South and East–South

The dramatic deterioration in the trade and payments position of the majority of developing countries during the 1980s, reflecting mainly the economic 'shocks' emanating from the Western industrial countries, had adverse effects on their other main flows of trade: trade among the developing countries themselves (or South–South trade) and trade with the countries of Eastern Europe (or East–South trade). The present chapter reviews briefly some of the major recent trends and considers how international policies in these areas might usefully be adjusted to support expansion in these trade flows, particularly in relation to primary commodities.

A. SOUTH–SOUTH TRADE

1. RECENT TRENDS

Developing countries' trade among themselves is still only a small part of their total foreign trade. Western markets remain by far the largest outlet for most developing-country exports. During the 1970s, however, South–South trade grew faster than developing-country exports to the rest of the world, and the share of South–South trade in total exports of developing-countries rose from 20 per cent to 25 per cent between 1970 and 1980. During that decade, the dominant feature of this trade expansion was the sharp rise in prices, particularly in petroleum exports, though price increases were also a marked feature of exports of both commodities and manufactures (Table 13.1).

By contrast, the 1980s have been dominated by price declines for developing-countries' non-oil commodity exports, as well as by a major collapse in petroleum prices in the second half of that decade. These price falls together accounted for a decline of some $40 billion in the value of South–South trade between 1980 and 1988.[1] However, these losses were partly offset by a substantial increase in the volume of exports, reflecting, in the main, continuing fast growth in exports of manufactured goods from the 'newly industrializing countries' (NICs) of East Asia. The volume of commodity exports also continued to rise—as already seen in Chapter 1—though their contribution to the overall volume growth in South–South trade was only one-quarter of that of manufactures.

The 1980s also witnessed marked changes in the geographical pattern of

---

[1] Over this period, the corresponding fall in the value of exports from developing countries to the rest of the world as a result of the price declines for non-oil commodities and petroleum amounted to about $90 billion.

Table 13.1. Exports from developing countries by broad destination and product group, 1970–80 and 1980–8

	Value ($ billion)			Value change (% p.a.)		Volume change[a] (% p.a.)	
	1970	1980	1988	1970–80	1980–8	1970–80	1980–8
Intra-trade of developing countries							
Commodities (non-fuel)	3.8	24.3	31.9	20.4	3.5	7.6	4.4
Fuels	3.8	75.9	42.4	34.8	–7.0	1.2	0.7
Manufactures	3.2	37.0	80.6	27.9	10.2	16.5	9.3
TOTAL	10.8	137.2	154.9	29.0	1.5	4.6	4.1
Exports to other countries							
Commodities (non-fuel)	23.2	82.3	95.5	13.5	1.9	2.4	2.8
Fuels	14.5	271.2	95.0	34.0	–12.3	0.7	–5.0
Manufactures	6.3	61.5	226.7	25.8	17.7	14.5	16.7
TOTAL	44.0	415.0	417.2	25.2	0.1	2.0	2.2

[a] Value change deflated by unit value indices of exports from developing countries to all destinations: for commodities, the unit value index in Appendix Table A.2 was used; for fuels, the unit value of exports from 'major petroleum exporters'; for manufactures, the unit value of manufactures exported by developing countries.

Sources: UN Monthly Bulletin of Statistics, Mar. and May, 1985 and 1990; UNCTAD *Commodity Yearbook*, 1989 and 1990a, and *Handbook of Trade and Development Statistics*, 1989.

developing countries' trade. In this regard, Hulugalle (1990) has usefully distinguished several notable trends. There was, first, a sharp contrast between the export experiences of developing countries in South and South-East Asia and those of other regions. High economic growth in the NICs and in neighbouring countries in South-East Asia, together with a marked trend towards greater integration and specialization in the region, contributed to fast expansion in their mutual trade. The region has also benefited from inward investment by developed countries, particularly Japan, and rapid growth in exports of manufactures to these countries. By 1987, the volume of exports from South and South-East Asia was about double the 1980 level, and by 1989, 2.5 times the 1980 level, whereas for Africa – at the other extreme – the export volume was down by some 15 per cent in both 1987 and 1989.

A second notable feature has been a clear shift in the direction of trade towards the developed countries. Exports to developed countries, particularly of manufactures, as a proportion of total exports rose for most developing countries (Table 13.1). This shift reflected, in part, the foreign exchange difficulties widespread among developing countries, which forced them to cut their imports; and in part, also, the pressure of debt service obligations which forced most developing countries to promote exports to convertible-currency markets.

Third, there was a sharp contraction in intra-trade within sub-regional integration and co-operation groupings, the contraction being particularly severe in both Latin American and African groupings. By contrast, the value of trade among countries of the Bangkok Agreement, which includes South Korea, and among ASEAN countries rose substantially between 1980 and 1988 (Table 13.2). Though a number of these groupings had established payments and clearing arrangements to promote their intra-trade, these generally failed to overcome the liquidity difficulties of their member countries in the 1980s. Many of these countries imposed restrictions on payments for imports, whether through the clearing arrangements or otherwise, following the severe contraction in the availability of foreign exchange. As a result, two clearing arrangements, for CARICOM and CACM, suspended operations, while for most of the other clearing arrangements the high proportion of settlements in convertible currency limited their value to member countries. Similarly, the five reserve funds in operation[2] have played only a marginal role in assisting their 44 member countries in dealing with their external financial difficulties, the total amount channelled to these countries by the reserve funds being relatively very small.[3]

Fourth, whereas during the 1970s the expansion of trade between developing regions (the 'inter-trade') was a marked feature of trade among developing countries, reflecting mainly the sharp increase in the value of oil shipments from Middle East countries, over the 1980s the reverse process set in. While trade within

---

[2] The Santo Domingo Agreement among ALADI countries; the Central American Monetary Stabilization Fund; the Andean Reserve Fund; the ASEAN Swap Arrangement; and the Arab Monetary Fund.

[3] Only $1.3 billion by the end of 1985.

Table 13.2. Intra-trade of sub-regional groupings of developing countries, 1970, 1980, and 1988

	Value of intra-trade ($ billion)			Intra-trade as % of total exports		
	1970	1980	1988[a]	1970	1980	1988[a]
ASEAN[b]	0.86	11.92	18.28	14.7	17.8	17.5
LAIA[c]	1.29	10.27	9.77	10.2	13.5	10.7
Bangkok Agreement[d]	0.05	0.52	1.11	1.5	1.8	1.4
CACM[e]	0.30	1.14	0.50	26.8	22.0	14.4
ECOWAS[f]	0.06	1.06	0.68	2.1	3.9	4.9
CARICOM[g]	0.07	0.35	0.17	7.3	6.4	3.3
Others	0.16	0.94	1.82	...	...	...
TOTAL[h]	2.79	26.20	32.33	7.4	10.9	9.7

[a] Provisional.
[b] Brunei, Indonesia, Malaysia, Philippines, Singapore, and Thailand.
[c] Latin American Integration Association (Argentina, Brazil, Chile, Mexico, Paraguay, Uruguay, *plus* Andean Group – Bolivia, Colombia, Ecuador, Peru, and Venezuela).
[d] Bangladesh, India, Republic of Korea, Laos, and Sri Lanka.
[e] Central American Common Market.
[f] Economic Community of West African States.
[g] Caribbean Community.
[h] In all, there are some 40 such groupings in existence.

Source: UNCTAD 1990*a*: Table 1.13.

regions (the 'intra-trade') grew modestly in value, there was a substantial fall in the value of 'inter-trade', especially after the fall in oil prices at the end of 1985.

The contraction in trade flows among developing countries in the 1980s was, moreover, accentuated in its effects by a decline in financial flows from OPEC countries to other developing countries. These flows, mainly on concessional terms, which had amounted to $11.0 billion in 1975 and $9.8 billion in 1980, fell to only $3.7 billion in 1985, and though there was a modest recovery, to $4.8 billion, in 1986, there was a sharp decline, to $1.7 billion, in 1987,[4] reflecting the contraction in oil revenues of OPEC countries.

2. POLICY RESPONSES OF DEVELOPING COUNTRIES

Apart from general policy changes to cope with their acute foreign exchange difficulties – such as currency devaluation, domestic income deflation, and other

---

[4] UNCTAD 1989*a*: Table 5.11.

measures associated with IMF stabilization programmes—many developing countries have also adopted a number of specific policies to foster their mutual trade.

Countertrade. The most important of such specific policies has been the use of countertrade deals or related compensatory trading arrangements, though such arrangements have also been used to increase trade between developing and developed countries. Of the 52 countertrade transactions among developing countries recorded for 1982–3, the most frequent (16) were for the exchange of non-oil primary commodities for manufactures, followed by the exchange of one or more non-oil commodities for others (11); oil was involved in 21 separate transactions, mostly in exchange for other commodities or for manufactures.[5] Recent estimates by Stewart and Singh put the value of countertrade at between 10 and 20 per cent of world trade (i.e. in the range of $200 to $400 billion a year),[6] and the evidence relating to the number of countertrade deals suggests that trade under this type of arrangement has grown rapidly since the early 1980s.

For developing countries, a major incentive to engage in countertrade is that it provides an alternative to the use of convertible currency as a means of financing essential imports. Moreover, many developing countries may prefer to receive goods under countertrade arrangements rather than be paid in convertible currency, if the latter is to be earmarked for meeting debt service payments under IMF stabilization programmes. The relatively large number of deals involving petroleum, noted earlier, might well reflect decisions by some OPEC countries to evade quota restrictions or to undercut agreed prices. Similarly, a number of deals have taken place involving tin or coffee, both commodities subject to market regulation at one time or another. More generally, also, many developing countries may perceive countertrade as a means of reducing the uncertainties of world markets for their commodity exports, thus allowing them to improve their forward planning of production and trade.[7]

Stewart and Singh, in their analysis of the short-run effects of countertrade deals, point out that for many commodities, such as sugar, bananas, bauxite, tin, oil, and wheat, the world market is dominated either by cartels (of producers or processing and marketing companies), or by developed-country governments. In such markets, individual developing exporting countries have much to gain by countertrade deals, which, in effect, bypass import restrictions or administered prices. There may, however, be an offsetting terms of trade loss if the importing country can exercise greater bargaining strength in fixing prices. The danger here, as Stewart and Singh rightly point out, is that if all developing countries try to gain market share by accepting reduced prices, their combined foreign exchange earnings may fall.[8] The key test of the net benefit of a countertrade

---

[5] Based on data in Ferenz 1984. [6] Stewart and Singh 1988.
[7] See ibid. for a detailed review of motives for countertrade.
[8] For a discussion of the significance of countertrade in manufactures exported by developing countries, see ibid.

deal in the short run is whether it results in greater purchasing power over imports than would obtain without it.[9] Moreover, if import volume can be increased, there would be additional longer-term benefits if productive capacity and/or productivity can also thereby be improved. In a wider perspective, countertrade deals among developing countries should help to strengthen South–South trading ties and reduce dependence on developed-country markets.

Trade preferences. Another policy development designed specifically to expand South–South trade has been the negotiation of a Global System of Trade Preferences (GSTP) among member countries of the Group of 77. The GSTP Agreement, signed by 46 developing countries in April 1988, is a contractual legal instrument providing for mutual trade preferences. The preferences listed in the Agreement were the result of a first round of bilateral negotiations, the concessions exchanged being extended to all the countries participating in the Agreement. In total, the concessions amount to only $4–5 billion (as against total South–South trade of some $155 billion in 1988). However, further rounds of negotiation are envisaged, and it also seems probable that additional developing countries will join the Agreement.[10]

The objective of the GSTP, as stated in the Agreement, is to constitute 'a major instrument for the promotion of trade among developing countries members of the Group of 77 and the increase of production and employment in these countries', through the exchange of tariff, para-tariff, and non-tariff concessions on the basis of mutuality of advantage. The GSTP – unlike the GATT – covers all products, both manufactures and commodities in raw, semi-processed, and processed forms.[11]

The GSTP does, however, have a wider significance than simply the quantitative expansion of South–South trade. To the extent that it succeeds in expanding this flow of trade and enhancing the economic development of the participating countries, it would thereby also strengthen the position of developing countries in their negotiations with developed countries on major trade and development issues. Moreover, the Agreement is based on principles which, if they were to be generally applied, would greatly strengthen the international trading system. The past decade has witnessed a serious erosion of the GATT principles – particularly those of non-discrimination and the banning of quantitative restrictions – which has led to a growing fragmentation of the GATT system.[12] The GSTP specifically incorporates the principles of equity and non-discrimination, together with an obligation to extend special measures in favour of the least-developed countries. This contrasts sharply with the granting of trade

---

[9] Stewart and Singh caution that countries need to exercise careful surveillance over countertrade deals, especially in those cases where hard currency markets are an option. The probable terms of trade loss must be offset, they argue, by identified gains which the country considers outweigh the loss. (1988: 176).
[10] China (not a member of the Group of 77) has expressed a wish to join the Agreement.
[11] *UNCTAD Bulletin*, 243 (May 1988), 3.
[12] See Ch. 12 for further discussion.

preferences by developed countries in favour of developing countries under the Generalized System of Preferences, which remains a voluntary act subject to unilateral modification or withdrawal.

Sub-regional groupings. A third policy response to the foreign exchange crisis has been a series of measures designed to foster the intra-trade of various sub-regional integration and cooperation groupings. The ASEAN group, for example, has agreed on across-the-board tariff cuts of 20–25 per cent on all items with import values above $10 million, and up to 50 per cent for certain items. Other sub-regional groupings have also negotiated measures to expand their intra-trade.

These various policy initiatives cover both primary commodities and manufactures, though manufactures have constituted the more dynamic element. None the less, there would seem to be much potential for a significant growth in South–South trade in commodities, in both crude and processed forms. Developing countries are already major buyers of a number of important traded commodities. For example, in 1987 they accounted for one-half or more of world imports of rice, soyabean oil, and palm oil, and for between one-quarter and one-half of world imports of wheat, coarse grains, sugar, tea, cotton, jute and jute products, and non-coniferous timber (Table 13.3).

For some of these commodities, particularly for wheat and coarse grains, the increase in developing-country imports since the early 1980s has been supplied mainly by developed countries. Increasing the incentives for South–South trade should enable some of any future increase in such imports to be met by greater supplies from other developing countries. Similarly for a number of other primary and processed commodities, particularly agricultural raw materials, the demand for which can be expected to grow in the future as the process of industrialization spreads in Third World countries.

3. POLICY PERSPECTIVES FOR THE FUTURE

Developing countries heavily dependent on primary commodities for the bulk of their foreign exchange earnings generally face an acute dilemma. The demand for their commodity exports in their major markets – the industrialized countries – cannot be expected to grow over the coming decade at any substantial rate.[13] Consequently, in order to attain the export growth required to support domestic economic recovery and longer-term structural transformation, including industrial development, these countries have perforce to turn to other potential markets to increase the overall growth rate in export earnings, at least over the short and medium term.[14] At the same time, however, their ability to shift towards other markets, primarily in other developing countries, is likely to

---

[13] See the projections discussed in Ch. 1.
[14] This is essentially the same argument as that advanced by Lewis 1980, who argued that the developing countries would have to expand their mutual trade in order to offset the slack in demand for their exports resulting from the slowing down of the rate of growth in the developed countries.

Table 13.3. Trade of developing countries in selected commodities: 1980 and 1987

	Trade of developing countries, 1987 ($ billion)		Share of developing countries in world imports[a] (%)		Change in developing-country imports 1980–7 (%)	
	Exports	Imports	1980	1987	Volume	Value
Foods and beverages						
Wheat[b]	0.64	6.62	46	47	13	−30
Coarse grains	0.87	3.58	26	39	31	−31
Rice	1.65	2.13	78	67	−21	−49
Sugar[c]	6.40	2.61	35	42	18	−52
Tea	1.46	1.04	37	43	36	41
Vegetable oilseeds and oils						
Soyabeans	0.98	1.41	12	22	88	40
Soyabean oil	0.63	1.05	71	64	11	−32
Palm oil	1.81	1.40	61	63	75	17
Agricultural raw materials						
Cotton	2.34	2.94	28	44	75	25
Jute[d]	0.61	0.35	36	45	1	−26
Natural rubber	3.66	0.85	16	21	61	8
Non-coniferous timber	7.72	3.17	29	28	6	5

[a] In terms of quantity
[b] Including wheat flour
[c] Raw and refined
[d] Including jute products

Source: UNCTAD *Commodity Yearbook*, 1990.

remain severely handicapped by the contraction in their earnings from commodity exports to the developed countries, which has been a major reason for the widespread import cuts enforced over the past decade in the developing world.

A significant and substantial expansion in trade flows among developing countries cannot, however, be expected to occur simply as a result of the operation of market forces, in view of the relatively gloomy outlook for real commodity prices. Rather, such an expansion would need to be promoted by positive and deliberate policies on the part of the developing countries themselves. The policy initiatives taken in recent years – the greater use of countertrade, the GSTP Agreement, and measures to expand the intra-trade of sub-regional groupings – all have a contribution to make to the expansion of South–South trade. None the less, it would seem unlikely that, by themselves, these initiatives will be able to reverse the setbacks to South–South trade experienced during the 1980s. New initiatives are now urgently needed to exploit the complementarities that exist between the economies of different developing countries. While these complementarities are more evident in the case of manufactures, with the development of modern industrial bases, including high-technology sectors, in a number of developing countries, there are also important complementarities in the commodities area which could be further exploited. There are three policy areas, in particular, relating to trade preferences, infrastructural links, and financial support, in which new initiatives could usefully be explored to this end.

(a) Trade Preferences

First, the move towards a comprehensive system of preferences favouring trade among developing countries could be expedited. More countries could join the GSTP, the tariff cuts could be increased over time, and the scope of the scheme broadened. So far, preferential concessions under the GSTP have related only to individual commodities or to individual tariff lines, though the Agreement has also a provision for across-the-board tariff cuts of up to 10 per cent. If some across-the-board preference could indeed be agreed, this could greatly enhance the impact of the preferential arrangement for South–South trade in a number of commodities (though the main impact would be on the intra-trade in manufactures).

Some assessment of the probable orders of magnitude of the trade-creating effects of a general reduction of tariffs on the intra-trade of developing countries is made in a recent simulation exercise by Erzan, Laird, and Yeats (1988). Assuming that export supplies are infinitely elastic, the simulations show that the value of the intra-trade would rise by about 3.5 per cent with a uniform 20 per cent cut in tariffs on imports from other developing countries, by 8.5 per cent with a 50 per cent cut, and by 17 per cent with a 100 per cent cut. At the same time, imports from developed countries would be reduced by amounts representing only about one-quarter of the rise in intra-trade, so that the tariff reductions would result mainly in trade creation, rather than in trade diversion. Relaxing the unrealistic assumption of infinitely elastic supply to, for example, elasticities of 3 or 1 yields correspondingly lower figures for the expansion in intra-trade (see Table 13.4).[15]

For both manufactures and commodities, the benefits of a uniform cut in existing tariffs would be concentrated on relatively few products (sugar, palm oil, soyabean oil, and tobacco would be the major beneficiaries among commodities).[16] Similarly, the benefits of a uniform cut in tariffs would vary considerably among different countries and regions, with some countries being net losers and others net gainers, so that some institutional arrangement for compen-

---

[15] For the assumption of a 50% linear tariff cut, for example, supply elasticities of 3 and 1 would result, respectively, in increases in intra-trade of 6.3% and 4.8%, as against 8.5% for infinite supply elasticity (Erzan, Laird, and Yeats 1988: Table 3).

[16] Erzan, Laird, and Yeats 1988: 1448.

Table 13.4. The effects of alternative GSTP tariff preferences on developing-country trade

Change from base year (1981)[a]	Exports to developing countries			Imports from developed countries		
	Preferential margin			Preferential margin		
	20%	50%	100%	20%	50%	100%
$ billion	2.91	7.23	14.31	−0.80	−1.96	−3.95
% of base year	3.4	8.5	17.0	−0.3	−0.8	−1.6

[a] Exports from developing countries to other developing countries in 1981 amounted to $85.0 billion, while their imports from developed countries in that year totalled $249.4 billion.

Source: Adapted from Erzan, Laird, and Yeats 1988: Table 1.

sating the net losers would be needed. In practice, a uniform tariff cut by a substantial number of developing countries might be difficult to negotiate in view of the wide differences among countries in the heights of their import tariffs. Some formula which allowed low-tariff countries to introduce smaller tariff cuts than high-tariff countries may thus be desirable. At a later stage, the more difficult problems involved in negotiating reductions in non-tariff barriers to trade among developing countries would also need to be resolved.

The greatest potential for expansion in South–South trade is for manufactures, especially as regards the mutual trade of the 20 to 25 countries which are already significant exporters of industrial products. As Hulugalle (1990) points out, an expansion of trade in manufactures would have a beneficial spin-off effect on a wider group of countries producing raw materials or processed commodities, as import demand for raw materials rises in resource-poor fast-growing industrializing countries. In any event, however, reductions in trade barriers will not be sufficient by themselves to evoke an expansion in South–South trade on the scale that is required, without supporting changes in the economic infrastructure and in financial provision.

(b) Infrastructural Linkages

A second area in which much greater co-operation among developing countries is required relates to the infrastructure of their mutual trade. There are a number of more obvious deficiencies in the existing infrastructure, such as the inadequacy and high cost of existing shipping freight services on many routes, especially between ports in Latin America, Africa, and Asia; the relative backwardness of inter-regional communications and information transmission; and the deficiency of export credit services – improvements in which are one condition for substantial growth in South–South trade in the future.

There are, in addition, other critical areas in which closer South–South co-operation is required to strengthen the economic infrastructure. A much larger Research and Development (R & D) effort, for example, is essential over the period ahead to meet the challenge of synthetics and the newer technologies to the markets for the traditional raw materials exports of developing countries.[17] This challenge can best be met by improving the technical characteristics of the competing natural products, by keeping costs and prices at competitive levels, and by promoting new end-uses. The success of Malaysia in increasing rubber tree yields and in developing technically specified natural rubber (now also produced by other countries in South-East Asia) is a good example of what can be accomplished. There is still an enormous gap between the resources devoted to R & D for natural raw materials and the far greater R & D resources employed in the synthetic materials industries. A cooperative effort by the scientists and technicians of countries producing particular natural raw materials could help to narrow this gap.

Moreover, there would seem to be much potential for useful collaboration by producing countries in the international marketing, distribution, and transport of their commodity exports to other developing countries.[18] Significant proportions of the inter-trade of developing countries in many commodities pass through entrepôt or re-export centres in developed countries, or are handled by transnational trading corporations as intermediaries. It should be possible to carry out much of this kind of intermediation by national or multinational enterprises of developing countries. Again, there should be scope for the establishment of multinational enterprises to market developing-country produce under their own brand names, thus competing directly with brand names of developed country enterprises. More generally, both state trading organizations and private enterprises of developing countries could participate in such South–South cooperation.

(c) Financial Support

Third, and perhaps of fundamental importance to the future of South–South trade, is the need to ensure adequate finance to support a major expansion in this flow of trade. Various possibilities could usefully be pursued in this context. One would be measures to strengthen the existing sub-regional clearing and payments arrangements and, in particular, to reactivate those arrangements which have had to suspend operations because of unsettled balances. This would require a new allocation of finance by the debtor governments. There may also be scope for some form of linkage mechanism among the various sub-regional arrangements, so that surpluses in one sub-region can be set off against deficits in others.

---

[17] The magnitude of the problem is discussed in some detail in Ch. 11.
[18] See the related discussion in Ch. 10.

An alternative approach would be the establishment of a new Third World clearing arrangement, which individual countries could join if they so wished, whether or not they were already members of an existing sub-regional clearing system. This approach might well result in a wider regional coverage of countries than merely linking the existing sub-regional schemes, and to that extent a Third World arrangement is more likely to include a high proportion of compensated trade. In the first instance, such a scheme could be confined purely to clearing activities, with balances to be settled within an agreed brief period. If successful, the arrangement could be extended at a later stage to the provision of trade credit.

The limited availability of trade credit in recent years has been a significant constraint on the ability of many developing countries to expand their exports of capital goods and other manufactures, while exports of traditional primary products have also been adversely affected by inadequacy of short-term credit facilities. This is an area in which the regional Development Banks, perhaps in conjunction with commercial banks, might play a useful role in assisting the expansion of existing trade credit facilities. A more comprehensive approach, proposed by Hulugalle (1990), would be the establishment of a multilateral trade financing facility for export credit arrangements, especially for capital goods produced in developing countries, but also for other manufactures and primary commodities. Such a multilateral facility would have access to finance from international capital markets on finer terms than could be obtained by any one national export credit agency. The possibility of a multilateral facility being supported by some form of interest subsidy by exporting countries could also be considered.

While such schemes would necessarily involve some injections of national or multinational finance, a more radical approach which would avoid the need for financial support is the proposal by Stewart and Stewart (1980) for the use of a 'new currency unit' (NCU) by developing countries. The new currency would be issued by an institution set up for the purpose by these countries.[19] As the authors of the proposal explain, participating countries would agree to accept NCUs from other participants in part payment for imports from them, the balance being paid in convertible currencies. Thus the scheme would provide credit by each participating country to all other participants, which would encourage such countries to buy more from each other. At the same time, no country need lose, since there would be no compulsion on it to sell to other developing countries if hard currency markets were available. Thus the new credits would provide a major incentive for developing countries to redirect their trading activities to other developing countries, as buyers if they were short of foreign exchange, and as sellers if they were short of markets.[20]

This proposal would seem to merit serious consideration by governments of

---

[19] If the separate proposal for the establishment of a 'South Bank' were to come to fruition, this bank might also be the issuing institution for the NCU.
[20] Stewart and Stewart 1980: 72.

developing countries, on the basis of detailed feasibility studies to determine critical principles and magnitudes: for example, how best to avoid unwanted accumulation of NCUs by surplus countries or a persistent shortage of NCUs by deficit countries. Moreover, the scheme would have important implications for the management of the international trade and payments system, at least as far as the developing countries are concerned. These countries have been pressing for many years, though without success, for a new and substantial issue of Special Drawing Rights (SDRs) by the IMF in order to improve world liquidity and, in particular, to alleviate their own acute foreign exchange difficulties.[21] The NCU—which, like the SDR, would consist of book entries—would provide developing countries with the additional liquidity which they have been seeking, so far in vain, from a new issue of SDRs by the IMF, and would thereby provide the additional liquidity to support the expansion in South–South trade which could be engendered by the GSTP Agreement.

B. EAST–SOUTH TRADE

The dramatic political changes in the countries of Eastern Europe during 1989 and the reorientation of their economic systems towards reliance on market forces are likely to have important consequences for the future growth of their trade with the outside world, including the developing countries.

Up to the 1990s, the countries of Eastern Europe were, in aggregate, a relatively small market for developing countries' exports. In 1980, for example, Eastern Europe took only 5 per cent, by value, of the total exports of developing countries (excluding exports from OPEC countries), the corresponding proportion for 1989 being only 4 per cent, reflecting the economic 'shocks' of the 1980s which had adverse effects on the trade of both Eastern Europe and developing countries.

The external payments position of the countries of Eastern Europe generally deteriorated during the 1980s. Exports of agricultural products from these countries fell off in the early 1980s as a result of exceptionally severe winters, while petroleum exports from the Soviet Union to Western markets also declined, especially in 1985. Soviet foreign exchange earnings were also cut substantially by the fall in petroleum prices in early 1986. Most of the other Eastern European countries also suffered from foreign exchange difficulties, particularly as a result of the general fall in the prices of their commodity exports, and the higher debt service payments which they had to make. Consequently, all these countries were constrained to take measures to reduce the growth in their imports while renewing their efforts to expand exports. These adverse changes coincided with the increased foreign exchange difficulties of developing countries which were discussed earlier. The main result of these various developments was a marked

---

[21] See e.g. the statement issued by the Intergovernmental Group of 24 on International Monetary Issues, 13 Apr. 1988.

decline in the annual growth rate in the value of East–South trade in the first half of the 1980s, compared with the 1970s, while the proportion of that trade conducted within bilateral trading arrangements tended to increase.[22] Moreover, the value of East–South trade stagnated over the second half of the 1980s.

The potential for expanding East–South trade in the future will depend heavily on the success of the Soviet Union and other East European countries in moving from a 'command economy' to reliance on market forces, in adopting the more productive technologies available in Western countries, in achieving faster rates of growth and higher living standards, while maintaining external financial balance. In this process, Eastern Europe will be assisted by new inflows of investment capital (e.g. through the newly established European Bank for Reconstruction and Development as well as by joint ventures between domestic and Western enterprises), and much closer trade and financial linkages with the economies of Western developed countries.

The transition to market-oriented systems in Eastern Europe seems likely to last for a number of years, with sharply reduced production, consumption, incomes, and foreign trade turnover. In the medium and longer term, with market systems operating and with closer economic ties with Western countries, output and incomes can be expected to expand, with associated increase in consumption of primary commodities, both of industrial materials and of tropical and other foods and beverages. This would, in turn, increase the potential market for the commodity exports of developing countries, possibly very substantially. Moreover, an expansion in East–West trade resulting from the closer economic ties between these two regions would have beneficial effects on the financing available for expanding the volume of East–South trade. The process of trade expansion would also be accelerated by a move to full convertibility of the currencies of the East European countries.

There might, however, be a significant element of trade diversion in the markets of Western developed countries. As Eastern European countries expand their trade with the West, their labour-intensive manufactures, such as textiles, clothing, and footwear, as well as a number of foodstuffs, could displace alternative supplies from developing countries. This possibility underlines the importance of further liberalization of trade barriers by Western developed countries on a non-discriminatory basis so as to minimize this potential trade diversion effect.

[22] UNCTAD 1987a: 165–6.

14
Diversification

1. DIVERSIFICATION AND GROWTH

The prolonged period of depressed commodity prices that began in the early 1980s, and the continuing instability in commodity prices and export earnings of developing countries, have greatly increased interest in the need to diversify their exports towards more dynamic products, particularly manufactured goods. Diversification of exports towards more dynamic markets would also raise the overall growth rate of a country's exports. Whether either commodity or market diversification would reduce the short-term instability of export earnings would depend on the relative stability of old and new export lines and export markets.

Export diversification has been described by Bond and Milne (1987), following Clark (1957), as a three-stage process coinciding with different stages of economic development. A first stage is diversification from one or a few primary commodities to a wider range of commodities, including processed commodities and rudimentary manufactures. This is the typical evolution of monocultural economies emerging from a relatively low stage of development. Second, export production is diversified from primary commodities into a wider range of goods, including more sophisticated manufactures. Finally, in a third phase, exports become still more diversified, including various kinds of services (such as financial, insurance, royalties, and management fees, in the case of developed countries), or income from tourism and workers' remittances (in the case of a number of developing countries).

Over the post-war period, there has generally been a movement among developing countries towards diversification in export patterns, though there have also been very great differences in the pace of diversification and in the relationship between export diversification and export growth. An analysis by Bond and Milne (1987) of export diversification for 59 developing countries over the period from 1964 to 1981 showed that there was no significant general relationship between export diversification and export growth, but that export volume growth was fastest where manufactures formed a high proportion of exports. Petroleum-exporting countries were exceptional, since their fast export growth in the 1970s resulted in their exports becoming more concentrated on petroleum, in value terms, and thus less diversified.

If the countries which were mainly exporters of manufactures or petroleum are excluded, there remain in the Bond–Milne sample 39 developing countries in Africa, Asia, and America which are dependent wholly or mainly on commodities for their export earnings. Of these, the majority, 29 countries, increased their export diversification between 1964 and 1981, though Africa lagged seriously

Table 14.1. Export diversification, export growth, and GDP growth of selected commodity-exporting countries,[a] 1964–81

	Africa		Latin America[b]		Asia
	Gp. A	Gp. B	Gp. A	Gp. B	Gp. A
No. of countries	10	8	10	2	9
Export diversification index[c]					
1964	35	55	46	51	58
1981	43	47	60	40	71
Share of manufactures in total exports (%)					
1964	15	18	9	22	21
1981	16	18	23	46	49
Purchasing power of exports growth rate[d] (% p.a.)					
1964–71	3.5	5.8	5.4	3.4	3.4
1972–81	1.3	7.6	4.2	2.9	9.5
GDP growth rate (% p.a.)					
1964–71	4.9	4.9	5.4	5.3	5.5
1972–81	2.1	3.9	3.9	2.8	5.5

[a] Group A = countries with increased diversification index; Group B = countries with reduced diversification index.
[b] Includes Caribbean countries.
[c] 100 *minus* Gini–Hirschman coefficient of export concentration expressed as percentage.
[d] Value of exports deflated by UN index of unit value of exports of manufactures from developed market-economy countries.

Source: Adapted from Bond and Milne 1987: Table 9. All indices and growth rates are unweighted means.

behind. This can be seen in several ways. First, nearly one-half of the African countries showed reduced diversification, compared with only one-sixth in Latin America and none in Asia. Second, the degree of export diversification in Africa was very much lower: for 1981, the African index for diversifying countries averaged 43 per cent, as against 60 per cent for Latin America and 71 per cent for Asia. Third, there was no significant additional export diversification in the African sample over this period, whereas both Latin American and Asian regions showed substantial progress (see Table 14.1).

Much of this latter progress reflected diversification into exports of manufactures, which accounted for one-half, by value, of Asian exports in 1981, as against one-fifth in 1964.[1] The shift to manufactures was more modest in the

---

[1] This compares with an increase in the share of manufactures in total exports from 53 to 77% (unweighted means) for five developing countries which are major exporters of manufactures (Brazil, Hong Kong, Singapore, South Korea, and Yugoslavia) over the same period.

diversifying Latin American countries, but for the African countries no increase was recorded in the share of manufactures in total exports. It would seem that it was the smaller, poorer, and least-developed countries—particularly in Africa—which faced the greatest constraints in export diversification.

Increased diversification was not, however, uniquely related to the growth rate of exports, either in nominal value or in terms of purchasing power over imports. Export growth depended heavily also on relative price changes for individual products, especially for traditional commodity exports, as well as on variations in export supply. Nor were export growth rates uniquely correlated with growth rates of GDP, though higher growth in import purchasing power was no doubt one important influence on domestic economic growth for the majority of countries.

With the collapse in commodity prices in the 1980s, and the rise in debt service obligations, most developing countries came under heavy pressure to expand exports, as already mentioned, and to diversify their exports towards products with better export prospects. However, relatively few countries succeeded in achieving any significant or substantial export diversification over the first half of the 1980s. Of the diversifying countries distinguished in Table 14.1, those in Latin America showed virtually no change in their mean diversification index from 1971 to 1985; for Africa the index rose slightly, from 43 to 47; while for Asia the increase was from 71 to 76.[2]

As in previous decades, the pace of diversification in the 1980s has varied greatly among countries. Among Latin American countries, Chile's dependence on copper exports fell, while El Salvador's dependence on coffee increased. In Africa, Mauritius increased its export diversification mainly by expanding sales of clothing, while its sugar exports fell sharply in value as a result of the collapse in prices. For most other African commodity-exporting countries, however, there was little change in export diversification levels. Of the Asian commodity-exporters, Thailand was the most successful diversifier, comparing 1971 with 1985, followed by Malaysia and Turkey.

The export diversification indices discussed above cover all export items, both commodities and manufactures. For present purposes, with a focus on commodity issues, it is useful to concentrate on diversification within the primary commodity sector itself—often known as 'horizontal' diversification—and on shifts towards processed commodities—the first stage of 'vertical' diversification.

2. HORIZONTAL DIVERSIFICATION

There are two distinct forms of diversification within the primary commodity sector that need to be considered. The first relates to the relative importance of food production for domestic consumption and of other commodity production

---

[2] Calculated from the export concentration indices for 1971 and 1985 in UNCTAD 1989*a* (and earlier issues): Table 4.5.

for export. For food-deficit countries, a shift of resources into traditional or non-traditional foodstuffs for domestic use could lead to improvements in nutritional standards and a more efficient workforce. It would also lead to improvement in the trade balance as a result of reduced food imports if the resource shift did not significantly reduce earnings from cash crop exports. The second form of diversification relates to an increase in the variety of primary commodities in a country's exports. Countries which have traditionally been excessively dependent on one or a few commodities for which world demand is sluggish and where the world market tends to remain depressed for long periods have particular need to diversify into more dynamic export products.

Table 14.2 lists 13 developing countries which were excessively dependent on a single commodity at the beginning of the 1970s ('excessive' being defined as over 50 per cent of earnings from all primary commodity exports). A decade later, in 1980, eight of these countries had reduced their dependence on their principal commodity by more than 5 percentage points, and five countries achieved a reduction of more than 10 percentage points. These were Chile (in regard to copper), Mauritania and Liberia (iron ore), Chad (cotton), and Senegal (groundnuts). However, no substantial reduction in dependency was achieved by the other countries listed, and in three countries (Zambia, Cuba, and Surinam) dependence on the main commodity export actually increased.

Over the first half of the 1980s, of the same 13 countries, only five managed to reduce their dependence on their principal commodity export by more than 5 percentage points. Ghana expanded into timber and fish exports, though exports of aluminium fell off. Gambia and Mauritania both expanded their fish exports, Surinam diversified into rice, while Sierra Leone expanded into coffee and cocoa. However, the majority of the countries listed, mostly having small-sized economies, were unable to achieve any substantial degree of commodity export diversification over this period.

This picture of limited success in diversification shown for the highly specialized exporters is consistent with the general finding, mentioned earlier, that the successful horizontal diversifiers have been the larger developing countries which already had fairly diversified economies and export structures. Smaller, poorer countries–particularly those in sub-Saharan Africa–clearly have much greater difficulties in restructuring to take advantage of possible new commodity export lines.[3]

3. VERTICAL DIVERSIFICATION

Vertical diversification into commodity processing can be regarded as an important element of economic development. Apart from its direct impact on the domestic economy (e.g. in employment, the acquisition of new skills, and the

---

[3] More recently, a number of countries have successfully developed the export of high-valued fruit, flowers, and other horticultural products (some Central American countries and, from 1988, Zambia also), but this does not change the general poor outlook for traditional commodity exports.

Table 14.2. Selected developing countries heavily dependent on exports of 'problem' commodities, 1970, 1980, and 1985

Country/Principal commodity	Exports of principal commodity (as % of total commodity exports[a])			Other commodities accounting for 5% or more of 1985 total
	1970	1980	1985	
Mauritius/sugar[b]	93	91	86	Tea (5)
Gambia/groundnuts and groundnut oil	83	77	61	Fish[d] (9), feeding stuffs (7)
Zambia/copper[c]	82	88	92	—
Chile/copper[c]	79	54	51	Fish[d] (12), forest products (9), grapes (6)
Zaire/copper[c]	79	71	70	Coffee (23)
Ghana/cocoa	77	74	55	Aluminium (11)
Cuba/sugar[b]	75	87	86	—
Mauritania/iron ore	74	62	47	Fish[d] (40), cattle (6)
Liberia/iron ore	72	52	63	Rubber (18), forest products (8), coffee (6)
Surinam/bauxite, alumina, and aluminium	63	86	78	Rice (15), fish (9)
Sierra Leone/diamonds	62	62	21	Coffee (38), aluminium (25), cocoa (20), fish (6)
Chad/cotton	60	30	28	Cattle (56)
Senegal/groundnuts and groundnut oil	51	20	16	Fish[d] (45), phosphates (18), cotton (5)

[a] Excluding petroleum.
[b] Raw and refined.
[c] Ore, blister, and refined.
[d] Including processed.

Source: UNCTAD 1987c.

adoption of new technologies), the development of processing will promote the evolution of a more diversified industrial base. Indirect benefits would also arise from backward linkages with commodity producers, and forward linkages with the manufacturing and services sectors, as well as from an income-multiplier effect. The foreign trade sector would also benefit from the expansion of domestic commodity-processing activities, either by import substitution or by export expansion, or both. The export of commodities in processed, rather than in crude, forms allows the producing country to benefit from the value added in processing, though the net benefit may be relatively small if there is a substantial import-content at the processing stage. Thus where commodity exports in processed forms add significantly to foreign exchange earnings the promotion of processing for export could provide a general stimulus to industrialization and development in commodity-dependent countries.

Developing countries have, in fact, expanded their processing industries for a number of important commodity exports over the past two decades. The proportion of imports into OECD countries from developing countries which are in processed forms has risen substantially for cocoa, copra/coconut oil (and for several other vegetable oilseeds/oils also), cotton, rubber, bauxite/alumina/aluminium, and tin. However, for many other commodities, such as coffee, sugar, tobacco, copper, and zinc, there has been little shift of any significance towards processed forms (see Table 14.3).

Positive factors for some commodities have been local availability of cheap energy, as required for the processing of bauxite into alumina and aluminium; or, where modern technology is involved, the active support of government research institutions and/or the involvement of foreign enterprises as, for example, in the case of Malaysian rubber (including rubber tyres). For many countries, however, there are some major constraints. First, many processing plants, particularly for smelting and refining mineral ores, for pulp and paper, etc., are capital-intensive and require the acquisition of foreign technology and know-how, as well as foreign financing, at least in part. Interest payments on foreign loans together with royalties on the use of imported technology might make such projects barely economic, especially if the value added by processing is not relatively great.

Second, for many commodities the markets for the processed forms are already controlled, to a greater or lesser extent, by transnational corporations (TNCs) operating from developed countries. Cartel arrangements, involving price fixing, market sharing, and joint marketing and distribution, often regulate the operations of subsidiaries of TNCs in developing countries. Other restrictive business practices, including price setting by a dominant firm, differential pricing for the same product by geographical area, and limitations on exports involving the use of technology acquired from transnational corporations create major barriers to entry to processing activities. For consumer goods, entry barriers are often created by the use of advertising by developed-country enterprises to establish consumer attachment to their own branded goods.

Table 14.3. Imports of primary and processed forms of selected commodities by developed market-economy countries from developing countries, 1965, 1975, and 1985 (% of import value of each commodity)

	1965		1975		1985	
	Primary	Processed	Primary	Processed	Primary	Processed
Food and beverages						
Cocoa	90.5	9.5[a]	79.9	20.1[a]	70.5	29.5[a]
Coffee	99.8	0.2	97.2	2.8	96.4	3.6
Sugar	53.1	46.9	66.9	33.1	53.1	46.9
Copra	72.6	27.4[b]	49.8	50.2[b]	13.7	86.3[b]
Agricultural raw materials						
Cotton	80.9	19.1[c]	60.7	39.3[c]	39.4	60.6[c]
Rubber	99.4	0.6[d]	93.0	7.0[d]	68.0	32.0[d]
Tobacco	97.2	2.8	95.6	4.4	94.8	5.2
Wood	82.2	17.8[e]	68.5	31.5[e]	59.9	40.1[e]
Minerals, ores, and metals[f]						
Aluminium	72.1	27.9	39.3	60.7	26.2	73.8
Copper	43.9	56.1	48.7	51.3	37.8	62.2
Iron	97.5	2.5	97.7	2.3	81.3	18.7
Lead	40.5	59.5	54.2	45.8	77.2	22.8
Phosphate	89.3	10.7	94.0	6.0	78.1	21.9
Tin	36.3	63.7	22.5	77.5	10.6	89.4
Zinc	74.8	25.2	75.4	24.6	71.2	28.2

[a] Mainly cocoa butter and cocoa paste.
[b] Coconut oil.
[c] Cotton yarn and woven fabrics.
[d] Mainly rubber tyres and other manufactures, including products containing synthetic rubber.
[e] Mainly wood manufactures.
[f] Primary = ores and concentrates; processed = metal and alloys.

Source: UNCTAD *Commodity Yearbook* (various issues).

A third constraint, particularly in small countries, arises in the absence of a domestic machinery industry to support the establishment and maintenance of new processing plants. A recent inquiry into processing in developing countries found that a domestic spare parts and machinery sector was in operation where commodity processing had been relatively well established, but was missing in most of the countries where processing had not been as successful.[4]

Fourth, the same inquiry found that inadequate government support for train-

---

[4] UNCTAD 1986. This inquiry covered the processing of four commodities (bauxite, palm-type oils, phosphates, and tropical timber) in a sample of 12 developing countries.

ing, technology and product research, and market promotion had been a crucial factor in the failure of efforts to establish processing industries in many developing countries on a competitive basis.[5] By contrast, where governments have provided support, for example by developing the necessary infrastructure (such as transport and storage facilities) and by promoting training, research, quality control, and marketing intelligence, this has been a major factor in successful development of local processing industries.

Finally — and probably the most important and widespread constraint — exports of processed commodities from developing countries are limited to a substantial extent by trade barriers imposed by developed countries. As was seen in Chapter 12, both tariff and non-tariff barriers facing imports by developed countries escalate with the degree of processing. The resultant trade barriers on the more processed forms of commodities are generally effective in substantially reducing the volume of imports that would otherwise enter the markets of developed countries. These trade barriers, together with the associated uncertainties created by the possibility of unforeseen changes in tariff and non-tariff regulations, act as major deterrents to investment in new processing industries in developing countries which aim to sell in world markets. It remains to be seen whether, and to what extent, such trade barriers are reduced as a result of the GATT Uruguay Round negotiations.

4. NATIONAL POLICIES TO PROMOTE DIVERSIFICATION

Successful export diversification is unlikely to arise in conditions of severe and prolonged external payments difficulties without appropriate and adequate support from national policies and from the international economic environment — which implies that the developed countries and the international financial agencies also have a major role to play.

Developing-country policies to promote export diversification can be designed consciously to reduce habitual instability of export earnings, or to enhance their trend rate of growth. Such policies can be predominantly specific, to overcome particular constraints or to promote exports of particular products; or they can be predominantly macroeconomic, providing an appropriate set of incentives for producing enterprises for the diversification of exportable production.

In principle, several policy options relating to specific measures may be available to a given commodity-exporting country directed towards reducing export instability or improving the trend of export prices and/or export earnings.

(*a*) Reducing Instability (see Section A of Table 14.4)

First, where the main cause of export instability is fluctuation in domestic supply, measures such as the construction of adequate storage facilities to avoid export sales on a falling market would reduce short-term variation in the volume

[5] Ibid. 5–6.

Table 14.4. Possible national policies to reduce export instability or to improve the trend of export prices and export earnings

	Would policy reduce instability (Section A) or improve the trend (Section B)?	
	Export prices	Export earnings
A. *Policies to reduce export instability*		
1. Reducing fluctuations in exportable supplies of traditional commodities	Only if country is a major supplier	Yes
2. Diversification of traditional commodity exports into more stable contractual arrangements	Possibly, depending on nature of contracts	Yes
3. Diversification into more stable non-traditional exports	Yes	Yes
B. *Policies to improve the trend*		
1. Increasing market share of traditional commodity exports	*Deterioration* if country is a major supplier	Only if country is *not* a major supplier
2. Restricting exports of traditional commodities	Only if country is a major supplier	Only if country is a major supplier
3. Diversification of exports into more dynamic commodities or into manufactures	Yes[a]	Yes[a]

[a] But see qualifications in text.

of exports and hence in export earnings instability.[6] Where, however, a country is a major supplier in the world market, a reduction in annual variations in the volume of its commodity exports can also be expected to result in a reduction in the degree of price instability for the commodity concerned, which would incidentally reduce export earnings instability for many, or most, other exporting countries. If, for example, frosts in Brazil's coffee-growing areas could be avoided (perhaps an unrealistic, though a striking, illustration), this would drastically reduce price and export earnings instability for the great majority of coffee-exporting countries. On the other hand, small producing countries, even if they reduce the fluctuation in their exports, are not likely thereby to reduce price instability of the world market.

Second, an individual country can seek more predictable institutional forms of export of its traditional commodities, such as long-term contracts, or bilateral

---

[6] As mentioned in Ch. 9, this was the new feature of the proposal for a commodity-specific compensatory financing facility.

intergovernmental agreements, giving assured export sales of specified quantities for a number of years ahead. Such contracts or agreements would normally provide for annual reviews of prices to be paid in the light of changing conditions in the world market, but even so, fluctuations in export earnings are likely to be significantly reduced, as would also the degree of uncertainty concerning the export outlook. Long-term contracts already play a major role in the marketing of many primary commodities (e.g. iron ore and other minerals), while bilateral trade agreements (e.g. between developing countries and countries of Eastern Europe) usually specify quantities of particular goods to be traded over the periods covered. The fast-growing use of countertrade in recent years is another example of the adoption of a new institutional form which, though arising from an acute shortage of convertible currency in the majority of developing countries, may incidentally help in reducing the degree of fluctuation in a country's exports.

A third approach would be for a country to diversify the range of its exports to include other, non-traditional, products which normally exhibit less instability in prices and earnings than do its traditional products. While such diversification – which may be either 'horizontal' into non-traditional commodities or 'vertical' into processed or manufactured goods – is not likely to have any effect on the level of instability of the country's traditional commodity exports, its overall instability, in terms of export unit values and export earnings, would necessarily be reduced.

This third approach is more practicable for large countries with a varied natural resource base, a skilled and adaptable labour force, adequate sources of finance, and the capacity to apply appropriate technology to the production of new goods on a competitive basis. Many small countries, by contrast, which have traditionally concentrated on the production of one or two major crops or minerals, may not have the variety of resources to allow them to shift successfully, or at all, to new export commodities. In fact, some small as well as larger countries have successfully diversified over the past decade into new export lines, particularly into fresh fruits and vegetables (e.g. Guatemala as well as Chile and Mexico), which are less subject to price fluctuations than the traditional commodity exports of these countries.[7]

However, in spite of growing diversification among the commodity exports of Latin American countries during the 1970s, the degree of instability in export prices and earnings in that decade was substantially greater than in the 1960s. This indicates that in some periods the major influence on export instability arises from fluctuations in world commodity markets, which can be only partly offset by commodity diversification programmes in the exporting countries. None the less, this type of 'horizontal' diversification could be a viable option for many commodity-exporting countries. A shift in the composition of exports from commodities to manufactures could bring a very substantial reduction in export instability, both in overall unit values and in export earnings. So far, such

---

[7] Labys and Lord 1990.

'vertical' versification of exports has proved possible on any substantial scale only for a relatively few developing countries—the NICs of East Asia and Latin America.

(b) Improving Export Trends (see Section B of Table 14.4)

Several policy options exist for national action to improve the trend of commodity export prices and/or export earnings. First, a country which can improve its competitive position in the world market can capture a growing share in world exports and, to that extent, can raise its export earnings, provided the country concerned is a relatively small source of supply, so that its action would not affect the world price significantly. However, if a number of small countries pursue this policy simultaneously, their actions are likely to be self-defeating in so far as the expansion in their aggregate exports results in a lower world price. Similarly, for a large exporting country, this policy is also likely to result in a decline in export earnings.[8] Moreover, there would be a consequential adverse effect on the export earnings of other countries exporting the commodity concerned, as a result of the price decline. The efforts of East African countries in the 1970s to increase their share of world exports of tea, and the more recent efforts of Chile and Brazil to increase their market shares of copper and iron ore, respectively, are notable examples of adverse effects of market share increases by significant exporters on export prices and on export earnings of competing countries.

Second, a major supplying country could impose some restriction on the volume of exports, or the rate of export growth, of a particular commodity the demand for which was price-inelastic. This would result in a rise in the world price and in export earnings, though the rise would be a 'once and for all' gain, rather than a continuing improvement in trend. Export restrictions of this type are generally rare, especially as governments of developing countries have traditionally been opposed to quantitative restrictions on their export trade (though many countries apply export taxes on their major commodity exports). The prohibition of exports of tea by India in 1983 was motivated by the need to avoid a sharp reduction in supplies for the large domestic market for tea; the action had, however, the incidental result of raising world tea prices substantially.

The possibilities for influencing world prices would, of course, be greatly enhanced for many commodities suffering from persistent oversupply if supply restrictions were applied by all producing countries acting in concert, or by

---

[8] The condition for a decline in export earnings is that:

$$\epsilon_d < \lambda_j - (1 - \lambda_j)\epsilon_s$$

where ϵ_d is the price-elasticity of demand in the world market (ignoring sign), λ_j is country j's initial share of world supply, and ϵ_s is the price-elasticity of supply from the rest of the world. In the limiting cases where $\lambda_j = 1$ (i.e. where country j is the sole supplier), or where $\epsilon_s = 0$ (i.e. where the rest of world supply remains constant), the condition reduces to $\epsilon_d < 1$, or $\epsilon_d < \lambda_j$, respectively.

supply management measures agreed with consuming countries in the framework of an international commodity agreement.[9]

A third policy option would be for a country to diversify its export structure towards relatively 'dynamic' commodities or towards manufactures, to the extent that this is feasible on the basis of its natural resource endowment, its technological capability, skills, and infrastructure, the availability of financing, and the assurance of export markets. As the proportion of exports consisting of such products increased over time, the average growth rate of export earnings should likewise increase. Moreover, if the diversifying country was a preponderant supplier of the traditional commodity, the latter's price would rise if the diversification process involved an absolute reduction in the volume of exportable supplies of that commodity.

However, in practice, 'horizontal' diversification into more 'dynamic' commodities frequently involves no cutback in output of the traditional, less dynamic, products, and may even be consistent with an expansion in output of the traditional sector, in which case producers in that sector will not benefit from a price rise, and may even suffer a fall in earnings. The other complication may be that commodities which are new for the diversifying country may be traditional for other countries, so that there would be a danger of the diversification resulting in a transfer of an oversupply situation from one commodity to another. This is likely to become an increasingly important problem in the years ahead as continuing depressed prices for the traditional exports of a wide range of developing countries force them to turn to alternative export lines, in many of which other developing countries have a major stake. Some form of harmonization of national commodity diversification programmes could thus serve a useful role in avoiding at least some self-defeating investments in additional productive capacity.[10]

A further complication in horizontal diversification programmes to reduce short-term instability or to improve the trend of prices and/or earnings is that these two objectives may be interrelated for a given shift in the export pattern. Thus, if among all feasible combinations of commodities that can be exported there is a positive correlation between instability and growth, there will be an optimum 'trade-off' pattern of exports which would provide the maximum rate of growth for a given level of instability.[11] Labys and Lord (1990) have analysed this problem for the major commodity exports of Latin American countries, using a portfolio optimization procedure. By evaluating each commodity in terms of its overall return (in terms of foreign exchange earnings) and its risk (in terms

---

[9] See the detailed discussion of the supply management issue in Ch. 3, Sect. 4.

[10] There could be a useful role here for the new Common Fund (see Ch. 15 for further discussion).

[11] Professor Spraos (private communication) has pointed out that an optimum trade-off is one that combines growth and instability in such a way as to maximize welfare. A sufficient condition for this is that the marginal utility from growth must be diminishing while the marginal disutility from instability must be increasing (which can be taken as the normal case).

of the variance in earnings), they showed how the composition of exports could be changed, by the addition of new products, so as to arrive at a risk–returns ratio lower than, or at least equal to, the current export composition. If, however, growth and instability are negatively correlated, then a shift of resources into commodities with above-average growth rates will also tend to reduce export instability. However, there are likely to be limits to such a shift, since the greater the shift to new commodities, the less likely is a country to enjoy a comparative advantage, so that the marginal cost of diversification designed to reduce instability could at some point rise steeply.[12]

Similar relationships are also likely to arise in regard to the geographic pattern of exports. Countries whose traditional markets are slow-growing have an incentive to diversify into faster-growing markets, though the latter may, or may not, be more stable than their traditional markets.

A more general complication arises from the inevitable margins of error surrounding any projections of future trends in world market prices. As noted in Chapter 5, the degree of uncertainty in the world economy in general, and in the major commodity markets in particular, has increased substantially over the past decade. The outlook is for continuing or even increasing risks and uncertainties, particularly in the light of the potential of new technologies to undermine markets for major industrial materials, and of the growing influence on world trade of often unpredictable policy changes by major governments. For many commodities, what appears to be a favourable trend in one period often reverses itself in a subsequent period as a result of changes in world market conditions, or in government policies, which were unforeseen.

Over the past decade, there have been many examples of such reversals of projected future market trends, as regards both major agricultural crops and a wide range of minerals. Price projections made by the World Bank, in particular, have often been influential in decisions to invest in non-traditional commodity production in the context of horizontal diversification programmes. However, these projections have on occasion encouraged an expansion of capacity while the price outlook was deteriorating.[13] Though projections of likely future market conditions are necessary for rational decision-making, an element of flexibility would also seem to be essential in the implementation of diversification programmes.

These and related specific policies, to be successful, generally need to be undertaken within a framework of appropriate macroeconomic policies. Bond and Milne (1987) place great emphasis on the need for consistent and coherent macroeconomic policies which provide a non-inflationary environment, and one where there is no strong bias against exports arising from the exchange and/or trade systems. As they point out, when macroeconomic policies are frequently modified, long-term investment decisions can be distorted, encouraging savings

---

[12] I am indebted to Professor Spraos for this point also.
[13] One example is the Bank forecast made in 1984 for a substantial rise in natural rubber prices in the following quinquennium, which encouraged the planting of more rubber trees and contributed to an over-supply situation in subsequent years.

to move into inventories of goods, financial investments, or abroad. Similarly, if there is inconsistency among policy instruments, unwanted results are likely to occur, as when excess demand pressures arising from fiscal deficits contribute to both internal and external imbalance, notwithstanding the stance of monetary or exchange rate policy (ibid. 115).

While, however, appropriate and consistent domestic macroeconomic policies are indeed necessary to achieve export growth through diversification, they cannot by themselves be a sufficient condition for growth and diversification. This is simply because the elements of the internal and external balances of individual countries are themselves heavily influenced by changes in the international economic environment, not only by changes in the prices and volume of world trade, in exchange rates of key currencies, and in financial flows, but also by changes – often large and unforeseen – in the domestic economic policies of the main developed countries.

For example, the objective of increasing domestic savings in developing countries by appropriate and consistent domestic macroeconomic policies could be effectively undermined by a deterioration in the terms of trade, in the case of countries where savings are closely related to earnings in the export sector. Again, the objective of diversifying the export pattern may not be achieved if it is frustrated by new or increased trade barriers in major developed-country markets. Thus appropriate international measures which provide a supportive external economic environment are essential for the success of national diversification programmes.

5. THE ROLE OF INTERNATIONAL POLICY

The various problems faced by developing countries in diversifying their economies have been discussed at length on many occasions in United Nations bodies concerned with trade and development issues, and particularly in UNCTAD. In a detailed analysis of diversification problems and policy options, published in 1971, UNCTAD's Advisory Committee on Commodities made a series of proposals designed to promote efficient diversification in developing countries.[14] The Advisory Committee stressed that it could not make recommendations on the appropriate diversification strategy for each developing country, in view of the great diversity in their circumstances. None the less, it made a number of general recommendations in regard to domestic policies, relating to the desirability of:

an overall economic development plan or strategy, which would greatly facilitate the identification and selection of diversification projects, mobilize the domestic resources of the country, and harmonize the diversification programme with other sectors of the economy;

[14] UNCTAD, 1971b. The Advisory Committee, now defunct, consisted of a small number of eminent experts on commodity issues, who were appointed in their individual capacities.

land reform, where concentration of land ownership was associated with an uneconomic balance between agricultural production for export and for domestic consumption;

government action to change the conditions of static comparative advantage so as to widen the range of economic production, while avoiding excessive protection of 'infant' industries;

evaluation of individual projects, taking into account both social and private costs and benefits, to help reconcile the objectives of maximizing immediate output, domestic employment, and long-term growth.[15]

The UNCTAD Advisory Committee emphasized that, to be effective, diversification programmes in developing countries required supportive action by developed countries to improve access to their markets for both crude and processed agricultural commodities and manufactures, and that a new international initiative was needed to bring about some progress on this issue.[16] The Advisory Committee also stressed the need to harmonize national commodity diversification programmes to ensure that they were mutually compatible;[17] recommended the systematic collection and dissemination to interested governments of information on resources, production costs and plans, and demand prospects for commodities in actual or potential surplus on the world market, or facing competition from synthetics; and advocated a greatly expanded research and development effort to improve the competitive position of natural products facing competition from synthetics, to improve the quality and yields of basic food crops in developing countries, and to adapt modern technology to the specific needs of the agricultural and industrial sectors in particular developing countries.[18]

The analysis made by the UNCTAD Advisory Committee of the problems of developing countries in diversifying their economies, and the associated recommendations for action by governments, underlay most of the subsequent discussions on this issue at the intergovernmental level. While most of the recommendations to the developing countries met with general approval, the major disagreement related to the recommendation to developed countries to reduce their barriers to imports of crude and processed commodities into their markets. After intensive discussion of the issue at UNCTAD III in 1972, the Western industrial countries submitted a draft resolution which, in its operative paragraphs, made no mention of trade barriers, whereas the corresponding draft of the developing countries urged the developed countries *inter alia* to adopt an adequate policy of access to their markets and an adequate price policy which would facilitate the complete execution of diversification programmes; to undertake to introduce appropriate structural adjustment; and to enlarge their systems of generalized preferences to cover, in particular, processed and semi-processed primary commodities.[19]

[15] Ibid. paras. 29–39. [16] Ibid. para. 41.
[17] Ibid. para. 45. [18] Ibid. paras. 59–61.
[19] Document TD/B/C. 1/L. 4, reproduced in UNCTAD 1973: i. 346–7.

The nearest that the Western industrial countries came to acknowledging the importance and relevance of improving market access to promote diversification in developing countries was the statement by a number of these countries that an improvement 'to a certain extent' of access to markets in developed countries 'might be required'.[20] However, the Western countries would not agree to any new international action in this respect being initiated by UNCTAD; and, as was seen in Chapter 12, no significant reduction in trade barriers in regard to crude and processed commodities was achieved in earlier rounds of negotiation in GATT.

The issue came under further discussion at UNCTAD V, held in 1979, where agreement was reached on the need for 'frameworks' of international co-operation in the areas of commodity processing and of the marketing and distribution of the commodity exports of developing countries.[21] However, no significant progress was made in reaching agreement on the specific elements of such 'frameworks', and by the time of the subsequent UNCTAD Conference, UNCTAD VI, in 1983, the developing countries argued for definite international measures to promote their commodity-processing industries, covering *inter alia*:

- reduction in trade barriers on processed commodities imported by developed countries;
- improvements in commodity market transparency;
- establishment of an investment facility to assist in financing new processing plants, especially in the mineral sector, with a lending programme of $5 billion for the period 1984–8.[22]

However, the Western countries were unable to agree on these or on other specific measures. Their view was that the problems of individual processing industries needed more detailed study, including study of the constraints within the developing countries themselves, before any general conclusions regarding desirable international action could be reached. They also insisted that the 'framework' should consist of guidelines or principles not legally binding, that it should not infringe on the responsibilities of existing international institutions, and that it should be compatible with free market principles.[23] Though this issue remains under discussion in UNCTAD, little if any agreement would seem likely, at least in the near future, to evolve a programme specifically designed to promote the diversification of the commodity sector of the economies of developing countries.

External Financial Support

One general – often critical – constraint in the implementation of diversification programmes is the inadequacy of available finance, from either domestic or

---

[20] Ibid. 174.
[21] Resolution 124 (v), in UNCTAD 1981: i.
[22] These and other possible elements of the proposed 'framework' for international co-operation were elaborated in UNCTAD 1984*h*.
[23] Statement at UNCTAD Committee on Commodities, Jan. 1985.

external sources. The processing of mineral ores in particular involves huge capital investments. The large sums involved,[24] and the difficulties for most smaller or poorer countries of raising finance in the private capital markets have led to suggestions for new institutional mechanisms, or at least collaboration between different sources of funds, both public and private, to ensure adequate financing of mineral-processing industries.[25]

Apart from the short-lived Coffee Diversification Fund set up under the 1968 coffee Agreement (which is briefly reviewed in the Annexe to this chapter), there has not been any agreed international strategy to promote the diversification of the economies of developing countries. In the absence of an international strategy, external financing has been forthcoming essentially on a project-by-project basis. With the sharp contraction over the past decade in commercial bank loans and in private foreign capital flows to developing countries, bilateral donors and the international financial institutions have become major sources of external finance for country programmes involving diversification and structural adjustment. Information is not generally available on how much of bilateral development finance has been used to support diversification projects, but a review has recently been completed of the commitments made during the 1980s by the main international development banks for the financing of export-oriented diversification in the commodity sector.

The results, summarized in Table 14.5, must be interpreted with some caution, partly because the definitions of 'export-oriented' and 'commodity-related' diversification may differ among the various institutions, and partly because it is not possible to divide some finance as between export and domestic diversification. It would seem, however, that in the later 1980s finance in the region of $1 billion a year was committed by the international development banks for commodity-related export-oriented diversification, representing about 5 per cent of their total annual commitments.

An examination of the individual projects which have been financed reveals two critical issues. First, loans for export-oriented diversification have been concentrated on the larger, more diversified, and generally less commodity-dependent countries. Even the African Development Bank, which has a large number of the least-developed countries among its membership, provided these countries, on average, with little more than one-quarter of its total loan commitments. The low-income countries in all developing regions find great difficulty in attracting private investment, are generally not 'creditworthy' as regards the commercial banks, and also have difficulty in formulating viable diversification projects for funding by the international development banks. This group of countries needs much greater technical assistance to identify and for-

---

[24] It has been estimated, for example, that merely to have maintained the trends of the decade up to 1982 would have required over $400 billion (at 1980 prices) between 1983 and 1985 for processing the main mineral ores of developing countries, not including investments in mining or infrastructure (UNCTAD 1982: para. 27).

[25] Ibid. paras. 29–31.

Table 14.5. Commitments by major international financial institutions for export-oriented diversification in the commodity sector, 1980–9

	Period	Total ($ million)	Annual average ($ million)	Average share of least-developed countries (%)	Total as proportion of commitments (%)
World Bank	1980–9	3,866	387	17	2.8
International Finance Corporation	1983–9	718	103	3	9.5
African Development Bank	1984–8	698	140	27	8.7
Asian Development Bank	1980–9	3,236	324	4	...
Inter-American Development Bank	1980–9	1,040	104	0	4.6

Source: UNCTAD 1990b: Table 1.

mulate projects to diversify and modernize their economies.

The second issue arises in relation to the particular commodities involved in the diversification projects covered by Table 14.5. A considerable amount of funds for commodity-related export-oriented diversification, particularly in the Asian region, has gone into projects in the larger, more diversified countries, involving traditional commodities, such as cocoa, coffee, rubber, and palm oil.[26] These financing activities were one element in the very substantial expansion in the exportable production of these commodities over the 1980s and, consequently, in the downward pressure on their prices in the world market. This reveals an underlying weakness in the country project approach used by the international development banks, since a project which appears viable for one country can result in a general fall in prices if its output adds significantly to supplies coming on the world market, in which case the export earnings of other producing countries are harmed.

Thus if the financing of country diversification projects were considered in the broader framework of the requirements for medium- and long-term balance in the world market for the individual commodities concerned, a shift towards lower-cost from higher-cost producing areas could be made over a period which gave the latter sufficient time to diversify into new activities in which they could develop some comparative advantage. As Avramović (1989: 11) comments:

The issue of lending for commodities in surplus has been extensively discussed within the [World] Bank, but it is not known that it has been satisfactorily resolved: it is a difficult issue as it sometimes affects the least advanced developing countries with few obvious non-commodity alternatives. Devaluations in commodity-producing countries, frequently a key element of IMF conditionality, also have a price-depressing effect on the world market as they stimulate additional export sales despite the surplus. What is missing is an international commodity production plan.

The Common Fund, as a new international agency concerned solely with international commodity problems, with a mandate to assist in financing commodity development in developing countries through its second window, should, in principle, be well placed to assume a central role in reconciling, to the extent possible, the diversification programmes of individual countries within an overall perspective of future growth and world market balance.

---

[26] UNCTAD 1990b: 13 and Tables 1–5.

ANNEXE

The Coffee Diversification Fund

A Diversification Fund was established under the international coffee Agreement of 1968. When that Agreement was under negotiation there was an over-supply of coffee in the world market, and there appeared every likelihood that the over-supply would continue. The Fund's objectives were therefore to divert resources from coffee growing to other activities in order to enhance the economic position of producing countries, and also to enable coffee growers to increase their income.[27]

Participation in the Fund was compulsory for those coffee-exporting countries, 30 in all, which had export entitlements of over 100,000 bags. Over the five years of the Agreement, contributions should have totalled about $142 million, though actual contributions amounted to $111 million (as the Fund was terminated in June 1973, before the end of the 1968 Agreement). Some $93 million was committed for 36 individual projects, though this amount was reduced to $72 million for 31 projects by the cancellation of five loan contracts while the Fund was in liquidation.[28] One-half of the total amount was committed for projects in Brazil designed to increase exports of agricultural products other than coffee by improving storage, processing, and shipping facilities, and to improve research and advisory services in food technology.

Most of the remaining funds were loaned to some 20 countries to help finance diversification away from coffee and into specified alternative crops or into livestock-rearing. The average loan for these diversification projects amounted to a modest $1.5 million, so that it was unlikely that the Fund would have had a significant impact in its objective of reducing the global coffee surplus. Though some loans were made to finance diversification from coffee to tea or cocoa production, these projects were too small to add significantly to the over-supply existing in the markets for the two latter commodities.

One clear lesson of the coffee diversification effort is that to attempt to deal with a longer-term process such as diversification by means of a short-term mechanism such as a temporary financing facility is hardly an efficient procedure.

A second lesson is that some effective institutional arrangement would seem necessary — as indicated earlier — in order to prevent diversification projects resulting in a transfer of surplus situations from one product to another. Such a transfer did not occur as a result of the coffee diversification experiment, but it might have done had larger sums been involved. Thus while the coffee experience indicates that an international commodity agreement can provide a useful framework for dealing with the diversification needs of developing countries, it also points to the desirability of operating diversification schemes for an individual commodity within a wider context in which the impact of such schemes on other producers of the commodity, as well as on other commodities, can be taken fully into account.

[27] International Coffee Organization 1979: 2.
[28] Ibid. 2-3.

IV
THE FUTURE OF INTERNATIONAL COMMODITY POLICY

15
The Future of International Commodity Policy

1. THE NEED FOR A NEW POLICY FOCUS

As the new decade of the 1990s opens, there is no end yet in sight of the economic crisis besetting the majority of the commodity-dependent developing countries. Not only have they generally been forced to make substantial cuts in their current levels of consumption and investment, but many of them have lacked the resources required to proceed very far with the necessary restructuring of their economies to meet the demands of a changed and largely hostile external economic environment. While there is now general awareness that the longer-term objective of economic restructuring should be diversification away from excessive dependence on primary commodities and towards industrial development and higher levels of skill and technology, the attainment of this objective has been made far more difficult by the prolonged period of depressed commodity prices, particularly for the smaller and poorer countries dependent on one or a few traditional commodities for the bulk of their foreign exchange earnings.

Much progress has, none the less, been made by many countries to adapt and restructure their economies, often supported by loans or grants from the international financial agencies and from other multilateral and bilateral donors. But the severity and persistence of the external financial squeeze has undermined such domestic efforts in many of these countries. All too often, the expansion in the volume of exports resulting from the diversion of investment to the export sector, more rational pricing systems, or currency devaluation has, in effect, been dissipated in helping to meet high debt service obligations, while adding further to the depressive forces on world commodity prices.

Many proposals have been advanced in recent years to reduce the debt 'overhang', and the burden of debt service payments, of the heavily indebted developing countries, and to expand the volume of financial flows to them. So far, however, little or no serious consideration has been given to the complementary problem of persistent depressed commodity prices, even though this has been an important element in the increase in the total foreign debt and in the debt-servicing burden. For the commodity-dependent countries, indeed, the loss of foreign exchange earnings associated with the deterioration in the commodity terms of trade has been of much the same magnitude as the rise in debt service payments in the deterioration of their balance of payments,[1] and, by implication, in the increase in their total foreign debt.

[1] See Table 2.3, and related discussion.

There would thus seem to be a general case for measures to alleviate the immediate commodity export problems of developing countries so as to complement measures to reduce debt service payments and to increase the flow of financial resources. Indeed, for a great many commodity-dependent countries, measures confined to purely financial flows are unlikely to be fully effective unless these countries are enabled to expand their export earnings at the same time. Moreover, as argued in Chapter 5, measures to reduce short-term commodity market instability would assist the developed countries in more effective management of their own economies, as well as reducing significantly the instability and uncertainties in the global economy which impinge adversely on both the developed and the developing countries.

In the discussion of the 1976 Integrated Programme for Commodities in Chapters 7 and 8, one major conclusion was that the conception of that Programme was a viable one, given adequate financial resources and a strong political commitment by governments to its objectives. There seems little doubt that the establishment of a series of ICAs with price-stabilization functions would have made a significant contribution to the attenuation of the commodity price recession in the early 1980s. The Integrated Programme was focused essentially on short-term commodity price stabilization (even though its objectives also covered longer-term issues), which was entirely appropriate for the experience of the 1970s. However, as argued in Chapter 3, the dominant problem over the past decade has been the persistence of depressed levels of prices, though short-term price and earnings instability have also remained important features of a number of individual commodity markets.

Thus it was suggested that the focus of international concern with the commodity problems of developing countries should shift from measures to reduce short-term price instability to mechanisms to raise persistently depressed levels of commodity prices and export earnings.[2] Three alternative possible mechanisms were considered, viz. supplementary financing, preferential prices for developing-country commodity exports to developed countries, and some form of supply management.[3] There may well be a place for each of these in a broad international strategy—in the context of the need to accelerate the process of diversification—to raise depressed export earnings of commodity-dependent countries, in so far as each may be the preferred mechanism for different commodity situations.

However, as indicated in the earlier discussion, any proposal for a mechanism designed to raise prices on international commodity markets, irrespective of whether or not those prices have been at historically low levels for many years, inevitably arouses strong opposition by the main Western developed countries. It was also suggested in Chapter 3 that there were two major reasons for this opposition.[4] First, the developed countries have greatly benefited from continuing low prices for their commodity imports in helping to reduce inflation, and

---

[2] See Ch. 3, Sect. 1. [3] See Ch. 3, Sects. 2–4. [4] See Ch. 3, Sect. 4.

they would not therefore support measures, such as supply management, which are likely to raise commodity prices and, to this extent, renew inflationary pressures. Second, the governments of the larger industrial countries during the 1980s have given strong support to the virtues of private enterprise and market solutions to international economic problems. Consequently, it was argued, these governments are reluctant to consider any proposals, however relevant, likely to promote interference with market forces.

There also appears to be a third factor operating, in the related area of international financial policy, which has repercussions on developed countries' attitudes to commodity markets. This is that, on present policies, the main industrial countries appear to believe that more remunerative prices for the commodity exports of developing countries would allow some of these countries to avoid having to accept IMF and World Bank stabilization and structural adjustment packages involving 'sound' domestic policies. One eminent economist much concerned with trade and development issues has recently expressed his disquiet over current international policies in this area as follows:

Why has there been such resistance to the provision of compensatory finance sufficient to offset greater proportions of externally caused changes in import purchasing power and thus to prevent much unnecessary disruption and suffering, particularly for the poorest countries who face the greatest difficulties both in making short-term adjustments and in acquiring finance (or holding reserves)? In part, it may be the product of today's dominant development/adjustment ideology. The current Washington obsession with conditionality on resource flows to the developing countries has stood the old 'trade not aid' slogans on their heads. Officials in both the US government and the international financial institutions can be heard complaining that the increased price of coffee allows some countries to evade 'sound' economic policies. Automatic resource flows and entitlements are 'out.' Targeted and conditional flows are 'in'. Needless to say, the developing countries do not see it this way. These differences and changes of approach are matters of ideology rather than economic analysis.[5]

On present policies, it would seem that the main industrial countries would welcome new approaches only if they support the policy changes imposed on developing countries as conditions for IMF and World Bank loans. Though the packages of such policy change vary somewhat from one country to another, they generally contain much the same prescriptions, including tight credit policies, higher interest rates, trade liberalization, substantial currency devaluation, and privatization of state or parastatal enterprises. There is now ample evidence that policy reforms on these standard lines have not worked well in many developing countries, partly because they have not been adapted to the particular structural problems of individual countries, and partly also because they are based in many cases on unrealistic assumptions, such as that domestic markets are always competitive; that high interest rates will attract more savings which, in turn, will lead to higher investment; or that the domestic private sector is strong enough, or

[5] Helleiner 1988: 207–8.

efficient enough, to take over state enterprises successfully.[6] It would appear from the experience of applying standard stabilization packages that economic growth has not thereby been uniformly improved, while income inequalities have generally worsened.[7]

The limited results of World Bank adjustment programmes are also revealed in a recent analysis by a World Bank economist, using a multiple regression approach to relate the application of such programmes to changes in the GDP growth rate, and changes in the ratios of investment, domestic saving, and exports to GDP. His results show that

> Bank-supported programmes have a small positive but not statistically significant effect upon growth rates. There is a significant positive effect on the changes in both domestic savings and export ratios, and a significant negative effect on investment ratios. The increase in saving associated with Bank-supported programmes appears to be going into interest on external debt rather than domestic investment.[8]

As regards the balance between the public and private sectors, while it is true that public enterprises have proved inefficient in many developing countries (in many cases, as a result of cuts in investment), and have often had to be subsidized from state funds, a number of countries have instituted policies designed to improve the managerial efficiency of these enterprises and restore their profitability. Moreover, many public enterprises were established because of the lack of private sector entrepreneurs with adequate capital, skills, and marketing expertise, a deficiency which is still apparent in many of the less-advanced countries. There is also the difficulty of privatizing those public enterprises based on a natural monopoly, such as exists, for example, with public utility concerns, since the resultant creation of a private monopoly is unlikely to prove a net gain to the economy. In other cases, privatization may lead to a more efficient use of resources, though there may be social offsets in the form of a worsened income distribution. Many developing countries have approached this issue pragmatically, taking into account the inherent strengths and weaknesses of market-based solutions, the stage of development reached, and the specific institutional characteristics of their economies. Governments of such countries have generally sought to enhance the contributions of both the public and the private sectors to the development process.[9]

Thus an optimal solution would depend essentially on the particular circumstances of individual countries, including the structural constraints faced by the public and private sectors, their relative efficiencies, and the nature of their complementarities. The insistence of the Bretton Woods institutions, in all the developing countries applying IMF and/or World Bank programmes, on a reduction in the role of the State in economic management, together with the sale of public enterprises to the private sector, is a strong indication of the injection of

---

[6] See, in particular, the discussion of these issues in Taylor 1988 and ECA 1989. For an opposing viewpoint see, for example, World Bank 1988a and World Bank/UNDP 1989.
[7] Taylor 1988.   [8] Holsen 1990: 17.   [9] UNCTAD 1987a: 43.

an ideological element into stabilization or structural adjustment programmes.

For these various reasons, economic, political, and ideological, the main Western industrial countries are likely to remain strongly opposed to proposals which might alleviate the financial pressure on developing countries by action to raise depressed levels of commodity prices. Thus to the extent that such action is feasible, it must be taken by the developing countries themselves – so long as the industrial countries maintain their present policy stance. However, before considering this issue further, the question arises as to whether some minimum programme of North–South co-operation in the area of commodity policy might none the less be practicable.

2. THE ELEMENTS OF A POSSIBLE MINIMUM NORTH–SOUTH PROGRAMME

It is important, to begin with, to relate the commodity problems of developing countries fairly directly to certain of the domestic economic policies of the main industrialized countries. Two issues are relevant here. First, as was pointed out in Chapter 1, the restrictive monetary policies of the major industrialized countries, aimed at reducing inflation, also greatly accentuated the severity of the economic recession of the early 1980s, and have continued to be a major factor in the slow growth rates of these countries since then. In turn, the growth slowdown has been one important cause of the decline in commodity prices throughout the past decade, as was also shown in Chapter 1. Thus the success of the main industrialized countries in dealing with inflation has been to a substantial extent at the expense of the developing countries, which have had to cope with both higher interest on their foreign debts and lower prices for their commodity exports. To the extent that policy can now be redirected to give greater priority to economic growth, this in itself could involve a significant improvement in demand for the commodity exports of developing countries and an alleviation of the depressing forces on world commodity prices. Such a reorientation in policy is still a contentious issue, particularly with revived fears of inflation in many industrial countries in the later 1980s and early 1990s: clearly, it would involve much closer co-ordination of national economic policies to minimize inflationary effects, and the adoption of effective measures to reduce the large payments imbalances among the industrialized countries.

Second, agreement by the industrialized countries in the GATT Uruguay Round negotiations to phase out existing systems of agricultural protection would result in significant increases in demand for many agricultural products exported by developing countries; world market prices would rise, in some cases (e.g. for cereals, sugar, and meat) substantially, while price instability in the world market for these products would be reduced, as indicated in Chapter 12. The success of these negotiations in phasing out such protection, or in reducing its level substantially over a short period, together with a major reduction in the escalation of trade barriers on processed commodities, should be regarded as one essential element in a wider strategy to alleviate the commodity crisis.[10] However, a rise in world prices for foodstuffs would impose an immediate extra import cost for food-deficit countries. Though one result, in some countries, may be greater domestic food production, there will be others which will suffer a fall in food supplies unless adequate compensatory financing is made available (see the discussion on this point in Chapter 12).

In addition to co-ordinated measures by the main developed countries to raise their growth rates and to phase out agricultural protectionism, a minimum programme should also include co-operative action by developed and developing countries. An immediate objective should be to resuscitate the various lapsed international commodity agreements, and to consider, within the framework of the Integrated Programme for Commodities, such agreements for one or two additional commodities for which excessive price instability remains a serious problem. This would require general agreement that the objective would be stabilization around the short-term trend, and not raising depressed levels of prices (in view of the opposition to the latter by the developed countries). The phasing out of agricultural support in the developed countries, by reducing the instability in world commodity markets, would in particular make the negotiation of a viable new sugar agreement much more possible.

A second immediate objective should be to reduce substantially the pressure on developing countries to expand exports of commodities which are already in surplus on the world market. Reducing the burden of debt service obligations or expanding financial flows to commodity-dependent countries would be indirect ways of reducing the pressure to expand the volume of commodity exports. But in addition, the international financial institutions need to drop their insistence on export expansion as an essential element of conditionality for countries faced with persistent over-supply in the world market for their major commodity exports.

Third, a substantial improvement in the present arrangements for compensatory financing of export earnings shortfalls should also form part of a minimum programme. The present schemes – of the IMF and the European Community – both suffer from serious inadequacies. The IMF Facility remains subject to strict conditionality, while neither scheme adequately addresses the underlying problem of supply instability.[11] Serious consideration should therefore be given to the need for a new facility with fully adequate resources which would make compensatory payments conditional on the adoption by the recipient country of measures to reduce supply instability (see the discussion in Chapter 9).

---

[10] The phasing out of agricultural protection would involve cuts in the output of many farm products in the industrialized countries, and consequently there would be a need for structural adjustment policies to assist in the redeployment of resources from high-cost agricultural production to more economic activities.

[11] However, under Lomé IV, compensatory payments under STABEX may be used, *inter alia*, for financing diversification in the affected sector (Article 209), which may indirectly reduce supply instability.

Fourth, new approaches would seem desirable to ensure a much larger flow of financial resources for development purposes. An expanded programme of loans by Japan – the principal surplus country – to developing countries, announced in 1989, is an important step in this direction, and needs to be complemented by similar programmes by other countries in persistent payments surplus. Developing countries could also take steps to encourage the inflow of investment, including easier provisions for joint ventures, consistent with their development objectives.

Fifth, common ground between developed and developing countries may also be found in proposals for expanded R & D programmes to improve the competitive position of natural raw materials in relation to synthetic materials and other substitutes, and for increased international financial support for diversification, both horizontal and vertical, in commodity-dependent developing countries.

Sixth, a minimum programme would need to include additional measures of support for the least-developed countries, and for other countries – particularly in sub-Saharan Africa – which have suffered most from the collapse in commodity prices. As pointed out in Chapter 2, the African region is more heavily dependent than other regions on the commodity sector for its export earnings, and the stagnation in the real value of Africa's commodity exports over the past decade has undoubtedly been a major reason for the continuing economic crisis there. A new programme of international measures would thus need to include special support for the region, in trade preferences and other trade-enhancing measures, in financial flows, and in debt forgiveness. This issue is taken up in more detail below, in relation to the recommendations made recently by a UN Expert Group to alleviate the commodity crisis in Africa.

The international economic agencies could provide a useful integrative framework in the evolution of a minimum programme of this kind. Here, the new Common Fund has the potential to play a lead role. As the only international financial agency concerned solely with the problems of international commodity markets, both agricultural and mineral, the Common Fund would be uniquely qualified – with support from the World Bank, UNCTAD, FAO, and others – to organize a series of in-depth reviews of the short- and long-term problems of each main commodity of interest to developing countries. Such reviews could consider, for example, the relationship between short-term price instability and longer-term structural characteristics (including the effects of protectionism, competition from synthetics, etc.), in the context of the outlook for future trends in supply and demand. The outcome could be an identification of the key problems to be tackled and, to the extent possible, a consensus on the policies needed to resolve them.

This might then lead to a co-ordinated approach by the different agencies to an international package of measures in support of such policies. Depending on the commodity concerned, such a package could include, for example, an expanded R and D programme (which could be co-ordinated by the Common

Fund), or increased finance for the diversification of production away from commodities in persistent surplus (which could be financed in part by the second Account of the Common Fund, as well as by the World Bank and the regional Development Banks). By injecting a much-needed overall view into international consideration of commodity problems and policies, the Common Fund could thus play a catalyst role in the evolution of the kind of minimum programme envisaged here. It remains to be seen, however, whether the Western industrial countries would agree to this kind of initiative by the Common Fund.

Even such a minimum programme—or, at least, many of its suggested elements—may not prove to be negotiable in view of both the present policy stance of the Western industrial countries, mentioned earlier, and the continuing weakness in the relative bargaining strength of the developing countries, which derives essentially from their severe financial difficulties and consequent heavy dependence on decisions by the industrial countries, not only in regard to bilateral aid but, more importantly, in regard to the stabilization and adjustment programmes of the IMF and World Bank.

A discussion of the measures which might be taken by the developing countries to improve their collective bargaining position falls outside the scope of the present book. However, as regards international commodity policy, it appears evident that the bargaining strength of the developing countries is reduced by the negotiations being conducted essentially in isolation from those on related issues (trade liberalization, the regime for foreign investment, trade in services, or the reduction in foreign debts). Some institutional arrangement which would bring the various key issues together so that their mutual interrelationships could be taken into account in the negotiations would be likely, by itself, to improve the developing countries' chances of arriving at a successful outcome.

3. MEASURES BY DEVELOPING COUNTRIES TO STRENGTHEN THE COMMODITY SECTOR

In any event, the developing countries need urgently to consider how best they can themselves improve the position of their commodity producers. Measures to this end can be divided into those involving co-operation among commodity-producing countries, and those related to the domestic economy.

(a) Co-operation among Commodity-Dependent Countries

Supply management. The key issue here is whether there are realistic possibilities for supply management schemes operated by producer countries themselves. If so, such schemes could become the centrepiece of an overall commodity recovery programme for the Third World. A recent preliminary study of the possibilities for such schemes indicated that the prospects for success are especially good for measures to remedy emergency situations (e.g. by the gradual depletion of large stock overhangs to more normal levels). Such schemes, having no explicit price objectives, should be relatively easy to negotiate.[12]

Schemes aiming to raise prices above depressed levels would, however, need to meet a series of stringent conditions to ensure success, as discussed in Chapter 3, including price-inelastic demand; a high proportion of initial output under the control of participating countries, with significant entry costs for non-participants; and a high degree of commitment by participants. It would also be important for the key producing countries to play a leading role; for the schemes to be flexible enough to allow for appropriate changes in the price objective, and in market shares, as market trends changed; and for prices not to be raised to levels which would cause concern to consumers. As indicated in the earlier discussion of the conditions for a successful supply management scheme,[13] it would appear unlikely that this approach would be applicable to more than a limited number of commodities, principally the main tropical beverage crops, some tropical fruits, and certain non-ferrous minerals and metals. None the less, countries highly dependent on income from the production and export of such commodities would stand to gain substantially by co-operation in supply management arrangements.[14]

Before any decisions are taken on whether or not producers as a group could negotiate such schemes, it would seem essential that they arrange for in-depth feasibility studies to be carried out, taking into account market structure, the potential for substitution by other commodities, the probable reaction of consumers, the relative merits of alternative mechanisms for raising depressed prices, and the estimated benefits for individual countries. Successful schemes of this type would also strengthen the bargaining power of producing countries in any later negotiations with consumers, and could lay the basis for later consumer–producer stabilization agreements for individual commodities.

While supply management has traditionally been conceived as involving some regulation of supply, either by buffer stock purchases or by export quotas, other approaches could also be considered as perhaps more appropriate in certain circumstances. The main alternatives would be the use by all producing countries of a uniform *ad valorem* export tax, or a minimum export price agreement, to affect the export of a particular commodity facing inelastic world demand. An *ad valorem* export tax would avoid the difficulties inherent in negotiating export quotas, while leaving intact the relative prices of different grades and varieties of the same commodity, as well as the relative competitive positions of different producing countries. In this case, the governments and not the actual producers would gain from the resulting increase in the world price.

A minimum price scheme would, if successful, also raise the average level of export prices, with the gain being captured by the commodity producers. This

---

[12] Kanan *et al.* 1989.
[13] See Ch. 3, Sect. 4.
[14] See Chapter 4, Section 3(*c*), for a discussion of some of the problems involved in operating supply management schemes using export quotas.

type of scheme is easier to operate when there are relatively few producing countries which together control the bulk of world supply of a commodity in inelastic demand. An informal minimum price scheme for mercury exports was successfully operated by Algeria, Italy, and Spain in the mid-1970s. More recently, in 1986, an agreement was reached between Indonesia and Grenada on minimum export prices for nutmeg and mace. This agreement, which also included sales quotas, seems to have been successful in raising export earnings from these two spices very substantially.

It is important to emphasize that, as stated in Chapter 3, supply management schemes designed to raise depressed levels of commodity prices would be essentially short-term expedients to help alleviate the immediate external financial difficulties of commodity-dependent countries, and thus to assist them in financing a greater volume of essential imports to speed economic reconstruction and development. In the longer term, these countries must give priority to policies to diversify their production and export structures away from commodities in structural oversupply.[15]

Research and development. A second important area in which developing countries could consider regular co-operation is in R & D, particularly (though not exclusively) in relation to natural raw materials. This has already been suggested above as one element in a minimum programme of international measures, but developing countries could also evolve their own institutional framework to accelerate progress in this area. There has long been a huge gap between R & D expenditures in developing countries in relation to natural raw materials, and the far larger R & D effort of the competing synthetic materials industries of developed countries. A useful start in closing this gap could be made by meetings among the scientists, technicians, and economists of the main producing countries, convened to identify the priorities for expanded, and co-ordinated, R & D programmes, and to provide budgetary estimates for funding by the relevant international institutions and bilateral donors.

The growing worldwide concern at the damage to the natural environment resulting from current production technologies and consumption patterns, particularly in the industrial countries, also has relevance for the competitive position of natural raw materials which have been displaced by synthetic materials in a wide range of end-uses. As suggested in Chapter 11, the magnitude of environmental pollution and degradation resulting from the use of synthetic materials and the disposal of synthetic waste now needs to be carefully examined and the policy implications widely disseminated. The hidden costs to the world community of the displacement of natural by synthetic materials could then more readily be assessed. The wider application of the 'polluter pays' principle would,

---

[15] In the event that the growth rates of GDP, and of demand for primary commodities, in the Western industrial countries increase substantially over the 1990s—a possibility which appears unlikely—so that commodity prices rise to levels generally considered remunerative by producers, then there would of course be no need for the adoption of short-term supply management schemes.

by raising the production costs of many synthetic materials, thereby improve the competitive position of the more 'environmentally friendly' natural materials.

Marketing, distribution, and transport. A third area of potential co-operation could be in the international marketing, distribution, and transport of commodities exported by developing countries. As pointed out in Chapter 10, many such commodities are effectively in the control of transnational corporations which can exercise their market power to increase their share of the overall benefits of international commodity trade. Developing countries, by co-operation among themselves, may nevertheless be able to increase their share of the final prices paid by consumers in developed countries. One possibility would be the use of a co-operative marketing organization, e.g. for processed commodities, such as packeted tea or instant coffee, which could bypass existing marketing and distribution channels by selling directly to wholesalers or retail chains in developed countries, using own-brand names as appropriate. There may also be scope for reducing excessive freight charges, particularly on processed commodities and on minor routes, by joint negotiations of producing-country interests with the shipping Conferences.

Closer co-operation among state trading organizations of producer countries to counteract the present dominant position of the TNCs in the international marketing and distribution of primary commodities is another area which would merit detailed feasibility studies. One possibility, mentioned in Chapter 10, might be to create a link between imports of manufactures into developing countries originating with TNCs, and counterpart sales of commodities to these TNCs at negotiated prices at levels remunerative to the producers.

The bargaining position of developing countries *vis-à-vis* the transnational corporations engaged in marketing, distribution, and transport would also be improved if greater transparency could be achieved in regard to the operation of these corporations. This could include, *inter alia*, information on prices paid in different producing countries by transnationals for the same or similar commodities and, where relevant, evidence of transfer pricing practices. Moreover, greater transparency should reduce or eliminate competition among developing countries in attracting TNCs by offering them excessive tax concessions.

Trade among Developing Countries

New policies and new mechanisms for expanding the intra-trade of developing countries have become urgently needed in view of the adverse impact of the external payments difficulties of the majority of developing countries on their mutual trade, and of the likelihood of continued slow growth in the period ahead in demand for primary commodities in the industrial countries. The Global System of Trade Preferences currently under negotiation is still limited in country and commodity coverage, and needs to be complemented by additional mechanisms, as suggested in Chapter 13, such as across-the-board relaxations of trade barriers; while the present infrastructure of trade among developing countries, including shipping availabilities, port facilities, insurance, and export credits, needs to be considerably improved to support a growing volume of transactions.

The potential of new mechanisms in the financial field also needs to be seriously explored. As also discussed in Chapter 13, various possibilities exist for strengthening the existing sub-regional clearing and payments arrangements, including the reactivation of those suspended because of unsettled balances; and for a formal link among these arrangements so that surpluses in one sub-region can be set off against deficits in others. A new Third World clearing arrangement should also be considered, to give a wider geographical coverage than the existing schemes.

The growing use of countertrade deals to avoid the problems caused by the shortage of convertible currency was an important feature of South–South trade in the 1980s, though there may well be economic losses associated with this new trade mechanism. A more fundamental approach would be the issue of a new Third World currency by an institution created for this purpose by the developing countries. Such a new currency, which was discussed briefly in Chapter 13, would act in a similar way to the Special Drawing Rights (SDRs) issued by the IMF. However, unlike the SDRs, the new currency would be issued in accordance with the liquidity needs of the developing countries. This proposal would merit serious consideration by these countries, based on a detailed feasibility study.

(b) Domestic Measures

Developing countries could also do more by changing or adapting their own policies and institutions to strengthen the commodity sector of their economies. An important distinction must be made in this respect between two groups of commodities. The first consists of food (for domestic consumption) and industrial raw materials (whether for domestic consumption or export). Measures to expand domestic food production and to improve the internal marketing and distribution system would be particularly important in food-deficit countries, especially if world cereal prices rise as a result of a reduction in agricultural protection in the industrial countries. Such measures could include more remunerative prices for producers, a greater R & D effort to improve productivity, improved extension services, and greater access to credit and marketing facilities for small farmers and women producers in this sector.

Similarly, for industrial raw materials, corresponding measures would be required to improve productivity and technical quality, and to reduce unit costs so as to lay the material basis for increased domestic processing and manufacturing activities, as well as for improved competitiveness in relation to potential synthetic substitutes in export markets (see the more detailed analysis of this issue in Chapter 11).

The second group of commodities consists of exportables other than industrial raw materials, i.e. essentially foodstuffs and tropical beverage crops. To the extent that world markets tend to be in over-supply for many of these commodities, measures to improve productivity and thus the volume of exports would increase export earnings only if the country concerned was not a major supplier. Similar measures by a number of countries, or by one or a few major suppliers, would be self-defeating, since prices would fall by a greater proportion than the rise in export volume (see Table 14.4). For commodities in persistent over-supply, then, the domestic policies of producer countries need to be co-ordinated in some form of supply management scheme (as discussed in Chapter 3).

For countries whose exports have traditionally been concentrated in one or a few commodities in persistent over-supply—such as cocoa, coffee, or sugar—an urgent priority must be to devise policies and mechanisms to develop non-traditional commodity exports enjoying more dynamic demand conditions and, even more important, to shift their production structures towards processed commodities and manufactured goods. The newly industrializing countries (NICs) of East Asia have built their high growth rates on precisely this kind of vertical diversification, and significant movement in this direction has also occurred in recent years in the 'second tier' NICs, such as Malaysia and Thailand. However, a similar process has been found very difficult to achieve in most other developing countries, particularly in the poor economies of sub-Saharan Africa.

As pointed out earlier (Chapter 14), in many developing countries—particularly small and poor ones—vertical diversification is subject to a number of constraints. Barriers to trade in processed commodities and manufactures are still of major importance in limiting access to developed-country markets, while the lack of adequate finance and of technical skills and know-how, as well as the absence of necessary infrastructure, all place strict limits, at least in the short and medium term, on efforts to shift production structures away from traditional primary commodities.

Africa's Acute Commodity Problems

Since the economies of African countries are much more heavily dependent on the commodity sector than are those of other developing regions, the adverse changes in world commodity markets over the past decade, and particularly the deterioration of the commodity terms of trade, have had a disproportionate negative impact on real incomes in Africa. As was shown in Chapter 2, the cumulative foreign exchange loss for African developing countries over the period 1980 to 1988 resulting from the deterioration in the commodity terms of trade amounted to as much as 16–17 per cent of their total GDP in 1980—an enormous loss, particularly bearing in mind the relatively high proportion of low-income countries in Africa and their generally low per capita income levels. Africa contains well over one-half (28 out of 42) of the countries designated as 'least developed' by the United Nations, which generally are the poorest, with insufficient domestic resources to respond adequately to unfavourable external changes without continuing and substantial external financial and trade-related support.

The income losses incurred by African countries as a result of the worsening of the commodity terms of trade was the major adverse change during the 1980s in Africa's balance of payments position, somewhat exceeding the increase in debt service payments (Table 2.3). Moreover, Africa's share of world commodity exports continued to decline, and many countries in the region became increasingly dependent on imports for their food supply. The stagnation in the commodity sector had clearly become a major cause of sluggish overall growth and of a decline in real GDP per capita for a large number of African countries.

To bring this issue clearly before the international community in order to evolve suitable remedial action, the Organization of African Unity requested the UN Secretary-General in 1988 to appoint a group of eminent persons to examine Africa's commodity problems and make recommendations. A Group of Experts on African Commodity Problems was accordingly established in 1989, and they issued a report in 1990.[16] This report—often known as the Fraser Report, after the Expert Group's Chairman—was very wide-ranging, placing Africa's commodity problems in the context of weaknesses in government policies, and in administration and organization, which resulted in an inadequate environment for maintaining productivity growth and competitiveness; of insufficient priority having been given to the commodity sector in planning, budgeting, and policy formation by governments; and of a lack of a coherent policy framework, essentially of specific measures to support a commodity strategy.

The report made a large number of recommendations designed to overcome these and related constraints. Those on attitudes to the commodity sector, on organization and administration, etc., are relevant and important, but essentially fall outside the scope of the present book. The central recommendation relevant here is that each African country should formulate a commodity strategy, and a comprehensive policy package to support it, within a long-term planning perspective, 'taking into account the macroeconomic environment, the resource needs, the requirements for human resources development, research and technological development and the potential benefits from regional co-operation, as well as specifically commodity sector matters' (United Nations 1990: 55–6).

There seems little doubt that if each African country evolved a coherent strategy to strengthen and develop its commodity sector on the lines set out in the UN report, this would be a great step forward. It would necessarily involve some analysis of the causes of stagnation in that sector, and provide higher priority in policy planning for overcoming that stagnation. In their discussion of the elements of such a commodity strategy, the experts considered a wide range of measures, some of which have been mentioned earlier in the present chapter (such as more effective agricultural research and extension services, and the encouragement of diversification), while others have not (such as the need for a

---

[16] United Nations 1990.

substantial reduction in military expenditures). These and many other detailed recommendations all need to be seriously considered by African governments.

However, the question arises whether individual countries, especially small poor ones, can in fact develop viable commodity strategies if the prices of their major commodity exports remain seriously depressed and if their diversification plans are not compatible with those of other countries. The argument in the UN report implies that African countries would base their plans, *inter alia*, on commodity price projections such as those of the World Bank, considered in Chapter 1. On this basis, their requirements for foreign financial assistance for diversification away from their traditional commodity production and export patterns could be very substantial. The prospects for success of this strategy will thus depend heavily on the ability and willingness of the principal bilateral and multilateral donors to finance the country policy packages.

In any event, problems of incompatibility between the commodity strategies of different countries could well arise, to the extent that these include plans for diversification of production away from traditional commodities into new primary or processed commodities which come into competition in export markets with supplies from other countries. Without some form of global harmonization of national commodity programmes, there would be a danger of shifting a structural surplus from one commodity to another, thus exacerbating the existing downward pressures on world commodity prices.

By contrast, the strategy discussed earlier in this chapter is based essentially on a global approach to the problem of depressed commodity prices. This would imply that African producing countries of cocoa and coffee, for example, should consider close co-operation with producers of these commodities in other regions in some form of supply management scheme, which would yield additional foreign exchange to help finance needed diversification, structural change, and improved living standards.[17] To the extent that such schemes are feasible, this approach would also improve the bargaining position of producing countries in negotiations with bilateral and multilateral donors.

4. THE CRUCIAL ROLE OF FINANCE

Many of the policies discussed above would require adequate financial support both from national governments and from external sources. For example, supply management schemes are likely to involve additional stocks being held by producers, and the required finance, e.g. for new storage facilities, will normally have a foreign exchange component. Similarly, a move away from producing commodities in structural surplus would be greatly facilitated if international support were available to help fund the cost of appropriate diversification

---

[17] The UN report approaches this issue in its recommendation that 'the attention of African Governments be directed to the possibility of gains from increased co-operation among African and other producers of these two commodities [cocoa and coffee], as well as renewed producer–consumer agreements' (ibid. 81), but stops short of raising the possibility of supply management schemes.

programmes; indeed, for many of the poorer developing countries the availability of external financial assistance would be essential for the implementation of such programmes. Equally, the possibilities of implementing greatly expanded R & D programmes for natural raw materials are highly dependent on adequate financing. The existing international financing facilities need to be reviewed, and greatly expanded, to give adequate support to these and other programmes in an overall policy for commodities.

One approach to meeting the need for increased finance for strengthening the commodity sector would be a multilateral financing 'package', whereby governments' own financial resources would be complemented by, for example, finance from the World Bank, the regional Development Banks, or commercial banks. The Common Fund could also play an important role in longer-term financing through its second Account, if its resources were substantially augmented at a fairly early date.

In addition, it would seem vital in the longer term for developing countries to have access to a much larger source of their own finance for development purposes. This would not only provide a much-needed addition to existing sources, such as bilateral donors and the international financial agencies, but would restore to developing countries the right to make their own decisions concerning their styles of development and their domestic priorities, instead of decisions on such strategic issues being imposed on them by the IMF and World Bank as part of loan conditionality.

The opportunity that arose during the era of high oil prices for Third World countries to create their own 'South Bank' for development financing was, unfortunately, not taken. Now, with continuing high interest payments and low commodity prices, the time may not appear propitious to propose a renewed effort on these or similar lines. Yet the issue remains a key one, not just for commodity financing, but for the future development of the Third World generally. A beginning with such a project, even on a small scale, perhaps with financial support from the relatively few developing countries in persistent balance of payments surplus, would be an important acknowledgement of the crucial role of development financing in a viable and coherent commodity policy.

APPENDIX

Terms of Trade Gains and Losses on Commodity Exports from Developing Countries

The 'terms of trade' of a given country is taken here to mean the ratio of its export prices to its import prices, a ratio usually known as the 'net barter terms of trade'. The foreign exchange gain or loss in a given year due to changes in the terms of trade from a specified base period can be derived by deducting the value of exports in the later year when revalued at base period export prices from the corresponding value when revalued at base period import prices (see Chapter 2, note 1). The dollar values of the gains and losses resulting from changes in the terms of trade of commodity exports from developing countries (the 'commodity terms of trade') have been calculated on this basis for each year from 1970 to 1988, while broadly corresponding estimates have been calculated for the 1930s.

More specifically, the calculations relate changes in prices of non-oil primary commodities exported by developing countries to price changes of manufactured goods imported by them. The methods used to arrive at the terms of trade gains and losses are described more fully below.

THE 1930s

Value, price, and volume series for foreign trade in the inter-war years were published by the League of Nations in its annual *Review of World Trade*. Separate series were compiled for the different Continental groups, and for three broad commodity categories: foodstuffs, raw materials (including materials partly manufactured), and manufactured articles. The League used the Brussels Classification of 1913 in distinguishing the three commodity categories, the major difference between this and the UN Standard International Trade Classification (SITC) being that base metals were included as raw materials by the Brussels Classification, but as manufactures (SITC 67 and 68) by the SITC. (There were other important differences also.) In the present book, non-oil commodities are defined to include non-ferrous metals (SITC 68), so that the pre-war series using the Brussels Classification should provide a reasonably reliable guide to annual movements in value, unit value, and volume of the two main commodity categories, primary commodities and manufactures, broadly comparable with the post-war series.

Values and prices of international trade were calculated by the League in terms of US old gold dollars, the conversion from other currencies being made according to par rates in the case of gold currencies. For paper currencies, the conversion was made monthly, when monthly figures were available, or annually using weighted monthly exchange rates. The price series for the three broad commodity groups were estimated mainly on the basis of the published national series for five large trading countries, viz. the United Kingdom, United States, Germany, France, and Italy, while the volume series was derived by dividing the indices for value by the corresponding price indices. The price indices were, in effect, current-weighted unit value series, since the 'most important national price indices employed are obtained by weighting the prices of individual commodities by the quantities entering into trade in each individual year' (League of Nations 1939: 59–60).

A close approximation to the present developing countries as a group can be derived by aggregating the pre-war series of export values for Africa (excluding the Union of South Africa), Asia (excluding China, Japan, and the Soviet Union), Latin America (including the Caribbean), Turkey, and Yugoslavia. A very high proportion of the total exports of this aggregated group of countries would have consisted of primary commodities during the inter-war period. This can be seen from an analysis of world trade in 1928 and 1937 made by Yates (1959), based on tables of world trade published annually by the German Statistical Office. His results are summarized below (Yates 1959: Tables A.18 and A.19), with values in US dollars at the new (1934) gold parity:

Exports from Latin America, Africa, and Asia	1928	1937
Total ($ billion)	9.51	8.20
Primary products ($ billion)	7.88	6.98

However, Yates's figures for Asia include Japan (about one-half of whose exports, by value, consisted of manufactures in this period) and China (which is now usually considered separately from the group of 'developing' countries). Excluding these two countries[1] from Yates's figures yields the following:

	1928	1937
Total ($ billion)	7.86	6.89
Primary products ($ billion)	7.46	6.59

so that in both these years, primary products on the Brussels Classification represented about 95% of the total value of exports from this group of countries.

To obtain a suitable unit value index for the total exports of this group of countries, the League indices of world trade prices of foodstuffs and raw materials have been weighted by their relative values in world exports in 1929. There were only marginal changes in the relative values of trade in these two commodity groups during the 1930s, so that the use of later year weighting would not have altered the combined index significantly.

The results of applying this combined commodity price index to the value of exports of those countries which, in aggregate, correspond closely to the present group of developing countries are summarized in Table A.1. This shows the annual movement during the 1930s in their terms of trade (commodity export unit values in terms of manufactured import unit values), and the corresponding terms of trade losses in relation to the level of exports in the pre-recession year, 1929.

---

[1] For 1937, exports from Manchuria—which was then a separate Customs jurisdiction under Japanese occupation—have also been excluded from Yates's total.

Table A.1. Exports and terms of trade of the present developing countries,[a] 1929–38

	Export prices[b] (1929=100)	Import prices[c] (1929=100)	Terms of trade[d] (1929=100)	Value of exports ($ billion, old gold)[e]			Terms of trade effect	
				At current prices	At 1929 export prices	At 1929 import prices	Value[f] ($ billion, old gold[e])	As % of 1929 exports
1929	100	100	100	7.73	7.73	7.73	...	...
1930	83	94	88	5.86	7.06	6.23	−0.83	−10.7
1931	62	78	79	4.19	6.76	5.37	−1.39	−18.0
1932	47	64	74	3.02	6.40	4.76	−1.64	−21.2
1933	42	57	74	2.83	6.71	5.01	−1.70	−22.0
1934	40	50	80	2.92	7.25	5.84	−1.41	−18.2
1935	40	48	83	2.98	7.53	6.21	−1.32	−17.1
1936	42	48	88	3.39	8.13	7.06	−1.07	−13.8
1937	46	51	90	4.24	9.14	8.31	−0.83	−10.7
1938[g]	43	51	85	3.47	8.13	6.87	−1.26	−16.3

[a] Africa (excluding Union of South Africa), Asia (excluding China, Japan, and the Soviet Union), Latin America and the Caribbean, Turkey, and Yugoslavia.
[b] League of Nations indices of world trade prices of 'foodstuffs' and 'raw materials' (which included 'materials partly manufactured'), weighted by relative values of world exports of these two groups in 1929.
[c] League of Nations index of world trade prices of 'manufactured articles'.
[d] Ratio of export prices to import prices (assuming that all exports were commodities and all imports were manufactures).
[e] The old gold (US) dollar was equivalent to 1.50463 grammes of fine gold. The parity was changed in 1934 to a new gold dollar of 0.88867 grammes.
[f] Value of exports at 1929 import prices minus corresponding value at 1929 export prices.
[g] The values and price indices for 1938 were labelled 'provisional' in the last issue of the *Review of World Trade* (published in 1939).

Source: Based on data in *Review of World Trade*, 1938 (and earlier issues), Annex 1, Geneva, League of Nations

THE 1970s AND 1980s

(a) Terms of Trade Gains and Losses

Several indices are available for the movement in primary commodity prices over the past two or more decades, the best known being those published by UNCTAD, the World Bank, and the IMF. However, none of these indices is suitable for calculating the effect of changes in the terms of trade, since each is based essentially on quoted prices of specific grades or varieties of different commodities, and not on the unit values of commodities exported from developing countries. The reasons why unit values can be expected to decline less than prices in a recessionary period are given on page 24, so that for the 1980s the use of a price index will give an upward bias to the calculation of the movement in the volume of commodity exports and this, in turn, will result in an overestimate of the magnitude of the terms of trade loss.

A new index of unit values of commodity exports is therefore required, and has been computed for 148 separate commodities, mostly at the SITC 4- or 5-digit level which, in aggregate, accounted for 92% of the value of all non-oil commodities exported from developing countries in 1980. The new export unit value index is shown in Table A.2, together with the calculation of the terms of trade effect on foreign exchange earnings of all developing countries from commodity exports, for the 1970s and the period 1980–8. This calculation implicitly assumes that the movement in the unit value of commodities not covered by the new index has been the same as for those covered. Indices of unit values and volumes for commodity exports by region have also been derived in a similar manner, and are shown in Table A.3 for the period 1980–8. As already indicated, the terms of trade effect, as defined here, relates to the exchange of commodity exports for manufactured imports. A wider definition – for example, in relation to total imports, including foodstuffs and fuels – might be relevant for other purposes.

For the years 1980 to 1987, the new export volume index shows a closely similar movement to the published IMF index (IMF 1989b), which covers 19 major commodities, but for 1988 there is a significant divergence, with the IMF volume index falling by 2%, and the new index based on Table A.2 rising by 4%. The actual indices (1980 = 100) are as follows:

	IMF	Present book		IMF	Present book
1981	101	102	1985	115	113
1982	102	104	1986	113	114
1983	107	106	1987	117	119
1984	108	109	1988	115	124

Commodity-Exporting Countries

For comparisons of the foreign exchange effects of movements in the 'commodity terms of trade', and of changes in debt service payments and other elements of the balance of payments of developing countries, it is convenient to exclude those countries which are major exporters of petroleum or of manufactured goods. In this context, the UNCTAD definitions of these categories have been used, as follows:

Table A.2. Effect of changes in the commodity terms of trade of developing countries, 1970–88

	Export unit value[a] (1980=100)	Import unit value[b] (1980=100)	Terms of trade[c] (1980=100)	Value of exports ($ billion)				Terms of trade effect	
				At current prices	At 1980 export unit values	At 1980 import unit values		Value[d]	As % of 1980 exports
1970	33	34	97	28.4	85.3	83.5		−1.8	−1.7
1971	33	37	112	27.4	84.0	74.1		−9.9	−9.1
1972	34	39	115	30.8	89.5	79.0		−10.5	−9.6
1973	47	46	103	43.1	91.3	93.7		2.4	2.2
1974	65	56	120	58.2	89.0	103.9		14.9	13.7
1975	63	63	102	55.3	87.4	87.8		0.4	0.4
1976	66	63	104	64.0	96.4	101.6		5.2	4.8
1977	80	69	116	75.1	94.3	108.8		14.5	13.3
1978	80	79	99	80.2	100.8	101.5		0.7	0.6
1979	91	90	99	97.1	107.2	107.9		0.7	0.6
1980	100	100	100	109.1	109.1	109.1		...	...
1981	93	95	98	103.2	111.0	109.6		−2.4	−2.2
1982	83	92	90	94.1	113.4	102.3		−11.1	−10.2
1983	83	89	93	95.8	115.4	107.6		−7.8	−7.1
1984	86	86	100	102.2	118.8	118.8		0.0	0.0
1985	79	86	92	97.7	123.7	113.6		−10.1	−9.3
1986	82	103	80	101.9	124.3	98.9		−25.4	−23.3
1987	82	116	71	106.2	129.5	91.6		−37.9	−34.7
1988	93	124	75	125.4	134.8	101.1		−33.7	−30.9

[a] Based on 148 commodities, accounting for over 90% of the total value of commodity exports from developing countries. Weights are based on the value of exports from developing countries in 1980.
[b] Unit value of exports of manufactures from developed market-economy countries.
[c] Unit value of commodities exported by developing countries as proportion of unit value of manufactures exported by developed market-economy countries.
[d] Value of exports at 1980 import unit values (of manufactures) minus corresponding value at 1980 export unit values (of commodities).

Sources: UNCTAD, Commodity Yearbook, 1989 and 1990; UN trade tapes; UN Monthly Bulletin of Statistics (various issues).

Table A.3. Unit value and volume of commodity exports of developing countries by region, 1980–8 (1980 = 100)[a]

	Unit value			Volume		
	Africa	Asia	Latin America	Africa	Asia	Latin America
1980	100	100	100	100	100	100
1981	86	95	93	101	101	104
1982	77	84	85	104	106	102
1983	76	85	85	100	108	106
1984	81	89	87	100	111	110
1985	79	80	78	98	115	119
1986	83	76	88	104	129	108
1987	81	83	81	103	135	113
1988	90	94	93	104	143	116

[a] These indices relate to commodity exports from all developing countries.

Source: UNCTAD, *Commodity Yearbook*, 1990.

Major exporters of petroleum: Algeria, Angola, Bahrain, Brunei Darussalam, Congo, Ecuador, Gabon, Indonesia, Iran, Iraq, Kuwait, Libya, Mexico,[2] Nigeria, Oman, Qatar, Saudi Arabia, Syria, Trinidad and Tobago, United Arab Emirates, and Venezuela.

Major exporters of manufactures: Argentina, Brazil, Hong Kong, Republic of Korea, Singapore, Taiwan Province of China, and Yugoslavia.

All other developing countries (except China) are treated here as 'commodity dependent' or 'commodity exporting' countries. The value of commodity exports (other than petroleum) from these countries for the years 1980 to 1988 are given in Table A.4 by major region – Africa, Asia, and Latin America – this table also showing the corresponding regional totals for all developing countries. A comparison of the two sets of regional totals shows that for Africa almost all primary commodities (95% in 1988) are exported by commodity-dependent countries; for Asia and Latin America, however, the corresponding proportions are over one-half (55% for Asia and 59% for Latin America in 1988).

For the three regional groups, the foreign exchange loss attributable to changes in foreign trade prices can be calculated for the period since 1980 by applying the relevant export and import unit values shown in Tables A.2 and A.3 to the export values shown in Table A.4. The results, given in Table A.5, indicate a cumulative foreign exchange loss over the period 1981–8 of some $80 billion, for the aggregate of commodity-dependent countries, an average annual loss of some $10 billion. It should be noted that the sharp rise in the dollar prices of manufactures after 1985 added substantially to the foreign exchange loss resulting from the fall in unit values of commodities, as compared with the 1980 levels. For the aggregate of commodity-dependent countries, the commodity terms of trade effect accounted for about two-thirds of that for all developing countries.

[2] Mexico was reclassified in 1989 as a major exporter of manufactures.

Terms of Trade Gains and Losses

Table A.4. Value of commodity exports of developing countries, 1980-8 ($ billion)

	All developing countries			Commodity-dependent countries[a]		
	Africa	Asia	Latin America	Africa	Asia	Latin America
1980	19.8	38.8	46.3	18.4	24.7	29.2
1981	17.3	37.3	44.7	16.1	24.7	26.9
1982	15.8	34.6	40.0	14.8	22.7	24.8
1983	15.1	35.7	41.5	14.0	22.7	25.6
1984	16.0	38.3	44.3	15.1	23.7	25.9
1985	15.3	35.7	43.3	14.5	21.6	25.9
1986	17.0	37.9	43.9	16.1	22.0	26.9
1987	16.5	43.4	42.4	15.8	24.8	24.3
1988	18.5	52.3	50.2	17.5	28.9	29.7

[a] See definition in the text.
Source: As for Table A.3

Table A.5. Commodity terms of trade effects by region, 1980-8 ($ billion)

	All developing countries			Commodity-dependent countries[a]		
	Africa	Asia	Latin America	Africa	Asia	Latin America
1980	–	–	–	–	–	–
1981	−1.8	0.1	−1.1	−1.8	0.0	−0.7
1982	−3.3	−3.5	−3.8	−3.1	2.3	−2.3
1983	−2.8	−1.8	−2.5	−2.7	−1.1	−1.5
1984	−1.2	1.5	0.4	−1.0	1.0	0.2
1985	−1.6	−3.1	−5.0	−1.5	−1.9	−3.0
1986	−4.1	−13.3	−7.6	−3.8	−7.7	−4.6
1987	−6.2	−14.8	−15.6	−5.9	−8.5	−9.0
1988	−5.6	−13.4	−13.4	−5.3	−7.4	−7.9

[a] The regional export unit values for all developing countries shown in Table A.3 were also used for the commodity-dependent countries.
Sources: Tables A.2, A.3, and A.4

(b) Terms of Trade Losses in Relation to GDP, 1980-8

The aggregate GDP of the commodity-dependent countries amounted to about $880 billion in 1980 (UN National Accounts data bank). Over the period 1980-8, the foreign exchange loss attributable to the deterioration in the commodity terms of trade – $10 billion a year, on average – represented 1.1% of total GDP, while on a cumulative basis,

Table A.6. Sugar exports from developing countries to the free market and to preferential markets, 1980-7

	To free market[a]			To preferential markets[b]		
	Quantity (million tonnes)	Unit value[c] ($ per tonne)	Value ($ billion)	Quantity (million tonnes)	Unit value ($ per tonne)	Value ($ billion)
1980	12.43	439	5.46	4.92	882	4.34
1981	12.01	426	5.12	5.94	662	3.93
1982	12.77	252	3.22	6.84	687	4.70
1983	12.72	228	2.90	6.09	842	5.13
1984	12.60	221	2.78	5.66	830	4.70
1985	11.13	161	1.79	6.57	781	5.13
1986	10.64	172	1.83	5.57	939	5.23
1987	9.99	170	1.70	6.17	976	6.02

[a] Gross exports to the free market from developing countries.
[b] Total exports from developing countries minus exports to the free market.
[c] Mean weighted unit value of sugar exports from eight developing countries (Argentina, Brazil, Colombia, Dominican Republic, Guatemala, Mexico, Philippines, and Thailand), each of which exports sugar only to the free market. These countries together accounted for 53% of total sugar exports from all developing countries to the free market in 1980, while for 1987 the corresponding proportion had risen to 60%.

Sources: International Sugar Organization, London; UNCTAD, *Commodity Yearbook*, 1989.

taking the period as a whole, the corresponding figure was 8.9%. The terms of trade loss in relation to GDP was much greater for Africa than for the two other regions; the mean annual loss for Africa ($3.1 billion) represented 2.4% of 1980 GDP, compared to 1.1% for commodity-dependent countries in Latin America and 0.8% for those in Asia. The relative foreign exchange loss increased substantially after 1985, as can be seen from Table A.5. The average annual loss for the three years 1986–8 represented 3.3% of 1980 GDP for Africa, and 2.1 or 2.2% for the two other regions. The corresponding percentages for the periods 1980–5, 1986–8 and 1980–8 are reported in Table 2.4.

(c) Sugar exports from developing countries, 1980–7

Annual figures of the quantity and value of sugar exports by individual countries for the period 1980–7 are given in the UNCTAD *Commodity Yearbook, 1989* (and earlier issues). Figures for gross exports from developing countries to the free market have been supplied by the secretariat of the International Sugar Organization, London. The quantity and value of developing country exports in preferential channels can then be derived by deducting exports to the free market from total sugar exports. The resulting series are given in Table A.6.

The purchasing power of sugar exports over imports of manufactures can be derived by deflating the value of sugar exports to the two areas of destination, as shown in Table A.6, by the unit value of manufactures exported by developed market-economy countries, as shown in Table A.2. The change from 1980 to 1987 in the purchasing power of sugar exports can then be divided into two elements, viz. the terms of trade effect and the volume effect. The terms of trade effect is calculated as in Table A.2, while the volume effect is the residual after deducting the terms of trade effect from the change in the purchasing power of exports. The results of this calculation are given in Table A.7, which also shows these changes as percentages of the value of sugar exports in 1980.

Table A.7. Terms of trade, volume, and purchasing power of sugar exports from developing countries, 1980–7

	Value change, 1980–7 ($ billion)			As % of 1980 sugar exports		
	To free market	Preferential	Total	To free market	Preferential	Total
Cumulative change						
Terms of trade	−15.23	−1.05	−16.28	−279	−24	−166
Export volume	−2.28	+7.39	+5.11	−42	+170	+52
Purchasing power	−17.51	+6.34	−11.17	−321	+146	−114
Annual average change						
Terms of trade	−2.18	−0.15	−2.33	−40	−3	−24
Export volume	−0.33	+1.06	+0.73	−6	+24	+7
Purchasing power	−2.51	+0.91	−1.60	−46	+21	−16

Sources: Tables A.2 and A.6.

REFERENCES

Acquah, P. (1972), 'A Macroeconomic Analysis of Export Instability and Economic Growth: The Case of Ghana and the World Cocoa Market', unpublished Ph.D. dissertation, University of Philadelphia, 1972.

Adams, F.G. and Behrman, J.R. (1982), *Commodity Exports and Economic Development*, Lexington, Mass., Lexington Books, D.C. Heath.

Adams, F.G. and Priovolos, T. (1981), 'Commodity Exports, Economic Development and Policy: Coffee and Brazil', unpublished report to AID; Philadelphia, Wharton Econometric Forecasting Associates, Inc.

Ady, P. (1969), 'International Commodity Policy', in I.G. Stewart (ed.), *Economic Development and Structural Change*, Edinburgh, Edinburgh University Press.

— (1980), Contribution to 'Proceedings of the Seminar', in A. Sengupta (ed.) (1980).

Anderson, K. and Tyers, R. (1986a), 'Agricultural Policies of Industrial Countries and their Effects on Traditional Food Exporters', *Economic Record*, 62/179 (Dec.).

— (1986b), *'Agricultural Policies of Industrial Countries'* (quoted in *World Development Report, 1986*, Washington, DC, World Bank).

Ansari, J.A. (1978), 'Environmental Characteristics and Organizational Ideology: UNCTAD and the Lessons of 1964', *British Journal of International Studies*, 4.

Athukorala, P. and Huynh, F.C.H. (1987), *Export Instability and Growth: Problems and Prospects for the Developing Economies*, London, Croom Helm.

Auty, R. (1985), 'Materials Intensity of GDP: Research Issues on the Measurement and Explanation of Change', *Resources Policy*, 11.

Avramović, D. (1978), 'Common Fund: Why and of What Kind?', *Journal of World Trade Law*, 12 (Sept.–Oct.).

— (1987), 'Commodity Problem: What Next?', *World Development*, 15/5 (May).

— (1989), *Conditionality: Facts, Theory and Policy*, Helsinki, WIDER (United Nations University).

Bale, M.D. and Lutz, E. (1978), *Trade Restrictions and International Price Instability*, World Bank Staff Working Paper 303, Washington, DC, World Bank.

Beckerman, W. (1985), 'How the Battle against Inflation was Really Won', *Lloyds Bank Review* (Jan.).

— and Jenkinson, T. (1986), 'What Stopped the Inflation? Unemployment or Commodity Prices?', *Economic Journal*, 96 (Mar.).

Behrman, J.R. (1977), *International Commodity Agreements: An Evaluation of the UNCTAD Integrated Commodity Programme*, Washington, DC, Overseas Development Council.

— (1987), 'Commodity Price Instability and Economic Goal Attainment in Developing Countries', *World Development*, 15/5 (May).

Bergsten, C.F. (1973), 'The Threat from the Third World', *Foreign Policy* (Summer).

Berthoud, P. (1985), 'UNCTAD and the Emergence of International Development Law', in M.Z. Cutajar (ed.), *UNCTAD and the South–North Dialogue*, Oxford, Pergamon Press.

Bird, G. (1987), *International Financial Policy and Economic Development*, London, Macmillan.

Bond, Marian and Milne, Elizabeth (1987), 'Export Diversification in Developing

Countries: Recent Trends and Policy Impact', *Staff Studies for the World Economic Outlook*, Washington, DC, IMF.

Bosson, R. and Varon, B. (1977), *The Mining Industry and the Developing Countries*, Washington, DC, Oxford University Press for the World Bank.

Bosworth, B. and Lawrence, R.Z. (1982), *Commodity Prices and the New Inflation*, Washington, DC, The Brookings Institution.

Brodsky, D.A. and Sampson, G.P. (1980), 'Retained Value and the Export Performance of Developing Countries', *Journal of Development Studies*, 17/1 (Oct.).

Brook, E.M., Grilli, E.R., and Waelbroeck, J. (1977), 'Commodity Price Stabilization and the Developing World', Bank Staff Working Paper 262, Washington, DC, IBRD.

Bureau of Agricultural Economics (1985), *Agricultural Policies in the European Community*, Policy Monograph 2, Canberra, Australia.

Caine, Sir S. (1954), 'Instability of Primary Product Prices: A Protest and a Proposal', *Economic Journal*, 64/255 (Sept.).

— (1958), 'Comment' (on paper by Nurkse), *Kyklos*, 11.

Chadha, I.S. (1980), 'The Common Fund for Commodities', *Trade and Development: An UNCTAD Review*, 2 (Autumn), Geneva, UN.

Chenery, H. and Strout, A.M. (1966), 'Foreign Assistance and Economic Development', *American Economic Review*, 56/4 (Sept.).

Chu, K.-Y. and Morrison, T.K. (1986), 'World Non-Oil Primary Commodity Markets: A Medium-Term Framework of Analysis', *IMF Staff Papers*, 33/2 (Mar.), Washington, DC.

Clairmonte, F.F. and Cavanagh, J.H. (1981), *The World in their Web: The Dynamics of Textile Multinationals*, London, Zed Press.

— (1988), 'World Commodities Trade: Changing Role of Giant Trading Companies', *Economic and Political Weekly*, 15 Oct., Bombay.

Clark, C. (1957), *The Conditions of Economic Progress*, London, Macmillan.

Cobban, M.A. (1988), 'Tropical Products in the Uruguay Round Negotiations', *The World Economy*, 11/2 (June).

Congressional Budget Office (1981), *The Effect of OPEC Oil Pricing on Output, Prices, and Exchange Rates in the United States and other Industrial Countries*, Washington, DC, Congress of the United States (mimeo.).

Coppock, J.D. (1962), *International Economic Instability*, New York, McGraw-Hill.

Corden, W.M. (1985), *Protection, Trade and Growth*, Oxford, Blackwell.

Cordovez, D. (1967), 'The Making of UNCTAD', *Journal of World Trade Law*, 1.

Corea, G. (1977), *New Directions and New Structures for Trade and Development*, report by the Secretary-General of UNCTAD to UNCTAD IV, 1976; New York, UN.

— (forthcoming) *Taming Commodity Markets*, Manchester University Press.

Council of Economic Advisers (1988), *Annual Report*, Washington, DC (Feb.).

Cuddy, J.D.A. (1976), *International Price Indexation*, Farnborough, England, Saxon House.

Dean, J. (1950), 'Pricing Policies for New Products', *Harvard Business Review*, 28.

Dell, E. (1987), 'Trade Policy: Retrospect and Prospect', *International Affairs*, 60/2 (Spring).

Dell, S. (1967), 'The Proposal for Supplementary Financing', *Journal of World Trade Law*, 1/4 (July/Aug.).

— (1985a), 'The Origins of UNCTAD', in M.Z. Cutajar (ed.), *UNCTAD and the South–North Dialogue*, Oxford, Pergamon Press.

— (1985b), 'The Fifth Credit Tranche', *World Development*, 13/2.
— (1990), *The United Nations and International Business*, New York, UN.
Deméocq, M. and Guillaumont, P. (1985), *Export Instability and Economic Development: A Cross-Section Analysis*, Washington, DC, World Bank (May).
Dornbusch, R. (1985), 'Policy and Performance Links between LDC Debtors and Industrial Nations', *Brookings Papers on Economic Activity*, 2.
Drucker, P. (1986), 'The Changed World Economy', *Foreign Affairs*, 64/4.
Durand, M. and Blöndal, S. (1988), *Are Commodity Prices Leading Indicators of OECD Prices?*, Paris, OECD (mimeo.).
ECA (1989), *African Alternative Framework to Structural Adjustment Programmes*, Addis Ababa, UN Economic Commission for Africa.
ECE (1951), *Economic Survey of Europe in 1950*, Geneva, UN.
Englander, A.S. (1985), 'Commodity Prices in the Current Recovery', *Federal Reserve Bank of New York Quarterly Review*, 1 (Spring).
Erzan, R., Laird, S. and Yeats, A. (1988), 'On the Potential for Expanding South–South Trade through the Extension of Mutual Preferences among Developing Countries', *World Development*, 16/12 (Dec.).
FAO (1983–4), *Commodity Review and Outlook*, Rome, UN Food and Agriculture Organization.
Ferenz, H.J. (1984), *Special Transactions in Third World Trade* (quoted in Avramović (1987: 653–5)).
Finger, M. and De Rosa, D. (1978), 'Commodity Price Stabilisation and the Ratchet Effect', *The World Economy*, 1/2.
Finlayson, J.A. and Zacher, M.W. (1981), 'International Trade Institutions and the North–South Dialogue', *International Journal*, 36 (Autumn).
— (1988), *Managing International Markets: Developing Countries and the Commodity Trade Régime*, New York, Columbia University Press.
Fleisig, H. and van Wijnbergen, S. (1985), *Primary Commodity Prices, the Business Cycle and the Real Exchange Rate of the Dollar*, Discussion Paper 90 (Dec.), London, CEPR.
Frank, I. (1968), 'The Role of Trade in Economic Development', in R.N. Gardner and M.F. Millikan, *The Global Partnership*, New York, Praeger.
Gardner, R.N. (1980), *Sterling–Dollar Diplomacy in Current Perspective*, New York, Columbia University Press.
GATT (1958), *Trends in International Trade: A Report by a Panel of Experts*, Geneva, GATT.
— (1987), *The World Market for Dairy Products, 1987*, Geneva, GATT (Nov.).
— (1990), *Focus: GATT Newsletter* (Mar.), Geneva, GATT.
Gilbert, C.L. (1987), 'International Commodity Agreements: Design and Performance', *World Development*, 15/5 (May).
— (1989), 'The Impact of Exchange Rates and Developing Country Debt on Commodity Prices', *Economic Journal*, 99 (Sept.).
Girvan, N. (1987), 'Transnational Corporations and Non-Fuel Primary Commodities in Developing Countries', *World Development*, 15/5 (May).
Glezakos, C. (1973), 'Export Instability and Economic Growth: A Statistical Verification', *Economic Development and Cultural Change* (July).
Goldstein, M. (1977), 'Downward Price Inflexibility, Ratchet Effects and the Inflationary Impact of Import Price Changes: Some Empirical Evidence', *IMF Staff Papers*, 24.

Gordon-Ashworth, F. (1984), *International Commodity Control: A Contemporary History and Appraisal*, London, Croom Helm.
Graham, B. (1937), *Storage and Stability*, New York, McGraw-Hill.
— (1944), *World Commodities and World Currency*, New York, McGraw-Hill.
Graham, F. D. (1942), *Social Goals and Economic Institutions*, Princeton University Press.
Griffith-Jones, S. (1989), 'Nicholas Kaldor's Contribution to the Analysis of International Monetary Reform', *Cambridge Journal of Economics*, 13/1.
Grilli, E. R. and Yang, M. C. (1988), 'Primary Commodity Prices, Manufactured Goods Prices, and the Terms of Trade of Developing Countries: What the Long Run Shows', *World Bank Economic Review*, 2/1 (Jan.).
Grondona, L. St. C. (1962), *A Firm Foundation for Economy*, London, Blond.
— (1971), *A Built-in Basic-Economy Stabilizer*, London, Economic Research Council.
Grubel, H. (1965), 'The Case against an International Reserve Currency', *Oxford Economic Papers*, 17/1.
Guillaumont, P. (1987), 'From Export Instability Effects to International Stabilization Policies', *World Development*, 15/5 (May).
Gupta, K.L. (1970), 'Personal Saving in Developing Nations: Further Evidence', *Economic Record*, 46.
Hahn, F. (1982), 'Reflections on the Invisible Hand', *Lloyds Bank Review* (Apr.).
Haji, I. (1985), 'Finance, Money, Developing Countries and UNCTAD', in M. Z. Cutajar (ed.), *UNCTAD and the South–North Dialogue*, Oxford, Pergamon Press.
Harling, K. (1983), 'Agricultural Protectionism in Developed Countries: Analysis of Systems Intervention', *European Review of Agricultural Economics*, 10.
Hart, A. G. (1966), 'The case for and against International Commodity Reserve Currency', *Oxford Economic Papers*, 18/2.
— (1976), 'The Case as of 1976 for International Commodity-Reserve Currency', *Welwirtschaftliches Archiv*, 112/1.
— Kaldor, N., and Tinbergen, J. (1964), 'The Case for an International Commodity Reserve Currency', in UNCTAD 1964, iii.
Hartman, D. G. (1985), 'Focus on Commodities', *World Outlook*, Lexington, Mass., Data Resources, Inc.
Hathaway, D.E. (1987), *Agriculture and the GATT: Rewriting the Rules*, Washington, DC, Institute for International Economics.
Helleiner, G. K. (1972), *International Trade and Economic Development*, Harmondsworth, Middlesex, Penguin.
— (1979), 'World Market Imperfections and the Developing Countries', in W. R. Cline (ed.), *Policy Alternatives for a New International Economic Order*, New York, Praeger.
— (1980), *Intra-firm Trade and the Developing Countries*, London, Macmillan.
— (1986), 'Outward Orientation, Import Instability and African Economic Growth: An Empirical Investigation', in Lall and Stewart (eds.), *Theory and Reality in Development: Essays in Honour of Paul Streeten*, London, Macmillan.
— (1988), 'Primary Commodity Markets: Recent Trends and Research Requirements', in K. A. Elliot and J. Williamson (eds.), *World Economic Problems*, Special Report 7 (July), Washington, DC, Institute for International Economics.
Herrmann, R., Burger, K., and Smit, H. P. (1990), 'Commodity Policy: Price Stabilization versus Financing', in L. A. Winters and D. Sapsford (eds.), *Primary Commodity*

Prices: Economic Models and Policy, London, Cambridge University Press for the CEPR.

Hewitt, A. P. (1987), 'Stabex and Commodity Export Compensation Schemes: Prospects for Globalization', *World Development*, 15/5 (May).

Holsen, J. A. (1990), *An Overview of Structural Adjustment*, paper presented to International Seminar on Structural Adjustment Policies in the Third World, Dhaka (Jan.; mimeo.).

Hondros, E. D. (1988), 'Materials: A Perspective', *ATAS Bulletin*, 5 (May), Centre for Science and Technology for Development, UN, New York.

Honma, M. and Hayami, Y. (1986), 'Structure of Agricultural Protection in Industrial Countries', *Journal of International Economics*, 20/1-2 (Feb.).

Hueth, D. and Schmitz, A. (1972), 'International Trade in Intermediate and Final Goods: Some Welfare Implications of Destabilized Prices', *Quarterly Journal of Economics*, 86.

Hulugalle, L. (1990), 'South–South Trade: Developments in the 1980s and Policies for the 1990s', *IDS Bulletin*, 21/1 (Jan.).

Humphreys, D. (1982), 'A Mineral Commodity Life Cycle? Relationships between Production, Price and Economic Resources', *Resources Policy*, 8.

IBRD (1965), '*Supplementary Financial Measures: A Study Requested by the United Nations Conference on Trade and Development, 1964*, Washington, DC.

IMF (1987), *Primary Commodities: Market Developments and Outlook*, Washington, DC, IMF (July).

— (1989*a*), *World Economic Outlook*, Washington, DC, IMF (Apr.).

— (1989*b*), *Primary Commodities: Market Developments and Outlook*, Washington, DC, IMF (July).

International Coffee Organization (1979), *Report on the Diversification Fund of the International Coffee Organization*, London (Aug.).

Jayawardena, L. (1990), *Development and Environmental Preservation: Management of Local and Regional Resources in an Interdependent World System*, paper presented to the Ninth General Conference of the International Association of Universities, Helsinki, WIDER (Aug.) (mimeo.).

Johnson, H. G. (1967), *Economic Policies towards Less Developed Countries*, Washington, DC, Brookings Institution.

— (1977), 'Commodities: Less Developed Countries' Demands and Developed Countries' Responses', in J. Bhagwati (ed.), *The New International Economic Order: The North–South Dialogue*, Cambridge, Mass. and London, MIT Press.

Kaldor, N. (1963), 'Stabilizing the Terms of Trade of Underdeveloped Countries', *Economic Bulletin for Latin America, UN (Mar.)* (reprinted in the author's *Essays on Economic Policy*, ii, London, Duckworth, 1964).

— (1972), 'The Irrelevance of Equilibrium Economics', *Economic Journal* (Dec.).

— (1975), 'What is Wrong with Economic Theory', *Quarterly Journal of Economics* (Aug.).

— (1976), 'Inflation and Recession in the World Economy', *Economic Journal*, 86 (Dec.).

— (1978), *Further Essays on Applied Economics*, London, Duckworth.

— (1980), *Essays on Economic Policy*, ii, London, Duckworth, 2nd edn. (Introduction).

— (1983), 'The Role of Commodity Prices in Economic Recovery', *Lloyds Bank Review* (July) (reprinted in *World Development*, 15/5 (1987)).

Kanan, N. *et al.* (1989), *Supply Management of Commodity Exports by Developing*

Countries, Report to UNCTAD; Amsterdam, Economic and Social Institute, Free University (mimeo.).

Kebschull, D. (1985), *Report on the German Round-Table on Commodity Export Earnings Stabilisation*, Hamburg, Institut für Wirtschaftsforschung.

Kenen, P.B. and Voivodas, C.S. (1972), 'Export Instability and Economic Growth', *Kyklos*, 25.

Keynes, J.M. (1938), 'The Policy of Government Storage of Foodstuffs and Raw Materials', *Economic Journal* (Sept.).

— (1942, 1943), 'The International Regulation of Primary Products', reprinted in D. Moggridge (ed.), *Collected Writings of John Maynard Keynes*, London, MacMillan and Cambridge University Press, 1980.

Killick, T. (ed.) (1984), *The Quest for Economic Stabilisation*, London, Heinemann Educational Books.

Knudsen, O.K. and Parnes, A. (1975), *Trade Instability and Economic Development*, Lexington, Mass., Lexington Books, D.C. Heath.

Kock, K. (1969), *International Trade Policy and the GATT, 1947–1967*, Stockholm, Almqvist and Wicksell.

Koekkoek, A. (1989), 'Tropical Products, Developing Countries and the Uruguay Round', *Journal of World Trade*, 23/6 (Dec.).

Kornai, J. (1971), *Anti-Equilibrium: On Economic Systems Theory and the Tasks of Research*, Amsterdam, North Holland.

Krishnamurti, R. (1985), 'UNCTAD as a Negotiating Instrument on Trade Policy: The UNCTAD–GATT Relationship', in M.Z. Cutajar (ed.), *UNCTAD and the South–North Dialogue*, Oxford, Pergamon Press.

Kuwayama, M. (1988), 'International Primary Commodity Marketing and Latin America', *CEPAL Review*, 34 (Apr.), Santiago, ECLAC.

Labys, W.C. (1980), *Market Structure, Bargaining Power and Resource Price Formation*, Lexington, Mass., Lexington Books, D.C. Heath.

— and Lord, M.J. (1990), 'Portfolio Optimisation and the Design of Latin American Export Diversification Policies', *Journal of Development Studies*, 26/2 (Jan.).

— and Maizels, A. (1990), *Commodity Price Fluctuations and Macro-Economic Adjustments in the Developed Countries*, WIDER Working Paper 87, Helsinki (Nov.).

— and Thomas, H.C. (1975), 'Speculation, Hedging and Commodity Price Behaviour: An International Comparison', *Applied Economics*, 7.

— and Waddell, L.M. (1989), 'Commodity Lifecycles in US Materials Demand', *Resources Policy*, 15 (Sept.).

Lahouel, M.H. (1981), '*Export Instability and the Developing Economies*', unpublished Ph.D. dissertation, Cambridge, Mass., Harvard University.

Laird, S. and Yeats, A.J. (1987), 'Empirical Evidence Concerning the Magnitude and Effects of Developing Country Tariff Escalation', *The Developing Economies*, 25/2 (June).

Lancieri, E. (1978), 'Export Instability and Economic Development: A Reappraisal', *Banca Nazionale del Lavoro Quarterly Review*, 125 (June).

Lasaga, M. (1981), *The Copper Industry in the Chilean Economy: An Econometric Analysis*, Lexington, Mass., Lexington Books, D.C. Heath.

Law, A.D. (1975), *International Commodity Agreements*, Lexington, Mass., Lexington Books, D.C. Heath.

League of Nations (1937), *Report of the Committee for the Study of the Problem of Raw Materials*, Geneva.
— (1939), *Review of World Trade, 1938*, Geneva.
— (1945), *Commercial Policy in the Post-War World*, Geneva.
Leontief, W. (1971), 'Theoretical Assumptions and Non-Observed Facts', *American Economic Review*, 61/1 (Mar.).
Lewis, W.A. (1980), 'The Slowing Down of the Engine of Growth', *American Economic Review*, 70/4 (Sept.).
Lim, D. (1974), 'Export Instability and Economic Development: The Example of West Malaysia', *Oxford Economic Papers*, 26/1 (Mar.).
— (1976), 'Export Instability and Economic Growth: A Return to Fundamentals', *Oxford Bulletin of Economics and Statistics*, 38 (Nov.).
— (1980), 'Income Distribution, Export Instability and Savings Behavior', *Economic Development and Cultural Change*, 28 (Jan.).
— (1988), 'Export Instability and Economic Growth in Resource-Rich Countries', in M. Urrutia and S. Yukawa (eds.), *Economic Development Policies in Resource-Rich Countries*, Tokyo, United Nations University.
Lira, R. (1974), 'The Impact of an Export Commodity in a Developing Economy: The Case of Chilean Copper, 1956–1968', unpublished Ph.D. dissertation, Philadelphia, University of Pennsylvania.
Loo, T. and Tower, E. (1988), *Agricultural Protectionism and the Less Developed Countries: The Relationship between Agricultural Prices, Debt-Servicing Capacities and the Need for Development Aid*, Canberra, Australia, Centre for International Economics.
Love, J. (1975), 'The Impact of Export Instability on the Ethiopian Economy', *Eastern Africa Economic Review*, 7.
— (1989), 'Export Instability, Imports and Investment in Developing Countries', *Journal of Development Studies*, 25/2 (Jan.).
MacBean, A.I. (1966), *Export Instability and Economic Development*, Cambridge, Mass., Harvard University Press.
— (1978), *A Positive Approach to the International Economic Order, i. Trade and Structural Adjustment*, London, British–North American Committee.
— (1980), Contribution to 'Proceedings of the Seminar', in A. Sengupta (ed.) (1980).
— and Nguyen, D.T. (1987), *Commodity Policies: Problems and Prospects*, London, Croom Helm.
McNicol, D.L. (1978), *Commodity Agreements and Price Stabilization*, Lexington, Mass., Lexington Books, D.C. Heath.
Maizels, A. (1963), *Industrial Growth and World Trade*, London, Cambridge University Press for NIESR.
— (1968a), Review of A.I. MacBean, *Export Instability and Economic Development*, in *American Economic Review*, 58 (Sept.).
— (1968b), *Exports and Economic Growth of Developing Countries*, London, Cambridge University Press for NIESR.
— (1982), *Selected Issues in the Negotiation of International Commodity Agreements: An Economic Analysis*, Geneva, UNCTAD (doc. TD/B/C.1/224).
— (1984), 'A Conceptual Framework for Analysis of Primary Commodity Markets', *World Development*, 12/1 (Jan.).
— (1985), 'Reforming the World Commodity Economy', in M.Z. Cutajar (ed.),

UNCTAD and the South–North Dialogue, Oxford, Pergamon Press.
— (1988), 'The Impact of Currency Devaluation on Commodity Production and Exports of Developing Countries', in S. Dell (ed.), *Policies for Development: Essays in Honour of Gamani Corea*, London, Macmillan.
— and Nissanke, M. K. (1984), 'Motivations for Aid to Developing Countries', *World Development*, 12/9 (Sept.).
Massell, B. F. (1969), 'Price Stabilization and Welfare', *Quarterly Journal of Economics*, 83/2 (May).
Matthews, A. (1985), *The Common Agricultural Policy and the Less Developed Countries*, Dublin, Gill and Macmillan.
Meadows, D. H. et al. (1972), *The Limits to Growth*, New York, Universal Books.
Mirakhor, A. and Montiel, P. (1977), 'Import Intensity of Output Growth in Developing Countries, 1970–85', *Staff Studies for the World Economic Outlook*, Washington, DC, IMF (Aug.).
Moggridge, D. (ed.) (1980), *Collected Writings of John Maynard Keynes*, London, Macmillan and Cambridge University Press.
Moran, C. (1983), 'Export Fluctuations and Economic Growth: An Empirical Analysis', *Journal of Development Economics*, 12.
Morgan Guaranty Trust Co., *World Financial Markets* (various issues), New York.
— (1987), 'Non-Oil Commodity Prices: Trends and Implications', *World Financial Markets* (Aug.), New York.
Morrison, T. K. (1979), 'Political Economy of Export Instability in Developing Countries: The Case of Ghana', *Journal of African Studies*, 6.
— and Wattleworth, M. (1988), 'The 1984–86 Commodity Recession: Analysis of Underlying Causes', *IMF Staff Papers*, 35/2 (June), Washington, DC.
Myrdal, G. (1956), *An International Economy*, New York, Harper and Brothers.
Nguyen, D. T. (1979), 'The Implications of Price Stabilization for the Short-term Instability and Long-term Level of LDC's Export Earnings', *Quarterly Journal of Economics*, 93.
— (1980), 'Partial Price Stabilization and Export Earning Instability', *Oxford Economic Papers*, 32.
Nordhaus, W. D. and Shoven, J. B. (1977), 'A Technique for Analyzing and Decomposing Inflation', in J. Popkin (ed.), *Analysis of Inflation: 1965–1974*, Cambridge, Mass., Ballinger.
Obidegwu, C. F. and Nziramasanga, M. (1981), *Copper and Zambia: An Econometric Analysis*, Lexington, Mass., Lexington Books, D. C. Heath.
OECD (1980), *Economic Outlook*, 27, Paris (July).
— (1990), *Agricultural Policies, Markets and Trade: Monitoring and Outlook*, Paris.
Oi, W. Y. (1961), 'The Desirability of Price Instability under Perfect Competition', *Econometrica*, 29.
O'Neill, Helen (1977), *A Common Interest in a Common Fund*, New York, UN.
Palma-Carillo, P. (1976), 'A Macro-Econometric Model of Venezuela with Oil Price Impact Applications', unpublished Ph.D. dissertation, Philadelphia, University of Pennsylvania.
Perlman, R. and Gilbert, C. (1987), 'The prospect for commodities', *The World Today*, 43/1, Jan., London, Royal Institute for International Affairs.
Pincus, J. A. (1967), *Commodity Agreements – Bonanza or Illusion?*, Washington, DC, Rand Corporation.

Popkin, J. (1974), 'Commodity Prices and the U.S. Price Level', *Brookings Papers on Economic Activity*, 1.
Prebisch, R. (1950), *The Economic Development of Latin America and its Principal Problems*, Santiago, ECLA.
— (1964), *Towards a New Trade Policy for Development*, in UNCTAD (1964), ii, Geneva.
Priovolos, T. (1981), *Coffee and the Ivory Coast: An Econometric Study*, Lexington, Mass., Lexington Books, D.C. Heath.
Radetzki, M. (1970), *International Commodity Market Arrangements*, London, Hurst.
— (1985), *State Mineral Enterprises: An Investigation into their Impact on International Mineral Markets*, Washington, DC, Resources for the Future.
Rangarajan C. and Sundararajan, V. (1976), 'Impact of Export Fluctuations on Income: A Cross Country Analysis', *Review of Economics and Statistics*, 58/3 (Aug.).
Rangarajan, L.N. (1978), *Commodity Conflict: The Political Economy of International Commodity Negotiations*, London, Croom Helm.
Rossen, S. (1981), *Notes on Rules and Mechanisms Governing International Economic Relations*, DERAP Publications 127, Bergen, Chr. Michelson Institute.
Rowe, J.W.F. (1965), *Primary Commodities in International Trade*, London, Cambridge University Press.
Rowlatt, J.A. and Blackaby, F. (1959), 'The Demand for Industrial Materials, 1950–57', *National Institute Economic Review*, 5 (Sept.).
Sampson, G.P. and Yeats, A.J. (1977), 'An Evaluation of the Common Agricultural Policy as a Barrier Facing Agricultural Exports to the European Economic Community', *American Economic Review*, 59 (Feb.).
Sengupta, A. (1980), (ed.), *Commodities, Finance and Trade: Issues in North–South Negotiations*, London, Frances Pinter.
Singer, H.W. (1950), 'The Distribution of Gains between Investing and Borrowing Countries', *American Economic Review* (May).
Siri, G. (1980), 'World Coffee Prices and the Economic Activity of the Central American Countries', unpublished report to AID; Philadelphia, Wharton Econometric Forecasting Associates, Inc.
Smith, G.W. and Schink, G.R. (1976), 'The International Tin Agreements: A Reassessment', *Economic Journal*, 86.
Spraos, J. (1983), *Inequalising Trade? A Study of Traditional North/South Specialisation in the Context of Terms of Trade Concepts*, Oxford, Clarendon Press in co-operation with UNCTAD.
— (1989), 'Kaldor on Commodities', *Cambridge Journal of Economics*, 13/1.
Stein, L. (1979), *The Growth of East African Exports and their Effect on Economic Development*, London, Croom Helm.
Stewart, F. and Sengupta, A. (1982), *International Financial Co-operation*, London, Frances Pinter.
— and Sengupta, A. (1984), *Framework for International Co-operation*, London, Frances Pinter.
— and Singh, H.V. (1988), 'Do Third World Countries Benefit from Countertrade?', in S. Dell (ed.), *Policies for Development: Essays in Honour of Gamani Corea*, London, Macmillan.
— and Stewart M. (1980), 'A New Currency for Trade among Developing Countries', *Trade and Development: An UNCTAD Review*, 2, Geneva.
Stoeckel, A. and Breckling, J. (1988), *Some Economy-Wide Effects of Agricultural Policies*

in the European Community: A General Equilibrium Study, Canberra, Australia, Centre for International Economics.

Stoltenberg, T. (1989), *Towards a World Development Strategy Based on Growth, Sustainability and Solidarity: Policy Options for the 1990s*, paper presented at OECD Development Centre 25th Anniversary Symposium; Paris, OECD (Feb.).

Stordel, H.E.W. (1988), 'Risk and Economic Growth: An Empirical Analysis of the Effects of Export Instability on Investment in Developing Countries', unpublished Ph.D. dissertation, Geneva University.

Tait, R.T. and Sfeir, G.N. (1982), 'The Common Fund for Commodities', *Journal of International Law and Economics*, 16/3.

Taylor, L. (1988), *Varieties of Stabilization Experience: Towards Sensible Macroeconomics in the Third World*, Oxford, Clarendon Press.

— (1990), *Foreign Resource Flows and Developing Country Growth*, Research for Action series, Helsinki, WIDER.

Thirlwall, A.P. (1987), *Nicholas Kaldor*, Brighton, Wheatsheaf Books.

Tilton, J.E. (1989), 'The New View of Minerals and Economic Growth', *Economic Record*, 65/190 (Sept.).

Tyers, R. and Anderson, K. (1986), 'Distortions in World Food Markets: A Quantitative Assessment' (quoted in *World Bank* (1986a: 112–13)).

UNCTAD (1964), *Proceedings of the United Nations Conference on Trade and Development, 1964*, New York, UN.

— (1967), *Supplementary Financial Measures: Final Report of the Inter-governmental Group on Supplementary Financing* (TD/B/260/Rev.1), Geneva.

— (1968), *Proceedings of the United Nations Conference on Trade and Development, Second Session, 1968*, New York, UN.

— (1971a), *Report of the Group of Experts on Research and Development for Hides, Skins and Leather* (TD/B/C.1/SYN/63, 15 Dec.).

— (1971b), *Report of the Advisory Committee to the Board and to the Committee on Commodities on its Sixth Session* (TD/B/348, 1 June).

— (1973), *Proceedings of the United Nations Conference on Trade and Development, Third Session, 1972*, New York, UN.

— (1974a), *The Indexation of Prices* (TD/B/503/Supp. 1, 30 July), Geneva.

— (1974b), *The Marketing and Distribution System for Bananas*, Geneva.

— (1974c), *Implementation of Resolution 50(III)* (TD/B/C.1/SYN/66, 26 Aug.).

— (1975), *The Marketing and Distribution System for Tobacco*, Geneva.

— (1977), *Proceedings of the United Nations Conference on Trade and Development, Fourth Session, 1976*, i, New York, UN.

— (1981), *Proceedings of the United Nations Conference on Trade and Development, Fifth Session, 1979*, New York, UN.

— (1981a), *Agreement Establishing the Common Fund for Commodities* (TD/IPC/CF/CONF/25), New York, UN.

— (1981b), *The Marketing of Hard Fibres (Sisal and Henequen): Areas for International Co-operation*, Geneva.

— (1981c), *The Processing and Marketing of Primary Commodities: Approach to a Framework of International Co-operation* (TD/B/C.1/PSC/23), New York, UN.

— (1982), *Approach to Frameworks of International Co-operation on Processing and Marketing of Primary Commodities* (TD/B/C.1/PSC/27, 14 Dec.).

— (1984a), *Report of the Expert Group on the Compensatory Financing of Export Earnings Shortfalls* (TD/B/1029/Rev. 1, Dec.), Geneva.
— (1984b), *The Processing and Marketing of Manganese: Areas for International Co-operation* (TD/B/C.1/PSC/20/Rev. 1), New York, UN.
— (1984c), *The Marketing and Distribution of Tobacco* (TD/B/C.1/205), New York, UN.
— (1984d), *The Marketing and Processing of Tea: Areas for International Co-operation* (TD/B/C.1/PSC/28/Rev. 1), Geneva (mimeo.).
— (1984e), *The Marketing of Hard Fibres (Sisal and Henequen): Areas for International Co-operation* (TD/B/C.1/PSC/21/Rev. 1), Geneva (mimeo.).
— (1984f), *International Co-operation in the Field of Marketing and Distribution of Commodities of Export Interest to Developing Countries: Elements of a Framework* (TD/B/C.1/252), Geneva (mimeo.).
— (1984g), *Trade and Development Report, 1984*, Geneva.
— (1984h), *International Co-operation in the Field of Processing Commodities: Elements of a Framework* (TD/B/C.1/253, 30 Aug.).
— (1984i), *Proceedings of the United Nations Conference on Trade and Development, Sixth Session*, 1983, New York, UN.
— (1985a), *The Role of International Commodity Agreements or Arrangements in Attaining the Objectives of the Integrated Programme for Commodities* (TD/B/C.1/270, 3 Apr.), Geneva.
— (1985b), *State of Progress and Elaboration, by International Commodity Bodies, of Development Projects and Programmes to be Presented to the Second Account of the Common Fund for Particular Commodities* (TD/B/C.1/279, 10 Oct.).
— (1985c), *Report of the Trade and Development Board on its 14th Special Session* (TD/B/1062, 9 July).
— (1986), *The Local Processing in Developing Countries of Primary Commodities* (ST/CD/2, Project GLO/82/A04, 13 Aug.).
— (1987a), *Revitalizing Development, Growth and International Trade: Assessment and Policy Options*, New York, UN.
— (1987b), *Commodity Export Earnings Shortfalls, Existing Financial Mechanisms and the Effects of Shortfalls on the Economic Development of Developing Countries* (TD/B/AC.43/5, 8 July), Geneva.
— (1988), *Commodity Yearbook, 1987*.
— (1989a), *Handbook of International Trade and Development Statistics: Supplement 1988*, New York, UN.
— (1989b), *Report of the Intergovernmental Group of Experts on the Compensatory Financing of Export Earnings Shortfalls* (TD/B/1216, 17 May).
— (1990a), *Handbook of International Trade and Development Statistics: Supplement 1989*, New York, UN.
— (1990b), *Financial Resources for Diversification Projects and Programmes* (TD/B/C.1/AC/12, 17 Aug.).
— (1990c), *Commodity Yearbook, 1990*, New York, UN.
— (1990d), *Report of the Sixteenth Special Session of the Trade and Development Board* (Mar.).
UNCTAD/UNDP/WIDER (1990), *Agricultural Trade Liberalization in the Uruguay Round: Implications for Developing Countries*, Geneva, UN.

UNCTC (1985), *Transnational Corporations in World Development: Third Survey*, New York, UN.
— (1988), *Transnational Corporations in World Development: Trends and Prospects*, New York.
UNICEF (1987), *Adjustment with a Human Face*, G.A. Cornia, R. Jolly, and F. Stewart (eds.), Oxford, Clarendon Press.
United Nations (1948), *Havana Charter for an International Trade Organization*, annexed to Final Act of the UN Conference on Trade and Employment, Havana, Cuba; New York.
— (1951), *Measures for International Economic Stability*, Report by the Group of Experts (Sales No. II.A.2), New York.
— (1953), *Commodity Trade and Economic Development*, Report by a Committee appointed by the Secretary-General (Sales No. II.B.1), New York.
— *Report of the UN Conference on the Human Environment, 1972*, New York, UN.
— (1989), *Report on the World Social Situation* (E/CN.5/1989/2).
— (1990), *Africa's Commodity Problems: Towards a Solution* (UNCTAD/EDM/ATF/1), Geneva.
Vastine, J.R. (1977), 'United States International Commodity Policy', *Law and Policy in International Business*, 9/2.
Vernon, R. (1971), *Sovereignty at Bay: The Multinational Spread of US Enterprises*, New York, Basic Books.
Vogely, W.A. (1976), 'Is There a Law of Demand for Minerals?', *Earth and Mineral Sciences*, 45/7 (Apr.).
Voivodas, C.S. (1974), 'The Effect of Foreign Exchange Instability on Growth', *Review of Economics and Statistics*, 56 (Aug.).
Wattleworth, M. (1988), 'The Effects of Collective Devaluation on Commodity Prices and Exports', *IMF Staff Papers*, 35/1 (Mar.).
Waugh, F.V. (1944), 'Does the Consumer Benefit from Price Instability?', *Quarterly Journal of Economics*, 58.
WIDER (1987), *Mobilizing International Surpluses for World Development: A WIDER Plan for a Japanese Initiative*, Study Group Series 2, Helsinki, WIDER (United Nations University).
Wilcox, C. (1949), *A Charter for World Trade*, New York, Macmillan.
Williamson, J. (ed.) (1983), *IMF Conditionality*, Washington DC, Institute for International Economics.
World Bank (1986a), *World Development Report, 1986*, Washington, DC, Oxford University Press for the World Bank.
— (1986b), *Price Prospects for Major Primary Commodities*, Washington, DC (Oct.).
— (1988a), *World Development Report, 1988*, Washington, DC, Oxford University Press for the World Bank.
— (1988b), *Price Prospects for Major Primary Commodities*, Washington, DC (Nov.).
— (1989a), *World Development Report, 1989*, Washington, DC, Oxford University Press for the World Bank.
— (1989b), *World Debt Tables, 1989-90*, i, Washington, DC.
— (1990), *World Development Report, 1990*, Washington, DC, Oxford University Press for the World Bank.
World Bank/UNDP (1989), *Africa's Adjustment and Growth in the 1980s*, Washington, DC.

Yates, P.L. (1959), *Forty Years of Foreign Trade*, London, Allen and Unwin.
Yeats, A.J. (1979), *Trade Barriers Facing Developing Countries*, London, Macmillan.
— (1981), 'Agricultural Protectionism: An Analysis of its International Economic Effects and Options for Institutional Reform', *Trade and Development: An UNCTAD Review*, 3, Geneva, UN.
Yotopoulos, P.A. and Nugent, J.B. (1976), *Economics of Development: Empirical Investigations*, New York, Harper and Row.
Zietz, J. and Valdés, A. (1986), 'The Potential Benefits to LDCs of Trade Liberalization in Beef and Sugar by Industrialized Countries', *Weltwirtschaftliches Archiv*, 122/1 (Mar.).

Index

Acquah, P. 69
Adams, F. G. 65n., 69n., 70n.
Ady, P. 65, 79
Africa
  commodity problems of 269–71
  commodity terms of trade 31, 33–4, 279
  exports: and balance of payments 30–2;
    diversification 235; instability 67;
    value and volume 278–9
  purchasing power 36
  foreign exchange losses 30–4; and
    GDP 33–5
  GDP growth rates 38
  imports and investment 35–7
  and supply management of commodities 54
  intra-trade 222–3
African, Caribbean and Pacific countries
  (ACP) 47, 161
agriculture
  protection: benefits and costs 208–13;
    liberalization: policies for 213–19,
    foreign exchange and welfare
    impact 217; world prices, changes
    in 212; monetary transfers 209; and
    non-tariff barriers 202; subsidies 203
  raw materials: consumption 186; export
    instability 141; non-tariff barriers 202;
    protection for 205; tariff rates 206;
    trade channels of TNCs 165
  subsidies 203
aluminium 205, 240
Anderson, K. 203n., 211n., 213n.
Ansari, J. A. 107
Argentina, 32n.
asbestos 184
Asia
  commodity terms of trade 31, 33–4, 279
  exports: and balance of payments 30–2;
    diversification 235; value and
    volume 278–9
  purchasing power 36
  foreign exchange losses 30–4; and GDP 33–5
  GDP growth rates 38
  imports and investment 35, 37
  intra-trade 222–3
Association of Southeast Asian Nations 222–3,
  226
Athukorala, P. 61n., 66n., 69n., 70
Atlantic Charter 101
Australia 155, 203, 211
Austria 203
Auty, R. 183n.
Avramović, D. 77, 119, 120n., 252

balance of payments 30–3
bananas 114, 161, 163–4, 165
Bangkok Agreement 222–3
Bangladesh 137
bargaining power in commodity markets 165–73
bauxite
  consumption and trade 192
  exports as 'problem' commodity 238
  integrated programme for commodities
    (IPC) 114
  trade channels of TNCs 160–1, 163, 165
Beckerman, W. 53n.–87n.
beef/veal 212
Behrman, J. R. 64, 64n., 65n., 69, 69n., 70,
  70n., 74, 77
Bergsten, C. F. 114, 182
Berthoud, P. 110n.
Bird, G. 95, 98
Blackaby, F. 185
Blöndal, S. 88
Bolivia, 56n.
Bollino, C. A., 146
Bond, M. 234, 246
Bosson, R. 160n.
Bosworth, B. 87
Brazil 30, 30n., 70
Breckling, J. 210n.
Bretton Woods Conference (1944)
  and Common Fund for integrated
    programme 119
  and emergence of UNCTAD 105, 107, 109
  and international commodity policy 260
  price raising and indexation 126
  and protection for agriculture 201
  and world economic fluctuations 93–4
Brodsky, D. A. 166n.
Brook, E. M. 72–3
buffer stocks
  Common Fund, struggle for 116; objections
    to 117–18
  integrated programme for commodities 112,
    115
  negotiations, political economy of 137–8
  post-war stabilization experience 132–3
  and world economic fluctuations 92–3
Burger, K. 52n., 130

Caine, Sir S. 63, 74, 77
Cairns Group 211
Canada 152–3, 155, 211
Caribbean Community: intra-trade of 222–3
Cavanagh, J. H. 163n., 174n., 175n.
Central America 70, 164, 222–3

Index

cereals
  integrated programme for commodities (IPC) 114
  non-tariff barriers 202
  trade by developing countries 227
  trade channels of TNCs 165
Chad 237-8
Chadha, I. S. 119n.
Chenery, H. 35n., 64n.
Chile 70, 237-8
China 37, 155
Chu, K. Y. 14n.
Clairmonte, F. F. 163n., 174n., 175n.
Clark, C. 234
Cobban, M. A. 208n.
cocoa
  exports as 'problem' commodity 238
  imports by developing countries 240
  integrated programme for commodities 113
  international agreements, objectives 130
  and liberalization policies 212
  mechanisms of price stabilization 132-33
  negotiations, political economy of 137
  price instability 90
  price ranges and cycles 134-6
  protection for 201-2, 205
  trade channels of TNCs 161, 164, 165
coffee
  imports by developing countries 240
  integrated programme for commodities (IPC) 114
  international agreements, objectives 130
  and liberalization policies 212
  and post-war commodity policy 104
  price instability 90
  price ranges and cycles 134-5
  protection for 201-2, 205
  trade channels of TNCs, 164, 165
Coffee Diversification Fund 250, 253
Commission on International Commodity Trade (CITC) 147
Commodity Credit Corporation 201
commodity markets 85-98
  and financial markets 89-92
  and industrial sector 85-9
  and post-war consumption trends of raw materials 185-91; impact on developing countries 191
  structure and control of 159-80; bargaining power 165-73; developing countries: policy options for 178-80; and TNCs 173-5; main enterprises 159-65; negotiations related to 175-8; trading channels 159-65
  and technology 181-2; dematerialization and transmaterialization 182-5; life-cycle theory of 184-5
  and world economic fluctuations 92-8

and commodity reserve currency 95-7; alternative linkages between commodity prices and international currency, 97-8
commodity policy
  early post-war developments 101-5
  and Havana Charter 101-5
  integrated programme for 114-16; commodity-by-commodity approach 112-14; Common Fund, struggle for 116-24; compensatory financing 140-55; negotiations on individual commodities 125-39, dual price objective 125-6, market share allocation 136, market stabilization, financial requirements for 133-6, political economy of 136-9, price raising and indexation 126-9, price range 131-2, price stabilization mechanisms 132-3, technical limitations 129-36
  post-war background to 101-11
Commodity Reserve Currency (CRC) 95-8
Commodity Stabilization Agency (CSA) 98
Common Agricultural Policy (CAP) 200-1
Common Fund for integrated programme
  and compensatory financing 154
  decision-making in 122-4
  international policies for diversification of exports 249
  market intervention in emergencies 119-20
  negotiations, political economy of 137-8
  objections to 117-18
  struggle for 116-24
  future potential role 263-4
Compensatory and Contingency Financing Facility (CCFF) 149
compensatory financing
  export earnings: effects of on economic development 145-7; fluctuations, origin of 140-2; shortfall, definition of 142-5
  in integrated programme for commodities 140-55
  international policies for 147-55; alternative or additional proposals 151-2; IMF compensatory financing facility 147-9; risk management 155; STABEX (European Community) 150-1; UNCTAD proposals 147, 152-5
  and price stabilization 78-80
compensatory financing facility (CFF)
  and export instability 79
  international policies for 147-55
  price raising and indexation 129
Congressional Budget Office, 91n.
Consultative Group on Agricultural Research 195
Consumer Subsidy Equivalents (OECD) 209-10

Index

copper
  consumption and trade 192
  dematerialization thesis and 183
  exports as 'problem' commodity 237–8
  imports by developing countries 240
  price instability 90
  protection for 205
  trade channels of TNCs 163, 165
Coppock, J. D. 65n.
copra 212, 240
Corden, W. M. 207n.
Cordovez, D. 105n., 109n.
Corea, G. 115–16, 117n., 118n., 119n., 120–1, 128n., 137, 138n.
Cornia, G. A. 38n.
cotton
  consumption and trade 192
  exports as 'problem' commodity 237–8
  imports by developing countries 240
  and liberalization policies 212
  protection for 205
  trade by developing countries 227
  trade channels of TNCs 161, 164, 165
countertrade in South–South trade 224–5
Cuba 237–8
Cuddy, J. D. A. 128n.

dairy products 111, 202
De Rosa, D. 87
Dean, J. 184
Dell, E. 108, 117, 118
Dell, S. 44n., 45n., 97n., 108, 147, 149n., 175n., 176
demand: decline in growth of 14–16
dematerialization of commodities and technology 182–5
Deméocq, M. 67
developing countries
  and agricultural protection 210–13
  commodity-dependent countries: co-operation among 264–7
  policy options for 178–80; and taxation 162–3; and TNCs 173–5, negotiations with 175–8
  and decision-making in Common Fund 122–4
  diversification of exports: growth of 234–6; international policy in 247–52, external financing for 249–52; national policies for 241–7
  domestic measures in commodity exports 268–9
  and emergence of UNCTAD 106–8
  exports 221; of 'problem' commodity 238–9; sugar 280–1; value and volume 28, 278–9
  impact of price collapse of 1980s 23–39; and exports: and balance of payments 30–3, losses and GDP 33–5; foreign exchange losses 23–35; and human resources 38–9; imports and investment 35–8; losses and gains (1970s and 1980s) 24–30
  imports by 240
  Integrated Programme for Commodities 112–14
  and international commodity policy 264–71; management of export earnings 264–6; marketing and distribution 267; research and development 266–7
  intra-trade of sub-regional groupings 223
  post-war consumption trends, impact on 191
  preferential prices for commodity exports 47–9
  tariff rates for processed commodities 206
  trade 267–8; changes in commodity terms 277; channels of TNCs 165; exports and terms of trade 275; in selected commodities 227
development process and price collapse (1980s) 7–9
diamonds 161, 167, 238
  marketing, distribution and transport and international commodity policy 267
diversification 234–53
  of exports 235
  external financing for 249–52
  financial institutions, commitments by 251
  and growth 234–6
  horizontal 236–7
  international policy for 247–52
  promotion of 241–7; export trends, improving 244–7; reducing instability 241–4
  vertical 237–41
Dornbusch, R. 17, 18
Drucker, P. 182
Durand, M. 88

earnings, *see under* exports
East–South trade 232–3
Egypt 35
Englander, A. S. 14n., 18
environmental degradation, 55, 195–8, 266–7
Erzan, R. 228
Ethiopia 68
European Community
  and Common Agricultural Policy 200–1
  and compensatory financing 155
  and international commodity policy 262
  and protection for agriculture 203, 208–13; monetary transfers 208–9
  trade channels of TNCs 161–2
export instability
  and compensatory financing fluctuations 140–1
  effects of 61–4

export instability – *contd*
  empirical evidence for 64–71; cross-country studies 64–7; individual country studies 68–71
  and market stabilization 71–84
  and price stabilization: and export quotas 80–4, and ceiling price 81–2, and price trends 80–1, and production patterns 82–4; 'harmful' 72–3; 'unnecessary' 73–80, compensatory financing 78–80, export earnings cycle 74–8
  reducing: and diversification 241–4; policies for 242
export quotas
  negotiations, political economy of 137–8
  post-war stabilization experience 132–3
  and price stabilization 80–4; and ceiling price 81–2; and price trends 80–1; and production patterns 82–4
exports
  diversification of 235
  earnings: and compensatory financing; fluctuations, origin of 140–2; cycle of in price stabilization 74–8; by developing countries 278–9; international action on 40–3; and preferential prices from developing countries 47–9; raising levels of 40–60; shortfall: definition of 142–5, effects of on economic development 145–7; and supplementary financing 43–7; supply management 49–60: forms of 56–8, and market intervention 49–56, and market solutions 58–60
  growth of 235; and diversification 234–6; and GDP 235
  and impact of price collapse in developing countries; and balance of payments 30–3; losses and GDP 33–5
  of 'problem' commodities 238
  and promotion of diversification 244–7
  terms of trade 273–82 *see also* trade

Ferenz, H. J. 224n.
financial instruments and compensatory financing 155
financial markets and commodity markets 89–92
financing
  and Common Fund for integrated programme 120–2
  compensatory, *see* compensatory financing
  and diversification 249–52
  requirements for market stabilization in commodity policy 133–6
  role of in international commodity policy 271–2
  supplementary and export earnings 43–7; support for South–South trade 230–2

Finger, M. 87
Finland 118, 153, 203
Finlayson, J. A. 104n., 110n., 123
fixprice markets for industrial products 85
Fleisig, H. 18n.
flexprice markets for commodities 85
Food and Agriculture Organization (FAO) 183
  and international commodity policy 263; synthetics: consumption trends 195, 197
foreign exchange losses and price collapse 23–35
France 118, 153
fuels
  exports from developing countries 221
  trade channels of TNCs 165

Gambia 238
Gardner, R. N. 101n., 103n.
General Agreement on Tariffs and Trade
  emergence of UNCTAD 105–10
  and international commodity policy 261
  international policies for diversification of exports 249
  and liberalization of trade 208, 214–215, 218
  and post-war commodity policy 104
  and minimum export prices for milk products, 57
  and preferential prices for exports 48
  and revenue taxes on tropical products, 208
  and trade barriers 197
  trade preferences in South–South trade 225
Generalized System of Preferences (GSP) 110, 226
Germany
  and compensatory financing 151–4
  and demand, decline in growth of 15
  objections to Common Fund 117
  and contribution of primary commodity prices to inflation 88
Ghana 68–9, 238
Gilbert, C. L. 14n., 17, 17n., 18, 131n.
Girvan, N. 163n., 164n., 168n., 174
Glezakos, C. 64n.
Global System of Trade Preferences (GSTP) 225, 267
  policy for future 227–8
Goldstein, M. 87
Gordon-Ashworth, F. 104n., 131n.
Graham, F. D. 94n.
grains, *see* cereals
Griffith-Jones, S. 86n., 94n., 96–7
Grilli, E. R. 10, 72–3
Grondona, L. St. C. 94n.
Gross Domestic Product
  and commodity demand, decline in growth of 14–16

Index

and export instability 61–2, 64–7
growth in commodity-dependent countries 38
growth of and diversification 235
and impact of price collapse in developing countries 33–5; and imports and investment 37; and terms of trade 33
and outlook for commodity prices 21
and raising levels of export earnings 41
Gross National Product and fluctuations in commodity markets 88–9
groundnuts 212, 237–8
Grubel, H. 95–6
GSP, *see* Generalized System of Preferences
Guillaumont, P. 67, 150n.
Gupta, K. L. 66n.

Haberler Report 207
Hahn, F. 52n.
Hart, A. G. 85, 94n.
Hartman, D. G. 14n., 18
Hathaway, D. E. 214n.
Havana Charter 101–5
Hayami, Y. 215–16
Helleiner, G. K. 52n., 62n., 63n., 67, 161n., 259n.
Herrmann, R. 52n., 130
Hewitt, A. P. 150n., 151n
hides and skins
  consumption and trade in raw materials 194
  protection for 205
  trade channels of TNCs 165
Holsen, J. A. 260n.
Hong Kong 35
Honma, M. 215–16
Hueth, D. 72
Hulugalle, L. 229, 231
Human resources 38–9
Humphreys, D. 184
Huynh, F. C. H. 61n., 66n., 69n., 70

Imperial Preference 102
imports by developing countries 240
  and impact of price collapse on 35–8
indexation and price raising in Integrated Programme for Commodities 126–9
India
  imports, and investment and GDP 37
  negotiations, political economy of 137
  trade channels of TNCs 163–4
Indonesia 30
industrial sector and commodity markets 85–9
Integrated Programme for Commodities (IPC) 114–16
  Common Fund for 116–24; objections to 117–18
  compensatory financing 140–55
  and international commodity policy 258
  negotiations on individual commodities 125–39; dual price objective 125–6; market share allocation 136; market stabilization, financial requirements for 133–6; political economy of 136–9; price raising and indexation 126–9; price range 131–2; price stabilization mechanisms 132–3; technical limitations 129–36
Interim Co-ordinating Committee for International Commodity Arrangements (ICCICA) 104, 107
International Bank for Reconstruction and Development (IBRD)
  letters from President to Secretary-General of UNCTAD, 44n., 45n.
  and Bretton Woods Conference 93
  and emergence of UNCTAD 107
  and supplementary financing 44–7
  see also World Bank
International Clearing Union 92–3
International Coffee Agreement 52n., 57
international commodity agreements
  and Common Fund for Integrated Programme 119–20; decision-making in 122–4; financing of 121–2
  and export instability 72–3, 78–9, 80–1
  and international commodity policy 258
  negotiations, political economy of 136–9, 258–61
  and post-war commodity policy 102–3
  post-war stabilization experience 129–31; mechanisms of price stabilization 133; objectives and instruments 130; requirements for market stabilization 134–6
  and preferential prices for exports 56
international commodity policy
  and Africa 269–71
  compensatory financing 147–55
  and developing countries 264–71; commodity-dependent countries: co-operation among 264–7; domestic measures 268–9; trade among 267–8
  diversification of exports 247–52
  and finance, role of 271–2
  future of 257–72
  need for new focus of 257–61
  North–South programme 261–4
  synthetics: challenge of 191–8
International Dairy Arrangement 111
International Investment Institution 92
International Monetary Fund (IMF)
  and commodity price fluctuations 94–5
  and commodity prices in 1980s 9–10
  and compensatory financing: and risk management 155; and STABEX 150
  compensatory financing facility (CFF) 147–9
  and emergence of UNCTAD 107

Index

International Monetary Fund (IMF) – *contd*
  and export instability 79
  financing exports from developing countries 45
  and international commodity policy 259–60, 262, 264, 268
  price raising and indexation 129
  and shortfall in export earnings 144
  supply, rise in growth of 16–17
International Trade Organisation (ITO) 102, 104
International Wheat Agreement 110
International Wheat Council 110–11
investment
  and price collapse in developing countries 35–8
  and price fluctuations in commodity markets 86–7
iron
  consumption and trade 193
  exports as 'problem' commodity 237–8
  imports by developing countries 240
  Integrated Programme for Commodities (IPC) 114
  protection for 205
  trade channels of TNCs 160–1, 165
Ivory Coast 70, 133

Jamaica 163
Japan
  and compensatory financing 154
  and financial flows to developing countries 54n.
  monetary transfers 209
  and price fluctuations in commodity markets 88
  and protection for agriculture 201, 203, 211
Jayawardena, L. 42n.
Jenkinson, T. 53n., 87n.
Johnson, H. G. 51n., 72, 74, 77, 96
Jolly, R. 38n.
jute
  consumption and trade 192
  dematerialization thesis and 183
  negotiations, political economy of 137
  protection for 205
  trade by developing countries 227
  trade channels of TNCs 165

Kaldor, N. 52n., 83n., 94n. 83–4, 85–7, 94, 96–8, 111
Kanan, N. 58n., 265n.
Kebschull, D. 151n.
Kenen, P. B. 64n., 65n.
Kenya 68, 164
Keynes, J. M. 59, 72, 85, 92–3, 116n.
Killick, T. 149n.
Klein, L. R. 146

Koekkoek, A. 208n.
Kornai, J. 52n.
Krishnamurti, R. 110n., 111n.
Knudsen, O. K. 65–6
Kuwait 14n.
Kuwayama, M. 179n.

Labys, W. C. 53n., 88, 90, 160n., 168, 170, 179, 184, 243n., 245
Lahouel, M. H. 64n.
Laird, S. 206n., 228
Lancieri, E. 64n., 65
Lasaga, M. 70n.
Latin America
  commodity terms of trade 31, 33–4, 279
  exports: and balance of payments 30–2; diversification of 235; value and volume 278–9
  purchasing power 36
  foreign exchange losses 30–4; and GDP 33–5
  GDP growth rates 38
  imports and investment 35–8
  intra-trade 222–3
Law, A. D. 104n.
Lawrence, R. Z. 87
lead
  consumption and trade 192
  imports by developing countries 240
  price instability 90
  protection for 205
Lend-Lease 101
Leontief, W. 52n.
Lewis, W. A. 226n.
liberalization policies in agriculture 213–19
  foreign exchange and welfare impact 217
  world prices, changes in 212
Liberia 237–8
Lim, D. 61n., 63n., 65, 65n., 68
Lira, R. 70
Lomé Convention 24, 47, 150, 151n., 262n.
Loot, T. 211n.
Lord, M. J. 243n, 245
Love, J. 68

MacBean, A. I. 49n., 61n., 62n., 64–65, 66n., 67n., 68, 71, 75, 87n.
maize 212
Maizels, A. 17n., 42n., 50n., 53n., 62n., 64n., 67n., 80n., 88, 90, 137n., 159n., 161n., 206n.
Malaysia 32–3, 68
manganese 193
market intervention
  arguments against, to raise levels of export earnings 49–53; and neoclassical theory 51–3
  arguments for, to raise levels of export

earnings 53–6
and Common Fund for Integrated Programme 119–20
market share allocation in commodity agreements 136
market stabilization
  Integrated Programme for Commodities: financial requirements 133–6
  price stabilization: 'harmful' 72–3, 'unnecessary' 73–80; compensatory financing 78–80; and exports earning cycle 74–8
marketing and international commodity policy 267
Marketing Boards 79, 146
Massell, B. F. 72–3
Mauritania 237–8
Mauritius 238
McNicol, D. L. 72
Meadows, D. H. 182
mercury 184
Mexico 30
Milne, E. 234, 246
Moggridge, D., 59n., 92n., 93n.
monetary influences on price collapse of 1980s 17–20
Moran, C. 65n.
Morgan Guaranty Trust Co. 14n.
Morrison, T. K. 19–20, 68
Mutual Aid Agreement (1942) 101–2
Myrdal, 61n.

Nairobi Conference (1976) 138
Namibia 167
narcotic drugs 55–6
Netherlands 118
New Currency Unit (NCU): financial support for South–South trade 231–2
New Zealand 203
newly industrializing countries (NICs) 7
  imports and investment and impact of price collapse of 1980s 35
  and international commodity policy 269
Nguyen, D. T. 61n., 62n., 64, 64n., 65n., 66n., 67n., 71, 73
nickel 192
Nissanke, M. K. 50n.
non-tariff barriers 204–7, 218
  and protection 202
Nordhaus, W. D. 87
Norway 118, 153, 203
Nugent, J. B. 65
Nziramasanga, M. 70n.

Obidegwu, C. F. 70n.
Oi, W. Y. 72
oil
  bargaining power of TNCs 167–8

post-war consumption trends 188
price fluctuations 88–9, 91–2
prices, collapse of 13–14
protection for 206
trends in terms of trade 10
Olano, F. G. 147
Organization for Economic Cooperation and Development (OECD)
  consumption and trade in raw materials 188, 190
  and demand, decline in growth of 15
  export losses of developing countries and GDP 34
  outlook for commodity prices 21
  and price fluctuations in commodity markets 88–9
  and protection for agriculture 203–4
Organization of Petroleum Exporting Countries (OPEC)
  bargaining power of TNCs 167–8
  and commodity price stability 96
  and Common Fund for Integrated Programme 117–18; decision-making in 122–4
  and East–South trade 232–3
  Integrated Programme for Commodities (IPC) 114
Organization of African Unity 270

palm oil 212, 227
Palma-Carillo, P. 70
paper, protection for 205
Parnes, A. 65–6
Perlman, R. 14n., 18
Permanent Group on Synthetics and Substitutes 194, 196–7
petroleum, see oil
phosphates
  consumption and trade 193
  imports by developing countries 240
  protection for 205
  trade channels of TNCs 165
Pincus, J. A. 49n.
Popkin, J. 87
Portugal 118
post-war materials consumption trends 185–91
  in developed countries 186, 188
  and developing countries 191
  and industrial production 187
Prebisch, R. 43, 105–6, 105n., 106n., 111n., 143n.
Preferential prices, 47–48
price stabilization
  in Integrated Programme for Commodities 129–36
  and market stabilization: 'harmful' 72–3; 'unnecessary' 73–80; compensatory financing 78–80, and exports earning cycle 74–8; mechanisms for 132–3

prices
    and unit values, 23-4
    changes in, contributions to 20
    collapse of 1980s 9-14: causes in non-oil
        commodities 14-20; developing
        countries, impact on 23-39; and
        balance of payments 30-3, foreign
        exchange losses 23-35, and human
        resources 38-9, imports and investment
        35-8, losses and gains (1970s and 1980s)
        24-30, losses and GDP 33-5; monetary
        influences on 17-20; in oil 13-14
    fluctuations and commodity markets 86-7
    in markets for commodities and manufactures
        85-6
    instability: and financial markets 89-92; and
        trends (1962-87) 13
    Integrated Programme for Commodities:
        dual objective in 125-6; indexation
        of 126-9; raising of 126-9; range of
        131-2
    oil 13-14
    outlook for 20-2
    preferential, for export earnings of
        developing countries 47-9
    recessions of 12
    trends and instability of (1962-87) 13
Priovolos, T., 70n.
Producer Subsidy Equivalents (OECD) 210
protection 200-19
    agricultural: benefits and costs 208-13;
        liberalization: policies for 213-19;
        monetary transfers 209; and non-tariff
        barriers 202; subsidies 203
    extent 200-8
    and tariff rates in developing countries 206
    and trade barriers, escalation 205

Radetzki, M. 62n., 174-5
Rangarajan, C. 67n., 69, 71, 83n., 104n.,
    128n.
raw materials
    export instability 141
    post-war consumption trends 185-91;
        decomposition of change in 198-9
    protection for 202
    trade and price instability 13
rice
    and liberalization policies 212
    trade by developing countries 227
    trade channels of TNCs 165
risk management and international policies for
    compensatory financing 155
Rossen, S. 102n., 104n.
Rowlatt, J. A. 185
Rowe, J. W. F. 49n.
rubber
    consumption and trade 192

dematerialization thesis and 183
imports by developing countries 240
international agreements, 130, 135
negotiations, political economy of 136-7
post-war consumption trends 185
post-war stabilization experience 134-5
price instability 90
protection for 205
trade of developing countries 227
trade channels of TNCs 161, 165

Sampson, G. P. 166n.
Schink, G. R. 130
Schmitz, A. 72
Senegal 237-8
Sengupta, A. 96-7, 153n., 154n.
Sfeir, G. N. 119n.
Shoven, J. B. 87
Sierra Leone 238
Singapore 35
Singer, H. W. 106n.
Singh, H. V. 224, 225n.
Siri, G. 70n.
sisal
    consumption and trade 192
    dematerialization thesis and 183
    protection for 205
    trade channels of TNCs 162, 164
Smith, G. W. 130
Smit H. P. 52n., 130
sorghum 212
South Korea 35
South-South trade 220-32
    developing countries, policy perspectives for
        future 226-32; countertrade 224-5
    financial support 230-2; infrastructural
        linkages 229-30; sub-regional groupings
        226; trade preferences 225-6
    trends in 220-3
Soviet Union 123, 232-3
soya 212, 227
Special Drawing Rights (SDR)
    and export instability 79
    financial support for South-South trade 232
    and international commodity policy 268
    post-war stabilization experience 132
    and price instability of commodities 96-8
    and shortfall in export earnings 144
Spraos, J. 52n., 57n., 86n., 96, 106n., 245n.,
    246n.
Sri Lanka 70-1
STABEX (European Community) 79, 150-2
stagflation and commodity markets 86, 94
Stewart, F. 38n., 96-7, 224, 225n., 231
Stewart, M. 231
Stoeckel, A. 210n.
Stoltenberg, T. 46
Stordel, H. E. W. 65n., 66n., 68n.

Strout, A. M. 64n.
sugar
  exports: from developing countries 47–9, 280–1; as 'problem' commodity 238
  imports by developed countries 240
  Integrated Programme for Commodities 113
  international agreements, objectives 130
  and liberalization policies 212
  and post-war commodity policy 104
  post-war stabilization experience: mechanisms of price stabilization 132–3; price ranges and cycles 134–5
  preferential prices for 47–9
  price instability 90
  protection for 201–2
  trade of developing countries 227
  trade channels of TNCs 161, 164–5
Sundararajan, V. 67n., 69, 71
Supplementary Financing Facility, 43–7
supply
  management 49–60; and co-operation among commodity-dependent countries 264–6; forms of 56–8; and market intervention 49–56; arguments against 49–53; arguments for 53–6; and market solutions 58–60
  rise in growth of 16–17
Surinam 237–8
Sweden 118, 203
Switzerland 152–3, 155, 203
synthetics 181–99
  consumption and trade 193
  dematerialization and transmaterialization 182–5
  international policy for 191–8
  trends in consumption 185–91

Tait, R. T. 119n.
Taiwan 35
Tanzania 191
tariffs
  barriers and protection 204–7, 218
  rates in developing countries 206
taxation and commodity markets 162–3
Taylor, L., 41n., 149n., 154n., 260n.
tea
  and liberalization policies 212
  protection for 201
  trade by developing countries 227
  trade channels of TNCs 161, 165
technology
  and commodity markets 181–2; dematerialization and transmaterialization 182–5; life-cycle theory of 184–5
  and post-war consumption trends of raw materials 185–91; impact on developing countries 191

terms of trade, *see* trade
Thailand 32–3
Third World and emergence of UNCTAD 106, 108
Thirlwall 86n., 94n.
Thomas, H. C. 90n.
Tilton, J. E. 188
timber
  consumption and trade 192
  and developing countries: imports by 240; trade in by 227
  protection for 205
tin
  consumption and trade 193
  dematerialization thesis and 184
  imports by developing countries 240
  international agreements, objectives 130
  and post-war commodity policy 104
  post-war stabilization experience: mechanisms of price stabilization 133; price ranges and cycles 135
  price instability 90
  protection for 205
  trade channels of TNCs 163, 165
Tinbergen, J. 85, 94n.
tobacco
  consumption and trade 192
  imports by developing countries 240
  and liberalization policies 212
  protection for 205
  trade channels of TNCs 164, 165
Tower, E. 211n.
trade
  barriers: escalation and protection 205; and vertical diversification 241
  channels in commodity markets 159–65
  cycle in world economic fluctuations 92
  East–South 232–3
  policy and emergence of UNCTAD 106–7
  preferences in South–South trade 228–9; as policy of developing countries 225–6
  and protection 200–19; agricultural: benefits and costs 208–13, liberalization, policies for 213–19; extent 200–8; in processed commodities 204–8; and trade barriers, escalation 205
  South–South 220–32; developing countries, policy perspectives for future 226–32; financial support 230–2; infrastructural linkages 229–30; trade preferences 228–9; developing countries, policy responses to 223–6; countertrade 224–5; sub-regional groupings 226; trade preferences 225–6; recent trends 220–3
  terms of: and balance of payments 30–3 effects of by region 31–3, 279; gains and losses on commodity exports: in 1930s

trade – *contd*
  terms of: and balance of payments – *contd*
    effects of by region – *contd*
      26–9, 273–5; in 1970s and 1980s, 24–6, 30–3, 276–9
    and GDP 33–5, 279, 281; trends in, 9–13
    and volume of exports 28
    secular tendency of, 105
transmaterialization of commodities and technology 182–5
transnational corporations and commodity markets: bargaining power 165–73; Code of Conduct in 175–8; developing countries, relations to 173–5; trade channels 159–65; transfer pricing 162–3
  and international commodity policy 267
  vertical diversification 239
tungsten 193
Turkey 32–3
Tyers, R. 211n., 213n.

Uganda 68
UNCTAD, *see* United Nations Conference on Trade and Development
UNICEF 38
United Kingdom
  and compensatory financing 154
  and demand, decline in growth of 15
  and supplementary financing 44
  early post-war developments 101–2
  objections to common fund 117–18
  trade channels of TNCs 164
United Nations
  and Africa's commodity problems 270–1
  Commission on International Commodity Trade (CITC) 147
  Expert Groups 147, 152–4; and Africa 270
  and international compensatory policies 147–55
United Nations Conference on Trade and Development (UNCTAD)
  and commodity prices in 1980s 9–10; developing countries, impact on 24
  and Common Fund: decision-making in 122–4; financing of 121–2; objections to 118
  and compensatory financing 152–5; fluctuations, origins 140–1; and STABEX 150
  developing countries: negotiations with TNCs 176–8
  emergence of in post-war commodity policy 105–11
  and export instability 76
  financing exports from developing countries 43–5
  GSP in 110
  Integrated Programme for Commodities (IPC) 114–16; commodity-by-commodity approach 112–14; dual price objectives 125–6; negotiations, political economy of 138; price raising and indexation 127; price ranges 131
  and international commodity policy 263
  international policies for diversification of exports 247–9
  and liberalization of trade 217–18
  mandate of 109–10
  and price instability of commodities 89–90, 94
  synthetics: consumption trends, international policy for 191–7
Trade and Development Board 109–10
United Nations Economic and Social Council (ECOSOC)
  and emergence of UNCTAD 109
  and post-war developments in international commodity policy 102, 104
United States
  and compensatory financing 151, 152, 155
  early post-war developments 101–3
  Integrated Programme for Commodities (IPC) 114
  and liberalization of trade 217
  mechanisms of price stabilization in cocoa 133
  monetary transfers 209
  objections to Common Fund 117–18, 123
  price collapse of 1980s 17–18
  and price fluctuations in commodity markets 87–8
  and protection for agriculture 201, 203, 211
  trade channels of TNCs 161

Valdés, A. 211n.
Varon, B. 160n.
Vastine, J. R. 117n., 118n.
vegetable oil 114, 141, 205
Venezuela 170
Vernon, R. 170
Vogely, W. A. 183n.
Voivodas, C. S. 64n., 65n., 66n.

Waddell, L. M. 184
Waelbroeck, J. 72–3
Wattleworth, M. 14n., 17n., 19–20, 42n.
Waugh, F. V. 72
Western industrial countries and Common Fund: decision-making in 122–4; financing of 121–2; objections to 117–18
  consumption and trade in raw materials 185–91
  and emergence of UNCTAD 106–11
  Integrated Programme for Commodities 114
  negotiations, political economy of 137–8
  and commodity reserve currency 97–8

and diversification 249
attitudes to compensatory financing 259; to price raising 53, 258-9, 261
wheat
and emergence of UNCTAD 110-11
and liberalization policies 212
and post-war commodity policy 104
supply, rise in growth of 16-17
trade by developing countries 227
trade channels of TNCs 165
WIDER, *see* World Institute for Development Economics Research
Wijnbergen, S. van, 18n.
Wilcox, C. 102n.
Williamson, J. 149n.
wool 192, 205
World Bank
and Africa's commodity problems 271
and commodity prices in 1980s 9-10
and Common Fund, financing of 122
and compensatory financing 154
and supplementary financing 44-7
financing exports from developing countries 44-6
imports and investment 36-7
and international commodity policy 259-60, 263-4
outlook for commodity prices 20-1
and commodity risk management 155
and supply management of commodities 58
World Conference on Trade and Employment 102
world economic fluctuations
and commodity markets 92-8; alternative linkages 97-8; and commodity reserve currency 95-7; linkages 91-2
World Institute for Development Economics Research (WIDER)
and financial flows from Japan, 54n.
and liberalization of trade 217-18
and raising levels of export earnings 41-2

Yang, M. C. 10
Yeats, A. 206n., 207n., 228
Yotopoulos, P. A. 65

Zacher, M. W. 104n., 110n., 123
Zaïre 68, 238
Zambia
consumption and trade in raw materials 191
and export instability 68, 70
exports of 'problem' commodities 237-8
Zietz, J. 211n.
zinc
consumption and trade 193
imports by developing countries 240
price instability 90
protection for 205